RURAL RESPONSES TO INDUSTRIALIZATION

Rural Responses
to Industrialization

A STUDY OF VILLAGE ZAMBIA

ROBERT H. BATES

NEW HAVEN AND LONDON
YALE UNIVERSITY PRESS
1976

Library of Congress catalog card number: 75–43301
International standard book number: 0–300–01920–3

Designed by Sally Sullivan
and set in Times Roman type.
Printed in the United States of America by
The Murray Printing Company, Westford, Massachusetts.

Published in Great Britain, Europe, Africa, and Asia (except Japan) by
Yale University Press, Ltd., London.
Distributed in Latin America by Kaiman & Polon,
Inc., New York City; in Australia and New Zealand by Book & Film
Services, Artarmon, N.S.W., Australia;
in Japan by John Weatherhill, Inc., Tokyo.

To
Elizabeth

Contents

Acknowledgments   ix

Introduction   1

Part One: The Preindependence Period

  1. The Local Setting: From Imperial Heartland to Industrial Periphery   9

  2. Investment in the Center: The Agrarian Response of the Periphery   16

  3. Migration in the Colonial Period   41

  4. Political Protest in the Nationalist Period   65

  5. The Rural Rebellion   80

Part Two: The Postindependence Period

  6. Postindependence Patterns of Public Expenditure   103

  7. The Impact of Expenditures in the Countryside   130

  8. Migration in Postindependence Zambia   160

  9. Migration from Kasumpa Village   188

  10. Political Responses at the Local Level   202

  11. Patterns of Party Conflict   226

  12. Rural Responses to Industrialization   252

Maps

  1. Line of Rail in Zambia   261

  2. Districts and Provinces of Zambia   262

  3. Luapula Province   263

  4. Kasumpa Village   264

A Note on Research Methods   265

Notes   274

Selected Bibliography   339

Index   371

Acknowledgments

This study has received the assistance of many persons and institutions, and this assistance has come in many forms. It is a pleasure to acknowledge the aid I have received. And it is with some urgency that I insist that the credit for the virtues of this study be shared while the blame for its shortcomings be confined to me alone.

The study was financed with grants from the Joint Committee on African Studies of the Social Science Research Council, the National Institutes of Health (grant number HD 05707–01/03), and the Division of the Humanities and Social Sciences of the California Institute of Technology.

Throughout the various stages of this study, numerous assistants contributed to this research and their aid has been invaluable. In particular, I wish to acknowledge the work of Margaret Kieffer, Bruce Wm. Bennett, Christine Partridge, Steven Mitchell, and Bellington Ndafuka. Mr. Ndafuka guided my efforts in a society and culture foreign to me; and his obvious tact, frankness, and graciousness were valued both by me and by the subjects of this research. Also helpful was the work of Kim Border, Jennifer Owen, Susan Williams, Ben Kalimukwa, Chintu Harringtone, Simon Munshimbwe, Joseph Chilafi, and Reuben Nyirenda.

Several organizations facilitated my work in Zambia. I was a research affiliate of the Institute for African Studies of the University of Zambia, and I gratefully acknowledge the assistance of its staff and its director, Jaap van Velsen. The faculty of the university and, in particular, Cherry Gertzel, James Fry, Sholto Cross, and Chris Hesse were of great assistance to me. Nchanga Consolidated Copper Mines Limited, the manager and the personnel department of Rokana Corporation, and the Copper Industry Service Bureau assisted in the urban portions of my work, and the aid of the Mindolo Ecumenical Centre was very helpful as well. I wish also to thank Ian and Susan Hodgkin for the gracious hospitality they extended to me.

In the rural areas, I received generous assistance from the Mbereshi Secondary School, and in particular from Tom Lynn and Dudley and Sarah Brown.

I wish also to acknowledge the aid and sponsorship I received from the officials of the United National Independence Party and the ministries, agencies, and departments of the government of Zambia. This cooperation was shown at all levels: in Lusaka, in Luapula, and at the district and local levels. Without the assistance, cooperation, and frankness of these officials, my study would not have been possible. I can only hope that its results will facilitate the welfare objectives to which so many of them are dedicated.

Most of all, my thanks go out to the subjects of this study. While they will remain anonymous, it was they, more than anyone, who made this work possible.

Numerous people read and criticized the manuscript for this book. Not all their suggestions were followed, if only because many were contradictory; and while the readers strengthened the work, they are not therefore responsible for the deficiencies that remain in it. The readers include Joan Nelson, Richard Sklar, Robert Rotberg, Lance Davis, Morgan Kousser, David Grether, Roger Noll, John Ferejohn, and Thayer Scudder. To Roger Noll and Thayer Scudder I owe special thanks.

My thanks go as well to Joy Hansen, Reiko Komine, Melinda Ziska, Linda Underwood, and Barbara Yandell for their aid in preparing the manuscript. Barbara Yandell typed and proofread the manuscript with infinite patience, care, and good humor. The population program of the California Institute of Technology provided equipment and bibliographic resources which aided the completion of this study; and Edwin Munger generously extended the use of his library.

This work could not have been completed without the use of materials from the collections of Margaret Rouse Bates and David C. Mulford.

Portions of this study have appeared elsewhere and are published with the consent of the University of California, the University of Denver, and the *Cahiers d'Études Africaines.*

Finally, I wish to thank Margaret and Elizabeth Bates for their support throughout this research effort. My last book was for Margaret; this one is for Elizabeth.

RURAL RESPONSES TO INDUSTRIALIZATION

Introduction

> In Africa [to focus on rural society alone is] conceptual butchery . . . for if one thing characterizes . . . behavior on the continent today it is the increasingly interlocked nature of the African . . . economy. To focus exclusively upon rural problems in an Africa of the late twentieth century is ingenuous . . . we must focus instead upon those functional relationships that bind the urban nodes to their rural hinterlands.[1]

To a greater degree than the vast majority of the nations of the world, Zambia has experienced rapid, precipitate, and comprehensive change. Less than a century ago, Zambia was exclusively agrarian; in the present era, it is a society dependent upon large-scale industry. Once characterized by village society, the territory that is now Zambia contains a score of cities of 100,000 or more persons, and these cities contain over 40 percent of its population. Where but a little over fifty years ago forests once stood, there now stand copper mines; and the marketed produce from these mines makes Zambia one of the world's leading exporters of this mineral. This study examines the rural responses to industrialization in this central African nation.

My principal thesis is that rural dwellers have responded in three distinct and important ways to the rise of industry and to the growth of towns. The first two responses are economic in nature: the spread of cash crop farming and the growth of migration from the countryside as rural dwellers enter the urban markets for produce and labor. The third response is nonmarket in nature and takes the form of political protest. In the early years, rural protest was marked by widespread participation in the nationalist movement; more recently, it has entailed rural support for forces of political sectionalism. This study examines the impact of industrialization upon the countryside of Zambia by analyzing the involvement of the villagers in cash cropping, migration, and politics.

A secondary thesis underlies the study: that much of the behavior of rural dwellers is based upon their desire for material gain. In making this assertion, I depart from the tradition that interprets the behavior of rural dwellers as being largely determined by cultural beliefs, the forces of tradition, or religious values. I also reject the interpretation of rural behavior that views villagers as too lazy, irrational, or unmotivated to take advantage of expanding economic opportunities. Instead, I make use of the assumption that the consistent preference for more income over less strongly shapes the economic, social, and political behavior of the village residents of Zambia.[2]

Conjoining these two theses, I will examine how the desire for material betterment has shaped the response of rural dwellers to the growth of industry in this central African nation. The literature on industrialization, and especially on peasant[3] responses to it, tends strongly toward romanticism. Industry tends to be seen as "evil" and rural life as "good," or at least unspoiled. The growth of industry and urban areas tends to be viewed in terms of increasing misery. There is, however, another way of regarding these trends, and I adopt this alternative perspective. The movement of capital into urban-based industry generates wealth. From the point of view of the rural dwellers, the influx of capital creates opportunities for higher incomes; and time after time peasant populations appear to have sought to exploit these opportunities. Their entrance into the urban market for produce and labor and their attempts to increase incomes by engaging in political action appear to represent alternative approaches to taking advantage of the new opportunities for material gain created by the rise of industry.

Seen from this perspective, the behavior of rural dwellers in Zambia raises several major questions which I will examine in this work. Given the growth of towns and industry, why do some villagers respond by engaging in cash cropping while others exit from the countryside and migrate to the towns? What determines why some rural regions become farming areas while others serve as labor pools for the major urban centers? And what are the relationships between the market and political responses of the village dwellers? In response to their relative poverty, why do some rural dwellers seek the riches of the cities by engaging in farming or migration while others take recourse to political action?

While pursuing answers to these questions, I also attempt to contribute to several areas of scholarly investigation. The analysis of agriculture and its role in industrialization is one such area. Thus, for example, T.W. Schultz, E.L. Jones, and a host of others have examined the transformation of agriculture in Europe and assessed its relationship to the Industrial Revolution in European society.[4] Maurice Dobb, Naum Jasny, Thomas C.

Smith, and others have studied the role of agriculture in the rise of Russia and Japan as major modern industrial powers.[5] Problems of contemporary agriculture in Africa, the role of agriculture in financing industrial expansion in the new African nations, and the responses of African peasant producers to the growth and penetration of market forces from the cities have also received the concerted attention of numerous contemporary scholars.[6] By investigating the rise of rural production in Zambia, and the determinants of the successful transformation from subsistence to commercial farming that has taken place therein, this study thus seeks to contribute to an area of continuing scholarly concern.

Another major body of literature centers on the subject of rural-urban migration. Students of British industrialization have long been preoccupied with the origins of the industrial labor force; and, while rejecting Oliver Goldsmith's portrait of a denuded and depopulated British countryside, they have nonetheless emphasized the shift of rural population to the major centers of industrial production in England.[7] Historians of industrial development in Russia and Japan have also studied the transfer of labor from farming to industry and have emphasized the characteristically confiscatory nature of this redistribution of human resources in the Soviet Union.[8] In Africa, scholars have noted and examined for years the movement of peoples from agriculture to industry and from the countryside to town. Indeed, of all the aspects of modernization in Africa, this phenomenon has received the greatest attention.[9] By focusing on the migratory response of the village dwellers to the growth of industry and the formation of towns, I hope to contribute to this area of scholarly investigation.

A third major literature centers on peasant politics. The transformation from a rural to an industrial society has been marked by outbursts of rural protest and of peasant violence. E. J. Hobsbawm, in his classic study *Primitive Rebels*, examined nineteenth-century protests against the rise of capitalism.[10] Historians of the United States, Japan, and the Soviet Union, to mention but three of the major industrial powers, have noted the rural protest and violence mounted in opposition to the industrializing strategies of their commercial and political elites.[11] So, too, in the modern era several contemporary scholars of Asia and Latin America have designated the peasantry as the revolutionary class of our time.[12] Scholars of Africa have been slower than their contemporaries elsewhere to recognize the rural base of political protest and violence.[13] Nonetheless, rural protest is now an acknowledged feature of African politics, and its relationship to the growth of wealth and the competition for developmental resources in the new African nations receives increasing attention.[14] By examining the political responses of village dwellers to the rise of industry in central

Africa, this study will therefore contribute to a third area of scholarly inquiry.

Of these literatures, the last has been of greatest concern to me. My own discipline is political science; and, within that discipline, I work in the subfield of political development. I am convinced that a major contribution can be made in this field by bringing the study of peasants and peasant behavior into the center of its concerns. With a few notable exceptions, political scientists working in the developing areas have tended to ignore the rural populations and the literature on peasant politics.[15] Instead, they have largely left the study of villagers to the anthropologists and historians while concentrating on the behavior of new elites, the conduct of national-level politicians and bureaucrats, and the interplay of pressure groups (students, ethnic associations, and the like), most of which are based in the cities. For political scientists studying the developing nations to ignore the affairs of the countryside is to commit a major error of omission. A defining attribute of the developing nations, after all, is the very magnitude of the proportion of the population which dwells in the villages. By focusing on the affairs of the rural areas, I attempt to rectify this deficiency in the discipline.

This volume strives to make one other contribution to the literature on the developing areas: it attempts to "get behind" and thereby to comprehend the long-familiar relationship between the great social and economic transformations—such as industrialization and urbanization—and the rise in political participation that seems to be characteristic of the developing areas.[16] The existence of such a relationship appears to be well established, but the causal basis for it is not well understood. By trying to disentangle the complex relationships between political behavior in the countryside and the growth of industry and towns, this study will attempt to explain why and in what manner social and economic modernization relates to the growth of political participation in the developing areas.

The Case Study

The material in this book is organized by topic and by era, the topics being areas of inquiry and empirical phenomena for which we seek explanations. The first is the spatial concentration of wealth. Along a narrow strip of Zambia, termed the line of rail,* lies perhaps one of the most developed areas in all of black Africa. Mines, railroads, industries, commercial enterprises, large-scale farms—all are concentrated in this area. The line of rail yields a standard of living that is prosperous even by world standards. Beyond the line of rail, however, there exists relative poverty:

*The phrase line of rail denotes the area lying along the railway in Zambia; it includes the copperbelt and runs from Livingstone to Chililabombwe (see map 1).

villages, whose modes of production, while skillfully utilized, nonetheless yield average incomes that are often dismally poor by comparison with the central portion of the nation. Only occasionally are the more remote districts prosperous. As two commentators have been quoted as stating, Zambia "give[s] rise in some respects to a sharper rural-urban contrast than can be found anywhere else in the world."[17] In spatial terms, prosperity in Zambia is highly constrained. This sharply delineated distribution of wealth is one of the phenomena I try to explain.

A second and related empirical phenomenon captures our attention: some rural dwellers in Zambia appear to have gained prosperity in the modern era while others have not. Some village areas have responded to the growth of the line of rail by entering commercial production and by marketing maize, cattle, fish, groundnuts, cotton, tobacco, and so forth, while others have remained in poverty. The question arises: why have some rural dwellers benefited from the expansion of wealth occasioned by the rise of industry while others have failed to do so? The question marks out the second kind of phenomenon I seek to explain.

Third, there is the fact of migration. For decades, villagers in Zambia have left the countryside and sought jobs in the cities. This phenomenon has attracted the attention of numerous and highly skilled social scientists, and they have established many of the empirical regularities that I attempt to account for. Among these there is, of course, the fact that migration does take place. There are also the facts that some kinds of people migrate while others do not, that some rural areas have higher rates of migration than do others, and that some people tend to stay in town while others return to the countryside.

There is also the phenomenon of rural political protest. Classically, politics in Africa has been seen as an urban phenomenon, but more recently scholars have uncovered the role of rural dwellers in mass political action. What studies of the Congo, Kenya, and West Africa have suggested, this study will seek to confirm: that rural dwellers participated extensively in the politics of the colonial era and contributed strenuously to the fight for political independence.[18] Indeed, as I will argue, they contributed to the wave of political violence that made it in the interests of Britain to make a rapid exodus from Zambia—and to do so on terms highly favorable to the local nationalist politicans. In addition, as studies elsewhere have suggested, the rural population of Zambia has contributed to the rise of patterns characteristic of postindependence politics in Africa: provincialism and the growth of political sectionalism.[19] These empirical regularities also demand explanation.

The concentration of wealth, the spread of agriculture, the growth of rural-urban migration, and the rise of political participation—these phenomena thus capture our attention. So too does change over time;

and this study therefore examines each phenomenon in both the colonial and the postindependence era. My interests are predominantly contemporary, and the postindependence era therefore receives the greater emphasis. But it is naïve to assume that contemporary patterns in Africa are the result of contemporary forces; as often as not, their causes lie in past decisions whose consequences are difficult to overcome. Moreover, there is a literature of very high quality, passed down from the colonial period, on the topics examined here. This literature amply rewards examination and analysis, and it must be utilized and spoken to. Part One of this study therefore examines each of these topics in the colonial period; Part Two examines them for the period since independence in Zambia.

Two basic methods will be utilized throughout this study. The first is the construction of verbal models. I posit actors of various kinds; I assume that they behave purposefully; and I assign rules by which they make choices so as to attain their goals. I then argue, in effect, that, given certain initial conditions, the choices these actors would make if their goals were in fact those I assigned to them and if the rules they observe were in fact those I set for them—the choices they would make if these things were "true" would then generate the empirical realities I seek to account for. The actors I posit are the following: public investors, private investors, producers, consumers, voters, and politicians. People acting in these capacities, I argue, have played the leading roles in the drama of rapid change in Zambia. And their behavior—the series and patterning of the choices they have made—largely accounts for the spatial allocation of economic resources in Zambia and the attempts to distribute these resources more broadly through migration, cash cropping, and political action.

The first method is thus one of abstraction: defining actors with objectives who behave according to the rules for choosing. The second method is one of particularization: to experience what social change in rural Zambia has meant to people, to make the experience of change visible and tangible through illustration and case materials, and to test our ideas against the actual experiences of one group of people. The case materials I employ to achieve these objectives come from Kasumpa, a village group in the Luapula valley of Zambia (see map 3). In this study I attempt to flesh out and to illuminate my analysis by examining the history of this village, the life of its people, and the ways in which they have sought to gain access to the wealth generated by the growth of industry and by the rise of the cities in central Africa. While time and again I move into the lives of these particular people, I keep a careful eye on the broader setting of the village. For while as citizens and voters, as investors in agriculture, and as proto-migrants these villagers have acted as choosers, the value of the alternatives from which they have chosen has been set largely by forces external to their village community.[20]

PART ONE

THE PREINDEPENDENCE PERIOD

1

The Local Setting: From Imperial Heartland to Industrial Periphery

The Luapula River flows northward, draining Bangweulu Lake and the adjacent swamp areas and debouching some 150 miles later in Lake Mweru. This river now forms the boundary between the Shaba Province of Zaire (formerly the Katanga Province of the Congo, Leopoldville) and the Luapula Province of Zambia. In the eighteenth century, however, it formed the easternmost perimeter of the most powerful central African kingdom of its time: the kingdom of Mwata Yamvo. From Mwata Yamvo's kingdom emigrated numerous groups, some led by conquering warriors dispatched by royal decree and others by dissident chiefs who were fleeing the king's disfavor. Many of these bands crossed the Luapula River and settled in Zambia; the history of many of Zambia's tribes reaches back to their origin in Mwata Yamvo's kingdom.[1] Among the tribes for whom this is true is the Lunda tribe of the Luapula valley.

The Lunda are the dominant tribe of the valley. In precolonial times they held military and political suzerainty over the area, albeit sometimes precariously, and received tribute from the chieftains on both sides of the Luapula River. The traditions of the Lunda allow us to date their arrival at approximately 1740; they came as conquerors, dispatched by Mwata Yamvo both to satisfy his ambitions for territory and to secure the production of important metal works and salt deposits in the area. Upon crossing the river, the Lunda rapidly subdued the major tribes of the valley—the Shila and Bwile—and established diplomatic relations with the principal tribes on the northeastern plateau—the Tabwa, Chishinga, and subgroups of the Bemba. While the early political system of the Lunda is poorly understood, it is known that the focus of the system was the tribal chief, Mwata Kazembe, who ruled through an intermediary group of military and political leaders, almost all of whom were recruited directly from the conquering Lunda and few, if any, from the indigenous groups whom they had conquered. It can be said that the Lunda tribal system was politically more highly centralized than were the systems of the majority of other tribes for whom we have early information.[2]

The Great Tradition

Within decades of their arrival in the valley, the Lunda and their chief, Kazembe, became a major focus of the attentions of the world outside of central Africa. More than any other group in contemporary Zambia, with the exception perhaps of the Lozi, the Lunda became the subjects of published commentaries by explorers, adventurers, and traders from Portugal, Britain, and the east African coast.[3] From an historical point of view, this notoriety reveals the importance of the Lunda in this period. Their early renown is also important to an understanding of contemporary relationships in the Luapula valley, for it has become a part of the "great tradition" of the Lunda aristocracy—the cultural and historical basis on which they seek to justify their supremacy in the social and political order of the Luapula area.[4]

There were several reasons why the explorers—most notably, Lacerda (1798–99), the Pombeiros (1805–11), Monteiro and Gamitto (1831–32), and Livingstone (1866–73)—sought out Kazembe of the Lunda. For Lacerda, at least, a major reason was political: with an eye to the threat of Boer and British penetration from the south, he wished to extend Portuguese influence to the interior from the Mozambique coast and, if possible, to link up with the Portuguese territories on the western coast of Africa. Both Lacerda and Livingstone were also motivated by religious zeal: to convert indigenous peoples to the Christian church, to civilize them, and to purge them of barbarity were important goals to both gentlemen. For some, the desire to comprehend the geographical features of central Africa gave impetus to their travels; Livingstone, for example, died just outside the Luapula area, having entered the Lunda territory in search of the headwaters of the Nile. But perhaps the major motivation behind all the explorations was the search for trade; and the major reason for Kazembe's prominence was that by controlling the Luapula valley he controlled access to the interior markets of Africa.[5]

The commodities traded in the interior are familiar to all students of nineteenth-century Africa. Guns, cloth, household implements and lesser ware from Europe were exchanged for ivory, precious metals, and slaves. Kazembe controlled access to two of the most desired of these commodities: slaves from the eastern Congo and precious metals (especially copper, either worked or in the form of malachite) from the watershed between the Zambezi and Congo rivers. To gain access to these commodities, expeditions from the east African coast had first to deal with Kazembe; and the diaries and commentaries that have been published reveal Kazembe's ability to exact monopoly profits from those who sought to trade in the central African markets.[6]

The profits Kazembe could extract soon led to the entrance of competitors. In the mid-nineteenth century, groups of Arabs established trading and military camps in the plateau area adjacent to the Luapula valley, and they soon became significant rivals to Kazembe in the trade in slaves and ivory. Another group, the Yeke, penetrated into the Congo and established in Katanga an empire that, by the late 1860s, had become fully the equal of the Lunda Kingdom in wealth and military power. The Arabs and the Yeke began to undermine the preeminent position of the Lunda. They extended their hegemony over lesser tribes that formerly had paid tribute to the Lunda. They joined with rival tribes, especially the Tabwa, in joint military campaigns against the Lunda. And, by providing shelter and support for rivals to Kazembe from within the Lunda ruling circles, they fomented internal conflict and instability within the Lunda empire.

This pattern of internal strife reached its peak in the 1870s and 1880s. As this era of turmoil has highly significant consequences for this study, it is worth examining a little more closely.

The Little Tradition

The central figure in the events of the mid-nineteenth century was one Lukwesa Mpanga, who had been selected to become Mwata Kazembe VII. Lukwesa's conduct prior to his installation generated widespread opposition to his succession, however; and one Muonga Sunkutu, with the support of many of the Lunda aristocrats, usurped the throne. Lukwesa took refuge among the Arabs; biding his time, he formed an alliance with important Arab leaders and the Yeke, and with their aid he seized back the throne from Muonga Sunkutu. Lukwesa's dependence on foreign powers, and his generally ruthless suppression of domestic dissidents, made him an unpopular chief. Thus a faction of Lunda aristocrats and military leaders sought to remove him from power again and to give the throne to Kanyembo Ntemena, one of the major princes. Toward this end, the "patriot" faction contracted with perhaps the most powerful Bemba king of the time, Chief Mwamba, for military assistance.

With the assistance of the Bemba, Kanyembo Ntemena (Kazembe X) succeeded in driving Lukwesa Mpanga from the kingdom. Upon his accession, Kanyembo sought to terminate the constant incursions of the Tabwa, the Yeke, and the Arabs and to restore peace to his kingdom; and so he turned once again to Chief Mwamba for military support. This time he secured a full brigade of Bemba warriors, under the leadership of Mwabamukupa. The Bemba assisted Kanyembo Ntemena in fortifying the capital city and then deployed in a defensive perimeter of fortified villages to the north of the capital. The largest of these villages was that of Mwabamukupa; in later years the village was to become known as Kasumpa village, and it is this village that forms much of the basis for my study.

The area that Kazembe allocated to the Bemba extended north from the Mbereshi River (see map 3). It was through that sector that the major attacks were expected from the north, and several were indeed mounted by the Arabs and by Shila and Tabwa warriors. Nonetheless, the perimeter held, and with the help of the Bemba, Kanyembo X was able to remain in power until subjugated by a new and overwhelming force in central Africa—the British South Africa Company.

The Bemba immigrants came to occupy a unique position within the Lunda kingdom. Unlike other groups in the valley, they resided with the Lunda not because they had been conquered by them but because they had been invited to live in the area. For years, they owed their fealty not to the Lunda chiefs but to their own chief, Mwabamukupa. This tradition of autonomy, equality and political independence formed a "little tradition" within the Lunda empire. While the Lunda perpetuated their "great tradition" in the pageantry of the Lunda court and the published works of the European explorers, the Bemba immigrants preserved their little tradition in the memories of their elders, the lineage histories of descendents of their chief, and in meaningful place names, like that of Mwabamukupa Stadium, the football field used by the youth of Kasumpa village, or chibolya, the tree-sheltered site of the first fortified village of the Bemba perimeter (see map 4).[7] This little tradition separated the Bemba immigrants from their Lunda overlords. It expressed their feelings of pride, autonomy, and independence, feelings which made it exceptionally difficult for them to accept a position of political subordination, with enduring consequences for themselves and for this study.

The British South Africa Company

The British South Africa Company (BSA) was a chartered company formed in 1889 to administer and develop the territories of central Africa for the benefit of its shareholders. The major interests in the company were held by its principal director, Cecil John Rhodes, who had made his fortune in the gold and diamond fields of south Africa. Attracted by the prospects of similar rewards from the minerals of central Africa, investors joined Rhodes in proposing a company that would gain rights to the minerals in the territories of the indigenous tribes of the region in exchange for political and military protection, money, and promises of industrial and social development. Upon the formation of the company, having gained the authorization of the British government for the venture, Rhodes enlisted several major agents to secure mineral concessions in central Africa, including a principal British consul in the area, Harry Johnston, who was stationed in Zomba.

The company extended its influence in three major separately administered spheres. In the south, it operated in what was to become known as Southern Rhodesia. In the northwest, it established its influence largely through the Barotse Protectorate, where it maintained a close relationship with Lewanika, the chief of the Lozi. In the northeast it operated throughout what now are known as the Eastern, Northern, and Luapula provinces of Zambia, its headquarters being located first in Zomba (in what is now Malawi) and later in Fort Jameson (now Chipata). While separately administered, each region nonetheless was responsible to a single board of directors; and the board, although entertaining imperial ambitions, was nonetheless primarily interested in gaining a profit. In this study, we will be concerned mainly with North-Western and North-Eastern Rhodesia, which later were amalgamated into Northern Rhodesia, and eventually Zambia.

Toward this end, the BSA dispatched its agents to secure mineral rights in these territories. From the accounts of the early explorers, the company was aware of the existence of copper deposits within Katanga and its environs, and they were eager to gain access to them. In addition, the company directors were struck by the geological analogy to the Rand represented by the watershed between the Congo and Zambezi rivers and were persuaded that the prospects of riches in the area were sufficiently great to warrant the costs of gaining control over it. Within weeks of the company's formation, Alfred Sharpe, one of its agents, left from the east coast of Africa to sign treaties with the chiefs in the Luapula valley and further inland in Katanga. In 1890, he entered the capital of Kanyembo Ntemena, who willingly exchanged rights over minerals in his territory for the company's assurance of military assistance. In a recapitulation of the policy of the previous Kazembes, however, Kanyembo sought to prevent Sharpe from dealing directly with the inland tribes of Katanga and severely delayed his departure for the court of the Yeke. When Sharpe did cross the Luapula he met resistance from Msidi, the chief of the Yeke; and so depleted had Sharpe's supplies become during the delay caused by Kazembe that he was forced to leave Katanga before signing the treaty he desired. Instead, shortly after Sharpe's departure the rights to the Katanga minerals were gained by a party in the pay of King Leopold of the Belgians. Upon recrossing the Luapula, Sharpe set up administrative posts to keep alive the presence of the British South Africa Company within striking distance of the Katanga concessions; one, at Chiengi, was on Lake Mweru, and the other was at Kalungwishi, near the lake and overlooking the river valley (see map 3). Both, but especially the latter, became centers of European influence over the affairs of the Luapula area. These were the earliest inland posts of the BSA in the northeastern territories.

After the initial period of treaty signing in the northeast, the British South Africa Company's primary concern was simply to establish order in the area. The buffeting of the Lunda empire by Arab slave traders and rival kingdoms found its parallel in numerous wars and skirmishes across the entire northeastern plateau. During the second half of the 1890s, the company mounted frequent raids and punitive missions against the Arab slave traders, and by 1898 they had defeated the most powerful of these marauding bands. In 1899 the Bemba were finally subjugated; and with their capitulation peace was brought to the plateau after almost a century of nearly continuous turmoil. Only Kazembe remained as an independent force within the northeastern possessions, preferring, despite his treaty agreements, to maintain a posture of armed neutrality vis-à-vis the company offices at Kalungwishi. Disturbed by reports from these offices telling of Kazembe's continued enmity, the company dispatched a military band to the Luapula in October of 1899. As had almost all the previous enemies of the Lunda, this force of men marched south from Kalungwishi along the Luapula River; unlike their predecessors, however, these men easily penetrated the defense perimeter along the Mbereshi River, and they laid waste to the capital city of Kanyembo Ntemena. Kanyembo fled to Belgian territory. When his negotiators were able to secure guarantees of his safety, he returned to his throne; but he was now as much a subject as a ruler in his own valley kingdom.[8]

One consequence of the Lunda capitulation was the worsening of relations between the Lunda rulers and the Bemba immigrants. The Bemba defenders had failed in their mission of defending the empire. Moreover, with the suppression of raiding and warfare, there was little need now for the services of the Bemba warriors; the Kazembes no longer needed to depend on the goodwill of the Bemba military captains. As a result, when Kanyembo Ntemena died in 1904, his successor sought to displace Mwabamukupa and to install his own appointee in charge of the territories the Bemba chief had governed.[9] Kazembe's initial attempts were successfully rebuffed by the immigrant community, who still enjoyed the influential support of Chief Mwamba of the Bemba nation. But in the 1920s Kazembe XII at last succeeded in terminating the independent power of the Bemba. Taking advantage of the first registration of the chiefs under the new British administration, he inserted the name of his own appointee in the list of chiefs as a ruler over the territories to the north of the Mbereshi River.[10] Kanyembo is now the official chieftainship of the area and the name of Mwabamukupa no longer appears among the names of the politically influential in the valley. His former village now bears the name of Kasumpa, the Lunda aristocrat directly appointed as village headman by Mwata Kazembe to govern the immigrant Bemba community. Kasumpa is only one of two villages in the entire Lunda kingdom whose headman is directly appointed by Mwata.[11] Thus did the Lunda king, while losing his sovereignty, yet gain greater control over a hitherto independent subgroup within his kingdom.

The major consequence of the entrance of the BSA, however, was to alter permanently the relationship between the residents of the valley and the outside world. The BSA came in search of profits from extracting minerals, but the richest ores were not to be found in Luapula. Consequently, the successful development of a mining industry—hundreds of miles outside the valley—moved the Luapula valley from the center of political and economic affairs in central Africa to their very periphery. Within three decades of the arrival of the company, the Luapula valley moved from the heartland to the hinterland of central Africa. The response of the valley's inhabitants to this change forms much of the subject of this study.

2

Investment in the Center:
The Agrarian Response of the Periphery

Patterns of Private Investment

Despite the imperial rhetoric of its most influential director, Cecil John Rhodes, the British South Africa Company was principally an economic enterprise and not a government. Its main purpose was not to conquer and administer but rather to generate profits;[1] indeed, the costs of administration were regarded as expenditures that had to be made in order to secure revenues. In accounting for the behavior of the BSA and for its historical legacy to Zambia, we can best analyze its conduct in terms of our notion of a private investor. Private investors, we assume, choose among alternative investment opportunities so as to maximize the present value of streams of future profits. And the present value of these profits is calculated in terms of their magnitude, temporal proximity, and degree of risk. Thus, according to this hypothesis, when confronted with a series of alternatives, private investors will choose to invest in those for which the profits are greatest, quickest, and most certain.

In the early days of the BSA's rule in central Africa, the location of the major mineral deposits was quickly established; virtually by 1910 the agents of various south African and British firms had discovered and registered the lodes that were later to be the sites of Mufulira, Roan, Rokana, Nchanga, and Broken Hill mines.* Initially, however, these claims lay for the most part undeveloped and almost all active mining in central Africa was confined to the territories in the south or in Katanga. Two related considerations account for the relative lag in the development of the Zambian mineral deposits. Because of inadequate subsurface explora-

*Roan is located in the town of Luanshya; Rokana in Kitwe; Nchanga in Chingola; and Broken Hill in what is now known as Kabwe (see map 1).

16

tion, the richness and abundance of the ores were not known. Moreover, the relative wealth of the Katanga surface ores was so overwhelming as to direct financial attention to the development and operation of that mineral field. As stated by J. Austen Bancroft in an oft-quoted passage:

> In the early days it was not uncommon for oxide ores containing 5 per cent copper to be used as ballast for railways and for road material. With the knowledge of this procedure in Katanga, numerous mining men who, from 1905 to 1926, examined the relatively low-grade oxide copper ores of the outcrops of the Roan Antelope, Nkana South, Chambishi and the first discoveries at Nchanga, considered them to be of very little or no value.[2]

Only two local deposits attracted serious financial attention: Broken Hill, where lead and zinc deposits were mined as early as 1904, and Bwana Mkubwa, a copper mine outside Ndola. While neither mine was in any sense a major producer, both attracted the participation of well-connected financiers. This became critically important when the world market in minerals altered in favor of African producers in the 1920s, for the financiers were in a position to channel investment funds rapidly into local mineral production through the intermediary of corporations that had been formed to develop these two local mines.

The turnabout in the fortunes of the local mining industry began in the 1930s. In 1922, the BSA altered its rules for obtaining mineral concessions so as to favor highly capitalized firms. To obtain concessions, companies now had to agree to "spend a minimum amount each year on prospecting with the right . . . to peg claims subject to the usual royalties and license fees payable to The British South Africa Company. . . . In the flotation of these Concession Companies, The British South Africa Company was entitled to a stated allotment of fully paid shares."[3] The rapidly changing structure of the world market provided an incentive for investors to utilize these new rules. Electrification, the development of the automotive industry, and other economic trends increased the demand for copper, and with the formation in 1926 of Copper Exports, Inc., a United States trust, producers came to control over 60 percent of the international trade in the commodity. The growth of demand and the cartelization of the market naturally resulted in price rise in copper and this price rise served as an incentive to increase investment radically; the incentive was strong enough to facilitate the organization of investments in the central African mineral fields.[4]

At Broken Hill, one Sir Edmund Davis was on the board of directors; a major partner of Cecil John Rhodes in the BSA and other ventures, Davis was able to attract south African investment to the local mineral deposits.

It was Davis who in the 1920s drew Anglo-American Corporation, the financial empire of Ernst Oppenheimer, into the development of the local mines, first as technical consultant and later as a major investor. A second key figure, Alfred Chester Beatty, was on the board of directors of Bwana Mkubwa mine. The director of Selection Trust, Ltd., of London, Beatty possessed an extensive knowledge of trends in the international copper market and a range of connections in American and British mining circles that enabled him to mobilize finances, engineering expertise, and managerial skills at short notice. Beatty quickly realized the potential value attached to mineral claims in central Africa and used his local companies to purchase major mineral concessions from the BSA on behalf of Selection Trust. In the mid 1920s both Selection Trust and Anglo-American began to prospect and map their respective concessions, to excavate and reinforce underground workings, and to import and erect the heavy equipment required in the extraction and treatment of ores. Both cleared and drained areas for factories and townships and established programs of medical care that would allow them to maintain a healthy and productive labor force for their enterprises. These initial, intensive investments stood the companies in good stead; for, although they had to close down their workings during the depression, their early efforts enabled them to bring the deposits into production rapidly and to capture a major share of the international market in copper that developed with Europe's economic recovery in the mid-1930s. Indicative of the rapidity of their ability to enter production after the depression is that the output of refined ore rose from 6,000 long tons in 1930 to 213,000 tons in 1938, making the territory's mines one of the major copper producers in the world.[5]

The incentive of the profits from mineral production was sufficiently strong to call forth major investments in other industrial sectors. Railways initially benefited the most. Just as the charter of 1889 endowed the British South Africa Company with exclusive title to mineral rights in the territory, so also did it endow the company with exclusive rights to the construction of railway transport in the area. In the early 1900s the development of the Broken Hill mineral deposit was hindered by the lack of transport. In 1906 the BSA helped to finance a rail link from its southern holdings to the Broken Hill mine. And, as a major shareholder in both undertakings, the BSA was in a position to utilize its earnings from mining to help finance railway construction.

The growing mining industry in Katanga supplied the next infusion of capital into the territory's rail network. Reaching an advanced state of development by the early 1900s, the Congolese mines required coke and coal for their smelting operations; the richest such deposits lay in Rhodesia. Moreover, until the completion of their own rail link to the sea, the

Congolese mines required access to coastal ports; the most efficient route to the coast was over the existing rail network in southern Africa. Both considerations led the Congolese firms to finance the extension of the rail line from Broken Hill to Katanga. The rail link reached the Congo border in 1909. The third major expansion of rail capacity was again financed in response to the prospects of mineral profits. As I have indicated, the alteration in the financial conditions of local mining in the mid-1920s led to a large-scale infusion of capital into the development of mineral production in the territory. A concomitant to the expansion of the mines was the construction of spur lines from the central line of rail to mine sites in Luanshya, Mufulira, Kitwe, and Nchanga. The completion of these spurs in the early 1930s marked the end of the formation of the physical basis for the line of rail in Zambia.[6]

Just as the development of the mining sector called forth investment in the railways, so too did it call forth investment in other sectors. Among the most important of these sectors was the power industry. A primary motivation for the construction of the railway was to provide the mines access to Rhodesian coal, but the collieries quickly proved insufficient to meet the energy requirements of the mines and the companies invested in alternative energy sources. The first such venture was a hydroelectric facility near Broken Hill in 1925; a second was completed during the Second World War. Following the war, the companies constructed an integrated electrical supply, the Rhodesian-Congo Border Power Corporation, and linked their energy network with that of the Katanga mineral producers. The culmination of these investments was reached in the mid-1950s when the companies invested heavily in the construction of the Kariba hydroelectric dam. Its completion in 1958 marked the end of the development of the preindependence power industry—an industry that sold over 60 percent of its output to the mines.[7]

The growth of the mines, the railways, the power industry—all these developments in the industrial sector entrained yet further private investments. For example, the creation of new hydroelectric capacity made investments in the cement industry profitable; and, with the backing of the Commonwealth Development Corporation, a facility for producing cement largely destined for the construction of the Kariba dam was constructed outside Lusaka. In addition a series of firms grew up around the mines: engineering services, construction firms, mechanical workshops, transport firms, and manufacturers of steel and metal products to be utilized by the mining companies. By the 1950s the mines were the major purchasers of acids, chemicals, quarry products, printing services, and wearing apparel. As Robert Baldwin wrote concerning the mid-1950s: "There are few domestic manufacturing activities left to be counted, once the local industries from which the copper companies make significant purchases are enumerated."[8]

Aimed as they were largely at supplying the mines, it is not surprising that these investments concentrated in the mining towns and along the line of rail. One index of this concentration was the distribution of the European population that immigrated in search of wages and profits. In 1921, 3,032 of the 3,634 Europeans in the territory, or over 80 percent, lived in the provinces along the line of rail; and by 1946 the figure had increased to 92 percent of the European population.[9] Another index is the location of the firms themselves; the earliest information available reveals that at least 95 percent of these establishments were located in the provinces on the line of rail.[10] A last index is the location of the employment opportunities generated by the capital investments. The earliest material available, which pertains to 1931, indicates that 77 percent of the jobs for Africans in the territory were located in provinces on the line of rail; by 1963 over 80 percent of the jobs were located in this area. At the latter date less than 50 percent of the African population lived in the line-of-rail provinces.[11]

The effect of the growth of the line of rail was thus to render the Luapula valley along with the areas of the Northern, Eastern, Barotse, and Northwestern provinces peripheral regions in the territory. These areas became rural hinterlands of the industrial center of Zambia, a complex that had been generated by investors who mobilized capital in search of the profits to be gained from mineral deposits in the territory. Though bypassed by the influx of industrial investments, the village population of this rural hinterland did have opportunities for sharing in the growth of industry. In 1938, according to Phyllis Deane's estimates, over four million pounds were spent locally by persons deriving income from employment in the territory; in 1945 the figure was over eight million pounds. In both years over 40 percent of this outlay was spent for food, drink, and tobacco—agricultural products that could be grown by farmers in the rural sector of the territory.[12] By meeting the demand for such products, the rural dwellers could benefit from the economic expansion.

The Agrarian Response

In agriculture as in mining, the incentive for private investment in increased production, and therefore the achievement of higher earnings, is the magnitude, certainty, and immediacy of the profits that can be obtained. In accounting for the patterns of the rural response to the opportunity for income from the line of rail, we can therefore best proceed by focusing on the major factors affecting the profitability of agriculture.

In the case of Zambia, perhaps the most important such factor was proximity to the urban markets. The demand for agricultural goods is concentrated in the towns, where the returns from cash employment are exchanged for basic commodities. In the rural areas families tend to produce their own requirements and so the market for agricultural produce is small. Significant advantages accrue to those producers who locate near the source of demand, for transport is costly, of course, especially in an area where the roads are poor and facilities scarce. As a result, the profitability of agriculture, and thus the incentive to invest in agricultural production, tends to be greatest in the areas close to the towns.

A second major factor is the cost of transport. E. A. G. Robinson, writing in 1932, noted that transport charges amounted to about one pence per pound for every 100 miles; a producer of a 200-pound (standard) bag of maize in Kasama wishing to sell his maize at the nearest copperbelt* town would have to pay 75 shillings in transport costs at a time when maize was selling at less than 10 shillings per bag.[13] Under these circumstances, prospective producers of agricultural commodities would therefore seek to locate their investments within sixty miles of the line of rail. As one more cautious scholar concluded in 1937: "Beyond 30 miles from the railway, it is not profitable to produce crops of low value."[14]

Particularly for this study, however, it should be noted that outlying areas could escape from the spatial constraints upon rural prosperity by producing crops especially suited to the peculiar natural conditions of the area; their advantage in production costs could offset the high costs of transport. As we shall see, villagers in the Luapula valley were able to share in the prosperity generated by the midcentury growth of industry in the central regions of Zambia by producing one such commodity, and they thereby became some of the more prosperous hinterland dwellers in the territory.

A third major determinant of the magnitude of rural prosperity in Zambia is the possession of readily mobilizable capital which could be invested in increased agricultural production. At the time of the development of the line of rail, money was scarce in the rural areas and institutions for mobilizing financial resources were almost nonexistent. Rather, capital consisted largely of productive assets, and the most critical of these assets was cattle. Cattle are particularly important to a people seeking to shift from subsistence to commercial production, for they are liable to be owned even by subsistence producers and they represent capital equipment. Cattle can increase the scale of rural production by providing traction power by which farmers seeking to increase their incomes can bring greater areas

---

*The word copperbelt refers to the collection of urban centers contained in the Copperbelt (formerly Western) Province, the majority of which have grown up around a major copper mine.

under production. Cattle can also influence the intensity of production. Fertilization can increase yields, and, where cattle are available, so too is manure. In addition, feed crops constitute a beneficial rotation, and foraging can improve the texture of soils; both feed-growing and grazing can therefore increase the productivity of existing acreages. Besides being a form of capital equipment, cattle also represent a final product, for they can be sold as meat to urban consumers and so can themselves constitute a major source of income for rural producers. The relationship between cattle holding and agrarian prosperity is thus close.

In Zambia, as elsewhere in Africa, the primary determinant of the distribution of cattle is the incidence of the tsetse fly. In the north, save in the area about Mbala (see map 2); in most parts of Luapula; in the east, save around Chipata; and in the northwest, the presence of the tsetse fly severely limits the level of cattle holdings by village dwellers.[15] In Barotse, the Chipata area, and the Central and Southern provinces, village dwellers can maintain livestock, and their herds have become sources of cash income. In the case of the Central and Southern provinces, this third major determinant of rural income coincides with the first, the proximity to markets. The result, as we shall see, has been that the center of rural wealth corresponds spatially to the center of industrial activity in Zambia; both areas abut the line of rail.

The Spread of Agricultural Production

The development of farming in Zambia reveals the effect of these major factors upon the pattern of agricultural investments. Commercial farming first arose in the areas adjacent to the headquarters of the BSA in the Eastern Province in the early decades of the twentieth century. With the development of the mines in the 1920s, however, the center of the industry shifted to the line of rail. Many of the Eastern Province farmers either switched into specialized production of a high-valued crop (tobacco) which could withstand transport costs or relocated closer to the industrial center of the territory, relocation being completed by the end of the early 1960s.[16] The mines, which provided rations for their employees, represented the principal market for the major agricultural products of the time—maize and beef. First exporting to the mineral centers in Katanga and then marketing to local mining firms, the commercial farms in 1937 sold 80 percent of their beef and over 25 percent of their maize directly to the mining companies.[17] Profits for farming were thus to be found in the markets along the line of rail, and major investments in agricultural production took place in this area.

Adding to the locational advantages of the line of rail were not only the magnitude but also the certainty of the returns from agricultural investments in the area. Seeking to promote farming and cognizant of the economic advantages of proximity to the railway, the British South Africa Company and the colonial government legalized the alienation of land to highly capitalized producers under freehold conditions in areas adjacent to the rail lines, thereby offering security to farm investments. These terms, by and large, were not offered in other areas in the country, which were left under conditions of native tenure and where the duration of leasehold agreements was too short to warrant major investments. The effect was to provide a legal underpinning to what market forces had already promoted —the restriction of highly capitalized farming to a narrow central band of Zambia near the railway.[18]

By and large it was European immigrants who invested in large-scale, highly capitalized farms in the country. Nonetheless, indigenous farmers also responded to the market for produce on the line of rail, and they soon became the most prosperous village farmers in the territory. Elizabeth Colson, in her studies of the Plateau Tonga, the dominant ethnic group of the area, notes that the Tonga began to market crops in the 1920s—the period of the expansion of the copperbelt and the growth of the demand for produce to feed workers in the new urban areas.[19] And L. H. Gann reports that in the early 1930s the Tonga, in search of farm profits, began to convert their cattle holdings into agriculturally productive resources; increasingly they converted portions of their cattle stock into oxen for drawing plows, sledges, and oxcarts, often with a measurable decline in the quality of their breeding herd.[20] Indicative of the extent to which farmers in this area reconstituted their cattle herds into capital assets is that, of the 22,700 plows in the territory in 1950, 18,000 were held by the indigenous farmers in the southern area along the line of rail.[21] William Allan points to the line-of-rail farmers at Pemba (south of Mazabuka) as being the first indigenous farmers to utilize manure for purposes of fertilization.[22] The result was that, by 1945, while 85 percent of the village farmers in the area about the railway in Southern Province remained subsistence producers, 15 percent had begun to specialize in the marketing of agricultural output to the urban centers. And the income of this group was over £33 per annum with the most prosperous 1 percent earning over £370 per annum; as a basis for comparison, the mean annual wage of the urban African laborer in 1945 was £21.8 per annum with the highest paid, the mineworkers, earning £41.2 per annum.[23]

Elsewhere, farming was not nearly so lucrative an enterprise. Barotse cattleholders did gain income from the export of their cattle, both to the mines of Southern Rhodesia and to the line of rail; but it does not appear that their earnings approached those of the line-of-rail farmers. In the

Eastern Province, local farmers were able partially to compensate for their remote location by taking advantage of favorable soil conditions to produce tobacco, cotton, and confectionary nuts. Eastern Province farmers also profited from both the sale and utilization of their cattle, the area being only partially subject to the tsetse fly.[24]

The only other sector of the country able to establish a major trade in rural produce was the Luapula valley. Luapula was not a viable area in which to invest in the production of most agricultural commodities. It is remote from the urban markets: from Kazembe's area to the nearest city, the distance is nearly three hundred miles.[25] Moreover, gaining access to the urban markets in both Katanga and Zambia involves crossing international borders if only to cross the Congo pedicle so as to reenter Zambian territory on the copperbelt. The formalities at the border can be costly to produce carriers whose cargoes are liable to inspection by customs officials and revenue collectors; to the costs of time must also be added the costs of occasional bribes to expedite the crossing. In addition, transporters must cross the Luapula River, and the ferry service is sometimes unreliable, traffic occasionally being delayed for hours. It can therefore be a very costly three hundred miles from Kazembe to the urban centers, making the province even more remote than its physical location would imply. In short, distance to the urban markets is such as to render the area relatively unattractive to investments in most kinds of agricultural production.

Even were Luapula closer to urban markets, it would be difficult to increase agricultural output from the area. For, like much of the territory in the north, Luapula is infested by the tsetse fly; and while eradication programs are currently underway, in most of the area, and certainly in most of the era of concern to this study, the presence of tsetse has historically made it impossible to maintain significant cattle holdings.

Basic determinants of agricultural profitability therefore constrained the capacity of the village dwellers of the Luapula area to respond to the growing urban markets by increasing levels of agricultural production. Fortunately, however, the lakes and river systems of the area did create a natural advantage for the production of one crop for which there was a great urban demand: fish, perhaps the basic protein ingredient in the diet of the growing African labor force. In the early years of the growth of the copperbelt, fish production brought prosperity to Luapula.

The demand for fish was created by the growth of the mines. The Katanga mines in the first decades of the 1900s, and later the mines in Zambia, issued rations for their employees as part of the conditions of service they offered; in addition to the maize and beef they purchased from the line-of-rail farmers, the mines purchased fish from the Luapula area.

The earliest figures available (for 1932) show a recorded export from the Luapula fisheries of 931 tons, a figure that grew to over 4,000 tons in 1942. By the mid-1950s, the export of fish to the Katanga and Zambian urban centers had increased to an average of over 9,000 tons annually, which at prevailing prices resulted in at least £300,000 in earnings per year by the upper Luapula fishermen. Table 2.1 shows what these tonnage figures imply for the per capita income of the Luapula fisherman under different assumptions concerning the conditions of sale and the number of fishermen. The per capita incomes earned in fishing compare favorably with those of the line-of-rail peasant farmers and those of the urban wage earners during this period, as recorded above.

In response to this opportunity to profit from the urban demand for fish, considerable investment took place in the marketing and production of this commodity. The center of these investments was Kasenga, a small town on the Congo side of the Luapula River (see map 3). In the early 1920s, immigrant Greeks established a depot at Kasenga, where they built an ice plant and packing facilities; contacting local fishermen, they commenced exporting their catches from the valley. By the end of the 1920s the Greek traders had purchased a steamer which made weekly runs along the Luapula River and into Lake Mweru, stopping at fixed points to exchange Congolese francs for the fish caught by the villagers.[26] By the end of the 1940s, the Greek traders had amassed a fleet of power boats for gaining access to the more remote fish camps; they also began selling plank boats and nets to the local fishermen, many of whom were investing their earnings in improved fishing equipment.[27] In addition, the traders purchased a fleet of lorries for transporting their purchases to depots in the interior whence they were distributed by rail to the main mining centers of Katanga.

Indigenous entrepreneurs also entered the fishing trade. By the 1950s, at least eighteen Africans owned motor boats and operated as major fish buyers.[28] Others invested in motorized land transport and supplied dried fish to the copperbelt by van, car, and even bus.[29] Some used their earnings from fishing to set up trading stores in the valley, which they used as fish-purchasing depots, retailing the fish to marketeers from the copperbelt. Still others remained in fish catching per se; but by purchasing engines and nylon nets, and by replacing their canoes with plank boats, they upgraded their production capacity by investing in new technologies.

As a consequence of the investment in the fish trade, the economy of the Luapula valley prospered. While the entrance of the BSA into central Africa had dislodged the valley from its position at center stage in the affairs of central Africa, the valley residents nonetheless had seized the advantages offered by their new status as dwellers in a rural hinterland. By

Table 2.1   Estimated Per Capita Income of Luapula Fishermen under Different Assumed Conditions

	Number of Fishermen					Number of Fishermen				
	2,000	2,500	3,000	3,500	4,000	2,000	2,500	3,000	3,500	4,000
	All Fish Sold Fresh at 2 d./lb.					*All Fish Sold Dried at 4 d./lb.*				
With total sales of:										
931 tons in 1932	£7.76	£6.21	£5.17	£4.43	£3.88	£15.52	£12.41	£10.34	£8.87	£7.76
4,000 tons in 1942	33.33	26.67	22.22	19.05	16.67	66.67	53.33	44.44	38.10	33.33
	All Fish Sold Fresh at 4 d./lb.					*All Fish Sold Dried at 1s. 1d./lb., (fresh weight equivalent)*				
8,655 tons in 1955	£144.25	£115.40	£96.17	£82.43	£72.13	£118.57	£94.85	£79.04	£67.75	£59.28

Sources: Prices obtained from: Northern Rhodesia, *Minutes of the Administrative Conference of Provincial Commissioners and Heads of Social Service Departments, 1949* (Lusaka: Government Printer, 1949), p. 25; and file LNA/F13/3, Kawambwa Local Council. Tonnage figures: Ian G. Cunnison, *The Luapula Peoples of Northern Rhodesia*, p. 9; and Northern Rhodesia, *Report of the Rural Economic Development Working Party* (Lusaka: Government Printer, 1961). The number of fishermen is calculated from S. K. Mayowe, "Mweru/Luapula Fishery: Commercial Fishing Survey, 8 September 1969," file FSH-5, Fisheries Officer, Nchelenge District Offices.

Notes: Average earnings per capita are expressed as decimal fractions. For the 1955 figures, the sales were recorded as fresh weight equivalents, and therefore the value of the sales was adjusted in calculating the earnings for dried fish sales (one pound of dried fish being reckoned as the equivalent of four pounds of fresh fish). From a study conducted in 1969 we know that there were roughly 2,000 fishermen in the Lake Mweru/Luapula fishery. Because of the previous decline of the fishery and the fact that new fisheries had opened and that fishermen had migrated to these new fisheries, we can assume that at least 2,000 fishermen worked the fishery in the earlier periods.

their response they had transformed their peripheral position into a position of advantage. The prosperity they gained from trading with the new urban centers struck many observers of the area. As early as 1929 a government official was impressed by the fact that 20 percent of the taxable males in the valley owned bicycles and "the number of licensed native traders . . . was rapidly increasing."[30] The government also noted the improvement in housing in the area; in 1931 it was reported that "in the Luapula valley, the people are building houses of burnt brick."[31]

Writing about the Luapula valley in the early 1950s, Ian Cunnison, an anthropologist, repeatedly commented upon the prosperity of the region. His accounts make the valley sound like a Latin Quarter in central Africa. Brick houses with verandas surrounded by decorative gardens, and possessing glass windows purchased from the city; men on bicycles or in motor cars; shops, tea rooms, and trading centers offering goods for sale from the urban centers; bus routes winding through the valley; gramophones, guitars, and radios—these signs of prosperity seemed to clamor for his attention. In recording his impressions of the area, Cunnison concluded: "There is a feeling that Luapula life is not rural, backwoods life. Commonly one hears: 'It is the Copperbelt here.' . . . There is much in this."[32] Earlier in the same book he wrote, "The people who throng the roads give the impression of sleek prosperity allied with great energy. The businesslike rags they wear on their fishing expeditions are replaced on Sundays by white shirts, creased trousers, polished shoes and felt hats."[33] This was a prosperity generated by trade with the city, and the government of the territory was perhaps correct in stating in 1948 that "the fishing trade on the Luapula River and Lake Bangweulu" is "the most important undertaking in the rural areas."[34]

Only a few of the people of Kasumpa, whose fate we shall follow closely throughout this book, benefited directly from the fish trade. Kasumpa village is too far inland from the river and lagoon and too far south from Lake Mweru to be a major producer of fish.[35] Out of a total sample of 105 household heads in Kasumpa whom I interviewed in 1971, 4 reported fishing as their primary source of income; 8 others reported supplementing their primary sources of income with occasional fishing; 3 others made their living as fish traders; in addition, another 3 entered fish trading to supplement their incomes from other occupations. All told, then, slightly under 7 percent of the sample of Kasumpa villagers were directly dependent upon the fishing industry, and an additional 10 percent entered it to supplement their incomes. Nonetheless, the economy of the village has clearly been affected by the prosperity of the surrounding fishing centers: Kazembe, the villages near the Chipita fish market north of Kazembe, and the villages and markets of the Kanyembo area of the Mofwe Lagoon.

Thus, as we shall see, one of the major cooperatives in the village, which has prospered sufficiently to purchase a lorry, imports mealie meal from the copperbelt and sells it to the fishermen; and they purchase the mealie meal itself with proceeds earned from transporting fish from town. There were but three persons involved in this activity; but the process is more widespread than this figure would suggest, for over five times that number of villagers (17) reported as their primary source of income the sale of crops—cassava, snuff, or fruits and vegetables—and many of these sales were made to fishermen from the river. An additional five reported supplementing their incomes in this way. And, lastly, there were five villagers whose primary source of income was from retail shops and groceries, and three others who occasionally sold retailed goods in the village. My own observations of their trade, as well as their own comments on these operations, suggested that a fair percentage of their business was with fishermen who were passing through the village on their way to the main highway of the valley, which bisected Kasumpa; on their way to the hospital at Mbereshi; or simply visiting relatives in Kasumpa or in neighboring villages. Nearly 30 percent of the villagers thus indirectly derived income from the fishing industry by selling goods to fishermen. The economic ties between the fishing industry of the valley and the descendents of the Bemba warriors are thus important, and the prosperity of Kasumpa village is dependent upon the economic fate of the surrounding fishing industry.

Patterns of Public Investment

Up to now I have focused on the investment choices of private individuals. My principal assumption has been that private investors choose those alternatives which promise the greatest expected discounted profits; on the basis of this assertion, I have accounted for the concentration of private investments about the line of rail. Private investment is not the only form of investment, however; nor, for some purposes, is it the most important. In continuing the study, we must also examine the financial behavior of the public sector in Zambia. Thus far, we have been able to employ an explicit and highly simplified notion of the behavior of private investors. Our notion of how public investors behave needs be, perforce, more complex.

Three primary factors, we shall assume, influence the decisions of public investors: ideological preferences, the need for political support, and the desire to augment the expected value of public revenues. Ideological and political considerations lead governments to invest in ways that private investors would not. Nonetheless, if only to secure revenues to spend for purposes that are of ideological or political significance, governments, like private investors, will seek to invest in areas that promise high rates of return, these returns accruing in the form of tax revenues.

A corollary of the last proposition is that, as public revenues become more abundant, public investments will be made in areas with lower rates of return, all other things being equal. This, of course, is a familiar tendency in all investment markets where an increasing supply of loanable funds, given a stable demand, allows borrowers (or projects) to obtain funds at cheaper rates (or with lower returns). This tendency has been noted by Albert Hirschman, who states that "paradoxically, *public spending on the poor area thus is likely to display the features usually associated with private spending on luxuries.*"[36] Only in cases of exceptional budgetary abundance, he concludes, are investment programs in poor areas liable to be undertaken.

In the sections that follow, the importance of these notions of government behavior will become increasingly apparent. To foreshadow this discussion, I will use these propositions to account for the varying behavior of the three major regimes that have held public power in Zambia: the British South Africa Company, the government of Northern Rhodesia, and the postindependence government of Zambia. The evidence I have so far presented clearly indicates that most areas off the line of rail offer returns to investments far below those to be earned from investments in the copper-based economy of the central zone of the country. My primary concern will be to understand the factors that promote or inhibit public investments in the hinterland areas where economic incentives have failed to attract investments by private individuals. The three regimes exhibit clear differences in their ideologies, their dominant constituencies, and their level of revenues. I shall use these differences to account for the variation in their efforts to alter the pattern of economic opportunities generated by the behavior of private investors in Zambia.

From Corporate Rule to Protectorate

As noted previously, the first government in Zambia was in fact a private corporation—the British South Africa Company. Being a corporation, the firm had little reason, either ideological or political, to invest in areas other than those that yielded superior rates of return; in seeking to maximize its profits, the BSA allocated its monies to the southern mining and farming areas in Rhodesia, while largely, and purposefully, ignoring the unremunerative areas to the north of the Zambezi. Even within the areas that were to become Zambia, a company memorandum of 1920 indicated that 41 percent of the total expenditures of the company went to the narrow railway strip at the center of its holdings—a strip that represented less than one-eighth of its total territory and population, but which contained the areas of mining and farming that were the chief source of the company's revenues.[37] The pattern of expenditures under the BSA thus reflected the desire of a private firm to maximize revenues and to minimize losses, thereby maximizing profits.

These attempts notwithstanding, the BSA was unable to turn a profit and for over thirty years it failed to pay out a single dividend. It was not until 1924 that the company made payments to its shareholders—6 pence on the pound—but the dividends stemmed from an inglorious source: while retaining title to the mineral concessions in the territory, the BSA transferred its other assets to the British Crown and virtually liquidated its administrative operations in central Africa. In 1924, in short, the BSA transferred public powers in central Africa to the British government and became purely a private corporation seeking to gain profits from the minerals of the territory. With the end of chartered rule came the transformation of the public sector in Zambia from a corporation to a government.

We have noted that it is reasonable to expect corporations and governments to diverge in their investment choices. If only for reasons of ideology, it could have been expected that the Northern Rhodesian government would have devoted a greater proportion of its financing to the more remote, hinterland areas of the territory than did the BSA. For Northern Rhodesia was a "protectorate," and its government was therefore officially committed to protecting and enhancing the well-being of the indigenous peoples of the territory. Moreover, the government officially subscribed to the colonial doctrine of indirect rule and to several of its normative corollaries: that the natives of the territory should maintain their commitment to their rural tribal communities, that the forces of modernity and civilization should be used to perpetuate and strengthen indigenous institutions, and that the role of government was therefore to maintain a rural focus in the lives of the indigenous population.[38] In pursuing their notions of the public interest, the colonial officials thus tended to see themselves as spokesmen for the indigenous population and as protectors of their welfare. These views naturally implied a budgetary priority on investments in the rural sector of the territory. As we shall see, these priorities were in fact reflected in the pattern of planned government expenditures.

For several reasons, however, the colonial government failed to invest public funds in the rural sector at a rate comparable to the rate at which it allocated funds to the line of rail. For one, the government of Northern Rhodesia for much of its existence had few funds. The depression of the 1930s deprived the government of revenues with which to do more than maintain the barest essentials in public services. No sooner did the depression recede than the government was embroiled in the Second World

War, and during the war it was impelled to order its budgetary priorities to conform to the needs of the metropole. In practice this meant that it surrendered control over the principal sources of its revenues—the earnings of the mining industry—to the British government and utilized most of the revenues that did remain for wartime mobilization rather than for development purposes.

The government of Northern Rhodesia therefore experienced long periods of financial scarcity. Moreover, the traumatic experience of the depression in the territory, during which the mines virtually closed and the government was literally put on a care and maintenance basis, generated a reluctance to mount major long-term investments. For the government's experience in the depression and its familiarity with the highly variable fortunes of the mining economy of South Africa made it extremely sensitive to the riskiness of its revenue base. The government therefore adopted a budgetary policy designed to enhance the *certainty* of its revenue position. And this entailed accumulating surpluses to tide the public treasury over years in which the adverse fortunes of the mining companies threatened to reduce severely the inflow of funds. Rather than risk the possibility of overextending itself financially, the government instead tended to retrench—to spend only on projects that would generate rapid industrial growth (and thus certain profits) while accumulating budgetary surpluses and thereby building up its financial reserves.[39]

During the late 1940s, however, the financial position of the government notably improved, for several reasons. With the end of the war the Ministry of Supply of Great Britain released control over the output of the mines, and copper commanded a better price on a competitive market than it had under the supply agreements of the war. For another, the government, under the urgings of local representatives in the Legislative Council, compelled the British South Africa Company to surrender to the government 20 percent of the royalties it received from metal mining in its old concession areas; this measure too substantially increased the government's revenues. Moreover, the government altered its taxation agreements with the United Kingdom so that rather than receive but 50 percent of the British tax on the mining companies, it could now tax up to the full local limit (7s. 6d. on the pound of taxable corporate income), with the residual balance going to the treasury of Great Britain. These measures plus the favorable effects of the postwar devaluation of the pound upon the world price of copper resulted in major increases in government revenues. From 1947 to 1950, for example, they more than doubled.[40]

According to our notion of the behavior of public investors, given this abundance of funds and given the ideology of the government, we should expect the government to increase its level of public investment in the countryside. Indeed, in response to its favorable financial position, the government set out to do precisely that. It set forth its goals in 1947 in a Ten-Year Development Plan. The plan restated the government's commitment to its protectorate role and its determination to advance the interests of the largely nonurban and nonindustrial African population. The financial power of the government was to provide the mechanism for upgrading the standard of living in the rural sector, and the government was to increase its level of public investment radically in the rural areas.[41] As the plan was devised on a sectoral and not a regional basis, it is difficult to determine the precise distribution of planned expenditures between the rural and urban areas of the country; nonetheless, we can make inferences concerning that distribution. Twenty percent of the planned investments were to be made in agriculture, rural marketing, forestry, and veterinary services; while involving the European farmers, these activities also impinged upon the primary productive activites of the African rural dwellers. A further 11.5 percent was to be made in rural development activities per se and thus clearly was intended to benefit the rural population. Altogether the plan unambiguously assigned a full 33.4 percent of its expenditures to the rural areas. And in other budgetary categories, such as African education (11.8 percent of the total planned expenditures), health, communications, and public works, the plan earmarked funds for activities that affected Africans off the line of rail. Given that, in 1963, 57 percent of the African population lived off the line of rail, and that it is reasonable to assume that in 1947 the proportion must have been higher, the planned per capita expenditure would have been greater for those dwelling on the line of rail than for those living off it. Nonetheless, compared with what had gone before, the plan was precisely what it purported to be: a significant redistribution of public expenditure programs from the urban-industrial to the rural areas, and the first major effort to make large-scale investments in the rural sector of the nation. This rural commitment was renewed a decade later in a supplementary plan aimed at the development of the Northern Province (now Northern and Luapula provinces). The plan called for an exceptionally high level of expenditures in areas thought to be particularly poor by comparison with the line of rail, the level of relative poverty having been signaled by the magnitude of emigration from the areas.[42]

Financial abundance and ideological preference thus led the colonial government to aspire to increase financial allocations to areas where economic conditions had failed to furnish an incentive for significant private investments. These aspirations were modified, however, by the fact that, like all governments, the colonial government operated within a constitutional order that vested influence over its decisions in certain constituencies. De facto, if not de jure, its major constituency was the immigrant-settler population. As these settlers had been attracted to the country by

Table 2.2 Distribution of the European Population of Northern Rhodesia

	1921		1946		1951	
	No. of	*% of*	*No. of*	*% of*	*No. of*	*% of*
Province	*Europeans*	*Europeans*	*Europeans*	*Europeans*	*Europeans*	*Europeans*
Line-of-Rail provinces						
Copperbelt			11,725	53.8	20,454	55.1
Central			5,867	26.9	10,027	27.0
Southern			2,450	11.3	4,779	12.9
Total	3,032	83.4	20,042	91.9	35,260	95.0
Other provinces	602	16.6	1,756	8.1	1,871	5.0
Total	3,634	100.0	21,798	100.0	37,131	100.0

Sources: 1921 and 1946 figures: Northern Rhodesia, *Report on the Census of Population of Northern Rhodesia Held on 15th October, 1946*, p. 12; 1951 figures: Northern Rhodesia, Labour and Mines Department, *Annual Report for the Year 1951* (Lusaka: Government Printer, 1952), p. 46.

Note: Totals will err because of rounding and because train passengers have been eliminated from the computations.

the economic opportunities created by copper mining, over 80 percent resided in the area of the line of rail (see table 2.2), while fewer than 50 percent of the African population resided therein.

Throughout the life of the colony, the settlers gained increasing power in the territorial government and thereby increasing influence over the pattern of public expenditures. Indeed, the political history of the colony has been interpreted largely in terms of the prolonged and consistent campaign of the settlers to gain constitutional revisions that would enhance their power within the government.[43] Demanding "responsible government," the settlers in 1918 compelled the British South Africa Company to concede to the formation of an Advisory Council of five elected members. The council had no formal powers, but it did provide a means by which the preferences of the European population could be registered in the making of governmental decisions. With the transition to colonial rule in 1924, the constitution was altered so as to provide a Legislative Council; though holding only a minority of the seats in the council (the majority being held by bureaucrats from the territorial administration), the settlers nonetheless benefited from their participation in an institution having significantly more than an advisory role in the governance of the territory. By 1938 the settlers' representatives gained parity with the government bureaucrats in the Legislative Council, and by 1945 they held a majority of the posts in that body. The settlers were excluded entirely from posts in the executive branch of the government (called the Executive Council) until 1939. Seeking to unite the territory in the war effort, the colonial administration in that year included political leaders of the settler community in the ranks of the Executive Council for the first time. In 1949, the settlers gained four posts in the Executive Council; more importantly, they also gained an official understanding whereby the executive branch of the government became in part accountable to the legislative branch within which the settlers' representatives held a majority of the seats. By the terms of this agreement, the territorial administration agreed to appoint representatives to the Executive Council only with the consent of the majority of the settlers' representatives within the Legislative Council; moreover, once the members of the Executive Council lost the confidence of their backers in the Legislative Council, under the terms of the agreement, they had to be dismissed.[44] Thus, through the successive modification of the territory's constitution, the settler community gained greater access to governmental power and a greater capacity to influence the decisions of government.

By comparison with the settlers, the African community lacked institutionalized means for compelling the government to take account of its preferences. While settlers' representatives entered the legislative arena in 1918, the first representative of African interests was not appointed until 1938; even then, the representative was a white European settler and not a black African. While Europeans had participated in elections since 1918, Africans virtually could not vote until 1959.[45] The settlers had been organized into political parties since the 1920s; until after World War II, African attempts to form political parties were deemed illegal and were prosecuted by the government as acts of sedition. Even at the end of the colonial era, the agencies that were formed to give voice to African opinion and to select spokesmen for African interests—the local and provincial councils—culminated in an advisory body, the African Representative Council, rather than in an agency vested with actual control over the making of policy.[46] While African representatives of African interests were admitted to the Legislative Council by that time, they were nominated to posts in that body by the colonial government rather than being elected by their own constituents. The African majority thus had less access to governmental bodies than did the settler community; and the greater weight of the settlers in the constitutional structure of the territory meant that it was they who were in a position to compel allocations by the public sector rather than the Africans who were, by the ideology of the protectorate, supposed to be the prime beneficiaries of colonial rule.

The consequences for the pattern of governmental expenditures in the colonial era were predictable. Despite its stated intention to divert investments to the districts off the line of rail, the government in fact modified its expenditure plans in favor of the line of rail. Perhaps the most dramatic illustration of this is its 1953 revision of the Ten-Year Development Plan. Not counting loans to local authorities, the amount unambiguously assigned to the rural sector fell from £4.11 million to £2.9 million; even counting those loans, the rural dwellers' unambiguous share of the proposed capital expenditures fell from 33.4 to 15.4 percent of the total planned investments.[47]

The main reason for the proportionate decline in rural expenditures was the vast increase in the planned expenditures upon public goods for the line-of-rail economy. The period of economic expansion after World War II led to vociferous demands by private industry for improved roads, more plentiful water supplies, housing, increased supplies of electric power, and more efficient railway facilities. Private industry by this time had come to dominate the tax base of the government. For example, while in 1947, when the first version of the plan was published, the mines contributed £1.189 million to the government revenues or 27.7 percent, when the plan was revised in 1953, the figure had risen to £16.771 million or over 55 percent of the government revenues.[48] The government, with a constituency based on the line of rail and anxious to sponsor the growth of its own revenue base, therefore diverted the flow of planned public investments to the benefit of the line-of-rail sector. As Robert E. Baldwin wrote of this period:

> Rapid expansion of the economy after the war created pressing needs for capital in the monetary sector. To take full advantage of these new capital opportunities, greatly enlarged outlays . . . were urgently needed, and gave every indication of yielding a higher short-run return than spending on . . . rural projects. The government soon shifted the main part of its development efforts toward the monetary sector. The urban African shared in the benefits from this change in policy but the rural, nonmonetary African sector did not receive proportionately much more in the way of development aid than it had in the thirties.[49]

Exemplifying this reordering of priorities was the increase of planned expenditures in the categories of "public works" and "communications." Within these categories fell the majority of the expenditures on economic infrastructure; and they rose from 24.0 percent of the plan in 1947 to 34.5 percent of the budgeted investments in 1953, an increase which in absolute terms amounted to 15.6 million pounds.[50] Illustrating the role of the European electorate in obtaining shifts in spending priorities was another major increase, this time in the level of planned expenditures upon European education. Increasing from £1.54 million to £5.1 million, the monies for European education rose from 1.9 to 9.4 percent of the total planned capital outlay; by contrast, the expenditures for African education remained virtually unchanged in absolute terms, resulting in a proportionate decrease from 11.8 percent to a mere 3.3 percent of the revised schedule of public investments. As Baldwin summarized the effect of the constitutional order upon the pattern of public expenditure,

> For years, government officials deplored the extent of the imbalance between economic development in the monetary versus the subsistence sector. But, under political pressures of the moment, the Legislative Council invariably responded to the wishes of the European electorate and channeled most of the funds available into the money economy. Without significant political representation, the rural African population, understandably, was seriously neglected.[51]

Public Investment in the Rural Sector

Before concluding our analysis of the public sector in preindependence Zambia, we should examine more closely that "lesser portion" of the government's program: its support for the development of the rural areas. The programs of the colonial government can best be studied by examining its policies toward agriculture. Two aspects of this policy are vital to our discussion. The policy aimed overwhelmingly at providing services and facilities to the central region of the economy where agriculture could most profitably be undertaken; it therefore helped to perpetuate the disparity between the returns to farming along the line of rail and those elsewhere in Zambia. In addition, insofar as agricultural policy impinged upon the subsistence farmers off the line of rail, it did so in a way that placed a clear upper bound on the incentives to invest in increased production.

One aspect of the government's policy has already been touched upon: the policy toward land. I have already discussed some of the factors that determine variations in the *magnitude* of the returns to investments in agriculture; and I have demonstrated the comparative attractiveness, in terms of these factors, of investments in line-of-rail farming. In addition to the magnitude of the returns, however, prospective investors also take into account the *certainty* of the returns. And it is here that the public sector has a critical role to play. Before investing heavily, a farmer wants to be certain that his rights over his land are clearly and enforceably vested; and to secure capital from commercial sources, the farmer must be able to minimize the risks to his creditors by possessing a title stating the enforceability of his rights and thus the recoverability of his assets. As I have suggested, the public sector in colonial Zambia established these legal preconditions for the capitalization of agricultural production primarily along the line of rail. Outside the line of rail, heavy investment by private individuals was discouraged by the multiple claims to land titles inherent in many areas under native tenure; by the inability of farmers in those areas to alienate land permanently save by subterfuge; and by the fact that the only legal form of alienation was by means of relatively short-term leases. In the words of one official who took part in the legislative debates that led to this pattern of land law, all of these factors made investments off the line of rail "an unattractive proposition for purchasers of virgin land requiring a great deal of initial capital."[52]

Besides providing a legal context within which agricultural investments took place, the colonial government also furnished agricultural services. As in the case of its legal reforms, the favorable impact of these services was largely restricted to the line of rail.

Perhaps the major such service was the government marketing agency for the major agricultural commodity in the territory: maize. The marketing agency was established shortly after the depression and was a critical element in the government's program to stabilize the price of this commodity. The government sought to control the level of production by small-scale African producers so as to prevent them from oversupplying the domestic market, thereby further depressing the already low price of maize and endangering the investments of commercial farmers. To obtain this objective, maize-control ordinances made the government marketing agency a monopoly buyer of maize in the major area of maize production in the territory: the area along the line of rail. The marketing agency was required to purchase all the maize sold by local producers, for only in this way could the agency gain control over the market for the commodity, thereby fulfilling its pricing objective.

After the creation of the marketing agency, economic conditions rapidly altered. With the end of the depression, the mines reopened and rapidly increased production. As output rose, so did the level of demand for agricultural products. Rather than controlling the supply of maize to a constricted market, the marketing agency therefore found itself supplying maize to a rapidly expanding market. And instead of suffering from the controls imposed by the marketing agency, the line-of-rail farmers found in the marketing agency a certain buyer for their produce. As the Department of Agriculture reported in 1937:

> The economics of Native maize production have been revolutionized by Maize Control. Formerly only a fraction of the surplus available for sale in good years was actually purchased; now a cash market is available for every bag of maize a Native cares to bring in. It was estimated that the average purchase of Native maize during the three years prior to Maize Control was 58,000 bags per annum. . . . In the first year of Maize Control, 234,000 bags of Native Maize were handled.[53]

For purposes of this study, the major effect of the government's marketing policy was to widen the differential in the profitability of farming between the line-of-rail areas and the rest of the territory. At no point did the government seriously commit itself to extending marketing services beyond the central section of the country. The costs of marketing in areas distant from the urban markets would have made such services a continuing drain upon government revenues, and there were no political incentives strong enough to cause the government to incur the real economic costs inherent in promoting crop production at great distances from the major markets. Public investments in the marketing services thus tended to reinforce, rather than to counter, the patterns of economic returns to farming that market forces and natural endowments had already established in the territory.

A similar areal bias existed in the provision of credit and extension services. Commercial farmers on the line of rail could secure credit from the Land Bank, a statutory agency of the government, or from commercial sources. Both accepted the farmers' fixed assets and titles as security for loans and therefore were willing to accept the risks involved in farming investments. Naturally, the small-scale farmer off the line of rail could furnish neither kind of security and therefore was excluded from using existing credit facilities.[54] In addition, the government helped to finance small-scale improvements on the part of peasant farmers through the African Farming Improvement Scheme. As described by John Hellen, the funding agency paid "bonuses on an acreage basis and . . . subsidies for Scotch carts [oxcarts], fertilizers and conservation work. This scheme was intended . . . to stimulate development at a lower level." However, because the scheme was funded by levies from produce marketed through the government marketing agencies, "the system operated only in the Southern and Central Provinces," that is, on the line of rail.[55]

The government thus maintained agencies and services designed to increase agricultural productivity and thereby increase rural incomes but confined these to a narrowly defined sector: the sector where output was already high, where the costs of production were relatively low, and where significant capital had already been invested by private individuals.[56]

There is one last significant aspect of government policy that deserves note, and this is the area of price policy. This policy can again best be discussed in terms of maize. With the growth of the urban industrial economy on the line of rail, the main purpose of government policy became the maintenance of a cheap and abundant supply of food to the urban consumer. The government therefore reimbursed the marketing agency for the difference between the earnings they realized in selling maize at a low consumer price and the expenses they incurred in purchasing the product from farmers. The result of the differential between consumer and producer prices was a consistent trend of oversupply for the local market and a continuing loss by the marketing agency as it sold the surplus production on the relatively depressed world market. The government offset this loss with public funds, and the resultant subsidy to the farmer has been estimated at approximately £2.5 million over the period 1955 to 1957.[57] The effect of this policy did not extend beyond the commercial farming sector, however, for the vast majority of African farm families lived in regions not serviced by the statutory marketing agency that benefited from the government's expenditures.

The more remote farm families faced an entirely different pricing policy. Rather than being subject to a policy whose main purpose was to encourage maximum production, even at the cost of expensive surpluses, they faced a policy whose goal was to generate regional self-sufficiency. The scale of provincial production was such that private entrepreneurs would not furnish transport and marketing facilities, nor, as we have seen, was government itself willing to absorb the cost of marketing, either by "exporting" produce from the more remote farms to the line of rail or by "importing" produce to these regions should local production fail to meet local demand. The government therefore set official prices at a level designed to make each remote region self-sufficient in food. The result was that, as local farmers became more productive and thereby generated a surplus, the government reduced the price offered to local producers. Beyond investing in productive capacity that could meet the level of local demand, they therefore had little incentive to invest in increased production in agriculture.[58]

In common with most of the areas off the line of rail, the Luapula valley received little public investment in agricultural production and was subject to a pricing policy for agricultural commodities designed to clear local markets. By and large, farming in the area was left at the subsistence level, villagers producing cassava as the staple crop, with some maize, groundnuts, curcubits, and other indigenous crops. Throughout the colonial period, commercial farming was almost unknown in the area. Indeed, while conducting my research, I often heard commercial farming referred to as a "new trade," brought into the valley by the new African government following independence. So backward was the production of cash crops in the Luapula that the colonial government, to my knowledge, simply never recorded marketed output from the area; the sole exchange of produce that was noted was the importation into the Luapula of basic agricultural commodities, such as mealie meal.[59]

The valley did, however, benefit from government investment in its fishing industry. It is difficult to estimate either the precise amount of funds or the percentage of the total public revenues devoted to these expenditures; my impression is, however, that both were small, in absolute amounts not exceeding £4 million. Nonetheless the expenditures did have an important impact on the promotion of the fish trade.[60] In 1954 the government constructed an ice plant on Lake Mweru so that traders from the urban centers could pack fresh fish for transport to the city. Beginning in 1957, the government constructed weighing stations and built marketing facilities along the river and lake so that the fishermen could sell their produce to the traders from the cities. The government also provided loans and training for fishermen and distributed improved nets and boats for purchase with the credit it had furnished. It upgraded the roads in the area to give easier access to the urban centers.[61] Lastly, it set up a special account so that Congolese francs could be exchanged for sterling currency—a measure that facilitated the investment of earnings from the fish trade in the construction of stores, the purchase of transport, or the undertaking of other enterprises in Zambian territory.[62] All these measures helped to underpin the private market in fishing that accounted for so much of the prosperity and well-being of the Luapula valley.

Among the more remote districts in Zambia, Luapula remained an exception both in the strength of its private markets and in the degree of government intervention. Nonetheless, Luapula does reveal the more general tendency for the government to reinforce rather than counter the distribution of wealth generated by the operation of private markets. The result was that rural prosperity tended to remain confined to the areas where private markets for agrarian produce offered the opportunity for laying hold of the wealth of the center; and these areas, by and large, lay in the central regions of the nation.

3

Migration in the Colonial Period

The choices made by public and private investors in Northern Rhodesia led, as we have seen, to the influx of capital and to the concentration of wealth along the central portions of Zambia. Some rural dwellers were able to respond to the opportunities created by the rise of industry by producing and marketing agricultural goods for urban consumers. This chapter will analyze a second kind of rural response: rural-urban migration.

In discussing migration, I must introduce a third idealized actor: the village dweller himself. Naturally the motivations of villagers are extremely complex, as was repeatedly illustrated in my field work in Zambia. Nonetheless, it was also apparent that the desire for economic gain influenced much of their social, political, and economic behavior. In many areas of significance to this study, villagers appeared to behave as if they chose among alternatives in terms of the magnitude of the economic benefits offered, the costs of obtaining these benefits, their certainty, and their proximity in time. This notion of their behavior certainly seems to apply to their decision to migrate. Studies elsewhere have underlined the importance of expected income maximization as a principle governing migration decisions. In this chapter I make use of this insight in interpreting rural-urban migration in colonial Zambia.[1]

Migration under the British South Africa Company

As the major private investor in central Africa in the early twentieth century, the BSA sought to allocate the factors of production so as to maximize its profits. In so doing, it manipulated the value of some of the principal elements that figure in the decisional calculus of potential migrants: the certainty of urban employment, the costs of migration, and the income to be had in the rural sector.

We have noted that, largely because of delays imposed upon them by Mwata Kazembe of the Lunda, the agents of the BSA failed to secure title to the mineral deposits of Katanga. The principal result was that the company failed to make profits during its period of suzerainty in Northern Rhodesia. As Kenneth Bradley states:

> It needs little imagination to see how bitter a blow . . . was the loss of the Katanga. The establishment of government, trade and settlement, and all the other trappings of civilization, in a wilderness was—even in those modest days—bound to be a very costly undertaking; and the only source from which enough money could possibly be found was the exploitation of the minerals.[2]

The interests of the company extended beyond North-Eastern Rhodesia, however. The company also administered Southern Rhodesia, and in that territory the situation was not nearly so bleak. There, mineral deposits were being actively mined, and commerce and agriculture were expanding as white settlers pushed northward from the Cape. Where minerals were worked, the company collected royalties;[3] where there was a demand for commercial plots, the company collected rents from the leases; and where farmers sought land, the company profited from the sales of land over which it had exclusive title. The earnings from its land and mineral assets were the company's principal source of revenues in the early 1900s, and both assets were far more lucrative in the south than they were in the north. In its search for profits, the company therefore devised policies to nurture the fledgling enterprises in the south, while at the same time reducing its losses from the northern territories that were proving so profitless a venture.

For a variety of reasons, in the early twentieth century the scarcity of labor was a major inhibitor of the expansion of economic enterprises in Southern Rhodesia. One reason for this scarcity was that native labor was thought to be unproductive, and European entrepreneurs were therefore unwilling to offer high wages. Moreover, Africans in Southern Rhodesia were able to sell their crops and cattle to the growing settler community and profit in this fashion. Since there was thus little difference between the earnings from labor and from village production, entrepreneurs faced a scarcity in the supply of labor. The farmers, miners, and businessmen petitioned the BSA to rectify the situation; and the company, desiring to enhance its earnings from these sources, implemented policies to render labor more abundant as a factor of production.[4]

The first of these policies was taxation. This was an elegant solution, for it simultaneously reduced the company's costs while promising to increase its profits. Starting with a three-shilling annual levy from each of its able-bodied male subjects age eighteen or over in North-Eastern Rhodesia, the company soon increased its levy to five shillings and then to ten by 1914; by means of this hut tax, the company offset for the period 1910–11 at least 68 percent of the costs of its administration in the northeast, leaving it with but 32 percent of the administrative bill.[5]

In addition taxation caused a flow of persons to the south, thereby obtaining the desired increase in the supply of labor. The reason for this flow is easily understood: the villagers' need to secure money to pay their taxes, for fear of imprisonment or property seizure for default.[6] As Robert Rotberg summarizes the position:

> The [administrators] of Northeastern . . . Rhodesia were subject to heavy pressure . . . from the British South Africa Company office in Salisbury. The Company, on behalf of farmers and gold miners south of the Zambezi River, sought to attract thither a steady supply of labor—generally unavailable in the Colony—from the northern protectorates. . . . Codrington [Administrator of North-Eastern Rhodesia] put his case simply: "the natives are able . . . to pay the three shilling . . . tax. It would prove . . . a means of getting a certain amount of work out of the natives, and would in this manner greatly assist."[7]

As a second device for moving labor to the more productive centers, the company supported the establishment of labor recruitment agencies. Initially, the company's own administrators acted as labor recruiters; in the early years its Department of Native Affairs enlisted workers on behalf of the mines and the farmers in Southern Rhodesia. Accused "of a lack of vigor in the recruiting policies" by the employers, however, the company in 1899 transferred this function to the Native Labour Bureau.[8] While the functions of the bureau altered with time, from the point of view of the rural dwellers the labor recruitment services played a critical function— that of enhancing the attractiveness of the employment alternative at a time when wages were low. The labor recruiters reduced the uncertainty of employment opportunities and increased the likelihood of securing a job; this must have been critically important at a time when urban employment was a new phenomenon and the labor market was still an unfamiliar institution. The effect on the migration decision would be to increase the *expected* income from wage labor, thereby rendering the alternative of migration attractive to village dwellers even though wage rates were low. Second, the recruiting agencies reduced the costs of migration. They provided food, shelter, and sometimes transport en route to employment centers; while "queuing" for jobs in the base camps of the recruiters, the migrants received food and sometimes clothing; the recruiters also returned the migrants to their villages, these costs being met by pooled subscriptions from the employers utilizing the services of the agencies. This reduction of the costs of migration would also enter the calculus of the migration decision in a manner that rendered the wage-seeking alternative more favorable by comparison with continued rural dwelling. Penalized for remaining in the rural areas by the hut tax, and induced by the enhanced certainty of employment and the reduced costs of job seeking, African rural dwellers in the early twentieth century therefore left the northeastern holdings of the BSA for wage employment to the south. As noted by one student of the period, "The Zambian African was the main source of labour in Rhodesia from 1898 until the First World War."[9]

A third company policy was that of withholding investments in the northern territories. Perhaps the best illustration of this policy is provided in North-Western Rhodesia, where the BSA, according to the terms of the treaty with Lewanika, chief of the Lozi, was specifically obligated to construct roads and manufacturing establishments in exchange for its rights to minerals and so to bring development and progress to Lewanika's domains. Despite repeated petitions by Lewanika and members of his court, the company refused to implement these policies. The company feared the costs of such investments, its ledgers already revealing considerable losses in the administration of its northwestern holdings; and it feared as well that, if it increased the incomes of persons residing in the rural areas, villages would no longer supply their labor at the cheap wages that the fledgling enterprises in its southern holdings were prepared to offer. As stated by Gerald Caplan in his study of this period in the history of the Lozi:

> The Company's policy was already set: Barotseland was to remain undeveloped, its primary function being the supply of cheap labour to . . . enterprises south of the Zambesi. The imposition of the hut tax assured the success of this objective. Lozi began streaming south in the tens of thousands, many on their own, many others recruited by the . . . Native Labour Bureau which the Administration had authorized to seek labourers . . . "for the purpose of benefiting the industries of (Southern) Rhodesia." . . . When Ngambela [the "prime minister" of the court of Lewanika] implored Wallace, the Acting Administrator, to find work for more people in the Valley, he was unceremoniously rebuffed; Lozi "boys", Wallace informed him, must continue to seek work . . . south of the Zambesi. This was the position in 1909.[10]

The result once again was a growth in the differential between the rural and urban income streams—a differential that promoted the redeployment of labor to the more productive areas.

Especially for this study, it is important to realize that not all labor migrants journeyed to the southern holdings of the BSA. Once the initial flow of migrants had satisfied the demand for labor in its southern territories, the BSA was willing to allow its northern residents to journey to competing employment centers. Thus, for example, the company authorized the Witwatersrand Native Labour Association to recruit specified quotas of workers from North-Western Rhodesia for the South African mines. More important for our analysis, it also allowed recruitment for the new Katanga mines to take place in North-Eastern Rhodesia, and in particular in the Luapula valley.

The rich ores of Katanga, which had been the source of the malachite and copper wares noted by the early explorers, had fallen under the control of the Belgians. Robert Williams, a colleague of Rhodes, formed Tanganyika Concessions, Ltd., in 1899 and secured the rights to prospect for minerals in Katanga from King Leopold. In 1900 George Grey, one of his agents, located immensely valuable copper deposits within the concession area. These deposits, known as the Star of the Congo, were soon to become one of central Africa's most prosperous mines. Further investigation confirmed the commercial viability of the Katanga deposits, and in 1906 Williams reconstituted Tanganyika Concessions as a holding company through which to help finance the Union Minière du Haut Katanga, a corporation organized to develop and manage mining operations in Katanga. The production and smelting of copper ores began in 1911; by 1917 annual production had risen to over 27,000 metric tons of copper; and by 1921 Katanga was yielding over 34,000 tons of copper a year.[11] To secure labor for these enterprises, Williams created a network of recruiting facilities, many concentrated in the Luapula valley of North-Eastern Rhodesia. These facilities and those of Williams' successor in labor matters, R. W. Yule, "specialized in finding Africans from what was then Northern Rhodesia"; they provided contracts and medical examinations for the recruits and maintained footpaths, campsites, and storehouses so that "the Africans . . . could have the quickest, most comfortable trip possible."[12] In 1913 the Katanga mines recruited 1,700 workers through these facilities; in 1917 the figure rose to over 4,000 and in 1920 to over 9,000.[13] During the period 1920–24, over 30,000 additional workers were brought to the Congo from the area.[14] As a result, by 1918, 48 percent of the labor force at the Star Mine in Elizabethville was composed of workers from North-Eastern Rhodesia, and the vast majority of these came from the Luapula area.[15]

The flow of labor from Luapula to the Congo in the early years of this century is reflected in the migration histories of the present residents of Kasumpa village. Of 105 sampled household heads in Kasumpa village, 85 had worked in town. As shown in table 3.1, the rate of migration to the

Table 3.1   Migration Histories of Kasumpa Household Heads

Have worked as migrant laborer	*First Instance of Migration*				
	Pre-1920	*1920–29*	*1930–39*	*1940–49*	*1950–*
Exclusively or primarily in Zaire	3	8	2	2	2
	(37.5)	(40.0)	(10.5)	(11.8)	(9.5)
Equally in Zaire and in Zambia	1	0	1	0	0
	(12.5)	(0.0)	(5.2)	(0.0)	(0.0)
Exclusively or primarily in Zambia	4	12	16	15	19
	(50.0)	(60.0)	(84.2)	(88.2)	(90.5)
Total	8	20	19	17	21

Note: Figures in parentheses are percentages.

Zairian labor market was relatively high in the early 1900s; later, with the development of the mines in Zambia, migrants tended to flow to Zambian labor centers (and particularly to the copperbelt). Nonetheless, for Kasumpa, as for other villages in Luapula, the Zairian market for labor, as well as the Zairian market for produce, was significant, and the residents utilized both markets in their attempts to take advantage of the flow of capital into the mining centers of central Africa.

Migration under Colonial Rule

In the late 1920s and early 1930s, intensive capital investment in mining and related businesses led to greater productivity on the part of labor; and while, as I shall argue, wage rates remained low, they nonetheless increased by comparison with those rates paid by the poorly capitalized firms of the precolonial period. Data on the early wage rates are difficult to find, but given that the BSA attempted to set the level of its annual tax at the value of a month's wages, wages apparently approximated 3 shillings a month in 1900 and about 10 shillings a month in 1914. Upon the opening of the Zambian mines, by contrast, money wages rose as high as 30 shillings for a month's labor, and real wages were even higher as employers provided food and housing.[16] In addition to wages, the number of jobs increased; employment on the mines alone rose from about 8,500 workers in 1927 to over 30,000 workers in 1930,[17] while for Northern Rhodesia as a whole employment rose from fewer than 80,000 Africans in 1931 to over 140,000 Africans by 1946.[18] The result of the increase in wages and jobs was that the expected value of the urban alternative rose for African village dwellers.[19]

Fortunately, migration attracted the attention of the academic community in this period. Scholars working in the 1940s and 1950s uncovered several empirical regularities in the phenomenon. These scholars were, by and large, sociologists. While they recognized that the rate of migration from the rural areas had fundamentally economic causes, they tended to argue that the incidence of migration was determined by the sociological features of the individuals involved. As J. Clyde Mitchell, perhaps the most important of these scholars, declared, "The level of or rate of migration is determined primarily by the *basic* (i.e. economic) causes. The *incidence* of migration—just when it takes place and who goes—is determined by the operation of a series of personal factors."[20] The distinction between economic and sociological causes seems overstated, and the sociological and demographic correlates of migration detected by these earlier researchers appear in fact to be the predictable consequences of maximizing behavior, given the conditions under which villagers were choosing at the time.

Age and Sex

As part of their research, the early sociologists compiled with meticulous care demographic profiles of the urban population in the principal line-of-rail cities. And whether the city was Broken Hill (now Kabwe), Livingstone, Ndola, Lusaka, or Luanshya, in each the population tended to be younger than the national population as a whole and to contain a greater proportion of men than did the overall African population of the territory.[21]

The results of these studies are perhaps best summarized in the demographic pyramids compiled by J. C. Mitchell. Figure 3.1 portrays the age-sex structure of the African population as a whole in the late 1940s and the early 1950s. In figure 3.2 this structure is broken down into its rural and urban components. The bulge in the working-age years for the urban population and the generally greater distribution of women in rural as opposed to urban centers is evident. Numerically, for the Livingstone and the copperbelt areas at least, nearly 50 percent of the urban population was found to be composed of working-age persons alone and approximately 60 percent were males.[22] Further evidence for the age and sex composition of the migrant population comes from another source: the sole reliable census of the colonial era, conducted in 1963. In support of these earlier findings the census revealed that (1) controlling for sex, working-age people more frequently resided in town than did persons of other ages; and (2) for each age group, males more frequently resided in town than did females (table 3.2). Other studies of migration in this period compiled further evidence of the selectivity of the migratory flow of persons from the rural areas in terms of age and sex; the data I present here document a general finding.[23]

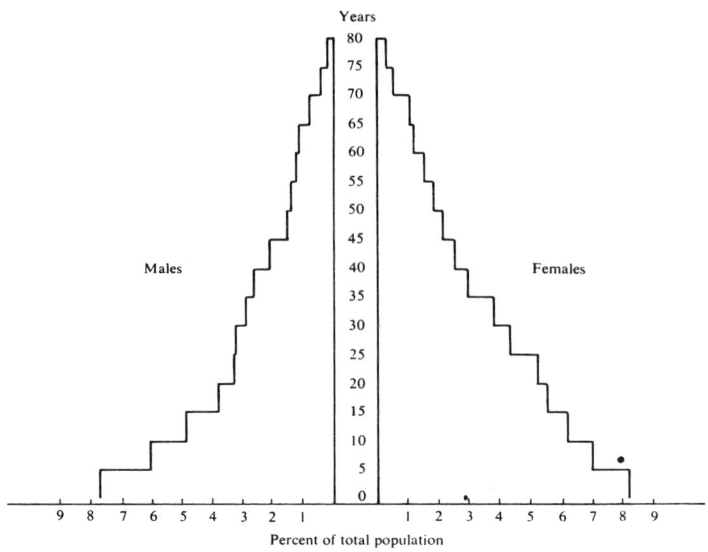

Fig. 3.1

**Age-Sex Structure, Total African Population,
Northern Rhodesia**

Source: Reproduced with permission from J. Clyde Mitchell, "Demographic Appendix," p. 13. Mitchell's data from circa 1950, variety of sources.

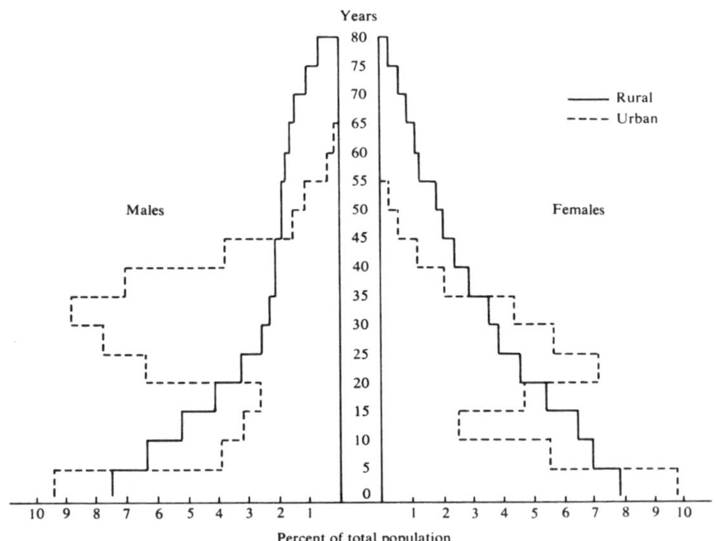

Fig. 3.2

**Age-Sex Structure of African Population of
Northern Rhodesia: Rural and Urban Areas**

Source: Reproduced with permission from Mitchell, "Demographic Appendix," p. 14. Mitchell's data from circa 1950, various sources.

Table 3.2   Age-Sex Distribution, National Population, 1963

	Males			*Females*			
	Over 45	*22 to 45*	*21 or less*	*Over 45*	*22 to 45*	*21 or less*	*Total Population*
African rural population							
Number	176,730	328,640	716,520	169,340	456,350	728,600	2,576,180
% of rural population	6.9	12.8	27.8	6.6	17.7	28.3	100.1
% of column total	85.2	60.8	76.0	93.7	77.5	76.8	75.6
Crown land population							
Number	9,610	41,880	42,110	3,880	27,930	39,910	165,320
% of crown land population	5.8	25.3	25.5	2.4	16.9	24.1	100.0
% of column total	4.6	7.8	4.5	2.2	4.7	4.2	4.8
Urban population							
Number	21,020	169,840	184,270	7,460	104,780	180,170	667,540
% of urban population	3.2	25.4	27.6	1.1	15.7	27.0	100.0
% of column total	10.1	31.4	19.6	4.1	17.8	19.0	19.6
Total*							
Number	207,360	540,360	942,900	180,680	589,060	948,680	3,409,040
% of total population	6.1	15.8	27.7	5.3	17.3	27.8	100.0
% of column total	100	100	100	100	100	100	100

Source: Adapted from Northern Rhodesia, *Final Report of the May/June 1963 Census of Africans* (Lusaka: Central Statistical Office, January 1968), pp. 35–40.

*Does not include railway passengers.

These data are readily interpretable in terms of our notion of the behavior of village dwellers. According to our model of how they make choices, we have every reason to expect young adults to migrate from the villages at a higher rate than either youths or older people. Persons deciding whether or not to migrate are choosing between alternative future streams of income which they evaluate with a bias for temporally proximate earnings. Persons of all ages—those under working age, young adults, and old people—know that they will have to pay costs in present time to secure these future earnings. But, while a young adult stands soon to gain benefits from this outlay, persons of less than working age will have to wait until a later time to secure these earnings; and, adjusted for the discount rate, these earnings will yield less of a benefit to persons under working age than they will yield to young adults. At a given earnings differential, the persons of working age thereby have a greater incentive to migrate than do the youths.[24]

By similar reasoning, these persons also have a greater incentive to migrate than do older people. While paying the same costs of migration, the young adults will receive the benefits of migration over a longer time span; the net benefit of migrating is greater for them than for the older persons, because their working life is longer. In addition, young adults stand in all likelihood a better chance of getting a job and thereby can reasonably place a higher expected value on the migration alternative. For both reasons, by our model, young adults can be expected to migrate more frequently than older persons.

Given this notion of how choices are made, we can understand the observed differences in migration rates for persons in different places in the life cycle. How then are we to understand the observed differences in rates of migration by sex?

The data suggest that men possessed a higher probability of employment; employers offered very few of their jobs to women. Thus, for example, the 1946 census of African employees found that less than 3.0 percent of the over 123,000 jobs held by Africans in the territory were held by women.[25] Moreover, apart from wage earning, there were very few income opportunities for Africans, and so women could not compensate for their disadvantage within the labor market. For example, David Bettison, in his analysis of the sources of the income of Lusaka residents, found he could justifiably ignore the financial contribution of women; very few were employed, and the magnitude of the cash earnings of those employed was too small to warrant his consideration.[26]

Even for those women who got jobs, the pay tended to be lower than that for men. Thus, for example, in the mid-1940s women who secured jobs tended to concentrate in agricultural labor or in mission work, for commercial farmers were willing to hire entire families and many of the missions placed a priority on the employment of women.[27] But, as Phyllis Deane's figures demonstrate, the European farmers and the missionaries paid the second lowest wage rate of any of the major employment sectors in this period; the annual average wage for the two groups was half the annual average wage paid to all employees (£10.3 and £11.7 respectively versus £20.2).[28] Given the women's low probability of employment and the lower wages they could expect to receive when they did in fact secure a job, and assuming roughly equal economic opportunities in the rural areas, the relative attractiveness of the urban alternative was therefore far weaker for women than for men. It would naturally follow that women less frequently chose to migrate. This point was perhaps best made by a female villager who told P. H. Gulliver during his study of migration from one of the hinterland areas of the copperbelt: "Men go away to earn money. We cannot earn money, so why should we go?"[29]

Education

The sociologists of the colonial period found a third characteristic of migrants: by comparison with the rural population, they were better educated. This characteristic too has been found in studies elsewhere in Africa as well as in other parts of the world.[30] The tendency for the educated to migrate was captured impressionistically in what Gulliver has termed the "bright lights" tradition of migration analysis. Exposed to Western culture and feeling confused and restless in the parochial world of the village, the educated young men, according to this literature, developed a " 'wanderlust.' Their desire to taste the novelties of modern life was reflected in their attraction to the 'bright lights' of the towns."[31] This interpretation dominated the administration's commentaries upon rural emigration in this period and much of the scholarly literature as well,[32] and it serves to underscore the role of education in rural out-migration.

More concrete is the evidence presented in the quantitative studies of the colonial period. George Kay, for example, found in his analysis of the colonial census that, among the adult males with no education, 77 percent lived in the rural areas and only 15.9 percent in the urban areas; by contrast, only 35.6 percent of those with a standard V or VI education lived in the rural areas, whereas nearly 60 percent lived in town.[33] Kay went on to relate: "Whereas 37 out of every 1,000 men in the towns have some secondary education, only 5 per 1,000 in the rural areas are so well educated. Similarly 183 per 1,000 men in the towns have attained Standards V or VI compared with 42 per 1,000 in the rural areas."[34] Given that mission-supported schools tended to be located in the rural areas and that they supplied the greater portion of African education in preindependence Zambia, it is plausible to conclude that these figures reflect the movement of educated persons rather than the distribution of educational opportunities.[35]

Again, the evidence indicates that the flight from the rural areas of those with education represents a rational response to the disparity in economic opportunities between the rural areas and the line of rail. Kay's data indicate that, whereas a person with no education had a 2 in 10 chance for a job in 1963, the chances of a person with a standard V were over 6 in 10, and those of a person with some secondary education were over 7 in 10.[36] The material presented in the last chapter indicated that most jobs were located in the central portions of Zambia. Further data suggest that education enhances not only the likelihood of employment but also the level of remuneration that can be gained once a job is secured. Thus, for example, Bettison found in the mid-1950s that educated persons in Lusaka tended to cluster in the most prosperous suburbs.[37] Merran McCulloch's study of Livingstone in the early 1950s reveals a strong correlation between the level of education and the level of employment, with illiterates disproportionately holding jobs as domestic servants or laborers, and persons with standard VI or higher education disproportionately holding jobs as white-collar workers.[38] McCulloch also reveals that, while the mean monthly earnings of those with no education were 63.95 shillings, the figure more than doubled for those with a standard VI or higher education (to 134.06 shillings per month).[39] Given that jobs were located in town, and that both the likelihood of employment and the value of employment increased with education, the educated rural dwellers confronted a more attractive urban alternative than did their less-educated brethren. It was therefore predictable that they would have a higher rate of emigration from the village areas.[40]

Distance

One of the major costs of migration is the cost of travel. Were they to maximize their returns from migration, prospective migrants, when confronted by similar wages at different distances, would therefore prefer to migrate the shorter distance. The data from the colonial period indeed substantiate such expectations.

The best data come from the employment records of the mining companies. Since their inception the mines have colluded in the labor market by offering similar conditions of service. Whatever the economic consequences, the consequences for researchers have been beneficial; for the similarity in wages enabled the scholars of the colonial era to hold constant the benefits of migration while observing the effects of variations in distance. After examining the provincial origins of the employees of the four major copper-mining firms, J. Clyde Mitchell concluded, "It appears that the distribution of African labour on the copper mines of Northern Rhodesia is determined mainly by ecological factors."[41] Thus the westernmost mine, Nchanga (in Chingola), had the greatest proportion of employees from the western provinces; the mine lying astride the principal entry point into the copperbelt from the north, Mufulira, had the greatest proportion of employees from the northern areas; and Roan (in Luanshya), the southernmost mine, attracted the greatest proportion of employees from the south.

As with the mines, so with the urban areas; for the earlier researchers found that the major employment centers on the line of rail also drew a disproportionate share of their immigrants from the rural areas to which they were spatially most proximate. Thus, the northernmost segment of the line of rail, the copperbelt, drew a greater percentage of its labor force from the northern areas than did any other segment; Broken Hill (now Kabwe) in the Central Province drew a greater proportion of its labor from the rural districts of the central areas;[42] Lusaka disproportionately tapped the Eastern Province, for which it was the nearest industrial area;[43] while the southwesternmost city, Livingstone, received a far higher proportion of its immigrants from the southwestern province of Barotse than did any other city on the line of rail.[44] Table 3.3 gives Peter Harries-Jones's summary of these earlier findings.

Three other findings from this early research are relevant. Our notion of the behavior of migrants supports the prediction that persons who possess a lower expected return from migration will be less willing to pay the costs of migration and therefore will travel shorter distances. In this regard it is interesting to note that women, whom we have seen to have a lower expected return from migration than men, tended to migrate shorter distances.[45] In addition, McCulloch's data suggest that it is the promise of high-paying jobs that furnishes the incentive to migrate great distances; thus she finds that persons migrating to Livingstone from the Northern Province tended disproportionately to cluster in the skilled work categories.[46] Finally, Harries-Jones, Ohadike, and others note the decline of migration to urban employment centers from various provinces when more

Table 3.3   Provincial Origin of African Urban Population

Province of Origin	Copperbelt Mines 1961	Broken Hill 1961	Lusaka Males 1957	Livingstone Males 1954
Northern	30.3%	16.6%	10.4%	6.4%
Luapula	16.0	—	—	—
Central	7.9	49.6	6.8	4.1
Eastern	9.5	13.3	45.1	11.2
Northwestern	5.9	6.5	3.5 ⎫	
Peri-Copperbelt	2.1	1.4	— ⎭	6.0
Barotse	2.1	1.6	3.7	45.5
Southern	0.6	2.6	3.7	17.0
Alien	25.6%	8.6%	5.8	9.8%
Unrecorded			21.0%	

Source: Peter Harries-Jones, "The Tribes in the Towns," p. 130.

Note: Peri-Copperbelt refers to the rural areas immediately adjacent to the mines and within the Copperbelt Province.

proximate economic opportunities arise.[47] These findings, all of which relate distance to migration, underscore the importance of income maximization as a principle underlying migratory behavior.

Rural Prosperity

A fifth major finding of the earlier researchers was that, as the prosperity of a rural area increased, the rate of emigration from that area declined; indeed, immigration appeared to be characteristic of the more prosperous rural areas. This finding was reported for two of the major areas of rural prosperity noted earlier in this study: the farming areas of the line of rail and the Luapula valley.

For the farming areas along the line of rail, Elizabeth Colson reports: "There was a dramatic fall in the migration rate when cash cropping developed in the late twenties and early thirties."[48] Researchers noted the relationship between declining rates of migration from the area and the rise of rural incomes in the labor histories they collected from local residents. As reported in one study:

> The oldest men spent far more of their time earning money out at work and all in distant labour. . . . The middle-aged men found very little work near at home . . . but went out less to work at a distance, according to their own statements because they were selling maize. . . . The younger men now hardly go out to work at a distance, but their chances of earning money in the [local] areas . . . have risen enormously.[49]

Not only did out-migration decline with the growth of rural prosperity, but the data also reveal that in-migration increased in response to the growth of economic opportunities from cash cropping. Thus, during her research in the area, Colson reported finding a "heterogeneous group of immigrants living either in Tonga villages or in separate settlements. . . . The maize-belt had . . . attracted settlers from an area with a radius of some 500 miles or more. Many had originally come to work on European farms and then settled in nearby Tonga reserves to grow maize for the market."[50]

Quantitative data on the relatively low rate of net out-migration are provided by government tax registers. These records indicate the location of the tax-age population for the administrative districts of the territory, and in the mid-1930s, after the opening of the mines, they revealed that a mere 25 percent of the taxable males from the line-of-rail farm areas were away at work. For the remote, non–commercially viable farming districts of the north, by contrast, the comparable figure was 50 to 60 percent.[51]

For 1941 the same records reveal that the percentage of taxable males outside the Southern Province—which contains the area under discussion —declined to 18 percent, in contrast to an average of 32 percent for all the provinces of the territory.[52] Urban studies from the era also yield empirical evidence concerning the reluctance of the residents of the line-of-rail farming areas to emigrate from the countryside. Thus, McCulloch, in her study of the nearest urban area, Livingstone, contrasts the number of immigrants from the surrounding Southern Province with the number of persons coming from the more distant Barotse Province. She notes:

> The Southern Province peoples have not readily adopted urban life. They have developed cash crop farming and are able to market their goods on the line-of-rail. Some get work on [commercial] farms. In Barotseland on the other hand there are few opportunities for earning wages, and local markets on a cash basis have not been developed. It appears that there is actually a slightly larger proportion of Barotseland men in wage employment than of Southern Province men, in spite of the geographical position of the Southern Province.[53]

Luapula Province, and in particular the Luapula valley, revealed a similar trend. Tax records indicate that in the 1930s the fishing areas possessed a rate of migration of taxable males precisely equal to that of the line-of-rail farmers: 25 percent.[54] And as late as 1960 Kay's material reveals that the percentage of taxable males working away from the fishing areas of the Luapula valley was the second lowest rate in the territory and closely approximated that in the Tonga farming areas.[55] That the rise of the prosperous fishing industry produced this low rate of out-migration is strongly suggested by the urban data sources. Both Harries-Jones and Ohadike note the relative stability over time of the distribution of mine-workers by their provinces of origin; but both also note the rather precipitate decline in the proportion of mine labor coming from the Luapula Province.[56] "In fact," comments Ohadike, "the relative flow of migrants during 1960–64 from Luapula declined to almost half its level [in the period] 1940–44. . . . The likely explanation for this change is that persons . . . had alternative sources of income. . . . In the case of Luapula, interest shifted to . . . the profitable trade in fish."[57]

Like the prosperous farming areas on the line of rail, Luapula appears to have sustained an influx of migrants. Thus, Ian Cunnison, in his study of the area in the late 1940s, stresses the great variety of ethnic groups in the valley and the mixture and diversity of the local population. This heterogeneity of the population, he contends, resulted primarily from the high rate of migration of foreign groups into the area. Cunnison argues that one of the primary attractions of the valley to these immigrants was

"the fishing industry and the obvious monetary wealth of Luapula inhabitants."[58] Dating the formation of the villages he researched, Cunnison
determined that "the peak period of village formation" corresponded with
the reign of Kazembe XII, who held the throne during the period of "the
expansion of the Luapula fishing industry."[59]

Thus, in the case of both the line-of-rail farming areas and the Luapula
fisheries, the evidence suggests that the more prosperous rural areas tend
to retain their populations to a far greater degree than do areas in which
agricultural production is less profitable and less developed. Urban labor
and local agricultural production are alternative sources of income, and
both have provided ways of benefiting from the growth of economic opportunities brought on by investments in the line-of-rail centers.[60] Where
village production increases in value, the evidence suggests, migration is
less frequently chosen.

The Character of Migration

There is a last set of empirical regularities in the data on migration from
the colonial period; although they from a cluster of traits, it is hard to
give them a single label. Some scholars interpret them collectively as
evidence of labor instability; others as the lack of severance of the working
class from agriculture; and others simply as evidence of the migratory nature of African labor. Whatever the label, the data do contain facts which
appear to go together and which are highly characteristic of migratory
flows in the colonial period. They are: (1) that men tended to leave their
wives and families in the village areas; (2) that the migrants tended to
work short periods and then return to the land, and that labor forces therefore exhibited high rates of turnover; and (3) that the urban migrants
maintained social and economic ties with the villages and retired there
after a period of work on the line of rail.

Family Separation: The Data

I have already presented material on the "imbalance" in the urban sex
ratios, and these data in themselves strongly suggest the bachelor status of
many migratory males. More direct evidence is contained in Godfrey
Wilson's 1940 data from Broken Hill which show that less than 50 percent
of the male immigrants had wives in town;[61] McCulloch's research in
Livingstone in 1952 yields almost precisely the same figure (46.3 percent of
the males in Livingstone were married and had their wives in town in 1952
as compared with 45.8 percent in Broken Hill in 1940).[62] Data from
Rokana Corporation are similar: the percentage of men with wives in town
was 46.1 in 1947, and it remained unchanged through 1951. A significant

percentage of migrants in the colonial period therefore appear to have left their wives and families in the rural areas.

Labor Turnover: The Data

The second characteristic of migration in this period was the frequency with which migrants returned to the rural areas and the degree to which they considered themselves to be but temporarily in town.

Wilson's data, for example, reveal that urban males in Broken Hill visited home on the average once every 3.3 years.[63] Data from Rokana Corporation reveal annual turnover rates throughout the 1940s of over two-thirds of the labor force;[64] at mid-decade, in 1945, the average length

Table 3.4   African Workers' Attitudes Toward Town Life, 1951–52
(in percentages)

Category	Roan Antelope Mine Township	Other Luanshya Townships	Ndola	Living- stone	Broken Hill
Labor migrants:					
Will return home as soon as possible	6.0%	3.3%	—	—	—
Working so as to go home soon	28.3	38.4	—	—	—
Will return home as soon as wealthy	24.2	15.1	—	—	—
Subtotal	58.5	56.8	54.7	39.0	55.5
Temporarily stabilized:					
Will return home at some future date	18.1	15.5	—	—	—
Will stay but keep contact with village	2.7	12.6	—	—	—
Will return home on retirement	14.4	5.7	—	—	—
Subtotal	35.2	33.8	32.6	50.8	37.9
Permanently stabilized:					
Thinks will always be on Copperbelt	5.5	6.1	—	—	—
Born and bred in town; "it is as if it were my village"	0.8	3.3	—	—	—
Subtotal	6.3	9.4	12.7	10.1	6.6
Total	100.0%	100.0%	100.0%	99.9%	100.0%

Source: Robert E. Baldwin, *Economic Development and Export Growth,* p. 116; J. Clyde Mitchell, "Urbanization, Detribalization and Stabilization," p. 708; and Merran McCulloch, *A Social Survey of the African Population of Livingstone,* p. 58.

Note: I have corrected an obvious error in Mitchell's figures on Ndola.

of service of all local mine employees was but 35 months.[65] These statistics suggest that the members of the urban labor force maintained a relatively free flow of persons between the urban and rural areas.

Compatible with this inference are attitudinal data which strongly suggest that few migrants had any intention of remaining permanently away from their homes. As shown in table 3.4, the urban studies of the period reveal that no more than 12 percent intended to remain permanently in town.

Participation in Rural Life: The Data

A last member of this cluster of characteristics is the extent to which urban dwellers continued to participate in rural life. Migrants tended to maintain close social ties with their villages. Thus, Bettison in Lusaka and Mitchell in Ndola and Luanshya found that a significant percentage of the children of urban dwellers lived in the rural areas;[66] both also noted the tendency on the part of migrants to board members of their rural kin in town.[67] Moreover, Wilson found that the average urban male had spent one quarter of the time since leaving the village "back home" in the rural area;[68] McCulloch, too, stressed the frequency of return visits. The data also suggest close economic ties with the village. Thus, among the children, those approaching working age were more frequently "repatriated" by their parents, according to Mitchell's data, than were those who were too young to work in the fields.[69] Financial contributions also flowed from the cities to the countryside. Wilson's data show that a full 10.5 percent of the wages earned in Broken Hill were sent as gifts and remittances to the rural areas;[70] and Kay's material from Fort Rosebery illustrates the economic importance of these cash flows from wage-earning migrants.[71]

Discussion

These facts constitute a challenge to our analysis. Family separation, high labor turnover, and flows of resources from the town to the countryside: how do they fit together and how can they best be explained?

SEPARATION AND TURNOVER

During the 1930s and 1940s, potential migrants faced a relatively low differential between urban and rural incomes; a principal reason for this was the relatively low level of urban wages. Until the early 1950s, wages in the territory, although high by comparison with the period of BSA rule, remained lower than would be expected given the increase of investment in the territory. There were several reasons for this. For one, the government limited foreign competition for the domestic labor supply; it renegotiated labor recruitment agreements with the southern territories so as to divert the formerly southward flow of migrants to the new industries being formed on the copperbelt and along the line of rail.[72] Moreover, the major employers for whom the marginal revenue product of labor must certainly have been the greatest—the mines—colluded in their bids for labor; the result most certainly was a lower monopsony wage than they would have been willing to pay in a competitive market.[73] A third major reason for the relatively low level of wages was the absence of unions among the African workers. While the employers maintained a monopoly on one side of the labor market, the employees competed among themselves on the other, with the result that they failed to control the price of their labor. During the depression the closure of some mines and the termination of the development of others led to an oversupply of labor and a consequent downward revision of wages. As a result of the relative power of worker and management in the labor market, the employees were in no position to prevent this downward adjustment; nor did they gain any upward revision of the wage rate after the end of the depression, when the reopening of the mines and the development of new ore bodies led to a scarcity of labor. Not until the war years did the African workers secure a raise in wages and then only after they began to organize to influence price levels in the labor market; when in 1940 they rioted and died in support of their demands for better conditions of service, they received their first raise in almost a decade.[74]

All of these factors—the lack of foreign competition, employer collusion, and the absence of unions—continued to operate through the war years in the territory and to influence the level of wages. The result was described by William Barber:

Broadly speaking, it is doubtful if the money wage received by Africans was on the average much higher in 1945 than it had been in 1930. Even in those industries in which the money wage rose, it is not clear that there was any improvement in real wages. In the early 1930's with prices of consumer goods dropping, it is possible that the real wage received by the African deteriorated little as his money wage fell. This situation was reversed in the war years. All consumer prices were rising rapidly, including those items normally included in the African budget. . . . Although there was a slight upward movement in the average money wage, it generally failed to keep pace with the increased prices of items consumed by Africans.[75]

From the point of view of the African villagers, the near doubling of the number of jobs over this period enhanced the expected returns from migration even though the real value of urban earnings stayed constant or declined. The urban alternative continued to be an attractive one, and people continued to migrate in great numbers. Low urban wages and, in particular, the low differential between urban and rural wages presented most migrants with a painful conflict, however: a conflict between their desire for economic gains and their desire to maintain the integrity of their families.

The best way to illustrate this dilemma is through the use of data compiled by Phyllis Deane and Robert Baldwin. Using Deane's figures, Baldwin notes that the 1938 annual real wage of employed Africans was £18, and the per capita subsistence income in that period was £4. On the assumption that the dependency ratio computed by demographers in the late 1940s held as well in 1938, Baldwin estimated that each wage earner had four dependents. Were the family to live entirely in the urban areas, the family head's annual share of his income would be £3.6; were he and his family to remain in the rural sector, he could then expect his income to be at most £4.[76] But were he to forsake his family financially and live alone in town, he could then keep for himself the full average wage of £18. Because of the low level of urban wages, the migrants were forced to choose between family integrity and economic gain. Most devised a painful compromise—one that enabled them to take advantage of the higher earnings to be got in the city while maintaining their family ties. The compromise took the form of circular migration: working for short periods in town, going home to their families in the villages, and returning once again to the urban labor market.

Using Baldwin's figures, by spending six months in town and six months in the village, total family earnings could reach £27 per year, or £5.4 each for the family head and each family member. While this alternative was economically more attractive than either moving the family to town or maintaining it in the countryside, it was nonetheless a costly compromise for most migrants (these costs being the difference between £18 per year and £5.4). And workers appear to have sought to mitigate the economic loss entailed by it, by timing their reunions with their families in the country-side to correspond with the periods at which their return would contribute most to agricultural production. As shown in the data from Rokana from 1949 and 1950 (fig. 3.3), monthly turnover in the labor force appeared to peak at the time of the harvest (May-June) and at the time of cultivating (September-October), that is, at the periods of peak demand for farm labor.

Remittances

Thus far, I have attempted to explain why, under conditions of low urban wages, we should expect to find high rates of family separation and labor force turnover in midcentury Zambia, given our notion of how village dwellers make choices. There remains the problem of the degree to

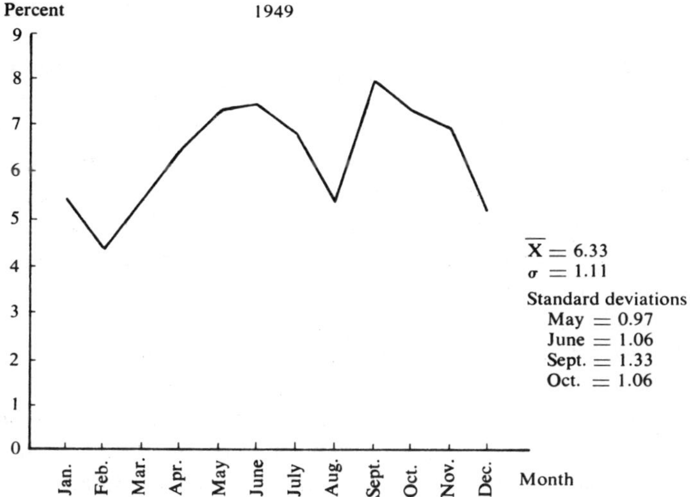

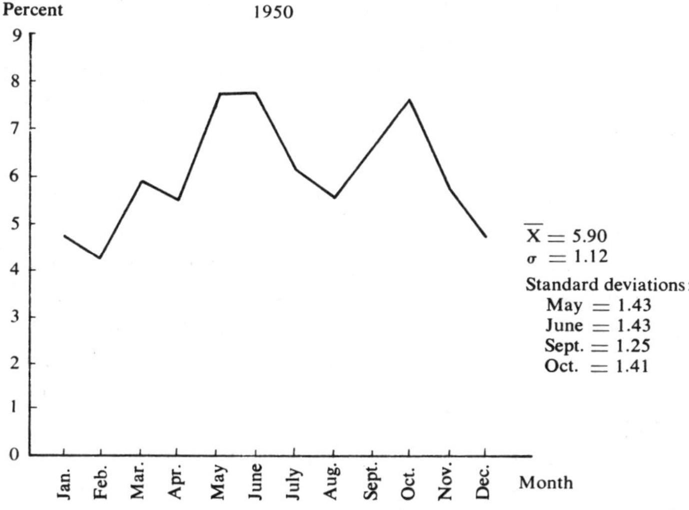

Fig. 3.3

Monthly Turnover of African Labor, Rokana Corporation

Source: Rokana Corporation, Manpower Services Department, Monthly Reports; and Copper Industry Service Bureau, File 5B, African Strength, Yearbook Statistics.

which the migrants dispatch resources to the rural areas, and in particular the extent to which they remit income to the villages. In attempting to comprehend this behavior, we can recall that according to our model the decisional calculus of migrants is future oriented. In effect, we can argue that, just as the migrants invested in the cost of migration from the village so as to secure higher future urban incomes, so too, at a later time, they invest in higher future incomes during their retirement years by sending remittances to the rural areas.

In the cities, cash earnings ceased at the time of retirement, but expenses did not. Only rarely were there pension funds, and those few funds paid poorly by conventional standards.[77] Upon leaving work, former job holders therefore experienced a radical decrease in cash income; but if they remained in town they experienced little decrease in living expenses, for several reasons. Almost all houses were rented and almost none could be bought; furthermore, housing was directly job tied, so that the retiring worker either had to continue to pay rent or had to leave after the termination of his employment. The retired worker did not have the alternative, save in the most exceptional cases, of building his own house, for the land about the cities could be leased only for approved purposes, and the public authorities actively discouraged self-constructed housing by African urban dwellers. Indeed there was an active policy of preventing the formation of, and, on the copperbelt at least, destroying "shantytowns" around the urban areas.[78] Not only housing but also food had to be paid for with cash. Regulations enforced by the government forbade the growing of most crops in the urban townships, and land in the areas immediately adjacent to the townships was often zoned for alternate uses—as forest reserves or as future industrial areas for instance—and so could not be legally converted into garden areas. The result was that few urban dwellers were able to maintain their own gardens, and thus most had to purchase their food supplies.[79] Upon retirement, therefore, a migrant's expenses were liable to remain high even while his earnings radically diminished; consequently he could best maximize his real income by returning to the rural areas where he need spend his meager income neither on food nor on housing.

As I have noted, in the vast majority of the areas off the line of rail, land had been left under native tenure, and the mechanism for securing access to the land upon which to build and grow was therefore the lineage or kin group. As a result, it was in the interest of urban residents to share their earnings with their rural kin during their period of migrancy, so as to create a willingness to grant rights in land at the time of retirement. Thus, as J. van Velsen writes concerning the Tonga of neighboring Malawi, "The migrants . . . during their absence, have been contributing actively and consciously to its continuance because they know that they may have to rely on [their kin] when they are no longer usefully employed in their urban habitat."[80]

Applying our notion of the migration decision to persons already resident in the urban areas, we can therefore interpret their tendency to contribute economically to the well-being of their village kin as an attempt to secure a high level of real future income after retirement from industrial employment in town. As we shall see, this interpretation derives additional support from the response of urban dwellers to trends in the postindependence period. By comparison with its colonial predecessor, the new African government has been relatively lax in its enforcement of housing and land-use regulations; and the chances for earning an income in town by means other than wage employment have increased since independence. Both trends appear to have reduced the incentive for making remittances to the rural areas, for they appear to have rendered the urban areas economically more attractive as a place to live after "retiring" from urban employment.

Before concluding this analysis of migration in the colonial period, it is instructive to return briefly to the political environment within which migration choices were being made. The role of the government in restricting competition in the labor market has already been discussed, as have the consequences for the pattern of migration. The government was important for another reason, however. What is at issue is its failure to make major public investments in the rural areas; although discussed in the last chapter, this failure is once again germane. For the government, confronted with scarce resources, an uncertain revenue base, and burgeoning settler demands for investments on the line of rail, was reluctant to make public investments in the countryside and sought instead to rely upon the private expenditures of migrant laborers to upgrade the standard of living in the rural areas. In effect the maintenance of these patterns of migration, in which families were separated, urban dwelling impermanent, and urban wages "repatriated" to the villages, became a major component of the government's rural development policy. As Elena Berger states, to the government:

It seemed that migrant labour would not only preserve the tribal society but would literally enrich it. In an ideal application of Indirect Rule native agriculture should have supported a stable tribal society, but most of the African Reserves in Northern Rhodesia were so poor, and the Administration's exchequer so depleted, that the best hope for any economic progress in those areas seemed to lie in the circulation of wages earned at the mines and elsewhere. Government representatives put this view to a Native Labour Advisory Board . . . : "A more rapid turnover of persons visiting the Mines would enable money to circulate more freely in rural areas and by its educative effect would tend to raise the level of the village, and the inequality between conditions in the industrial areas and the villages would be less apparent."[81]

Private remittances thus took the place of public investments as a key source of capital for the government's rural development program during much of the colonial period.

Confronted with the growing wealth of the cities, some rural dwellers sought access to it through the exchange of agricultural produce in the urban food markets. Others sought access to it by entering the urban labor market. These responses to the growth of industry in Zambia were alternatives: where one response was made, the other was unlikely to be found. There was another response, however, and this was political in nature. We turn now to the politics of the nationalist period.

4

Political Protest in the Nationalist Period

Numerous motivations for participation in politics exist in Zambia. In the nationalist period such diverse objectives as the desire for equality, a hatred of racism, and a longing for an end to foreign rule, to mention but a few, spurred people to political action. In the Luapula valley these motives were reinforced by the passion of age-old rivalries, as immigrant communities sought to use the nationalist movement to escape from the political dominance of the Lunda.

This chapter will examine the full range of objectives that underlay nationalist protest; however, for two reasons I give particular attention to the desire for material betterment. First, the evidence in fact suggests that this desire provided an important stimulus to political action. Moreover, by closely examining the role of this factor, I can begin to come to grips with one of the central problems this study seeks to explore: the relationship between political and economic behavior in rural responses to industrialization in Zambia.

The chapter begins with a brief overview of the course of nationalist politics and the transfer of power to the African majority. It then examines the pattern of political protest in the urban centers where the nationalist forces first organized in the colonial period and from whence they penetrated to the village populations. By examining the basis of the nationalist alliance between the urban and rural populations, this chapter prepares the way for the subject of the next: the nature of rural protest in the era of nationalist politics.

The Basic Chronology of the Nationalist Period

Until the 1960s, African politics in Northern Rhodesia was primarily a response to European politics in the territory. I have already indicated the manner in which the European settler community achieved a position of power within the constitutional structure of Northern Rhodesia and the way in which it utilized this position to influence the policies of government. The primary goal of the African political leaders was at least to share in this power and at best to wrest it from the Europeans; for African leaders wished to alter the policies to which the European community had committed the government. The most basic of these policies was that of federation: the merging of the Northern Rhodesian protectorate with the settler-dominated colony of Southern Rhodesia.

Federation had long been an objective of the European politicians of Northern Rhodesia. Their goal appeared always to be the same: through federation with the white-dominated colony of the south, to weaken the power of the colonial office over the government of Northern Rhodesia and thereby gain greater latitude in implementing policies which, while favoring their community, might be at the expense of indigenous Africans.[1]

In the 1920s the European representatives in the Legislative Council pushed for amalgamation with the south; the government successfully resisted. Following the declaration of the principles of the Passfield Memorandum by the colonial government in 1930, the incensed leaders of the European community in the Legislative Council passed a declaration in favor of "amalgamation" with Southern Rhodesia.[2] In October of that year they met with the leaders of the colonists of Southern Rhodesia; this conference of European politicians resolved unanimously in favor of amalgamation of the two territories. Once again, however, the British government refused to implement policies that would lead to closer association between the two territories and would thereby diminish its control over the internal affairs of Northern Rhodesia. The government's decision was largely based, reports one analyst, "upon an appreciation of the restrictive racial policies of Southern Rhodesia," and its fears of creating any constitutional order that would limit its ability to counter their implementation in the north.[3]

Like other issues, the issue of federation was withdrawn from the political agenda of territorial politics during the era of World War II. Following the end of hostilities, however, the issue arose once again; and this time it did so in an environment more favorable to the proponents of amalgamation. The surge in the price of copper after the war had led to a demand for capital in central Africa to finance the expansion of the mines, the upgrading of the rail system, and the creation of new energy supplies. It was felt by the British government that the central African territories, if united together, would better attract foreign capital than would the territories singly. Moreover, the British were alarmed at the 1948 rise to power in

South Africa of the Nationalist Party—a party that explicitly endorsed settler domination, and whose aims and objectives could well extend northward unless stable patterns of multiracial politics could be institutionalized in the British possessions.[4] Again, this threat seemed to make it advisable to create a powerful and stable state in central Africa.

With these goals in mind, the Colonial Office responded much more favorably to the resolutions in support of federation passed at the 1949 and 1951 meetings of the European politicians of Northern and Southern Rhodesia. The British were also impressed by the apparent (though temporary) conversion to the cause of federation of Sir Stewart Gore-Browne, the spokesman for African interests in the Executive Council of the Northern Rhodesian government and one of the most widely respected politicians in central Africa. In March of 1951, the government of the United Kingdom published a report endorsing federation;[5] in June of 1952, it published a Draft Federal Scheme which outlined its proposals concerning the structure and organization of the new federal government;[6] in 1953 it implemented these proposals; the federal government began to function in October of that year,

The federation, from its inception, was predominantly organized by and run to serve the interests of the European electorate. The government was dominated by the United Federal Party, which drew its membership and support from the European communities of the territories. African parties had virtually no chance of organizing the government, for African voters comprised less than 7 percent of the electorate (although they accounted for more than 96 percent of the federal population), and what representation they did have (two African members from each territory) was sure to be overruled by the far more numerous European legislative members.[7] To this European-dominated federal government were reserved the areas of predominant concern to the settler community. European education and European agriculture, for example, were serviced by federal departments while African education and agriculture remained the concern of the governments of the member territories.

African politics developed in Northern Rhodesia primarily in protest to the settlers' campaign for federation with Southern Rhodesia. As elsewhere in Africa, local "welfare societies" served as the first forums for political expression in Northern Rhodesia; and opposition to amalgamation formed a major topic of their deliberations. Where these societies gained membership in the local councils, a study of the minutes of these councils revealed that "the members . . . constantly raised their voices in one . . . major refrain: we want no part, they said, of amalgamation with Southern Rhodesia in any form. Each of the councils voted yearly against amalgamation."[8]

The postwar surge toward federation with the south on the part of the

European politicians led to a parallel increase of political activity on the part of their African counterparts. In 1948 the leaders of the welfare societies met in Lusaka. Condemning European domination in the councils of government, they also attacked the settlers' policy of amalgamation with the south; more importantly, they formed the Northern Rhodesia African Congress, the first African political party in the territory.[9] And when in 1951 the British government first indicated its active support for federation, this stimulated indigenous political activity yet further. Following the publication of the government's report endorsing federation,[10] the leaders of the Congress met once again. They replaced the president of the Congress, Godwin Lewanika, with Harry Nkumbula; at the time, Nkumbula represented the militant wing of the party. The leaders of the Congress changed its name to the Northern Rhodesia African National Congress and sought to involve other associations—trade unions, cooperative societies, youth, and women's organizations—within the structure and affairs of the party. Last, and most important for this study, the Congress for the first time dispatched local organizers to the rural areas of the country. According to A. L. Epstein, following Nkumbula's accession he "at once set out to build up Congress organization. Leading figures in Congress toured the whole country, addressing Chiefs and mass gatherings of villagers, forming new branches, and collecting funds."[11] And as L.H. Gann reports:

> In 1951 Congress for the first time began to appoint field officers, one for each province, and branches opened up in various parts of the territory, the regional organization being subsequently strengthened by the creation of Provincial Headquarters with their own Presidents, and Secretaries and Financial Secretaries, with District and Branch Organizing Secretaries lower down the hierarchy.[12]

Following the imposition of federation in 1953, the goal of the African politicians altered only slightly: rather than seeking to prevent Northern Rhodesia's entrance into the federation, they sought Northern Rhodesia's withdrawal from it. Despite this consensus regarding ultimate objectives, serious differences over tactics soon arose within the nationalist movement. The most important concerned the 1959 elections. For the first time in the history of the territory, significant numbers of Africans could vote and Nkumbula resolved that the African National Congress (ANC) should contest the elections. But his major lieutenants—Kenneth Kaunda, Simon Kapwepwe, Munu Sipalo, and Reuben Kamanga—contended that by boycotting the elections ANC could better register its opposition to the prevailing political order and give stronger voice to the political sentiments of the African majority, and especially to their opposition to federal government. Nkumbula's disaffected lieutenants formed the Zambia African Nationalist Congress (ZANC); their vigorous organization of the electoral boycott led, in March 1959, to the imposition of a ban on the party and to their own detention. Upon the lifting of the detention orders, the militant group of leaders regrouped as a new party, the United National Independence Party (UNIP).

It was UNIP that brought independence to Zambia. In accordance with the federal agreements, the Colonial Office in 1960 appointed a commission of inquiry, the Monckton Commission, to examine the operation of the federal constitution. Because it worked under terms of reference that did not allow consideration of the dissolution of the federation, the Monckton Commission was boycotted by the nationalist parties. Despite its terms of reference, however, the commission concluded that African political sentiment so strongly opposed federation that the federal agreement should in fact be terminated. Northern Rhodesia, like so many of the other nations in Africa, was thus to become an independent territory; what remained to be determined were the conditions of independence and, in particular, who was to hold power.

From opposition to federation, the goal of all African political leaders now shifted to the negotiation of a constitutional order that would maximize the power of the African majority. The negotiations over the new constitution were intricate and protracted. Voter qualifications, the apportionment of legislative seats, and the creation of two voting rolls—one, in effect, "African" and the other "European"—with candidates having to gain a minimal number of votes from each: all these devices had to be negotiated in a way that would secure the transfer of power to the nationalist parties, while at the same time gaining acceptance by the white settler community. The negotiations came to a head in June of 1961, when the secretary of state for the colonies, Ian Macleod, presented to the representatives of the African and European interests proposals under which the African parties could obtain a majority in the new legislative bodies; however, Duncan Sandys, the secretary of state for commonwealth relations, in negotiations with the settler representatives in Salisbury, revised the proposals in a way that enabled the most powerful settlers' representative in Northern Rhodesia, John Roberts, to state: "It was virtually certain . . . that Northern Rhodesia's next Legislative Council would have a white majority."[13]

In response to this crisis in the negotiations, UNIP, on 6 July 1961, held an emergency meeting at Mulungushi (just north of Kabwe) where, "after a day-long closed debate, Kaunda [its president] was unanimously granted 'emergency powers' to implement UNIP's widely publicized 'master plan,'"[14] a plan purported to involve widespread boycotts, positive action, and possibly acts of force and violence. Widespread violence did in fact break out in early August; and for obvious reasons UNIP's national leaders disassociated themselves from it. Nonetheless, they benefited immeasurably from the unrest, for it provoked the British government once again to revise its constitutional proposals in a way that favored the negotiating position of the African politicians. In February 1962 the negotiators agreed upon a document that guaranteed a government ruled by Africans for the first time in the history of the territory. In the subsequent series of preindependence elections, UNIP secured the majority of votes and it was therefore a UNIP government that brought Zambia to independence in October of 1964.[15]

These, then, are the highlights of the political history of the territory. They can be found in all the major studies of the politics of the nationalist era; and analogous accounts can be found in the histories of other nationalist movements.[16] The accounts of the meetings, the negotiations, and the declarations of public figures—all focus on the high politics of the nationalist era and involve the elite politicians, indigenous and colonial. What is missing in these accounts are the answers to fundamental questions: at the mass level, what was it that provoked opposition to colonialism? Why did people support the efforts of politicians to overthrow the colonial order and to seize power from the Europeans? It is to these questions that we now turn.[17]

The Urban Nexus

While primarily interested in political protest in the rural areas, this study cannot afford to focus solely on the rural sector. Rather, we are compelled to recognize that in Zambia, as elsewhere in Africa, political organizations began in cities, and their headquarters remained in the urban areas throughout the nationalist period. A discussion of the nature of urban politics is therefore essential in order to offset any unintended implication of rural political primacy in the events of the nationalist era. In addition, insofar as I can demonstrate the utility of my interpretation of politics in discussions of the urban materials—materials many readers are liable already to know—then the interpretation may gain greater credibility when we turn to a discussion of rural politics and in particular to politics in Luapula, where the major events are far less likely to be familiar.

As we have seen, the major issue of the nationalist movement was the issue of racial domination. Federation was the most visible manifestation of settler supremacy; but racial domination had pervaded the economic as well as the political life of the territory, and it was most often at the economic level that it generated the sense of grievance that motivated the mass support for the nationalist cause. One of the primary reasons for the primacy of urban protest was that the racial issue was simply most relevant to urban dwellers.

Urban Africans frequently took recourse to political protest to counter racial biases in the urban marketplace. One of the major markets in which such biases prevailed was the market for labor. The mines provide the most vivid example of discriminatory labor practices. During World War II the European union, taking advantage of the need for the sustained output of copper, obtained a closed-shop agreement from the mining companies. Having gained an agreement in 1941 that no European could be hired who refused to join the union, in 1945 the union secured an agreement from the company that included the notorious clause 42: "The Company agrees that work of the class or grade that is being performed or job that is being filled by an employee at the time of the signing of this agreement, shall not be given to persons to whom the terms and conditions of this agreement do not apply."[18] As Epstein comments, "Since the terms of the agreement applied only to . . . [the union of the] European employees, this meant in effect that no job performed by a European in 1945, when the agreement was made, would be given thereafter to an African."[19] While discrimination in the hiring of mine labor was the most flagrant and visible instance of racial bias, the pattern prevailed elsewhere as well. Thus, Elena Berger notes that on the railways "the Southern Rhodesian policy that Europeans be used for all skilled and semi-skilled work was followed in [railway] operations";[20] she also notes that in the building trades the Europeans' Building Artisans Trade Union demanded agreements guaranteeing that at least 50 percent of the artisans employed by contractors be Europeans.[21] The pattern of racial bias in the urban labor markets provoked some of the more explosive moments in the early history of African politics in Zambia. Official inquiries into the repeated outbreaks of industrial unrest in the copperbelt in the 1940s and 1950s stressed that racial inequities furnished the basic source of grievance that led to industrial unrest; and it was this sense of grievance that fueled the currents of protest which nationalist politicians sought to organize in the colonial period.[22]

Racial bias also characterized the consumer markets of the urban areas. Under pressure from their European clientele, retailers frequently established market conditions that placed Africans at a disadvantage by comparison with European consumers; for the same money, African consumers frequently could not receive the same service as their white counterparts. The most galling example of discrimination was that practiced by the urban butchers. The butchers did not allow African customers within their shops; rather, they served Africans through a special "hatchway" on the side of their stores. Under these circumstances, the African consumers could not examine and choose among cuts of meat. The butchers prepackaged the cuts most favored by Africans; wrapped in newsprint or brown paper, the meat could not be inspected prior to purchase. Often the African consumers were convinced that they had been cheated, as they would later discover that bone, fat, or gristle made up much of the weight of their purchase. The African consumers bitterly resented such conditions and were convinced that they could spend their money more effectively were they allowed to shop in the same manner as the European customers. To improve their standing in the consumer market, they therefore resorted to political protest. It was by organizing and orchestrating this protest and by handling negotiations with the governmental authorities and the urban chambers of commerce, that the African National Congress generated much of its political support after its failure to prevent federation.[23]

Africans were also convinced that racial discrimination prevented them from enhancing their incomes by engaging as sellers in the urban marketplace; and this too led to participation in politics. The best example is contained in A.L. Epstein's study of the African National Congress in Luanshya. In Luanshya, as in the other towns of Zambia, municipal regulations controlled the number of licenses for retailers in the urban townships, and these licenses were held by European and Indian traders. As Epstein states: "Denied the facilities for trading available to the European and the Indian shopkeepers, the hawkers shared a deep sense of grievance and frustration. . . . They bitterly resented the barriers which stood in the way of their economic progress, and saw themselves as the victims of racial discrimination."[24] In response to these sentiments, the hawkers joined en masse the African National Congress, which championed their position before the municipal authorities; in furtherance of its political objectives, the Congress was able to gain a change of policy in the issuance of licenses, and the hawkers, by supporting the African National Congress, were able to further their economic interests by gaining access to increased trading opportunities and to wider markets.[25]

The nationalist movement therefore tapped the desire of African urban dwellers to enhance their incomes in the major private markets. Besides trying to influence conditions in private markets, the nationalist movement sought to alter the distribution of public goods; indeed, this was perhaps its major objective. The nationalist leaders realized that the provision of public goods was radically biased in favor of the Europeans. The government provided, for example, secondary schools and hospitals for Europeans which compared favorably with those throughout the world. But for Africans there was but a single secondary school in the territory which offered a preuniversity training, and the quality of medical care available to the average African was well below that which the average European could expect to receive. The political leaders also realized that the structure of public finances insured that expenditures on different kinds of public goods favored the European residents and left the "protected" African population at a great disadvantage. A primary basis for their oppositon to the federation was that the fiscal portion of the federal agreements helped to insure that this would be so. Because over 60 percent of the revenues collected in the territories were reserved to the federal government, the European-oriented services it provided were far more lavishly financed than were those mounted by the governments of the member territories. Thus, for example, Europeans, whose education was federally financed, received an average of £18.4 per capita in expenditures on education in 1957–58, while Africans, whose education was financed at the territorial level, received an average of £0.624 in educational expenditures in that same year.[26] In addition, the African politicians realized that the structure of federal finances diverted funds from mineral-rich Northern Rhodesia to the white-dominated colony in the south. The magnitude of this diversion of resources has been most rigorously analyzed by Arthur Hazlewood and P. D. Henderson, who determined that Northern Rhodesia contributed approximately £10 million per annum more to the federal territory than it gained from it in goods and services (see table 4.1).

Through speeches at meetings and through the nationalist press, the African politicians of Northern Rhodesia informed their constituents of these economic facts.[27] And the constituents, already aware of segregated lines at post offices and segregated accommodations on the government-run railways, became convinced that the allocation of goods in the public sector was fully as biased as the allocations made through the private marketplace. The Africans therefore supported their leaders in their quest

Table 4.1   Estimated Direct Gains or Losses on Current Account
(in millions of pounds)

	1954–55	1955–56	1956–57	1957–58	1958–59
Southern Rhodesia					
Payments to					
federal government	19.9	23.9	29.3	32.1	36.4
Share of total receipts	28.6	32.2	38.5	41.5	36.7
Difference	+8.7	+8.3	+9.2	+9.4	+0.3
Northern Rhodesia					
Payments to					
federal government	25.8	26.9	36.1	36.6	25.4
Share of total receipts	15.1	16.1	22.5	23.4	21.3
Difference	−10.7	−10.8	−13.6	−13.2	−4.1

Source: Arthur Hazlewood and P. D. Henderson, *Nyasaland: The Economics of Federation*, p. 46.

for political power, and thus the power to alter the financing and distribution of public goods through governmental authority.

Be the issue job discrimination, consumer boycotts, health care, or education, the very fact that the major private markets existed in the cities, and that the majority of public facilities were based there, was sufficient reason to insure that the impetus for the nationalist movement originated in the urban areas. Nonetheless, when in 1951 Nkumbula dispatched political organizers to the rural areas, his organizers found ready support for the nationalist cause.[28] Though they did not take the initiative in the formation of the nationalist movement, the rural dwellers vigorously responded to it: they opposed federation, participated in the era of agitation, and joined in the violence that culminated in independence for Zambia.

The Rural-Urban Coalition: The Role of Urban Migration

When ANC began organizing the rural areas in the early 1950s, it was attempting to create a coalition of all Africans against colonial rule. We have noted the set of issues it exploited in recruiting support in the urban areas. In its quest for national support ANC was aided by the fact that the issues in the urban sector were of great importance to the rural dwellers as well. A basic reason for this was the steady current of migration between the rural and urban areas which took place during the colonial period.

As noted in Chapter 3, urban migration was a pervasive fact of life in central Africa. In 1962 an average of 48 percent of Northern Rhodesia's taxable males were away from their villages at work.[29] At any given time for any given rural area, most of the old men of the villages would have worked in the cities; most of the working-age men would be away in the cities; and most of the young men would be planning to migrate in search of employment. The patterns of discrimination in the urban labor market were therefore relevant to almost everyone; and the discriminatory practices in butcheries, stores, and public services were familiar and disliked features of urban life. The rural dwellers easily identified with the actions of their urban brethren who sought through politics to alter these unjust practices.

Like their urban counterparts, the villagers opposed federation. They were aware that the rules they resented in the urban sector were enforced even more harshly in the white settler colony to the south. And they feared that these practices would be irreversibly institutionalized were their own land to come under the control of a settler-dominated federal government. Urban migration played an important part in the formation of these expectations. For, as we have seen, from the early days of the protectorate, many villagers worked in the south; at the time of federation thousands of villagers from Barotse and the Eastern Province still worked there. In addition, many of those who had worked in Northern Rhodesia felt that employers from south of the Zambezi, particularly "the Boers," were even more racist than those from Britain. The "tradition" of rural emigration in the territory thus led to an identity of political viewpoints between the urban and rural areas which made it easier for the nationalist parties to form a political coalition encompassing both sectors.

Evidence for the contribution of migration to the formation of the national coalition comes from the assessment of the colonial officers in the field. Thus Gann noted: "In the opinion of many Government officials, the migrant[s] . . . were often inclined to 'leave their country to seek employment as ignorant and tiresome children but return offensive and often rebellious men.' "[30] And no less a figure than the governor of the territory was aware of the contribution of migrant labor to the opposition to federation. In 1939 the governor wrote:

> There is no contesting the fact . . . that a very large number of the natives of this territory have worked in Southern Rhodesia and have an intimate knowledge of conditions there, and that though their views may not have been formed with the clarity of a jurist or the profundity of a political philosopher, they were held none the less stoutly and they were unanimously opposed to amalgamation with Southern Rhodesia.[31]

Further evidence is contained in the propaganda issued by the nationalist parties themselves. Thus, for example, the broadsheets that found their way to the village level in the Luapula valley stressed a mixture of both urban and rural grievances, revealing the publicists' apparent perception that the affairs of the city were of great relevance to the residents of the countryside. For example, one propaganda sheet I located in Kasumpa village attacked federation on the grounds that it increased the likelihood that urban jobs would be taken by the children of settlers; and it cited the statistics on educational expenditures to demonstrate the advantages given European children in the competition for urban employment. The circular went on to stress that Africans in Northern Rhodesia are "remaining in poverty because the money [from our mines] is sent outside the country . . . to the south by Welensky [the Prime Minister of the federation] where it is being used for . . .the Boers."[32] Another circular emphasized the progress being made by the nationalist movement; in appealing to the *village* dwellers for support, it cited as progress the movement's fight against discrimination by the retailers in town. The circular urged its readers to recall that in "the butcheries and stores there were only shopping windows, where Africans were standing in order to be served" and indicated that, through the power of the nationalist movement, these practices were being ended. Now, it went on, the nationalist movement was seeking to fight poverty elsewhere, even in the villages where the Europeans "had prevented us to live by keeping away sources of money." It concluded: "Let us unite together like the bundle of firewood, where each alone can be broken but where together it is strong. Workers and villagers together, . . . we can chase those people in the House of Parliament in Lusaka so that we can choose our own people, Africans, who will be looking out for our African interests."[33]

Similar appeals, emphasizing discriminatory patterns in the labor and consumer markets and in the provision of public goods by government, were contained in letters sent by villagers abroad in the urban areas to residents in the countryside. The private correspondence of party leaders in Kasumpa village contains many letters exhorting them to support the fight against these practices; and the files of Mwata Kazembe contain similar exhortations from prominent "Luapulists" in town.[34] For example, after the London Conference of 1951 recommended federation in British Central Africa, Mwata received a letter from Elder Kafuti Kasembe of the Ndola African Location, stating: "We have received some news . . . [about] the decision in London to have the government force the people of Northern Rhodesia to accept Federation. . . . Mwata . . . here in the copperbelt all the people have started to pay subscriptions to ANC to fight this. . . . You should spread the news to all people that you should pay subscriptions."[35] Mwata replied:

> Thank you for your letter . . . which explained about unity. Your thinking my brother is good. Even we people who are living here in the rural areas are not pleased to Federate our countries. . . . We are receiving plenty of letters about the same matter of refusing Federation. We are very strong against it and yourself you should be very strong against it. We have started giving subscriptions. You in town and we here in the villages should unite together.[36]

Rural-urban migration thus furnished a basis whereby village dwellers could learn about and come to identify with the demands made by their urban brethren. Equally as important, the "character" of migration created a sensitivity on the part of *urban* dwellers to one of the major issues of relevance to the villagers: the issue of land.[37]

As we have seen, urban migration in the colonial period was characterized by the maintenance by the urban dwellers of close ties with the village; it was the intention of most migrants to return to the village, and the high rates of turnover and short lengths of service, as well as the remittance of earnings and the frequency of rural visits, strongly suggest that large numbers of urban dwellers actively pursued the goal of a rural retirement. It will also be recalled that the colonial government promoted the transformation of land rights from native to freehold tenure along the line of rail. Land reform in itself promoted rural protest. And the coexistence of migration and land reform led to the conjoining of urban and rural political forces in the nationalist period.

For the rural areas, the land issue was most important along the line of rail. The first political societies were formed in this area, and Robert Rotberg notes the prominence of the land issue among the grievances registered by these associations.[38] The impact of land on nationalist sentiment in the area was also documented by agricultural researchers working in the Mazabuka area. They discovered that the village farmers readily and bitterly assigned the responsibility for their low agricultural incomes to land policies of the government.[39] Village farmers, because they were prevented from encroaching on freehold lands, could not extend their acreages and were compelled to overcultivate the lands they held. Moreover, the farmers were reluctant to invest in land improvements for fear that the investments would be appropriated by commercial farmers who might "rezone" these holdings. Government policy thus adversely affected the ability of the line-of-rail village dwellers to respond to the growth of the urban demand for agricultural produce. And the villagers, first through the political societies and later through the nationalist movement, took recourse to political protest to remove this limitation upon their well-being. As Gann states in his discussion of this area, "the land question remained the Party's most powerful talking point."[40]

Even in areas where land alienation had not taken place and where land was rarely a commercial asset, fear of land seizure was a leading issue in local politics. One of the primary reasons was that, though commercial farmers had not received extensive land grants, mission stations had. In the Luapula valley, for example, several major missions had been granted large acreages. And, at Mbereshi Mission, just to the north of Mwansabombwe and bordering on Kasumpa village, the London Missionary Society possessed several hundred acres of land. The society erected a school, a hospital, a church, and other facilities—a bakery, a carpentry shop, and a mechanical workshop—with which to support their religious operations. Much of the land stood vacant, however, and neighboring villagers often sought to establish gardens on the unused portions. The missionaries attempted to prevent their encroachment, and the employees of the Lunda Native Authority (see Chapter 5) enforced the missionaries' policy. The policy of the mission generated anger and resentment in the neighboring villages, and the nationalist movement identified with these sentiments.

Perhaps the most vivid illustration of the political consequences of the mission's policy took place in 1954, when a former mission teacher, an African, established a garden of cash crops on the mission land. Having left his job with the mission, this gentleman nonetheless sought to maintain himself and his family by selling produce to the mission school and hospital. The director of the mission tried to dissuade him from maintaining the garden on mission grounds; failing that, he had the garden uprooted by the messengers of the Lunda Native Authority. The outraged ex-teacher then "turned to politics," as he expressed it, and later became one of the leading political organizers in the valley. He rose to a high rank in the party organization in Kawambwa District, and his greatest satisfaction now comes from the return, after independence, of many of the mission lands to conditions of native tenure.[41]

The fear of land alienation was exacerbated by talk of federation, for rural dwellers knew that in Southern Rhodesia commercial farmers had seized nearly 60 percent of the land, and they were concerned that the settlers, through their control of the federal government, would lay hold of further lands to the north.[42] With each proposal of federation, these fears rose to new heights. When federation was proposed in the 1930s, the Africans opposed amalgamation on the grounds that "south of the Zambezi . . . white pioneers came to the country as conquerors and occupied vast tracts of native land."[43] When the issue of federation was renewed in the late 1940s, African sentiment throughout Northern Rhodesia again focused on the land issue. As Gann recounts the position of the African population: " 'Without land we shall be like wild pigs, driven from place to place,' they said, and no arguments would convince the doubters; land rights might be entrenched, but the whites were so clever, they would get around these clauses somehow. . . . The land-fear . . . became a real obsession with many Africans."[44]

In the Luapula valley, as elsewhere, politicians articulated these fears; in the words of one informant, "We politicians were certain that because the land of the valley was good land the Europeans would seize it." The nationalists attacked the government on the grounds that it planned to bring settlers to the valley. They also informed the valley residents of the events in the Zambezi valley, where thousands of Tonga tribesmen had been moved away from the rich lands of the Zambezi River to make way for the rising waters of Lake Kariba. They contended that power projects were being planned for the Luapula River; and only by supporting the nationalist movement could the villagers protect their lands from the schemes of the government.[45] The villagers of the valley thus came to fear that the federal government would seize their primary economic asset; and they joined the currents of political protest that had been unleashed by their urban brethren and backed the nationalist movement.

Just as the villagers identified with the position of their urban compatriots and joined in their opposition to the market inequities and discriminatory treatment to which they were subjected, so too did the urban dwellers support the position of their rural counterparts in opposition to the alienation of land. Once again, the pattern of labor migration facilitated this coalition of urban and rural interests. For, as I have argued, just as land was an economic asset to the villager, so too was land an asset to the urban dweller. For some, part of their earnings derived from the land, for they kept their families there and joined them at the times of peak demand for agricultural labor. For many, the right to land was an asset in which they invested by remitting earnings during their years of employment. In this way many urban dwellers enhanced the level of the real incomes they could realize upon their retirement from wage labor. Threats to native tenure land thus affected many urban dwellers as well as villagers, and the land issue became one that encouraged a coalition between villagers and laborers during the nationalist period.[46]

5

The Rural Rebellion

The last chapter concentrated on the issues that drew the villagers into a coalition of the whole: the coalition forged by politicians in the era of nationalist protest. There were other issues, however, which affected rural dwellers as such, and they were uniquely the stuff of rural politics in Zambia. By intensively examining the politics of one place and time—the Luapula valley during the nationalist period—this chapter will analyze these issues and attempt to better comprehend the reasons for rural support for the nationalist cause. In so doing it will provide further insight into the role of politics in the attempts of rural dwellers to gain access to the economic opportunities generated by the growth of industry in central Africa.

Kasumpa Village and the Luapula Valley

When, in the early 1950s, the African National Congress dispatched an organizer to Luapula—one Banda, whose first name is no longer remembered—he moved from village to village, spending no more than three or four days in each, and returning once or twice to each major village "to guide those who had turned to the path of politics," in the words of one informant. Banda avoided the major towns—Mwansabombwe, the Lunda capital; Kawambwa, the *boma*;* and Nchelenge, the major sub-boma—for fear of the governmental authorities. He preferred instead to work in the countryside, out of range of the police and of the boma messengers.†

Banda found ready converts in the Luapula valley. And, of all his con-

---

**Boma* is the colonial term for an administrative center; most often it refers to the governmental headquarters of a district.

†The messengers were just that; in areas where postal communications were poor and telecommunications nonexistent, they served as vital links in the government's communication apparatus. In addition, they served as police, apprehending and delivering to the authorities any violators of the law.

verts, those in Kasumpa village appear to have been among the most dedicated. The political militancy of Kasumpa was repeatedly stressed by my informants, and their assertions are confirmed by governmental records, where the level of sedition emanating from Kasumpa village received repeated comment.[1] For a while during the formation of ANC, Kasumpa village served as the organizing headquarters for the nationalist movement in the Luapula valley; and during the period in which ZANC was re-forming as UNIP, the nationalist leaders maintained the provincial headquarters for Luapula in Kasumpa village.[2] As a result of the political prominence of the village in which my research was conducted, we are in a position to assess with some confidence the nature of the nationalist movement in the valley.

There were both economic and historical reasons for the prominence of Kasumpa village in the nationalist movement. Unlike most of the major villages in the Luapula valley, it was but partially involved in the fishing trade. Other Luapula villagers could enhance their incomes by participating in the fishing industry, but because of their distance from the river many Kasumpa residents lacked this alternative. In order to make themselves better off, they instead turned to politics. My informants in the village explicitly interpreted their behavior in this way and explained that other villages tended to be "lazy politically" because they were "rich" and were "too busy fishing to do party work." This assessment was shared by the political authorities; noting the lapse in political activity in the valley following the protests over federation, a member of the district administration commented, "The tendency is for the Luunda in the valley to concentrate more and more on the catching of fish"[3] and "to abandon politics for business,"[4] something most Kasumpa villagers could not do.

Economic circumstances thus rendered political activity more attractive to Kasumpa villagers than to most other residents of the valley. But historical circumstances also played a part in placing them in the forefront of the nationalist movement. We have seen that Kasumpa village occupied a unique position in the political structure of the valley. Its residents had been invited into the valley by their Lunda overlords; for decades, the villagers gave allegiance to their own chief; and only by deposing Mwabamukupa and by imposing his own headmen had Mwata Kazembe achieved political suzerainty over the immigrant Bemba warriors. Because of this history, the Kasumpa villagers regarded themselves as independent and equal to the ruling Lunda of the valley. While they came to respect and to honor the headman imposed upon them, the Kasumpa villagers nonetheless refused to acknowledge their position of subordination to the Lunda Superior Native Authority. When, in the 1950s, political organizers attempted to rally the villagers against the native authority, they found enthusiastic adherents in Kasumpa village. Habits of deference to Lunda rule were weakly established in Kasumpa by comparison with elsewhere in the valley; and the villagers could therefore take the lead in the rebellion against the native authority.

While history provided a basis for the particular sensitivity of the Kasumpa people to Lunda rule, the grievances championed by the Kasumpa politicians in the nationalist period were widely shared. They stemmed by and large from the role and function of the native authority in the life of the valley. To this we now turn.

The Native Authority

Applying the doctrine of indirect rule to Northern Rhodesia in 1930, the colonial government designated many of the local chiefs and their advisers as native authorities. In the Luapula valley, the Lunda king, Mwata Kazembe, and his councillors were registered as a superior native authority; and the lesser Lunda chiefs were designated as subordinate chiefs to the native authority, responsible for maintaining law and order and for adjudicating minor cases in their areas. To support these minor bureaucracies, the colonial government in 1936 empowered the native authorities to raise revenues by collecting license fees and court charges and by keeping a portion of the taxes levied from people in their jurisdictions.[5]

As part of the postwar surge of interest in the development of the rural areas, the government began to rebate larger amounts of tax revenues to the local treasuries so that the native authorities could expand their activities and upgrade their salaries and, by doing both, attract well-trained and progressive commoners into the public service. The government helped to recruit and train staffs for the native authorities: clerks, messengers, accountants, and later departmental councillors. It also encouraged the authorities to reorganize into substantive departments—finance, health, and public works, for example. With the growth of their finances and the upgrading of their personnel, the native authorities expanded their programs and services. They began clearing minor roads, building bridges, and constructing local facilities, such as dispensaries, rest houses, and welfare centers. At the urging of government, they also began to regulate agricultural practices, protect forest reserves, and administer local fisheries.[6]

Where their financial base allowed, the native authorities became very prominent indeed. Such was the case in the Luapula valley. With the growth of the fish trade in the 1940s and the resultant spread of prosperity in the valley, the treasury of the Lunda Native Authority expanded; indeed, it soon became one of the largest in all Northern Rhodesia. For example, figures from 1954 indicate that while the revenues of the Bemba Native Authority—politically, one of the most significant native authorities in the territory—amounted to £2,546, that of the Lunda Native Authority amounted to £11,802; and in 1956, while the Bemba Native Authority collected £3,554 in revenue, the Lunda Native Authority collected £21,380.[7] Though the Lunda Native Authority derived its revenues from the usual sources available to all local governments—licenses, court fees, and rebates from the head tax—it derived the largest share of its monies from the fishing industry: license fees for boats, nets, and engines, and a levy imposed on every shipment of fish to town. In 1954, for example, the fish levy alone brought in over £4,000, more than 30 percent of the revenue;[8] and as early as 1949 the administration lauded the Lunda Native Authority as "lead[ing] the way" in Northern Rhodesia.[9]

In response to this prosperity, the Lunda Native Authority recruited a bureaucracy, and undertook new tasks and programs. In the late 1940s and early 1950s, it attracted a number of able white-collar personnel away from urban employment and placed them in charge of its newly created administrative departments. Its educational councillor, Dauti Yamba, helped to found a native authority school in Mwansabombwe and instituted a scholarship program to finance the education of promising youths from the valley. An agricultural councillor oversaw the development of a nursery and seed farm and distributed new kinds of cassava plants to villagers to counter the spread of a pernicious blight in the valley. He also imposed new rules which required minimum cassava acreages, as a means of reducing the possibility of famine. The health councillor created and implemented regulations concerning the construction and depth of village latrines; the fabrication of drying racks to keep chickens, goats, and children from soiling eating utensils; and the building of houses in a way that let in sunshine and fresh air and reduced the dampness of the village living quarters. He also oversaw the construction of village clinics. Most importantly, however, following the government's investments in the fishing industry in the early 1950s, the Lunda Native Authority recruited a fisheries councillor who took over the day-to-day regulation of the fishing industry in the valley. The councillor posted fish guards to the newly built markets in the valley, and they oversaw the weighing and selling of fish, enforced the gazetted prices, and imposed the appropriate levies. They also policed the river and lakes, making sure that the fishermen used nets of sufficient gauge, that they stayed clear of the breeding grounds of the fishery, and that they refrained from fishing during the spawning season. In addition fish guards of the native authority issued the necessary licenses and imposed fines upon violators of the fishing ordinances.

The Lunda Native Authority therefore became a major presence in the valley. Possessing its own resources and personnel, the native authority was nonetheless vulnerable to political attack in the nationalist era, for it served and was seen to serve as the lowest rung in the colonial administration. The regulations it enforced in the fishing industry were regulations drawn up and urged upon it by the central government in Lusaka; its policies on village health were designed by the provincial administration; and its agricultural ordinances and especially its policy of famine prevention were similar in origin.[10]

The colonial administration not only controlled the policies of the native authority; it controlled its personnel as well. Thus, for example, when the district commissioner visited the native authority offices in 1963 and found a clerk absent from duty, he fined him £5. The clerk protested in writing, declaring, "I have no direct responsibility to you but to the Lunda Native Authority where I am employed."[11] In reply, the district commissioner wrote to the native authority, "The tone of this letter . . . discloses an attitude that I will not tolerate. . . . The clerk will be suspended immediately."[12] The district commissioner's oversight extended from control over clerks to the hiring and firing of full councillors as well. In 1962, the district commissioner summarily terminated the appointment of the chief secretary—the councillor who was in charge of the entire staff of the native authority and the day-to-day management of its affairs.[13] And in the mid-1950s he successfully prevented the promotion of the fisheries councillor to the post of chief councillor and instead filled the post with an inexperienced man who had just completed an administrative course at a government training center.[14]

Perhaps most revealing of the dominance of the district commissioner, however, was his relationship with Mwata Kazembe, the head of the Lunda Native Authority and the personification of the Lunda government. The files of the native authority revealed that the district commissioner was not above instructing Mwata Kazembe to prepare for important visitors by clearing up the roads of Mwamsabombwe, routing out all the native authority's staff to warmly greet the visitor, wearing his traditional robes, and inviting the visitor to tea at his personal quarters.[15] The records also reveal that the district commissioner brooked no opposition from Mwata. Mwata Kazembe once failed to meet with the district commissioner because he was "performing traditional duties"; the latter left a letter declaring: "I require [an] . . . explanation from you, and you will come to my office in person to deliver this explanation on Wednesday, 27th March, 1963 at ten o'clock in the morning."[16] Mwata arrived on time and received a vigorous dressing down from the colonial official.

In its policies, in the recruitment and supervision of its staff, and in the conduct of its "monarch," the Lunda Native Authority was thus a subordinate element of the colonial administration. Consequently, at the time of the rise of the nationalist parties, the Lunda Native Authority was vulnerable to the political attacks of those who sought to overthrow that administration. The native authority was vulnerable on other grounds as well, for the mass of the valley residents were convinced that the native authority operated in a way that was harmful to their economic interests, and that, were it to be overthrown, their incomes would rise.[17]

The Basis of Opposition to the Native Authorities

As much as anything else, the rural rebellion in the nationalist era was a rebellion against taxes. This should not be surprising, for, like all people everywhere, the villagers hated to be taxed; and everywhere grievances over taxation have fueled the fires of political protest and have generated large-scale rebellions.[18] The native authority directly taxed its people 2s. 6d. a year, and it assisted the district commissioner in levying the taxes of the national government. Because much of its revenues came from rebates from the capitation tax fund, the native authority had a strong incentive to guide the district commissioner to all the villages; to deploy its messengers so as to marshal all the villagers for tax payment; and to apprehend and convict tax defaulters. The villagers resented these levies and the public authorities that made them.

The villagers also resented the efforts of the native authority to divert to the public coffers the wealth they generated through their own enterprise in the private marketplace. The levies and license fees charged fishermen were the most obvious taxes of this kind. Also readily visible were the charges imposed upon beer brewers, shop owners, and hunters. Lastly, the villagers protested the fines imposed by the native authority. Not only did these fines depress their cash earnings; but they also necessitated expenditures that most residents would not choose voluntarily to make— expenditures on the fines themselves, of course, but also expenditures, if only in time and effort, to correct the offense, be it substandard housing, inadequate sanitation facilities, or failure to grow the number of mounds of cassava required by the agricultural ordinances of the native authority.

The reaction of the valley residents to these public levies is perhaps best portrayed in the recollections of one villager from Kasumpa:

> First the messengers of the chief came to our village and told us the day that the district commissioner would come to inspect the village and to collect the taxes. All the people of the village were to be in the village on that day. They were not to go to the lake or to their fields. They were to wash themselves and their clothes for that day and they were to learn songs. Then the district commissioner would come. He would camp near the village; his messengers would use a house in the village, and the people would have to sleep elsewhere. His messengers would take him eggs and chickens from the village, and the owner would be paid a very small price, even though [the district commissioner] was paid a salary by the government.

When the district commissioner at last entered the village, we would form lines. We would clap and cheer and sing what his messengers had said was his favorite song. We put on our happy faces. Then the district commissioner would come pushing his bicycle and he would wave as if he were happy to see us, but letting us know that he was only seeming to be so as he was our superior.

Then he would put up a shelter and take the personal levy. If we did not pay it, we went to jail. Then he inspected the houses and the latrines and saw if there were drying racks to keep our dishes off the ground. If there was poor thatch, pah! You paid a 5-shilling fine. A poor latrine, pah! 5-shillings. The fines and the taxes continued, even though you may have no work.

During all this, we had to stand. We feared if our children cried. It was forbidden to sit until you were told to do so. Then, you had to sit. One man from the copperbelt was here with a new suit on. He refused to sit on the ground because his suit was clean. The district commissioner shouted at him for being insolent. The messengers made him carry the district commissioner's tent on his tour for the next two weeks, even though he only had five weeks leave in the village to visit with his family.

Thus it was to be taxed and fined in the villages during the colonial era.

Adding to the resentment of the villagers was their conviction that the services received from the native authority failed to equal in value the income lost to it. The villagers did not particularly regard the primary service rendered—law and order, as administered by foreign rulers—as a benefit. And they felt that even the development-oriented policies of the local administration tended to reduce rather than to enhance their incomes. The best illustration of this was in the fishing industry. Out of a regard for the long-term yield of the fisheries, the native authority forbade the catching of fingerlings, imposed a closed season during spawning, and prevented fishing in the breeding grounds at the shallow end of Lake Mweru. While observance of these regulations may well have been in the long-run interest of all the fishermen, they were in the short-run interest of none of them; rather, they imposed limits on their immediate incomes. Opposition to the fish guards, who enforced these regulations, became a regular feature of the life of the valley.

The nationalist movement harnessed the protest against taxes. On behalf of the villagers, political officials argued before the public authorities that it was inequitable for the poor villagers to pay taxes when the government failed to provide employment; they also dwelt upon the fate of wives and children who must wait while their husbands and fathers languished in jail because they were too poor to pay the levy.[19] At Kasumpa village, the party leaders organized youths to jeer at, harass, and occasionally attack messengers and revenue collectors who were searching for tax defaulters. And because Kasumpa village lay along the main road from the boma to the valley, the political leaders of Kasumpa were also able to delay the progress of these officials while sending youths ahead to warn "targeted" villages of the impending arrival of the tax collectors.[20]

The protests against the fishing regulations were also channeled through the nationalist movement. Upon entering the valley the African National Congress, as one of its first campaigns, protested the imposition of the fishing regulations. Thus in 1953 the colonial administration reported: "At the beginning of the year there were serious disturbances which arose from resentment over the fishing control regulations. There was active opposition for a few months and feeling ran high throughout the valley. Compliance . . . was, however, enforced with the aid of police reinforcements."[21] Later, in 1956, ANC organizers from Kasumpa promoted large-scale protests against the enforcement of net-size regulations. They criticized the conduct of the fish guards, who were seizing "the nets all along the lake . . . [and] pushing people cruelly in their boats," and threatened violent reprisals unless the fish guards stopped harassing the fishermen and "left them to freely and peacefully earn their wages and provide for their families, who have no employment here in the rural areas."[22] The next year, ANC officials promoted the wholesale withdrawal of fishermen from the native authority markets and built alternative markets at which they could sell their produce to traders from the city without having to pay market fees.[23] By helping to organize the protests of fishermen, just as by helping to organize the protests of the taxpayers, the ANC indicated its willingness to use political power to alter the conduct of the public authorities so as to enhance the economic well-being of the valley residents.

Economic Recession and Its Political Effects

In the late 1950s and early 1960s there occurred a series of events that severely disrupted many of the private markets from which the residents of the valley derived their incomes. The prosperity that had so characterized the Luapula region gave way to a severe recession; and partially as a result, political protest gave way to political violence in support of the nationalist cause.

The Imposition of Customs

The first major shock to the Luapula economy took place in 1955. Under agreements that dated back to the 1880s, Luapula, along with other areas of Northern Rhodesia, had been part of the Congo basin free-trade area. No customs or tariffs were levied on international trade in that area; and, given the extent to which the valley derived its revenues from fish sales to the Katanga, the Luapula region, more than other sectors of Northern Rhodesia, benefited from its free-trade status. In the mid-1950s, however, the federal government sought to promote the formation of domestic industry by erecting tariff barriers around the domestic market. Toward this end it abrogated the Congo basin agreements, and among the first to be affected were residents of Luapula.[24] The federal government constructed customs posts along the border with the Congo and dispatched officials to tour the villages and the waterways of the area. Fishermen who spent their francs on marketable produce from the Congo—blankets, petroleum products, bicycles, cooking utensils, and the like—now had to pay duty to these federal officials. Labor migrants returning from the Congo, who often sought to repatriate their savings in the form of commodities, also suffered from the imposition of customs duties, as did retailers who purchased stocks from the distributors in the nearby Katanga rather than from the more distant urban centers within Northern Rhodesia itself. Naturally, the Luapula residents were angered at the price rises forced upon them by the new tariff policy. So too were those who attempted to escape the price rises and were arrested for smuggling.

So great were the political tensions that resulted from this change in federal policy that the provincial commissioner of Luapula petitioned the chief secretary of Northern Rhodesia to withdraw customs officials from his area. The chief secretary replied that he was unable to dissuade the federal officers; the federal government, in his words, was determined to "show the Federal Flag," and appeared to welcome the confrontation which was being provoked by its actions.[25]

The Franc Crisis

The second major blow to the economy of the Luapula valley came in 1960. In that year the Congo attained independence, and Katanga Province, which bordered upon Luapula, attempted to secede from the new nation. From the point of view of the Luapula residents, perhaps the most important consequence was the sudden nonconvertibility of the Congolese franc. Given the turmoil within the Congo and the widespread disruption of the production and export of minerals from the country, the federal government refused to underpin the trade between sterling and the franc, for fear that it would accumulate stocks of a currency liable to decline precipitately in value. The result was a major shock to the Luapula economy, where for decades both currencies had served as mediums of exchange. Fishermen no longer dared make major sales in the Congo, for they could no longer trust the coinage they would receive there. And traders, who had accumulated francs, were left with nothing of value; many were unable to pay off wholesalers who had advanced them goods on credit.[26]

Unwilling to use public monies to cushion the economic impact of Congolese independence by issuing sterling for the now worthless franc, the government forced private residents of the valley to absorb the economic consequences of this "act of God" themselves. Indeed, the government went so far as to enforce bankruptcy proceedings against those whom it had failed to assist in the monetary crisis: it posted writs against the village storekeepers, seized their assets, and placed their goods on auction to pay off their creditors.[27] Ingenuously, one official who had supervised over one hundred such proceedings commented in a report, "It has been found that when seizure is effected it is normally the case that the defendant has few goods, but frequently he has substantial holdings of worthless Congo francs."[28] He went on to note that the villagers were "generally restive and discontented with their reduced income."[29]

The Decline of the Fish Trade

Compounding the injurious effects of the new tariffs and the non-convertibility of the franc was the decline of the Luapula fishing industry. During the mid-1950s the fishing industry produced over 7,000 short tons of fish per year;[30] as we have seen, the industry made Luapula one of the most prosperous rural areas in the territory. In the late 1950s and early 1960s, however, the industry was subject to a series of shocks, and the prosperity of the valley suffered a reversal from which it had not yet recovered by the early 1970s. The precipitate decline of the economy of the valley led to renewed attacks upon the government.

The first blow came in 1958, when the mines of the Congo terminated their bulk purchases of agricultural commodities; instead of paying their employees partly in kind, the companies began paying higher money wages. The mines left it to traders and distributors to supply food to their labor force; the result, for producers, was a reduction in the demand for fish, as these suppliers failed to adjust quickly to the new marketing conditions.[31] It was in 1960, however, that the real blow hit the fishing trade. The outbreak of civil war in the Congo completely disrupted the supply routes to the Katanga mining towns,[32] and fishermen were left with a reduced volume of sales. Conditions made it difficult for them to adjust by increasing their sales in the domestic market. For one, fish prices were controlled, so the market did not readily clear. For another, new fisheries had entered production in the late 1950s and had strongly penetrated the domestic fish market; these included Mweru Wantipa in Northern Province, which quadrupled its sales over the period 1956 to 1960, and Lake Kariba, which made its first major domestic sales in 1960.[33] Adding to the woes of the Luapula fishermen was that it was increasingly in the interest of the traders to patronize these alternative suppliers. The Lunda Native Authority, its revenues now reflecting the effects of the recession, imposed an ill-timed increase in its levy upon fish traders—an act that the native authorities in other areas saw fit not to follow. The natural result was a decline in the number of buyers.

Incredibly, two other shocks—apparently accidental quirks of nature —hit the industry at this time. The *mpumbu*, a fish considered a delicacy in the urban market, suddenly and completely disappeared from the waters of the fishery, and heavy floods in 1961 cut the fishery off from the urban markets as the height of the marketing season.[34] Both acts of fate served to divert traders to new sources of supply. The statistics reveal a 24.3 percent drop in sales from the Luapula fisheries over the period 1959 to 1962. In money terms, assuming that all fish sold at the lowest price, this represented a loss to the valley dwellers of £179,000 per year in income over those years.[35]

Political Protest

During this period, politics in Luapula shifted from political agitation to violence. The above account of the economic conditions of the valley suggests in part that this should have been a probable transition. In response to the growing urban demand for food, the economic fortunes of the Luapula residents had improved markedly; in the late 1950s and early 1960s, however, they suffered an abrupt and severe reversal. As such, the course of Luapula prosperity conformed with almost unsettling precision to the path traced by the fortunes of other societies entering periods of political violence. For, as James Davies, Ted Gurr, and others have argued, societies in which growing prosperity has been abruptly checked by circumstance are highly prone to rebellion.[36] Luapula, in this period, was clearly a society tracing the course of probable revolution, as outlined by Davies and Gurr. And like others of its kind, Luapula did indeed experience an outbreak of political violence.

The rise in tariffs, the nonconvertibility of the Congolese franc, and the decline of the fish industry all led to protests and violence. In attempting to enforce the new tariffs, customs officials were attacked and assaulted when they toured the villages demanding custom receipts from the owners of imported goods and searching for contraband merchandise. Villagers also abused messengers sent to serve notice on store owners who had been bankrupted by the fall of the franc, and they attacked the government employees who had been sent to impound their merchandise. The nationalist officials joined with the impoverished traders in seeking the removal of branches of European-owned retail companies from the valley in order to enhance the prospects of the beleaguered African traders.[37] More than anywhere else, however, the acts of protest focused upon the fishing industry.

The fishermen had always opposed the levying of taxes upon their trade; now, with the industry in decline, they pressed strongly for tax relief and doubled their resistance to taxation. As the fish councillor of the native authority wrote in 1960, "Fish guards, levy-clerks, and even Departmental Councillors [had a] tough time to persuade people to pay their licenses and levies; often they were attacked. . . . Many people were arrested and given cases in the Native Courts."[38] The fishermen also sought permission from the native authority to raise their prices. But the core of the conflict between the fishermen and the native authority was the fishermen's resistance to the fishing regulations.

As we have noted, the regulations were imposed by the native authority to protect the long-run interests of the fishing industry. To refrain from fishing in the spawning season and in the breeding grounds, and to use gill nets of sufficient size to protect fingerlings, were in the long-run interests of all the fishermen. But each fisherman, in the short run, could do better by violating these regulations. Careful policing of the industry was therefore essential. The native authority provided such enforcement, and it did so in close collaboration with the Congolese officials, whose border also ran along the Luapula River and Lake Mweru, and whose nationals shared the fishing grounds.

With the Katanga rebellion, however, the Congolese officials no longer could enforce the regulations against their nationals; and given the proliferation of arms in Katanga and the sighting of disaffected and armed members of the Force Publique* in fish camps and on the river, the fish guards of the Lunda Native Authority were not about to impose the regulations on the Congo side of the river.[39] The Zambian fishermen, increasingly losing money as a result of the disruption of their markets, were strongly committed to short-term gains; and with the breakdown of the enforcement of regulations on the Congolese fishermen, it was no longer plausible to them that their adherence to the fishing regulations was of any benefit. As a result, the Zambian fishermen turned against the native authority and resisted the fish guards and messengers with force and violence.[40]

In the period 1959 to 1961, therefore, economic circumstances furnished strong incentive for the masses of the valley to engage in acts of political protest. Adding to the explosiveness of the situation was the fact that the

*The Congolese army whose mutiny had sparked the early turmoil in the Congo.

political organizers had strong reasons for wishing to tap this potential for violence. For, as the opening narrative of the last chapter pointed out, the nationalist parties were engaged at that time in engineering a critical series of constitutional reforms and they had to demonstrate continually the intensity of their popular support in order to exact a more favorable distribution of power.

In 1959, as we have seen, the colonial government allowed elections to be conducted under a franchise which for the first time permitted Africans to vote in significant numbers. Differences over tactics led to a split in the nationalist forces. While the "old guard" in the nationalist movement—Nkumbula and the African National Congress—determined to contest the elections, the militant wing of the party determined to boycott them. This militant wing therefore withdrew from ANC and organized a rival party, the Zambia African National Congress (ZANC), through which to pursue its objectives.

The nationalist leaders of the Luapula valley attended the conference at which this split took place. During the conference, they caucused to determine which group to follow. They recalled the strength of the popular resistance to the government and its agency, the Lunda Native Authority, at home in the valley. They recalled the timidity of the leaders of the African National Congress, who had in recent years failed to tour the villages in the valley or to speak before local audiences in their area.[41] They felt they had been fighting the government "single-handedly." As one recalled in an interview with me:

> We battled fish guards and messengers. We beat people and we were not afraid. But the big leaders from Lusaka, they did not visit us. When they did, they spent all day talking with the district commissioner or the chiefs. They were afraid of the jails here, and afraid of coming to our villages by the river; they lived too well for too long in the cities, and they feared the mosquitos in our houses.

The Luapula nationalist leaders therefore chose to support ZANC, because only its leaders "seemed willing to go to jail, to fight, or to die, to get rid of the Federation."[42]

In conformity with ZANC policy, the nationalist leaders returned to the valley to organize a boycott of the elections. They maintained their headquarters in Kasumpa village, both because of its central location in the valley and because a large number of the local organizers from the valley were residents of that village. In Kasumpa they began to recruit "freedom fighters." The freedom fighters served as party messengers; for the party leaders, given their plans, now feared to put into writing the communications they wished to send. The freedom fighters also fashioned crude weapons and amassed stores of petrol; armed with these, they engaged in programs of selective political violence.

The new party soon began to organize a boycott and disruption of the March 1959 elections. The government had dispatched touring teams to inform the people about the elections and to enroll them as voters, and the freedom fighters harassed these teams, disrupted their meetings, and occasionally beat them and destroyed their records. The government had decided that local schools were to serve as voting centers, and the district administration posted on the school walls information about the elections, statements of the party platforms, and biographies of the candidates. Meeting during the night in the bush, the freedom fighters would dress in skins ("so that others would know that we could not be expected to act as people"); then, having decided upon a particular school as a target, they would silently move in, douse it with petrol, and burn it to the ground. They continued this program of intimidation and arson for several months prior to the 1959 elections. Finally, in March of 1959, the government could no longer tolerate the disruption. At the urging of the native authorities, it brought mobile police units into the province; after officially declaring a state of emergency, the government unleashed these forces against the local party units. On 12 March 1959, the mobile units descended upon Kasumpa village. Breaking down the doors of houses, the police herded the villagers and their families into the clearing under the mango trees—the place of Mwabamukupa's original stockade. Informers, dressed in straw costumes and with their faces hidden beneath cloth hoods, circled through the crowd of villagers and selected for detention and trial the political organizers of the nationalist movement.[43]

From the nationalists' point of view, the prosecutions that followed were highly successful affairs; for want of evidence, the magistrate refused to convict the local leaders of the party. The leaders returned to their villages to assess what should be done, given the ban that had been placed on their party and the jailing of its national leaders. In search of guidance, the local officials established contact with the detained national leadership and secured authorization to re-form the banned party under a new name and so to continue the struggle for independence. Meeting once again at Kasumpa village, the former leaders chose a provincial executive committee and full slates of officers for constituency posts in Kawambwa, Nchelenge, and Mwense. At the urging of Huggins Chewe, who served as liaison with the national leaders, they resolved once again to

> form Action groups whose function will be to destroy bridges and attack property; recruit "policemen" whose main function will be the guarding of party leaders and protecting them from arrest. . . . A courier system will be established between Provincial Headquarters

and Districts and branches . . . and postal services will not be used. . . . In the concluding stages of the conference, speakers reflected the prevalent atmosphere when they spoke in . . . praise of [a] campaign of violence . . ., of their willingness to die in the struggle for freedom, of seizing self-government by force; and by asserting that nothing would be achieved without loss of life.[44]

Centered in Kasumpa, the stronghold of the resistance to the Lunda Native Authority and the administration of which it was a part, this new party organization soon spread out once again and penetrated almost all the villages of the valley.

As detailed by David Mulford, the national-level leaders of ZANC, after emerging from detention, soon coalesced into a new nationalist party: the United National Independence Party (UNIP). Dispatching officials and facilities to Luapula, UNIP forged a link with the local party units there.[45] The local units were to prove valuable allies. For after the Monckton Commission recommended that the federation be terminated the UNIP leadership faced a series of tough and protracted negotiations; and the Luapula branch's willingness to employ violence proved to be a valuable asset in the bargaining for a new constitution.

The Monckton Commission reported against the continuation of federation in 1960, and the new constitutional conference began in London in December. The conference continued on for months; it nearly broke down several times, with delegations temporarily withdrawing and returning home to reformulate their proposals prior to reentering the bargaining sessions. The national-level elite of the nationalist parties conducted the negotiations; but they were closely and painstakingly followed at the local levels. Village radios carried the news of the conference and the party newspapers contained detailed accounts of the various negotiating positions, the differences between and within the delegations, and the practical implications of what appeared to be esoteric differences between the fine points of the different constitutional proposals.[46] The local party units were not merely passive audiences to the proceedings, however; they also responded to the news and tried, as best they could, to fortify the bargaining position of their delegates. On the nineteenth of December, for example, the local party units of Kasumpa wired their delegation in London that they were "ready to pay any price for freedom. If Kaunda be ignored in his demands for an African majority, Britain would have long chaos. . . . No toleration with sell out. Endless chaos immediate."[47] When the UNIP delegation found it necessary to walk out of the conference at one point, the local party units deluged it with telegrams of commendation; to shore up the position of the delegates, the telegrams went on to express tacit threats of insurrection: "You may command us if Macleod ignores you over secession [from the federation] and majority rule."[48] The London delegation telegraphed back that there was "no need for action until letter of instruction"; but no doubt the threat of action had been useful to them.

As a result of the negotiations, the nationalist parties secured a favorable draft constitution for the territory. But while the African population was pleased with the progress that had been made, the settlers were severely alarmed. Duncan Sandys, secretary of state for commonwealth relations, sensing that the settlers were on the point of rejecting the proposals, agreed to several revisions that appeared to undo much of the progress the nationalists had made.[49] In response, the UNIP leaders called for a national conference of party leaders at Mulungushi, north of Broken Hill, to determine what steps should be taken to arrest the apparent weakening of their position. The public statements from the meeting declared that the nationalist politicians had rejected the alternative of violence but also indicated that the delegates had accepted a secret master plan to resist through "positive action" the continuation of colonial rule in the territory. The statements did not outline what was meant by positive action; but the impression was left that the plan detailed several levels of mass action, beginning with boycotts and strikes and possibly culminating in insurrection and violence.

Whatever was agreed at the conference, the Luapula delegates returned to their villages convinced of the need for violence. As they recounted their feelings at that time: "We found our national leaders troubled by the British. They could not tell us to fight; then, they would all be arrested and the Europeans would run the country. But if they did not fight, the British would agree with words but would give everything to Welensky [the leader of the United Federal Party]. We decided that we had to fight here in the villages. The British would have to leave, or else be left with nothing to rule but ashes."

The UNIP leaders in the Luapula valley went about their normal political tasks in the daytime: enrolling members, organizing new party branches, selecting leaders to fill posts in the new party units, and speaking at public meetings. But at night they met in the bush out of sight of the headmen, the messengers of the native authorities, and the informers paid by the colonial government. There, in liaison with the provincial headquarters of Luapula and Northern provinces, they formulated a carefully scheduled program of civil disobedience and insurrection.

The campaign began early in August of 1961. Party leaders held a series of meetings in the villages, and at each the proceedings were the same. A hole was dug in the ground; a casket, representing the federation, was blessed by a "priest" and then lowered into the ground. Then the villagers filed by, paying their last respects to federation and dropping into the grave their hated tax booklets. To destroy the tax booklets was, of course, to violate the law, but when the native authorities' messengers swarmed into one village to arrest the lawbreakers, they quickly got word that a meeting had commenced in another. Soon the forces of law and order in the valley were in disarray.

An African representative in the Legislative Council who had visited his constituency during these events later reported:

> It [had been] said that on [the] 29th of July there would be something strange in the area. Indeed after two days or so, 17 people who intended to burn . . . certificates . . . were arrested by the . . . Kapasus [messengers]. A report was sent to the Boma to collect these people, but just as the Mobile Units [came] many people burned their *situpas* [tax booklets]. . . .
>
> This . . . happened in every corner. . . . This made the Native Authority surprised, . . . but [it] tried its best to arrest many. . . . People were forced to pay the fines by the Native Authority, but were saying that they were prepared to be jailed.
>
> At many times people were asked why they were so wild, but the answer was that . . . they were prepared to break and destroy the present Government's rules and orders so that they could get African self-rule in Northern Rhodesia.[50]

At first, despite the arrests and the attendant beatings, the campaign of resistance had a festive air. Perhaps the high point of this stage came when troops of children from the villages entered the boma towns and headquarters of the chiefs carrying buckets filled with ashes. Care had been taken to insure that the ashes could easily be identified as the remnants of burned tax booklets.

The native authorities responded to the crisis by exercising their legal right to ban UNIP meetings and gatherings of UNIP officials in the area on the grounds that such meetings were inimical to law and order. They also arrested and detained all those whom they thought were organizing and promoting the illegal campaign in the area. Further, they urged the district administration to send mobile units to make a show of force in the valley. The banning, arrests, and tours of armed personnel only increased the unrest, however; and, with the rise of tensions in the valley, the party leaders now implemented the second stage of their campaign.

This stage of the campaign was the same in the valley as elsewhere in Luapula Province. First, on the twelfth of August, parents were persuaded to keep their children home from school and teachers were prevented from reporting to work. Then the fires began: first a school building in a distant village; then, while attention focused there, another at the mission station; then a third building, this a customs station on the river; then others—the chief's house, the court buildings, and the houses of messengers at Kanyembo. Before long, arsonists had burned a fair percentage of the governmental structures in the area. Naturally, the native authority sent word of the outbreak to the boma officials, who promptly dispatched units of the mobile police. The party units had prepared for the arrival of reinforcements, however. Their scouts reported the location of the mobile units; and their freedom fighters burned bridges and felled trees in the path of the approaching forces. At one point, a mobile unit approached Kasumpa village at high speed and, cresting a hill, discovered too late a blockade of rocks and trees that had been concealed in its path. As the armed forces camped for the night while awaiting the completion of repairs to their vehicles, the freedom fighters shot at them from the dark. Upon returning from the province, one reporter wrote that, although the towns were quiet,

> life in the . . . bush is far from normal. Two R.R.A.F. Provost aircraft, kept busy throughout the day scouting the area, continually report sabotage and arson in the villages. . . .
>
> The police are working untiringly on the ground. They have completed their job of establishing contact with all the Europeans in the area. But it took days to accomplish. I rode with one patrol to a mission station. . . . In under two miles, we met seven road blocks. Four were felled trees. One deep ditch had been dug across our path, and two bridges had been destroyed. . . . [Police] make anyone they find in the vicinity help to shift the trees or rebuild the bridges. Roughing-up by African constables speeds them along.[51]
>
> It was learnt today that four men were wounded when a security force patrol was attacked near Mbereshi Mission. . . . An African member of the security forces was wounded on the head and three of the attackers were injured. . . . After the casualties had been taken to the mission hospital, about 200 armed rioters attacked the security forces' vehicles. The attackers were dispersed, but the patrol was heavily stoned as it left the scene.[52]

Like the violence of 1959, however, the insurrection did not last long. In the third week of August, the government banned the party in Luapula Province. Federal troops entered the valley. Garrisoning the towns, the troops relieved the mobile units, which once again entered Kasumpa, rounded up all suspected party leaders, and transported them to jail. They also destroyed the party headquarters in the village, smashing its furni-

ture, leveling the walls, and setting fire to the remaining debris. Angered
and embittered by the police's response, the Kasumpa villagers nonetheless soon had reason for satisfaction. While suppressing the rebellion
on the one hand, the government felt compelled to reopen negotiations on
the other. The British government modified the concessions it had made
to the settlers and reaffirmed its commitment to majority rule in the territory. And in February 1962 the territory adopted a new constitution—one
under which, for the first time, the political leaders of the African majority
were to govern Northern Rhodesia.

The people of the Luapula valley vividly recall this period of the nationalist struggle. They feel, and rightly, that they made great sacrifices to
overthrow the colonial regime. They recall the beatings they suffered at
the hands of the chiefs' messengers. They remember the descent of the
mobile units upon the village, and the interrogations and jailings that
followed. Many carry the scars of wounds sustained in combat in the villages or while under interrogation in the police offices. Others still suffer
from the years of schooling lost, either as a result of being expelled from
classes because of their political involvements, or as a result of the destruction of the schools in the area. The people of the valley had chosen to invest
time, effort, pain, and opportunities foregone, in the political struggle
against the colonial regime. The battle won, they began to expect benefits
from their labors.

With the shift of power from the federal forces to the African majority,
the people of the valley realized the first fruits of their political toil. After
news of the implementation of a new constitution, they sharply cut back
on their payment of taxes. This alarmed the native authority, which was
dependent upon these revenues, as well as the central government, which
was upset that the spirit of disobedience remained unbroken. Nonetheless,
the refusal to pay taxes, condoned and encouraged by party leaders in the
area, represented the first harvest of the benefits from the political struggle,
and the government could not refuse it.[53] In addition, the people would
no longer abide by the regulations imposed upon the fishing industry.
Acknowledging the fait accompli, the government in 1961 simply gave up
attempting to prevent fishing in the spawning season and in the spawning
areas; it ruefully acknowledged that the "fish levy collection has been
affected by the . . . political instability," with the native authority's
revenue in "nets and boats hav[ing] dropped down very considerably."[54]
As another official put it, "Our fishermen look upon all conservation regulations as nothing more than a piscatorial equivalent of humanitarian-
ism."[55] By not paying the license fee and by successfully resisting the
regulations imposed upon their major industry, the people of the valley
took advantage of their new position of power to remove the limitations

which had been placed by public authorities upon their ability to enhance their private incomes.

In conjunction with the transfer of power at the national level, a similar transfer of power took place at the local level. In 1963 the local UNIP politicians assumed elected posts on the council of the Lunda Native Authority. The debates of the council reveal that the politicians sought to purge the old staff of the native authority, both because these employees were opponents whom they had just vanquished in the political struggle and because they sought jobs for their political supporters, who were clamoring for employment.[56] The councillors also sought to implement local tax reform. They strongly urged the provincial administration to shift from a flat capitation tax to a graduated tax, so that "those who have no work" would not have to pay, while "those who are rich" would.[57] They legislated new license and market fees in the fishing industry which were to be paid only by "those with plenty of nets who [fish] as a business," and they instructed the fish guards to make levies on this basis.[58] The councillors went on to reduce the tax on sawyers, who had had to pay the council £1 per tree, and to remove the taxes on beer brewing and hunting.[59] This minor outpouring of local reforms clearly revealed the commitments of the nationalist leaders to utilize their newly attained positions of political power to alleviate the economic grievances that had helped to bring them to power in the first place.

Another theme, apparent in the deliberations of the local councillors, characterized the expression of political sentiment in other forums as well. Not only did the UNIP politicians seek to lighten the tax burden of the villagers, but they also sought to increase the quantity of public services provided to those "who had fought so hard and so long to bring an African government." The councillors petitioned the government to survey the valley for mineral deposits and to open mines there "so that our people could have opportunities for employment."[60] It petitioned for more government construction in the valley so that "we can have facilities and so that there will be plenty of jobs."[61] It asked the government to erect more refrigeration plants for the fishing industry, and a factory so that "we can tin fish." And, outside the council walls, there were mounting demands for government "schemes" to be brought to the valley—fruit-growing schemes, banana schemes, dairy-farming schemes, mango schemes—and for the distribution by government of cash loans—loans for fishermen, prospective farmers, and businessmen; loans for making home improvements, for buying lorries, for starting a bakery or for constructing a filling station.[62] Thus, almost immediately after the transfer of power, the people of the valley demanded that their political sacrifices pay off, that their incomes and economic opportunities be enhanced by increased expenditures by the public sector, which their own representatives now controlled. The villagers had wrested power from the colonialists and handed it to the nationalist politicians; now they wanted results.

Indeed, in the postindependence period, as the remainder of this book will show, the demands for benefits from the government would be, if anything, more intense than ever. For not only had the people put their own kind in power; not only had they fought and suffered and so earned future benefits; but also, with the end of rural taxation they now could get public benefits seemingly for free. In effect, a major consequence of the nationalist rebellion in the rural areas was a transfer of the tax burden to the cities. Rural dwellers could now benefit from the growth of industry not only through the private urban markets for produce and labor; but also, through agitation, pressure, and politics, they could now transfer the wealth of the cities to the countryside through public channels. Furthermore, such benefits as they could obtain from government would now come without a visible price. Their appetite for government investments would therefore seemingly be insatiable.[63] As one colonial official stationed in Luapula commented, after the demise of the British administration in the area: "Perhaps our only consolation is that [these people] will be equally troublesome to an African government."[64]

PART TWO

THE POSTINDEPENDENCE PERIOD

6

Postindependence Patterns of Public Expenditure

Part One of this book examined the concentration of capital in the urban and industrial regions of colonial Zambia and the response of the rural dwellers to the growth of the wealth of the towns. Rural dwellers, as we have seen, sought access to the wealth of the cities by entering the urban markets for produce and labor. In addition, they engaged in politics. In pursuit of their political objectives villagers enlisted in the nationalist cause, significantly contributing to the installation of a new government in Zambia.

Part Two concentrates upon the fortunes of the rural dwellers under the regime they had helped place in power. In particular, it examines the degree to which the new African government has improved the material well-being of the countryside by levying the wealth of the cities and distributing it to the village areas in the form of programs of rural development.

In analyzing the government's investments in the rural areas, we will utilize our model of the financial behavior of the public sector. Governments, we have hypothesized, choose to spend so as to increase their level of political support, to fulfill ideological objectives, and to enhance the expected level of public revenues, if only in order to generate the resources through which to attain their political and ethical objectives. We have also hypothesized that governments will invest in projects with lower rates of return, the greater the magnitude of available revenues. Differences in the nature of their constituencies, their ideologies, and their revenue base should therefore relate to variations in the way governments allocate funds. These propositions help to clarify the way in which public monies were spent by the new African government, and in particular the government's use of its resources to develop the rural areas in the postindependence period.

The Effect of the Revenue Base

Upon independence, the new government of Zambia had access to a tax base composed almost exclusively of mining and industrial firms located along the line of rail. The tax returns for 1963—the year prior to independence in Zambia—indicate that the mining companies alone paid over 60 percent of the total taxes of the territory, and that taxes on companies constituted over 95 percent of the revenues of the state.[1] As over 95 percent of the industrial establishments fell in the line-of-rail provinces of Zambia, it is obvious that the geographical origins of the government's revenues were highly concentrated.[2] The copper and copper-related industries provided the vast bulk of the government's revenues; and it was in the interest of the newly independent government to spend its funds in a manner that would increase the value of their taxable profits.

However, governments are interested not only in the magnitude but also in the certainty of the returns to their expenditures; what governments seek to maximize are *expected* revenues. Because the economy in Zambia was so narrowly based, the fiscal revenues available to the newly independent government were extremely uncertain. Thus, for example, the price of copper stood at £230 per ton of electrolytic wirebar on the London Metal Exchange in the year before independence; by the year after independence, the price of copper had risen to £462, or more than doubled. Given that the marginal tax rate on copper profits was over 70 percent, public finances were highly sensitive to fluctuations in the copper industry;[3] and, while the government initially benefited from the fluctuation in the copper price, it was aware of the possibly disastrous effects upon its revenues of a sudden movement downward. In its program of public investments, it was therefore in the interest of the government to diversify its tax base—to generate an element of "redundancy" in the industrial economy—so as to reduce the variability and increase the certainty of its revenues. The diversification of the copper-based economy consequently received high priority in the government's investment program.[4]

On the basis of these considerations, the new African government sought to channel public investments onto the line of rail and to do so in a way that would sponsor the development of nonmining enterprises. Figure 6.1 compares the estimated capital expenditures for the ten urban and thirty-three rural districts of Zambia from 1961 to 1968. Even after independence, it can be seen, well over half of the capital investments made by the government went to the urban districts of Zambia. Corroborating evidence comes from the Planning Office's description of planned and actual government expenditure over the first planning period, 1966 to 1971 (see

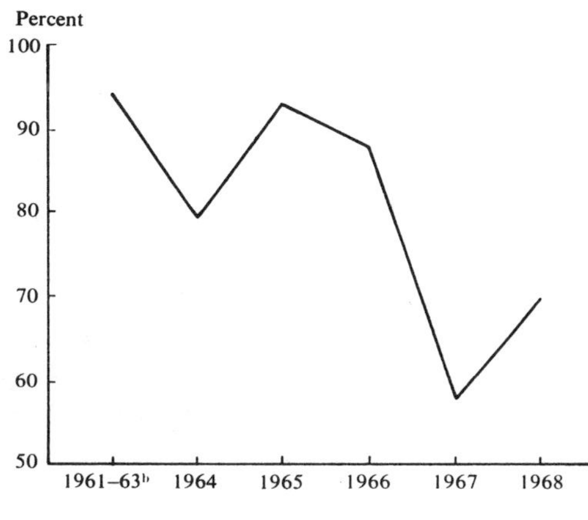

Fig. 6.1

Percent of Total Annual Government Capital Investment Allocated to Urban Districtsᵃ

urce: Republic of Zambia, *Estimates of Revenue and Expenditure for the Year[s] 1961–1968.*

ı. The ten line-of-rail urban centers: Livingstone, Lusaka, Kabwe, Ndola, Kitwe, Luanshya, Chingola, Mufulira, Kalulushi, and Chililabombwe.

ɔ. Average annual.

table 6.1). By plan, the urban provinces would have gotten over half of the government's funds; in actuality, they got over two-thirds of the government's investments. The government therefore spent, and intended to spend, in the area from which its revenues derived.

Because of the structure of the Zambian economy, the government found it could best diversify its tax base by promoting economic activities that took advantage of the demand for goods and services on the part of the dominant copper companies.[5] Robert Baldwin, writing in the mid-1950s, described the linkages between the mining industry and other sectors in the following terms:

> Of the main supplies used for operational purposes in the copper mines—explosives, timber, coal, furnace and firebricks, mill balls (used to crush ore), rails and fittings, and steel—about 15 percent of the timber is cut within the territory, and a large share of the mill balls are manufactured in Northern Rhodesia. The rest of the articles are imported.[6]

This list anticipates accurately many of the major investments in the post-independence period. Among the major achievements of the first planning period (1966–71) were the construction of a nitrates and explosives in-

Table 6.1 Distribution of Capital Expenditures in First National Development Plan

| | Planned | | Actual | | Ratio of Actual to Planned Capital Expenditure |
	Total (*K million*)	Per Capita (*K*)	Total (*K million*)	Per Capita (*K*)	
Urbanized provinces	294.6	188	448.0	286	152
Rural provinces	269.6	104	211.9	82	79
Three line-of-rail provinces	389.1	188	539.4	260	141

Source: Republic of Zambia, *Second National Development Plan, January 1972– December 1976*, p. 167.

Note: Urbanized provinces: Central and Copperbelt; rural provinces: all others. Line-of-rail provinces: Central, Southern, and Copperbelt.

dustry, which sold most of its product to the mines; the development of major local deposits of coal, almost all of which is consumed by the refineries and smelters of the mining industry; and the creation of an industry to manufacture clay pipes and firebricks, most of which again are consumed by the mines.[7] In addition, the metal-working group of industries, which produced mill balls, fittings, rails, and so on, grew rapidly over this period. As one source stated, referring to 1966–71, "The total number of industrial establishments increased . . . [by] 30 percent. The largest among existing industrial units belongs to the metal working group —largely subserving the mining industry and economic activities connected therewith."[8] A similar case was the cement industry, which expanded its capacity by 80 percent, principally by creating a new plant on the copperbelt itself; and the construction industry, which in 1965 received more payments from the mines than any other domestic industrial sector, nearly tripled its capacity over the first planning period. An oil refinery, which would sell most of its output to the mines, was nearly completed by the end of this period.

Diversification of the industrial economy thus characterized much of the investment activity in the initial postindependence period. The success of the program is perhaps best measured in terms of the changing import content of the purchases made by the mining companies. Norman Kessel's evaluation of the input-output matrix for the Zambian economy in 1966 indicates that direct imports by the mining companies plus the import component of purchases from local companies constituted 50 percent of the value of nonlabor inputs into the mines; an analogous evaluation of the 1969 input-output table yields a comparable figure of 28.3 percent, suggesting the formation of local sources of supply for the productive requirements of the Zambian copper mines.[9]

The new African government played a complex role in promoting industrial expansion and diversification. Occasionally, it "invested" in new forms of industries by foregoing tax revenues from the new enterprises in their initial years in order to secure revenues in later periods. Thus, it declared tax holidays for new industries; in at least one case—the establishment of a glass-making plant in Kapiri Mposhi—the tax holidays purportedly attracted investments that otherwise would not have been forthcoming. Moreover, the government encouraged private investments by offering generous capital depreciation allowances and tax credits for capital expenditures; in this way too it in effect "spent" public revenues in support of its economic objectives.[10]

The government also used its legal power literally to force local investments. By regulating the purchase of foreign exchange, for example, it limited the repatriation of corporate profits by foreign-owned enterprises, thereby compelling international corporations to maintain their earnings in local capital markets.[11] In some cases, the government simply nationalized firms which it felt were increasing local sales by mobilizing slack capacity abroad rather than by creating new productive capacity within Zambia; this motivation apparently underlay the government's takeover of industries within the building trades in 1968.[12]

Finally, the government also acted as an entrepreneur. Through its Indeco group of industries, for example, it invested in an oil refinery, the cement industry, the nitrates and explosives industry, and a clay and firebrick works. It also made major investments in the textile industry, in automobile assembly and in metal fabricating. In this way, it utilized public revenues to expand and diversify the urban-industrial economy.

Perhaps most important, however, were the government's investments in infrastructural goods which would serve to underpin a high rate of return on private capital formation and thus produce investments by private entrepreneurs. The government made major capital outlays to modernize and upgrade the equipment of the national railways. It facilitated the purchase of supplies and equipment abroad by creating a transport fleet and depot facilities for trade with the coast, by resurfacing the road system to coastal ports, and by expanding harbor and warehouse facilities in the port areas. It expanded the energy supply available to industry by laying an oil pipeline to the coast and by investing in major hydroelectric projects: a new power facility at Kafue, in Central Province, and a major addition to the existing facilities at the Kariba dam in Southern Province. By Dennis Dresang's estimates, on the basis of the pattern of government investment in 1969, direct investments in business enterprises constituted 19 percent of the government's capital expenditure, while a full 55 percent of the government's capital expenditures went to the formation of infrastructure of this kind.[13]

The magnitude of the government's effort is suggested by the rate of investment it achieved: gross fixed capital formation remained at a rate of nearly 20 percent of the gross national product (in 1965 prices) between 1964 and 1969.[14] The success of the government's effort is suggested by the rate of economic expansion attained in this period. Measured at factor cost, the gross domestic product increased from K465 million to K979 million* over the six-year period.[15] Paralleling the growth of the economy, the recurrent revenues accruing to the government increased from just under K160 million in 1964 to over K400 million in 1969.[16] And whereas the copper industry contributed over 60 percent of the revenues in the year prior to independence, in 1969 its share was only 45 percent.[17] These figures suggest that by investing in the line-of-rail economy the government both increased the magnitude of the revenues available to the public treasury and diversified its sources of income.

Shifting Priorities

Factors other than a concern for expected revenue influence public spending, and they do so in ways that promote public investments in areas where the rate of return is low. Factors that can lead to such expenditures include the quantity of public revenues, the values of politicians, and the political incentives confronting public officials who seek to remain in power.

In postindependence Zambia, the government possessed an abundance of capital. With independence, the funds that had hitherto gone to the government of the federation reverted to the government of the territory, and the new African government therefore had access to greater revenues than had its colonial predecessor. Moreover, with independence, the Zambian government acquired the mineral rights of the British South Africa Company and so became the recipient of the mineral royalties paid by the mining corporations.[18] Lastly, the achievement of independence coincided with a favorable and major upswing in the price of copper (see table 6.2). The result was a surge in government revenues from company taxes and mineral royalties, plus new earnings from an export tax which the government imposed to capture the windfall resulting from the soaring price of copper.[19] All told, in the first fiscal year of independence (1964–65), the government was able to lay claim to an estimated K160 million in recurrent revenues, a figure that represented a doubling of the actual revenues of the last fiscal year prior to independence.[20] With funds so abundant, the government could therefore afford to invest in projects and

*K stands for kwacha, the new currency issued after independence. Two kwacha equal one pound.

Table 6.2   Copper Price: Annual London Metal Exchange Mean
Cash Price per Ton of Electrolytic Wire Bars, 1962–71

Year	£
1962	230
1963	230
1964	346
1965	462
1966	541
1967	411
1968	517
1969	611
1970	589
1971	444

Source: Mindeco, *Mindeco Mining Year Book 1971* (Kitwe: Copper Industry Service Bureau, n.d.), p. 33.

in areas where the revenue returns would be relatively small, uncertain, or long term.

Not only were funds more abundant with independence, but also the transfer of power to an African government took place in conjunction with a reconstitution of the political structure of the territory. The primary characteristic of the transformation was an enormous expansion of the electorate, as the de facto racially constrained franchise was replaced by universal adult suffrage. In practice, this change meant a transformation from a colonial electorate that was overwhelmingly urban, employed, and European to a postindependence electorate that was predominantly rural, agricultural, and black. As shown in table 6.3, the result was that the new UNIP government was based largely upon a rural set of constituencies, as any other government would have had to be under the circumstances. Under conditions of competition, to remain in power, the new government therefore had to give greater weight to the preferences and demands of

Table 6.3   1964 Election Results

	UNIP		*ANC*		*Total*	
	Rural	*Urban*	*Rural*	*Urban*	*Rural*	*Urban*
Contested seats	19	12	10	0	29	12
Uncontested seats	22	2	0	0	22	2
Total	41	14	10	0	51	14
	55		10		65	

Source: Parliamentary Elections Office, "Analysis of Polling, Northern Rhodesia General Election of 1964," mimeo. (28 January 1964).

Note: Main roll seats only; for an explanation, see n. 45 in this chapter. Constituencies counted as urban are those in the major urban centers, plus immediately adjacent peri-urban districts (e.g., Kafironda, Ndola West).

rural dwellers than had the colonial government. And this change implied a higher level of public expenditure in the rural areas.

The normative values of the new African government reinforced the priorities dictated by these political considerations. These values were articulated in terms of the philosophy of Humanism—a doctrine elaborated and propagated by its originator, President Kaunda, through numerous speeches, seminars, and governmental publications.[21] The philosophy stressed the equality of all men and the dignity of even the most impoverished individual; no man, it emphasized, was to be excluded from the benefits and opportunities created through governmental action. Humanism also extolled the moral virtues of village life—equality, cooperation, and mutual interdependence—and emphasized the necessity of fostering and perpetuating village society in order to preserve a moral resource for the nation. By implication, the philosophy therefore made it imperative that the government spend its resources so as to enhance the well-being of the village communities. As President Kaunda stated in a speech on Humanism:

> Government is vitally interested in participating actively in the economic life of the country. But . . . ALL OUR PEOPLE MUST BE BROUGHT INTO THIS . . . How can it be done? To be effective we must think in terms of the smallest unit . . . the village.
>
> . . . I must admit that I hesitate to interfere to any great extent with village life as it is today for the very reason that culturally we may be committing suicide—we might—without being aware of it, destroy some of the best things in our national culture. At the same time, to leave our villages as they are today means stagnation and the last may be worse than the first.[22]

The president therefore advocated expanded programs for agriculture and rural education, health care, and sanitation. The ideology of the new African political elite thereby seemed to encourage greater public expenditures in the village areas.

The Rural Development Program

In response to the changes that took place at the time of independence in the magnitude of the government's revenues and in its ideology and constituency, the government of Zambia made major efforts to upgrade the standard of living in the countryside. Evaluations of these efforts in later chapters will demonstrate that they fell far short of fulfilling their objectives. Nonetheless, major commitments were made by the new African government. Clinics, hospitals, schools, and roads were important symbols of the new commitment, but so too were programs designed to increase the profitability of cash crop production. These latter programs were central to the government's rural development program and will be of primary concern here.

The Initial Commitment

Zambia became independent on 24 October 1964. The first occasion on which the leaders of the new government publicly met the UNIP workers who had placed them in power was at a public meeting in Chifubu, outside of Ndola, in mid-January 1965. At this meeting, the government announced the first major benefits to be realized from the struggle for independence. As related by one observer:

> The *Northern News* reported on 18 January that "The President called on all unemployed in Zambia to form themselves into co-operative societies and to put their various skills to work on the agricultural and construction projects planned." President Kaunda declared: "The money is there and the know-how is there. You can form these co-operative societies anywhere in Zambia and we shall assist you in getting on."[23]

Three of the leading politicians from Kasumpa village attended the Chifubu rally and heard the president's message. They rejoiced that their leaders had remembered their electoral promises, and they determined to take advantage of the opportunities that were being created by the government. Upon returning to the village, they spread the news of the cooperative program. One of the politicians, a constituency secretary at the time, helped to organize the Katofyio Building Cooperative. A second, vice president of the constituency, gathered friends and fellow party workers together and organized Chikalamo Farming Cooperative. The third, a branch chairman in the village, also formed a farming cooperative, named Lukungwe. As they had been instructed to do, the founders registered their cooperatives with the government. They also sought financial support for their cooperatives. In the case of the building cooperative, the money was used to purchase building equipment; in the farming cooperatives, the members used the initial funds to maintain themselves and their families until they had cleared their land and begun agricultural production. While the officers of the building cooperative had to journey to Lusaka to register their society—the district officers were not sure whether building cooperatives qualified for governmental support—the story they tell about the formation of their cooperative nonetheless parallels the stories told by the officers of the farming cooperatives, and it is worth recounting.

We went to Chifubu in 1965 and brought back the President's speech. It said: "We want you to form cooperatives." I gave the speech to my friends, and we said: "We must do that." So we went to the boma to register with the government and to get help, like the President had told us. But the officer said, cooperatives are only for planting. We were afraid to go back to the village for we had promised work and K15 a month and we were now not able to give it. We would have been beaten. So we decided to go to Lusaka.

When we got to Kabwe we were out of money. So I went to my brother Oliver and got some and we went on to Lusaka. It was so big, but we got the way to Freedom House [national headquarters of UNIP] and they gave us directions to the cooperative department. We got there and told them that we were from Kasumpa and asked for papers. The secretary looked in many files but could find nothing about Kasumpa there. We could do nothing. So, we asked to see President Kaunda, but the secretary said he was in the United States. So we asked after the Vice President, but he was in Ethiopia. So we asked after the General Secretary of the party, but he was away. So then we said: "Well, let us see the director."

After having to wait for a day, we went in. The director said, "Where are you from?" "Oh, you are from Luapula. Where?" "Kasumpa—oh, my ancestors are from there." He gave us forms and a booklet and a copy of the ordinance and we walked out of there dancing. We walked about the streets of Lusaka, happy, reading those things.

Then we went back into the office and filled out the forms to register our cooperative. While we sat there, the orderly came out and said: "Don't you want a loan?" We looked at him and tried not to show how amazed we were and said coolly: "We were about to bring this important topic up." We asked for a loan for a vehicle, tools, lathes for shaping our wood, and so on.

Now we were a cooperative, and we went back to our village to work.

The government assisted the cooperatives in several ways. It sought to provide the training and skills necessary for their work. Government workers instructed the secretaries and treasurers of the cooperatives in the rudiments of record keeping and accounting. For the building cooperative, the government organized courses on the copperbelt and dispatched the officers for instruction in construction work. The government organized courses for the officers of the farming cooperatives as well. The courses were held at the provincial capital and featured instruction in land preparation, the use of fertilizers, and the planting and spacing of basic cash crops. In addition, the government posted extension workers to the rural areas to advise the cooperative farmers. These extension agents were particularly important for the farming cooperatives, as farming skills, by contrast to construction skills, were poorly developed in the Kasumpa area.[24]

Equally as important as the training was the infusion of capital from government sources. In the case of the building cooperative, the government loaned the group K3,880 for the purchase of tools and equipment. For the farming cooperatives, the government helped finance the transformation of bush lands into productive acreages by paying K30 an acre for "stumping"; and it attempted to enhance the productive potential of the farming sites by advancing credit for the purchase of fertilizers, pesticides, and improved seeds. In addition, the government purchased tractors and stationed them in Kanyembo, seven miles from Kasumpa. By federating with other local cooperatives and contributing funds to a tractor pool, Chikalamo and Lukungwe gained access to mechanical power and thus the potential for more productive farming. Given the absence of oxen in the area because of the tsetse fly, this was a major step toward commercial-level farming. And in view of the fact that private sources had never invested heavily in agricultural production in the area, the government's efforts represented a radical departure from previous levels of agricultural investment.

What happened in Kasumpa appears to have taken place elsewhere as well. After the Chifubu political rally in January 1965, the news of the cooperative program passed down through the party structure and out into the villages of Zambia. At a rate that nearly overwhelmed the administrative capabilities of the new government, local party units organized themselves and their fellow villagers into productive units, be they construction workers, brickmakers, or farmers. Two thousand applications for registration were received in the first five months of 1965 as compared with five for all of 1964.[25] Within the year, the number of registered cooperatives in Zambia more than doubled; within two years, the number had doubled again (see table 6.4). So too went the mechanization of agriculture: by 1967 the government had distributed over 170 tractors, valued at approximately one million kwacha, to serve these societies; it had distributed these throughout all the rural areas in Zambia and had set up repair facilities and maintenance stations to service the mechanical units.[26] Also, as it had done in Kasumpa, the government spent great sums for stumping new agricultural lands and distributed generous loans for the cooperative societies; between 1964 and 1969 it distributed over

Table 6.4   Number of Co-operatives, by Year

Year	Total Number of Societies at End of Year	Societies Newly Registered During Year	Societies Dissolved During Year
1964	220	8	9
1965	468	264	16
1966	601	135	2
1967	875	279	5
1968	1,069	195	1

Source: Adapted from Republic of Zambia, Department of Co-operatives, *Annual Report of the Department of Co-operatives for the Year 1968* (Lusaka: Government Printer, 1969), p. 7.

Note: There appear to be minor errors in these figures.

K1.2 million in stumping subsidies and advanced over K1.3 million in loans for seeds and fertilizers in Zambia as a whole. All told, by 1969, after six years of independence, the government had invested over K14 million in the cooperative movement.[27] The intervention of the public sector in Kasumpa was therefore apparently neither unusual nor atypical in postindependence Zambia. And although, as we shall see, the investments made by the government were deficient in critical respects, they nonetheless represented a totally unprecedented departure from previous patterns, wherein investments were concentrated on the line of rail, while the more remote areas were largely ignored.

The Farmers

Not all residents of Kasumpa sought increased incomes through the cooperative movement, however; nor did the government confine its efforts to upgrading the rural standard of living through the promotion of cooperative societies. Instead, ten of the villagers and their families set themselves up as independent cash crop farmers; like the members of the cooperative societies, these farmers too received the support of the government. With the backing of the Agricultural Department, the farmers obtained land in an area that had been set aside for peasant production in the late 1950s by the Lunda Native Authority.[28] The area, called Tusha, contains soils which are moist and well watered, for water rises in the high ground and seeps down across the farmlands to the Mbereshi stream (see map 4). The soils are dark and loamy, and in their natural state they support an abundant grass cover. By appearance, and according to the commentary of the local extension agents, the soils appear to conform to C. G. Trapnell's early description of the valley basin lands; in the valley, he stated, there are many signs of . . . quality. These signs are marked in the composition of the vegetation and in the height and luxuriance of the grass which is equalled only in the best soils in the territory. This striking luxuriance is probably due primarily to the richness of the soil in organic matter and its favorable physical and moisture retaining properties.[29]

The sole deficiency in the soils was their acidity—a trait shared with other soils in Zambia—which made the application of bases necessary to gain high yields from farming.

The first farmer in Tusha was an evangelist and school teacher who had retired from the Mbereshi Mission and entered farming as a means of support in his retirement (*ukutusha* means, in Bemba, to rest or to retire). The evangelist had been popular with the villagers as well as with the native authority, and so, with the backing of the European missionaries, he was assigned land in the 1950s by the village headman. Three other retired mission workers joined this "pioneer" over the next ten years and sought to earn a comfortable living by growing the fruits and vegetables required by the inpatients and staff at the mission hospital and by boarding students and teachers at the mission school. The first major influx of farmers into Tusha, however, took place at independence. In 1964–65 the four old-timers were joined by six new entrants into farming. When interviewed, two stated that they had seen that the original settlers "were rich" and they too wanted to be farmers, while the four others had "heard that the government was going to provide loans and money" and so entered farming. In each case they contacted, at their own initiative, extension workers who helped them secure an allotment of land from the chief; after consulting with the first settler in Tusha, who had acquired the informal status of a headman in the area, the chief then assigned them land. As one farmer told me, "I noticed that the first farmers here . . . seemed to be getting rich as there was fertile land. With independence the government announced that it would take a list of names of people who wanted to farm here and I applied. They then sent me to the farm institute for training, and they helped me with growing. And they provided loans and their trucks came to buy from me."

Like the cooperative farmers, the individual farmers received training from the government in cash crop production, government loans to purchase seeds and fertilizers, and services from the local tractor depot. In contrast to the members of the cooperative societies, the individual farmers had not gone through the party to upgrade their standard of living; nonetheless they were equally the creations of politics. For rather than entering farming through private initiative in existing markets, the majority of the farmers entered production by being selected, trained, and capitalized by public servants of the new African government. They too represented an attempt by the government to bring the benefits of independence to the villages and to upgrade the standard of living therein.

The Creation of Rural Services

Thus far I have stressed the initial capitalization of rural production by the new government. But the government went beyond merely making a "lump-sum" distribution of training, capital goods, and financial credit; it also sought to furnish for the first time permanent services in the more remote districts of Zambia. The new services were to perform functions that the forces of the private market had not performed. One such function was the provision of funds for agricultural credit. Another was the virtual creation of means of exchange: a mechanism for bringing the urban demand for agricultural produce to the village level and the supply of farm requisites, manufactured in the city, to the village areas. While, as we shall see, these services in fact operated in a way that tended to undermine the government's rural development effort, they nonetheless represented a commitment to the development of the countryside which was unprecedented in the history of this nation.

The Credit Organization of Zambia (COZ) was formed by an act of Parliament in 1966. Though it handled loan applications by small businessmen as well as by farmers, the principal purpose of COZ was to finance rural agricultural production; over two-thirds of its loans went to small farmers. By the end of 1967 the government had lent the organization over 18 million kwacha. This figure constituted an increase in the level of credit available to small-scale farmers on the order of K9 million by comparison with the period prior to independence.[30] Backed by the security of the national treasury, suppliers of seed, fertilizer, and tractor power were willing to advance their goods and services to the small-scale producers, despite the latter's lack of freehold tenure and the paucity of their possessions. In Tusha, for example, until independence and the formation of the credit agency, not a single farmer had been able to secure seasonal credit to finance the planting of their year's crop; consequently, only four persons had farmed. Following independence, no Tusha farmer received less than K360 in loan funds; and the number of producers from Kasumpa more than doubled.

The creation of a marketing agency for the more remote areas was also begun in this period; hitherto, such an agency had been maintained only for the line of rail. Late in 1964 the Ministry of Agriculture assumed direct responsibility for the Agricultural Rural Marketing Service which hitherto had served African farmers on the line of rail, and extended its facilities to

Northern and Luapula provinces. In 1965 the ministry reconstituted the agency as a statutory board entitled the Agricultural Rural Marketing Board and extended its facilities to cover Northwestern, Barotse, and Eastern provinces as well. At the inaugural meeting of this new agency, the minister of agriculture outlined the rationale for the marketing service.

> It was Government's intention to develop the rural area, particularly in view of the fact that 70% of the population is on the land and, therefore, to improve the lives of the majority of the population of Zambia. . . . He appreciated that the services to be provided in certain areas may prove to be uneconomic, but if Government did not take the initiative to provide such services these areas will stagnate, so that Government is prepared to give financial support to the Board in order to indirectly support the people.[31]

Pursuing this commitment, the government built depots and storage houses in the rural bomas; it hired personnel and transport services; and it designated a series of pick-up points where it would accept delivery of cash crops and where it would deposit orders of seed, pesticides, and fertilizers. In many cases, the marketing board would make such exchanges at the farm site; this was particularly important in farming areas like Tusha, where the farmers lacked oxen and ox-drawn implements to assist them in transport. By providing an institution for distribution and exchange in the rural areas, the government attempted virtually to create a market through public intervention where private markets had failed to function.

The posting of extension agents, the provision of mechanical power, providing credit, training in farming skills, and the creation of marketing facilities—in all these ways, the government attempted to promote productive enterprise among village dwellers in the years right after independence.

The Recommitment to Rural Development

In 1968 and 1969 the government made major alterations in its rural development program. Once again the factors previously noted appear to have strongly influenced the behavior of the government. For one, the price of copper had steadily increased. Since the achievement of independence in 1964, it had attained levels never previously reached in the international market. The result, as shown in table 6.5, was a continued increase in government revenues and a vast expansion in the capacity for public spending. The government was therefore in a better position to undertake financial commitments that promised relatively small, uncertain, or long-term revenue returns.

Table 6.5   Government Revenues and Expenditures (K million)

Revenue Source	1964/65	1965/66	1966/67	1967	1968	1969
Copper companies	90.7	141.5	169.5	76.2	176.2	235.1
Other sources	66.4	75.9	103.2	69.1	129.9	166.1
Total revenues	157.1	217.4	272.7	145.3	306.1	401.2
Total spending	129.1	186.6	252.0	166.5	406.2	367.4

Source: Charles Harvey, "The Control of Inflation in a Very Open Economy," p. 45.

Note: The figures for 1967 are those which actually accrued during the second six months of the year. The budget year was then shifted to the calendar year. The figures must therefore be "doubled" to give annual levels for comparative purposes.

Second, the government was obligated under the terms of its constitution to renew its mandate by holding general elections within five years of independence. The government determined to hold the elections at the end of 1968, and this meant that the politicians would again be made accountable to an electorate which was overwhelmingly rural in composition. As seen in table 6.6, with the expansion of the postindependence Parliament from 65 to 105 seats, a full 83 of the 105 seats were from rural constituencies. Political considerations therefore furnished an incentive to expand and perfect the rural development program.

The government first announced its recommitment to the rural development program during the 1968 election campaign. Its major campaign pledge was to decentralize and politicize its administrative agencies so as to upgrade their operations in the rural areas.[32] The governing party pledged that it would appoint political officials—governors for each of the districts and ministers for each of the provinces—who would be responsible for coordinating the operations of governmental agencies in their areas and for making them more responsive to the needs of the citizenry. The performance of governmental departments, the UNIP candidates contended, would be enhanced were they overseen and scrutinized by such political officials who perforce would be more responsive to the needs and demands of the populace than would bureaucratic officials located at the political center. To assist these political officials, the government would form district and provincial development committees; the people could

Table 6.6.   1968 Election Results

	UNIP		ANC		Independent	
	Rural	*Urban*	*Rural*	*Urban*	*Rural*	*Total*
Contested	30	22	23	0	1	76
Uncontested	29	0	0	0	0	29
Total	59	22	23	0	1	105

Source: Parliamentary Elections Office, "Summary of Election Results, 1968," mimeo. (Lusaka, n.d.).

lodge their complaints with the development committees, and the political appointees could then pressure the bureaucrats to respond to them.

UNIP was returned to power in the 1968 elections (see table 6.6), and immediately after the elections the government implemented its decentralization reforms. In conjunction with these measures, it regrouped all the relevant departments—the departments of agriculture, cooperatives, land, natural resources, marketing, community development, and so on—into a single major ministry: the Ministry of Rural Development. The ministry was charged with coordinating and implementing all rural development programs and with overseeing the performance of the relevant parastatal agencies, particularly the credit organization and marketing services.[33]

The Reform of the Services

The reconstruction of the rural marketing and credit agencies was among the most important of the reforms undertaken in this period of recommitment to rural development. In both cases, the government sought to restructure the agencies so as to reallocate resources from the line of rail to the more remote districts. It did so by combining the services to the economically viable producers—the commercial farmers on the line of rail—with the services to the hitherto uneconomical village producers. By linking the fortunes of the two classes of producers, the government in essence attempted to use the "profits" generated by the one to offset the losses generated by the other.

In the case of the marketing agencies, the provinces off the line of rail had been served by the Agricultural Rural Marketing Board and those on the line of rail by the Grain Marketing Board. While the latter organization had consistently operated at a loss, this loss represented largely the difference between the producer and sales prices of agricultural commodities, a difference the government willingly subsidized as a means of keeping down the prices paid by urban consumers. These externally imposed losses aside, the Grain Marketing Board appeared to operate relatively efficiently and economically. It was able to do so because of the central location of its operations, the efficiencies it could achieve from handling large deliveries from producers who were concentrated in a relatively small area, and the expertise of the managerial, financial, and technical officers it employed. By contrast, as shown in table 6.7, the Rural Marketing Board was uneconomical and was running up large unit losses. It was, in effect, absorbing the real costs of marketing in areas where distances from the consumer market were great; where the number of farms and the distances between them were large; and where the volume

Table 6.7   Losses of the Agricultural Rural Marketing Board by Province
for the Years Ending 31 December 1967 and 1968 (in kwacha)

	Northwestern Province		Barotse Province		Luapula Province	
	1967	1968	1967	1968	1967	1968
Expenses	77,646	245,268	70,222	168,887	118,256	227,514
Subsidy	22,908	52,400	22,910	23,000	17,256	42,600
Total loss	100,554	297,668	93,132	191,887	135,512	270,114
Loss per 200 lb. bag	10.16	20.96	17.24	10.32	8.47	12.06

Source: Agricultural Rural Marketing Board, "Annual Report[s] of the Agricultural Rural Marketing Board, Profit and Loss Account for the Year[s] Ending December 31, 1967, and December 31, 1968," mimeo. (n.p., n.d.).

of goods for delivery was small—sometimes as low as four to six bags of maize per producer.[34] In effect, the Rural Marketing Board was utilizing public funds to counter the costs that had prevented the formation of private markets in these areas.

When in September of 1969 the government compelled the Grain Marketing Board to merge with the Rural Marketing Board, the government was seeking to upgrade and augment the services of the rural marketing agency, and to do so by making available to it the resources and economies that had been developed in servicing the more central producers. Thus, for example, the line-of-rail depots were made available for stockpiling fertilizers and seeds prior to distribution to the more remote provinces; orders for the imports of farming requisites for the more remote producers could now be combined with those for the commercial farmers and so be made more cheaply; transport could, if necessary, be diverted from the pool available to commercial farmers to the provincial producers; and the accounting, technical, and managerial expertise that had been concentrated in providing services to the large-scale farmers was now made available to service the emergent producers.

The combination of the two agencies into what was called the National Agricultural Marketing Board (NAMBoard) thus made it possible to share the superior services of the center with the relatively impoverished services available in the more remote areas. To help finance the operations of the marketing agency, the government then sought to render the servicing of the commercially viable sector of its operations even more "profitable" so as to offset the losses incurred in providing services to the more remote farms. Toward this end, the government chose to continue its policy of making the marketing agency the monopoly buyer of the major commercial crops. For farmers in the outlying provinces, this choice was of little significance, as few alternative markets existed. For the commerical farmers, however, the policy had the effect of stabilizing the price of produce. At times of reduced demand, this policy would have been to their advantage. But the late 1960s was a time of increasing demand, and the policy meant that the commercial farmers had to sell at lower prices than they would otherwise have been likely to obtain. The gains from the monopoly market therefore accrued to the marketing agency and helped to finance the expansion and maintenance of its services off the line of rail. In addition, the government also decided literally to close down the major private fertilizer-distributing companies in Zambia, leaving NAMBoard the exclusive supplier of fertilizer and chemical products in the agricultural market. In part, this measure was taken in order to protect the domestic market against foreign competition, thus benefiting the newly completed Zambian fertilizer manufacturing plant.[35] But the measure also had the effect of assuring the marketing agency monopoly profits from trade in this commodity.

The government followed an analogous pattern in providing rural credit. Given the uneconomic nature of production in the outlying areas, the rate of default on government investments in rural farming was bound to be high;[36] and, given conditions of traditional tenure and the low value of farm assets in those areas, the government was unable to recover assets to cover its losses. Consequently, the government sought to improve the actuarial basis of its investments by compelling commercial farmers to participate in its rural credit programs. In September of 1968, the Ministry of Finance announced that no farmer could obtain credit from commercial sources if he owed money to the government's credit organization. Since an estimated 95 percent of the commercial farmers had seasonal debts with the credit organization which could not be paid until harvest time, virtually all commercial farmers had to turn to the credit organization for all other forms of financing—financing they hitherto had sought from private sources. As a result the government's organization received a radical increase in the volume of commercially viable loans; and, by charging interest higher than that charged by commercial sources, the government was able to offset in part the losses it incurred by investing in economically marginal agricultural producers.[37]

Pricing Policy

Thus far I have emphasized the institutional reforms that characterized the government's rural development program. While I will argue that the actual operations of the credit and marketing structures substantially compromised the government's efforts in the countryside, the very formation of these new agencies nonetheless represented an unprecedented commitment to upgrading the standard of living in the more remote rural areas.

The changes initiated in the late 1960s were not confined to institutional reforms, however. They also involved changes in agricultural prices, where, after a long delay, the government in the late 1960s reversed a pricing policy that had seriously weakened the incentive of rural producers to respond to the rural development program.

In promoting rural production, the government emphasized the production of maize. Not only was this a basic crop in Zambia, but also successful maize production required less intensive training and subsequent extension support. Land preparation, planting, spacing, weed and pest control—all were relatively straightforward by comparison with, say, the cultivation of tobacco or vegetables. Finally, maize was not highly perishable and so could withstand transport to urban markets from the more remote areas. The government therefore encouraged the emerging commercial farmers to plant high proportions of their acreages in that crop.

However, while using its extension agents to encourage maize production, the government, through its pricing policy, in fact discouraged the production of that crop in the years right after independence.[38] As can be seen in table 6.8, the price offered for maize by the marketing agency declined throughout the first several years under the new regime.

The fact of independence was itself the principal reason for the change in price. Prior to independence, the commercial farming settler population had been an important source of support for the colonial government. These commercial farmers had been able to gain a pricing policy which generated production far in excess of national demand, and the government assisted in disposing of the surpluses in the world market, frequently

Table 6.8   Maize Price and Output

Crop Years	Producer Price (K per 200-lb. bag)	Marketed Production (1,000 bags)	Local Sales (1,000 bags)	Surplus or Deficit (1,000 bags)
1963/64	3.45	2,139	1,939	+200
1964/65	3.45	2,804	2,184	+620
1965/66	3.32	4,163	2,262	+1,901
1966/67	3.10	4,131	2,548	+1,583
1967/68	2.90	2,748	2,928	−180
1968/69	3.20	2,791	3,199	−408
1969/70	3.50	1,371	3,804	−2,436
1970/71	4.00	4,109	3,844	+265
1971/72	4.30	6,851	3,859	+2,992

Source: United Nations, Food and Agricultural Organization, *Report to the Government of Zambia on Agricultural Marketing and Pricing Policies,* p. 8.

Note: The price is the line-of-rail price for Grade A maize.

at a loss which was offset with public revenues. With independence, of course, the political base of the government altered, and there was little inclination to use public funds to dispose of surplus production by large-scale producers, most of whom were Europeans. The new government instead changed to a policy of encouraging production to supply only the national market; to implement this policy the government reduced the price of maize. The deliberations of the Agricultural Marketing Committee which formulated these recommendations reveals little consideration of their implication for the newly emergent rural producers—precisely those who were the least able to take refuge in the marketing of alternative crops.[39]

For a variety of reasons, the reduction of maize prices at first had a muted impact upon the level of national production. The primary reason appears to have been the level of uncertainty in the commercial farming community. Unsure as to their fortunes under the new regime, and facing increasingly difficult problems in repatriating earnings abroad and in securing credit, the large-scale producers on the line of rail apparently changed their pattern of production by shifting away from produce promising only long-term returns, such as beef production, and into crops like maize, which required little investment and had short-run returns. The result, in the mid-1960s, was a level of maize production that far exceeded domestic consumption despite the lower prices. And so, once again, the government reduced the price of maize.

In the late 1960s, however, the government was compelled to alter its policies and to revise the trend of falling producer prices. Political incentives played an important part in this shift in policy. By this time the damage to the government's rural constituency was becoming well known. While the governing party in fact won the 1968 elections and over 70 percent of the rural parliamentary contests, it nonetheless lost one major province off the line of rail (Barotse, now Western Province); and the percent of the registered voters supporting UNIP in the rural districts declined from 87 percent in 1964 to 71 percent in 1968. In addition, the party itself was wracked by internal factionalism, and the plight of the rural dwellers was being emphasized by politicians seeking to advance their positions in these factional disputes. I will discuss these patterns of rural protest in greater detail in later chapters; we need only note here that these currents of political disaffection provided a political incentive for reversing the government's pricing policy.

Secondly, as seen in table 6.8, the decline in maize prices finally led in the late 1960s to a major decline in maize production (contributing to this result was the inclement weather of the 1969/70 crop year). In fact, so great was the decline in production that major imports became necessary, and in the late 1960s these imports appeared to threaten the capacity of the government to attain its major economic objectives. In 1968, despite the high prices of copper, Zambia for the first time sustained a negative balance of payments on current account;[40] and it was anticipated in government circles that the balance of trade would shift to a negative position in the early 1970s, given the level of capital imports required to maintain industrial expansion and diversification along the line of rail.[41] To limit the drain on foreign reserves and to minimize the cost of foreign borrowing, the government therefore sought to decrease the level of imports, especially imports of food.[42]

The first price rise took place in 1968, and entailed simply a slight increase in the overall price of maize. A second increase took place in 1969, but this one was linked with a "floor price" of K3.20. The floor price insured that, no matter how remote the farmer, the price he received would never be below K3.20 per standard bag; in effect, the economic costs associated with his distance from the market would be absorbed by the public sector. After making large maize imports during 1970 and 1971, the government announced even more extensive price changes. For the 1972 season, the government announced an increase in consumer prices and an increase in the rural floor price of maize to K3.50; in addition, it offered a 30 percent subsidy for seeds and fertilizer. Both changes were announced well before planting and thus could more effectively be taken into account by agricultural producers.[43] As table 6.9 shows, however, the new price structure, by raising line-of-rail prices more than rural prices, reduced the subsidy to outlying farmers and so also, in effect, the incentive for new investors in farming to locate off the line of rail.

In the late 1960s the government thus modified its pricing policy so as to increase the incentive for village producers to engage in commercial production. In conjunction with the changes in the organization and extent of rural public services, this shift represented a major improvement in the government's rural development program. Nonetheless, as I will show, the increase in prices apparently was not sufficient to guarantee the profitability of cash crop production in the more remote areas. Whether because the price rise was so long delayed, or because it was insufficient or because of imperfections in the operation of rural services—for whatever reason, the increase in prices failed to bring about the major transformation in rural incomes that was the objective of the government's rural development program.

The Effect of Party Competition

Thus far, I have analyzed the pattern of government investment, stress-

Table 6.9 Maize Producer Prices (K per 90-kilo bag)

	(1) Line-of-Rail Price		(2) Producers' Price[a]		(3) Producers' Price Were it "Economic Price"[b]		(4) Effective per Bag Subsidy[c]	
District	1968/69	1972/73	1968/69	1972/73	1968/69	1972/73	1968/69	1972/73
Western Province								
Mongu	3.20	4.30	5.05	5.00	1.84	2.94	3.21	2.06
Kaoma	3.20	4.30	3.80	3.80	2.31	3.41	1.49	0.39
Senanga	3.20	4.30	4.10	4.19	2.18	3.28	1.92	0.91
Shesheke	3.20	4.30	4.60	4.35	2.68	3.78	1.92	0.57
Kalabo	3.20	4.30	4.30	4.30	1.71	2.81	2.59	1.49
Northwestern Province								
Kabompo	3.20	4.30	4.80	5.00	2.16	3.26	2.64	1.74
Solwezi	3.20	4.30	3.60	3.80	2.75	3.85	0.85	−0.05
Mwinilunga	3.20	4.30	4.20	4.40	1.07	3.13	3.13	1.27
Kasempa	3.20	4.30	4.00	4.20	2.30	3.40	1.70	0.80
Zambezi	3.20	4.30	4.75	4.95	1.78	2.88	2.97	2.07
Luapula Province								
Mansa	3.20	4.30	3.90	4.30	2.80	3.90	1.10	0.40
Kawambwa	3.20	4.30	3.40	3.80	2.42	3.52	0.98	0.28
Samfya	3.20	4.30	3.70	4.10	2.61	3.71	1.09	0.39
Nchelenge[d]	—	4.30	—	3.55	—	3.31	—	0.24
Mwense[d]	—	4.30	—	3.80	—	3.54	—	0.26

Sources: NAMBoard Circular E/26/72; and Bastiaan de Gaay Fortman, "Zambia Markets," in *Constraints on the Economic Development of Zambia*, ed. Charles Elliott, p. 210.

a. The producers' price is the price paid to producers by the government.
b. The "economic price" is the line-of-rail price less the costs of transport (0.06 kwacha per bag per kilometer).
c. The subsidy equals col. 2 minus col. 3.
d. Nchelenge and Mwense districts were not officially created until 1968, and the roster of prices does not list them in that year.

ing the effects of financial abundance, ideological priorities, and political incentives upon the apportionment of public resources between the rural and urban areas. As indicated in Part One of this book, however, not all rural districts are remote districts; and in fact the districts of greatest agricultural potential lay along the line of rail. In understanding the patterns of governmental expenditure, it is important to note that the government faced strong incentives to concentrate rural investments in these central farming areas.

Political Incentives: The Quest for a One-Party State

Like other parties in Africa, the governing party in Zambia sought to make theirs a single-party state. In contrast to many others, however, UNIP, throughout the first years after independence, sought to attain this objective at the polls. According to an interview with President Kaunda shortly after independence,

> President Kaunda . . . repeated his determination to make UNIP the only political party in Zambia. But he emphasised that this would not be done by legislating against existing parties or the formation of new ones. Legislating for a one-party system, President Kaunda told a press conference, would be "bottling up the anger of our people" and added: "This, we are not prepared to do."[44]

To obtain a 100 percent victory, UNIP contested every parliamentary seat in both the 1964 and 1968 elections.[45] And, as interviews with its campaign managers and the writings of scholars testify, UNIP concentrated the vast bulk of its electoral resources in the constituencies that were the strongholds of the major opposition party, ANC.[46] As President Kaunda stated: "UNIP had to organise itself so effectively that the voter would have only UNIP in mind at the next election."[47]

UNIP utilized other tactics, however. To win votes from the opposition party, UNIP bid for them with governmental funds. The government attempted to skew its pattern of expenditures so as to demonstrate to opposition voters that the governing party was able to make them prosperous. In the words of UNIP's own slogan, the UNIP government attempted to show that it "paid to belong to UNIP."

This financial strategy is suggested in the public statements of UNIP party officials. Thus, for example, a UNIP youth secretary stated, "This country is on the way to a one party state, because all the people are benefiting from what the Government is doing for the country. All ANC members should be happy that the Government abolished poll tax, bicycle tax and [that] schools will be free soon. The £35,000,000 development plan will give a chance to everyone."[48] The tendency is also suggested in the statements of the UNIP government officials. Thus, one parliamentary secretary, touring in opposition area, was quoted as

> appeal[ing] to the people to come forward and obtain farming loans from the Government. "You are refraining from getting these loans from the Government because of cheap party propaganda from some individuals. . . . The money is yours because the Government gets it from . . . taxes. . . . And even if it was Kaunda's money, wouldn't you say 'Thank you for being so kind,' " he asked.[49]

The government's position, in the areas of opposition strength, was summed up as follows by one source:

> massive . . . development schemes there could go a long way to convince the people that the Government—though at the moment a UNIP one—is for every citizen. . . . This does not by any means mean that the Government should concentrate on developing the [opposition areas] at the expense of other parts of the country. All that is being said here is that the [opposition] province is a special case calling for special treatment.[50]

The tendency for the government to bid for votes from the opposition areas is suggested in the distribution of its investment expenditures. Through regression analysis the 1964 voting patterns can be related to the subsequent patterns of capital investment by the UNIP government. As shown in equation 1, the government tended to concentrate its expenditures in areas that had voted for the opposition party. Thus, the coefficient linking the per capita expenditures by district in 1964–68 with the percent of registered voters in the district voting ANC in 1964 is significant and positive in sign. The equation implies that, if one district had a percentage point more ANC voters than another in 1964, it received roughly 7 kwacha per capita more in government investments over the next five-year period.[51]

Eq. 1: 1964–68 Capital Expenditures as a Function of 1964 ANC Vote

$$Y = 1.825 + 7.131\ X$$

Coefficient of determination $= 0.1082$; $t = 2.15$, significant at 0.025 level

where:

$Y =$ total per capita government capital expenditures, 1964–68

$X =$ percent registered voters voting ANC in 1964

Financial Incentives: High Returns on Expenditures

There were other reasons for the government to spend this money in the ANC districts; the low value of the coefficient of determination alone suggests this. The opposition areas were grouped in Central and Southern provinces, along the line of rail; and all that has been said thus far about the financial incentives to spend on the line of rail constitutes reason as well for investing in the areas that voted for the opposition party. Moreover, the ANC districts clustered in the rural centers of these provinces, and so the opposition voters tended to concentrate in the most productive agricultural zones of Zambia. This clustering of the opposition voters in areas of high agricultural potential can be demonstrated by regressing 1964 ANC votes in districts against the per capita number of plows and cattle in those districts; this yields positive relationships between opposition voting and those indices of agricultural development.

Eq. 2: Opposition Voting and Measures of Agricultural Development

$$Y = 4.192 + 222.1X_1 + 23.88 \, X_2$$
$$(1.418)^* \quad (2.595)^{**}$$

* t score significant at 0.10 level, one-tailed test

** t score significant at 0.01 level, one-tailed test

$R^2 = 0.6489$; $F = 34.19$, significant at 0.01 level

where:

$Y =$ percent registered voters voting ANC, 1964

$X_1 =$ per capita number of plows, 1963

$X_2 =$ per capita number of cattle, 1963

Being centrally located and endowed with cattle, and revealing a tendency for these cattle to be transformed into farm assets by being harnessed to plows, the ANC districts were the districts of highest agricultural potential in Zambia. Expenditures in these areas could therefore yield rapid and certain increases in agricultural production. These considerations provided even further reason for concentrating agricultural investments in the ANC areas.

The question then arises: controlling for the economic incentives to invest in the line of rail, do the political incentives remain significant? To answer this question, we can place the political and economic measures in a multiple regression equation. We then find that, controlling for the economic variables, the percent opposition votes remains positively and, given the level of multicolinearity, nearly significantly related to subsequent levels of government capital spending (see equation 3).[52] If we examine the pattern of governmental expenditure more closely, restricting our attention to capital expenditures on agricultural development, the above results are even more pronounced, as shown in equation 4. The significance of the political variable as a determinant of government spending is thus underscored by the data.

Eq. 3: Total Capital Expenditure Per Capita as a Function of Political and Economic Indicators

$$Y = 4.187 + 0.1845X_1 + 10.98X_2 - 11.31X_3$$
$$(1.100)^* \quad (0.0633) \quad (-1.108)^*$$

* t scores significant at the 0.25 level, one-tailed test (see note 52)

$R^2 = 0.0580$; $F = 0.7392$, not significant

where:

Y = total per capita government capital expenditure in districts, 1964–68

X_1 = percent registered voters voting ANC, 1964

X_2 = per capita number of plows, 1963

X_3 = per capita number of cattle, 1963

Eq. 4: Total Capital Expenditure Per Capita in Agriculture as a Function of Political and Economic Indicators

$$Y = 0.1342 + 0.1581X_1 + 7.235X_2 - 0.8696X_3$$
$$(1.969)^* \quad (0.9230) \quad (-1.783)^*$$

* t scores significant at 0.05 level, one-tailed test

$R^2 = 0.1417$; $F = 2.161$, significant at 0.10 level

Y = total per capita government capital expenditure on agriculture, 1964–69

X_1 = percent registered voters voting ANC, 1964

X_2 = per capita number of plows, 1963

X_3 = per capita number of cattle, 1963

Its abundance of revenues, its ideology, and the nature of the constituency within which it competed for power thus led the government of newly independent Zambia to increase radically the level of public investments in the rural areas. This trend was in part countered by the government's desire to enhance the value of its revenue base and by the strategy it adopted in the competition for electoral support. Nonetheless, insofar as the residents of the more remote regions had participated in the nationalist struggle in order to install a government that would divert the wealth of urban industry to the rural areas, their political labors clearly bore fruit in the postindependence period. It remains to evaluate the degree to which increased spending resulted in higher rural incomes.

7

The Impact of Expenditures
in the Countryside

The principal component of the government's rural development program was the sponsorship of cash crop production in the more remote regions of Zambia. Through the creation of the cooperative movement and the provision of services to rural cultivators, the government attempted to underpin profitable farming in areas where market forces had failed to furnish the appropriate environment. How did the government's policy fare? In attempting to answer that question, I will again focus on Kasumpa village and follow the fate of the cooperative and farming programs started there.

The Cooperatives

It will be recalled that the UNIP leaders in Kasumpa formed three cooperative societies following independence in Zambia: a building cooperative, Katofyio, and two farming cooperatives, Lukungwe and Chikalamo. Of the three, by 1972 only Katofyio was functioning.

Katofyio

Katofyio began with eighteen members. After registering with the government and securing a loan for initial capital purchases, the founders returned to Kasumpa village. While searching for building contracts, they began to function as suppliers of building materials. They gathered and sorted stones and washed gravel, then sold these materials to Mbereshi Mission, which was constructing new school facilities. Cooperative members also began to burn bricks. Locating clay deposits near the river, they molded the clay into blocks which they stacked into kilns. They burnt charcoal and with it they fired the kilns. They sold the bricks which

130

they thus fashioned to the school and the hospital, and also to store owners in the nearby towns.

The leaders of Katofyio were constituency-level party leaders. Though they were willing to work and to work hard for a living, they nonetheless were impatient to begin construction work and to gain greater incomes than those they could receive from the fabrication of building materials. In their meetings with government officials and their visits to the district headquarters—meetings that occurred naturally as part of their party work—they prompted and cajoled the government administration. "Our men are without work," they said. "We are staying idle." "When is the government going to call us for building?"

By 1967 the contracts began to arrive. Katofyio became a prime beneficiary of the expansion of governmental services into the rural areas. The government, as a matter of policy, purchased the services of the building cooperatives when building new rural classrooms, new houses for the extension agents it was now posting to the countryside, and office buildings and depots in the rural areas. Rather than relying solely on the resources of its own public works department, the government also employed the services of the local cooperatives as part of its rural development effort. Because of the low level of skill and capital equipment of the cooperatives, the government provided supervisors and inspectors to oversee work on the construction projects; and the government, rather than the cooperatives, supplied the building materials and transported them from the copperbelt to the building sites. All told, between 1966 and 1971, Katofyio received 14 contracts from the government, valued at a total of K61,520. The cooperatives' actual revenues were less than this figure would suggest, as the government deducted the costs of supervision, materials, and transport from its payments to the society. Nonetheless, the earnings were great enough to pay back the government's loan of K3,880, to purchase a six-ton van worth nearly K6,000, and to have funds left over for consumption purposes.[1]

The story of Katofyio is not a story of pure success, however. For the leaders, the cooperative has been a profitable venture, but for the vast majority of the members it has not. The leaders include the secretary, who handles all the correspondence with government departments; the treasurer, who handles the accounts and records; and the chairman, who convenes meetings and moderates their debates. At work, the treasurer serves as the interpreter of blueprints and building designs; he is the best educated of the three officers, having received government training on the copperbelt. The secretary acts as the building foreman; he is a skilled manipulator of men and can smooth over disputes, motivate people, and elicit both humor and commitment. The chairman serves as the driver and transporter at the building site; by using the cooperative's lorry, he minimizes the deductions for transport services made by the government on the value of its contracts. As the executive committee of the cooperative—and the committee that makes the decisions governing finances—these three officers pay themselves liberally by rural standards: while on the job they receive K80 a month; while not working they receive K35. That the officers have prospered is shown by the fact that two of them are building houses for themselves on a newly cleared road slightly apart from the village and slightly above it on the slope rising up from the Mbereshi River (see map 4). Two of the officers are also building grocery stores: one is already completed; the bricks have been burned and construction will soon start on the other.

While the officeholders in the cooperatives have prospered, the rank and file have not. The rank and file constitute the labor force of the cooperative. They prepare the mortar, lay the bricks, and construct the building frames. The rank and file join the cooperative when there is work to be done. When the work is completed, they put aside the skills they acquired either through instruction at the mission or in construction gangs on the copperbelt, and they return to subsistence production in the village, there to await word of new contracts.

While the officers have remained committed to the cooperative, many of the rank and file have not. Many of the latter explicitly stated to me that they had in fact withdrawn from the cooperative and would refuse future work offers from it. Many stated that the cooperative has been "a waste of time" for them; that in financing the cooperative the government failed to solve the problems of "starvation which we face in the villages"; and that, while the party leaders who founded the cooperative have prospered, the members have not, and so they have been "exploited" by the nationalist movement.

The reasons for their complaints are easily identifiable. Most basically, while the executive committee paid itself handsomely, it did not pay the workers as well. The best-paid worker (the mason) received at most K35 a month, by contrast with the K80 a month earned by the officers; the rank and file earned around K15 a month.[2] In addition, the development of the cooperative has inevitably entailed sacrifices in the form of deferred gratification, and as a result of their higher rates of pay, the officers appeared to have felt compensated for the delays in financial benefits; being paid less, the workers have not. As noted by one of the officers after the initial government loan was repaid, "We worked hard and we paid out nothing, even to ourselves. Me and my family, we dressed in rags until we paid back the loan and got money in the bank. But many of the members got mad and left because they thought we should pay out the money for salaries." Later, when the executive committee asked the government to credit nearly K6,000 of their earnings on a major contract to the purchase of a lorry, the officers were nearly beaten by the members, who resented the diversion of earnings to the formation of capital. And since, as we shall see, the officers later turned the lorry into a source of additional personal income, the members had further reason to resent this decision. In sum, both the rank and file and officials would naturally have preferred immediate returns from the cooperative effort, and both had had to suffer through the initial period of capital formation. But, thereafter, the officers compensated themselves handsomely for the delayed benefits, while the workers, who were paid much less, received no comparable compensation. The natural result has been different levels of satisfaction with the cooperative movement.

The strong preference for immediate returns caused further problems. Among the most important was the anger and dissatisfaction over the bureaucratic delays that arose in payments to the cooperative upon completion of building projects. The government departments were abysmally slow in issuing payments for the finished buildings. The building first had to be inspected. When it was approved, the local officers had to file inspection certificates with their provincial supervisors, who in turn forwarded pay claims to the central headquarters in Lusaka, upon completing further forms. Central headquarters then had to draw payment vouchers from the Ministry of Finance, and these were then sent back down through the department to the district level. Careless clerical work, officers away on leave, and the backlog of work facing understaffed bureaucracies with greatly expanded programs all caused delays in payment. While the officers of the cooperatives tolerated such delays and compensated themselves for the inconvenience, they did not compensate the rank and file.[3] In anger and distrust the ordinary members turned against the cooperative and contended, in the words of one member, that "when the government gave us the cooperatives for independence, it gave us nothing."

Another problem led to splits between the officers and the rank and file. From time to time, there would be no work. Such things as budget constraints, interruption in the delivery of supplies, lags in gaining administrative approval for site selection or building plans would lead to periods in which government construction would cease in the Kasumpa area. At that point, the officers had no work to offer, and the members had to return to farming. But the officers did have control of the lorry, and, by hiring a work force of one or two other people, they could continue to earn money by entering the major private market in the valley, the market for fish.

The first time the officers entered the fish trade, they did so as transporters. They drove to the major producing area, Mweru Wantipa, and on the way they carried buyers who had arrived in Luapula by bus from town. Charging the buyers a fee for transport to the fishing camps, the cooperative officers then spent twenty-four hours at the fishery. They received room and board from a local store owner in exchange for space on the lorry for the transport of his retail goods. After spending the night at the fishing camp, the officers toured the various loading points of the lake, collecting bales of dried fish, the goods of the fish traders (who had lived at the camp while processing, drying, and baling the fish), and the traders themselves. That day, they left for the copperbelt. En route, the officers spent the night at a local council rest house. They then passed through the Congo pedicle, paying the obligatory bribes to the Zairian customs officials on the way, and entered the copperbelt at Mufulira. They spent their first night in town with relatives of the treasurer, the next with relatives of the secretary. At both places they were given food and lodging in exchange for news from the village and the free transport back to the village of letters, gifts (powdered milk, a bag of mealie meal, cloth and enamelware), and persons who had been visiting in town. During the two days they spent in town, the officers delivered the traders and their bundles of fish to the markets and collected payments from them.

On leaving town, the officers entered another market between the copperbelt and the Luapula valley: the market for manufactured goods and processed foods. For a local schoolteacher, they purchased and transported to the village a divan and two armchairs from the furniture factory in Ndola. And they used their earnings from fish transport to buy at wholesale prices bags of mealie meal which they later sold at a K1.05 markup to teachers, mission employees, and store owners in the valley. For these five days of intensive labor—from the time of leaving the village to the time of their return—they netted approximately K379 or about K125 each.[4] During this time the rank and file of the cooperative netted nothing (see table 7.1).

By working Luapula's private markets, the Katofyio officials were thus able to generate incomes in between work on government contracts. But the officers were not pleased with the quantity of these earnings. The work days on the trip described above had been long—12 to 14 hours—and the work had been hard; they had lifted and moved 200-pound bales of fish and spent some days virtually without eating until well after dark. They felt they should have received greater returns for such labor. In addition, the officers felt that they had not earned enough to cover the depreciation on their vehicle. The roads to the fishery had been merciless. Large potholes, swampy areas, and the occasional hillsides of large stones that the truck had had to climb punished the lorry and threatened to

Table 7.1   Accounts from the Katofyio Fish-Marketing Trip, First Week of April, 1971

Trip to the fish camp
    Earnings
        6 private passengers, transported en route K3.00
        10 fish traders transported to camps K50.00
    Expenditures
        1 drum diesel oil K5.80
    Net earnings K47.20
Trip to town
    Earnings
        6 traders, transport fees...K29.40
        37 bundles fish, at 0.04 kwacha per pound K206.68
        3 private passengers, transport fees K13.20
                                                   K249.28
    Expenses
        Rest house fee K1.00
        1 drum diesel oil 5.80
        1 bribe/customs fees...8.00
        Market-scale fees 3.00
                                                   K17.80
    Net earnings K231.48
Return trip to village
    Earnings
        Transport of furniture K30.00
        Sale of mealie meal K320.00
                                                   K350.00
    Expenses
        Purchase of mealie meal K236.00
        Bribes/custom fees 8.00
        Diesel oil 5.80
                                                K249.80
    Net earnings K100.20
    Previous net earnings .... ⎰ 47.20
                                                          ⎱231.48
Total net earnings K378.88

destroy the cooperative's primary capital asset. To recover the costs of depreciation and to gain greater rewards for their efforts, the officers therefore altered their operations so as to make each trip more profitable. In a visit to town, they stocked up on commodities that were desired by the fishermen at Mweru Wantipa but were scarce in so remote an area: oilskins, knee-high boots, boat paint, several drums of petrol, flashlights, and packets of sugar. They transported these goods to the fish camps and bartered for fish at a rate of exchange well above the money rate of exchange for the commodities.[5] Two of the officers remained at the camp for a month with these goods. They spent the days trading for fish, drying them, and packaging them in bundles. Despite losses of fish due to their inexperience in drying and a loss of time due to the burning out of a wheel bearing on the lorry, the officers claimed to have realized vastly increased earnings by comparison with what they had gained from transporting fishermen. These earnings and the money they gained from the sale of the mealie meal they had brought back from town tided them over nicely until the next contract: building houses at a new agricultural station being opened in the valley. Between public contracts, the officers of Katofyio had done well in the private markets of the valley. But the members had not.[6]

The Farming Cooperatives

By contrast to Katofyio, which continued to operate even at this low level in 1971 and 1972, the two farming cooperatives in Kasumpa were simply not functioning at all; they had closed down. The officers had sold off some of their assets. The members were "on strike against the government." And the government was planning to deregister these cooperative societies and to "wind up" their affairs. How did the farming cooperatives decline to such a state?

Following the initial registration of the cooperatives in 1966, the members set out to prepare cooperative farms in the forested margin well above Katofyio stream, where the lands required extensive stumping and clearing before they could be cultivated. While preparing their lands, the members drew subsistence allowances from the cooperative department; and when they had finished their preparations they petitioned for—and eventually got—payment from the government for having brought new land into production. Lukungwe cleared 100 acres and Chikalamo 50; for the effort, each cooperative received K30 an acre in cash.[7] In 1967, the two cooperatives commenced production. In both cases, they farmed about a seventh of their cleared acreages, Lukungwe growing a total of fifteen acres of maize, groundnuts, and beans, and Chikalamo a total of seven.[8] Like nearly all the cooperatives in the area, Chikalamo and Lukungwe received generous credit from the government to help with their farming.[9] With the aid of these loans, on a total area of 22 acres the two cooperatives achieved an average yield of five bags an acre of maize, one bag an acre of groundnuts, and one bag an acre of beans. These yields were low— about one-half the yields achieved by the individual farmers in Kasumpa— but they nonetheless represented a significant increase in production above the levels of the preindependence period. The yields did not improve from year to year, however, and they were not sufficient to repay the cooperatives' government loans.[10] Similar shortfalls in each farming season meant increased indebtedness to the government.

Becoming concerned about the poor record of loan repayments, the government decided to deduct the loan payments from the proceeds of the sales by the farming cooperatives to the government's marketing agency. The proceeds therefore went to the credit agency and not to the cooperative members. The effect was devastating. In 1970, for example, after the sale of their produce to the marketing agency, the members were left with an average of K5.00 each for their year's labor. In protest, they went "on strike" in 1971 and refused to plant the seeds or to use the fertilizers the government had distributed to them. Instead of using these farming supplies for cash crop farming, they used some on their own gardens and sold the remainder to the individual farmers. The cooperative officers investigated the sale of the farming supplies and recommended the cooperatives' liquidation. As the credit officer wrote regarding Lukungwe, "to continue assisting a group of people of this kind is a matter of wasting the nation's funds."[11] He therefore instituted proceedings to have the cooperative "wound up."

This spare account of the demise of the farming cooperatives does not explain why they did in fact fail. Two major kinds of reasons were offered for their failure. From the members came bitter attacks on the government departments responsible for overseeing their development and well-being. From the government officers came commentaries upon the attitudes and conduct of the members. The factors cited on both sides deserve consideration.

The Effect of the Bureaucracy

It will be remembered that Luapula was ill favored for agricultural production. Its remoteness from the urban markets, as well as the absence of cattle to convert into farm assets, meant that other more proximate and more favorably endowed rural areas could capture most of the national market for food. In response to the political demands of the nationalist party in the area, however, the government set about creating public agencies to promote village-level farming as a means for enhancing rural incomes. The purpose of these agencies was to perform in the more remote districts the functions the private market did not perform: to offer credit for producers, to distribute agricultural inputs—fertilizer, seeds, pesticides, and tractor power—and to purchase agricultural commodities. With the initiation of the cooperative movement, the government hastened to form and staff the credit agency, the marketing services, and tractor points in the Luapula area to support the village-level producers. By all accounts, however, these agencies failed to allocate services properly. The result was that profits were not made and village incomes stagnated. Indeed, the agencies appear to have operated in a way that plunged many producers into debt.

The best way to understand the effect of the agencies upon the operation of producers is to envisage not a competitive market but a series of bureaucratic hurdles. The first of these is the extension agent of the agricultural department. His goal is to increase agricultural production in the area; his resource for achieving that goal is his ability to recommend farmers for loans. Without loans, most farmers could not contract for tractor hire or purchase seeds and fertilizer; therefore producers are strongly motivated to adopt the practices suggested by the agent, in order to secure his loan recommendations. The second hurdle is the credit organization. The credit officers receive and process the loan applications which have been received and evaluated by the extension agents. Once a loan application is approved by the credit organization, the credit officer issues purchase orders for tractor power and for seeds and fertilizers. The purchase orders are sent directly to the mechanization department and to the marketing agency and constitute payments by the government for the goods and services provided by these agencies. The last step is the actual allocation of tractor services and the distribution of fertilizer and seeds to the funded producers. This step is a crucial one from the producer's point of view. It must be completed by the end of October, generally speaking, so that he can complete the preparation of his land prior to the onset of the rains and finish seeding his lands early in the rainy season. Unless the deliveries are made properly and on time, the producer will fail to do these things and so be unable to grow enough crops to repay his loan and still make a profit.

It was the experience of the cooperative producers that year after year they failed to clear this series of bureaucratic hurdles. Thus, for example, the records reveal the delivery dates for tractor services displayed in table 7.2. In every year for which I got information, the tractor arrived late or performed improperly; the last year it did not arrive at all. It was the failure of the tractor to arrive in 1971 that precipitated the strike of the cooperatives, for the members knew that in the absence of cattle they could not plow enough land or achieve great enough yields to repay their loan debts, much less gain a profit.[12] They therefore refused to plant.

Similar problems occurred with the marketing services; more often than

Table 7.2 Performance of the Mechanical Services Department

Year	Date of Tractor Arrival	Comments
1967/68	6 December.	Too late. Did not complete job, as broke a plow share.
1968/69	Don't know.	Don't know.
1969/70	22 December.	Too late. Improper depth of plowing.
1970/71	8 January.	Too late.
1971/72	Did not arrive at all.	

not, fertilizers and seeds arrived late or in improper amounts, or were left miles down the road from the more inaccessible producers. Not only did erratic deliveries lead to late planting and therefore lower yields and earnings; but, at least in the case of Lukungwe, the sporadic deliveries also led to the over-ordering of farming requisites, as the cooperative officers sought to accumulate inventories so as to safeguard against the uncertain provision of essential supplies. The result was even greater indebtedness as the cooperative amassed stocks of greater value than could easily be paid for by its marketed output.

Behind the problems of both the tractor and marketing services lay the performance of the credit agency. For the agency was often so slow in processing its applications that it was difficult for the mechanical services to devise plowing schedules or to order proper amounts of fuel, with the result that tractors often stood idle. And it was also difficult for the marketing services to order proper inventories and to devise efficient routing schedules; this problem was particularly severe in an area where there were over 200 farmers, each an average of 55 miles from the marketing depot.[13] As figures 7.1 and 7.2 reveal, the marketing services, rather than being given lead time by the credit agency, instead received the bulk of its orders at virtually the last minute, that is, with the start of the rains.[14]

There were many reasons for the inefficiency of these agencies. For one, their personnel had been hastily assembled and were often unskilled and untrained. Thus, for example, the reports of the tractor inspector cry out with anguish at the brutalities inflicted upon the machines by their unskilled drivers;[15] and the marketing service in 1968 tersely notes in its annual report: "There cannot be too many organizations who have been able to report a 20 fold increase in activity . . . without also having to report that some staff who were recruited to do 'x' are finding it difficult to do 20x."[16] For another, as already noted, the large number of producers and the small scale of their operations made it extremely difficult to provide effective services to them, especially given the poor roads and the tendency of the roads to deteriorate during the rainy season.[17] Further, the very remoteness of the producers added to the problems of providing services to them. Thus, for example, it was extremely difficult to keep tractors and vehicles in good repair in areas where mechanics and workshops as well as parts and equipment were scarce. Partially as a result of this, of the five tractors in Nchelenge District in 1971, four were out of commission.[18]

But apparently at the bottom of the problem of the inefficiency of these agencies was simply their lack of incentive to be efficient. Having been instituted in areas where private markets did not function and where other suppliers of services therefore did not exist, there was little need for

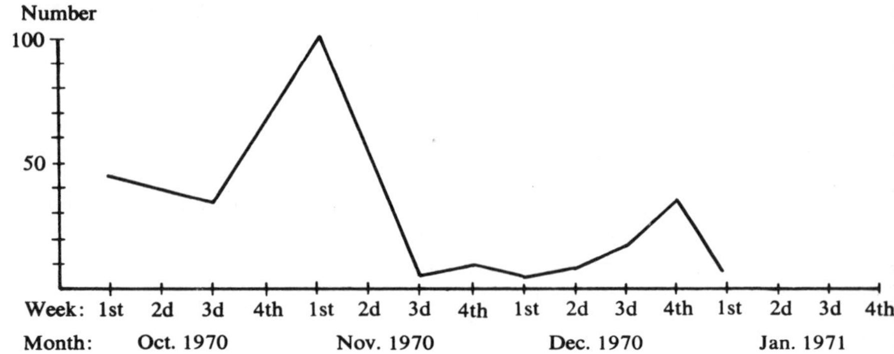

Fig. 7.1

Purchase Orders Received from Credit Agency by Marketing Agency, October 1970–January 1

Source: Files of NAMBoard District Depot, Nchelenge.

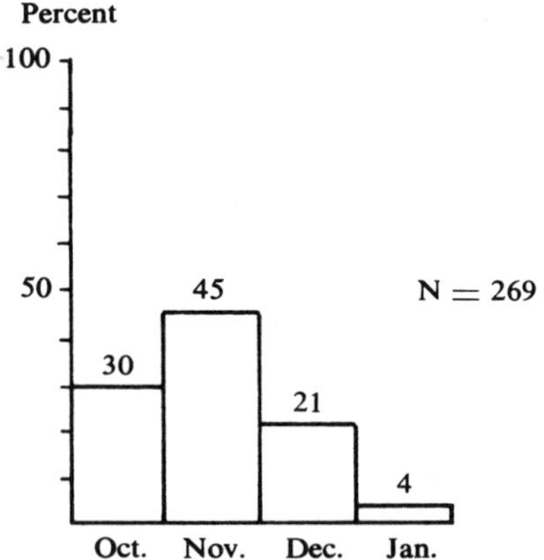

Fig. 7.2

Monthly Breakdown of Purchase Orders Received from Credit Agency
by Marketing Agency, October 1971–January 1972

Source: Files of NAMBoard District Depot, Nchelenge.

them to upgrade their performance; for there was little prospect that they would lose their business to other suppliers. Thus it mattered little if the tractors were late; the producers could not place their orders elsewhere. And of what consequence was it that the orders of seeds and fertilizers were not properly fulfilled? The producers would not cancel their orders and place them with other organizations. Given the lack of competition, the agencies had little incentive to be efficient; the number of their clients would, within vast limits of performance, remain the same, and there was little prospect of their being put out of business by competitors. Rather than themselves, it was the producers who would bear the costs of their inefficiencies in terms of lower yields and lower earnings. The record of these agencies in this region of Zambia thus calls into question whether the government could intervene bureaucratically where markets did not function, and do so in a way that was efficient and thus beneficial to the producers whom the government sought to sponsor.

MOTIVES OF THE FARMING COOPERATIVES

The above critique is based upon the cooperative farmers' perception of the failure of the bureaucracies involved in the rural development effort. But the bureaucrats themselves had substantial criticisms to make, and more often than not these criticisms were aimed at their clients: the co-operative farmers. The cooperatives failed, the bureaucrats claimed, because the farmers had the wrong attitudes. The farmers were not interested in long-run results, but only in getting "cash on the barrel." As a result, they did not plan; they were unwilling to sacrifice present gain for future profits; and, because each was out for himself, they lacked the "cooperative feeling" supposedly necessary to make the cooperatives work. These criticisms bring into focus the attitudes of the cooperative farmers and the way they affected the operations of the cooperatives.[19]

It is absurdly obvious but fundamental that the members of the cooperatives wanted to earn money. More accurately, they possessed very high discount rates and hence were particularly interested in short-term returns. In their minds they had fought hard to get a new government which would develop programs that would allow them to earn money. When the co-operative program was announced after independence, they joined the cooperative movement so as to receive higher incomes. And so long as the members could earn money from the cooperatives, they supported the cooperative movement; when they could not, they quit.

This desire to profit is reflected in the members' preference for stumping as opposed to planting. In the case of both Lukungwe and Chikalamo, the members had stumped more land then they had planted. The reason for this was that the returns to stumping were K30 an acre. At an average of five bags of maize per acre, the returns to planting (assuming a price of

K3.20 a bag) were K16 an acre; were the crop beans or groundnuts (assuming an ideal of three bags an acre), the returns to planting would be K24.00. It is therefore little wonder that one cooperative officer was moved to comment that the cooperatives were planting a farm of "grass" and not "crops."[20]

The desire for quick returns is shown in the intense pressure members place on the officials of the cooperatives for immediate cash payments. Thus, for example, after stumping, the members of Lukungwe demanded their money immediately and placed their chairman under intense pressure for their earnings. He and his fellow officers sent a veritable barrage of letters to the district offices demanding payment of the stumping subsidy. Becoming more frustrated, the officers began to send copies of their letters to the regional secretary of the party, the minister of state of the province, and even the minister of cooperatives in Lusaka. In these letters the chairman threatened, "We shall never continue as cooperative members. Because we do not want to go naked through co-operative way. . . . To make it short, we shall not compromise with words only. What we want is to withdraw our subsidy."[21] When the subsidy was late in arriving, the chairman wrote again:

> We officers are badly treated. . . . [People are saying] "If you are not going to pay us, we shall go to the court of law to report or summon you." It is not only that, but they do come to insult us as if we are children. . . . Apart from that, the chairman of this so-called cooperative does not sleep in his house but sleeps in the jungle for fear of being attacked . . . during the night.[22]

The government officials replied to these appeals by demanding further information so that they could fill out the forms necessary to secure the release of the subsidy by the central ministry. For example, in response to the last letter, the provincial cooperative officer replied:

> Before the money is drawn the following procedure is to be followed:—
>
>   (i) A list of members and money required. . . .
>   (ii) Acreage you stumped. Acreage you planted . . . and condition of crops.
>   (iii) A resolution from the committee stating that the money should be withdrawn;
>   (iv) . . . the work must be certified by my Farm Manager or Agricultural Officer.[23]

Without the information and testimonials, the provincial cooperative officer simply could not get his superiors to authorize the release of funds.

But the procedure was time consuming, and, as the officers of the cooperative wrote the district cooperative officer, "We are demanding money for our fields and many people are running away because of lacking money. They are saying that we shall come back when we receive money for the field. . . . There cannot be a job without any wages. You are the people who have caused people to run away because of your cruelty."[24] Protesting the lack of immediate returns for their labor, the chairman of the cooperative noted another alternative: "I can't keep on working because I am fed up for I have nothing which I can feed my family. . . . Please, if there is no money, I will go to the copperbelt."[25] The officer did not migrate, but he did quit his office. As he explained his actions to me, "I quit because I couldn't take a position between the government departments and the members. I would be sent to the cooperative department officers for money and they would refuse it saying that there was no money today; and as a result, when I came back to the village, I would be very badly insulted. I started the post in 1965, and I quit in 1969."[26]

In the case of payment for stumping, it was the lack of immediate payment that caused dissatisfaction and discontent. In the case of the money for crop production, it was the size of the returns that caused dissatisfaction. Having received large loans, and having over-ordered fertilizers and seeds, the cooperatives received little money for their deliveries once the loan payments were deducted. The current chairman of the cooperative stated, "We are deadlocked with the government. We are on strike with the government. They just take our money for loans; they take out bags without money. We will stop our cooperative to stop these people who take money and do not give us anything. We talked with the government, but they said 'We gave you much money and you have lots of debts.' How can we work for no money?"[27] Another said, "There is no profit in it. When we got money, we just saw it in writing. The money never reached our people. The profits were taken by the government, and we never saw the money."[28]

The attitudes of the members thus affected their response to the cooperative movement. When they found that their earnings from the cooperatives were neither large in magnitude nor immediate and short run in nature, they turned away from the movement. The farming cooperatives failed simply because they failed to serve the financial interests of the villagers.

THE FATE OF THE COOPERATIVES

After independence the national government supported the development of the cooperative movement as a means for upgrading the economic well-being of persons in the countryside. As we have seen, for the mass of the members of the building cooperative, the program had failed to furnish a sustained source of rural cash incomes, and most had withdrawn from Katofyio. By 1971 both farming cooperatives had ceased to function. In general the cooperative movement had failed as a means of enhancing the standard of living of the members of Kasumpa village.

There were important differences, however, between Katofyio and the two farming cooperatives. Whereas both of the latter had ceased functioning, the former continued to operate, albeit in a highly altered form and with a greatly reduced membership. And for the officers, if not the members, the building cooperative still represented a major source of income. The distinction between Katofyio and the farming cooperatives is sharp enough to invite exploration.

The basic difference between the building and farming cooperatives appears to be that there was a major demand for construction services whereas there was no comparable demand for food. In the postindependence period the government sought to expand its rural administration and therefore devoted a major portion of its resources to constructing houses and office blocks for its rural personnel. While the expansion of the rural administration brought an immediate increase in the demand for building services, it brought little increase in the demand for food. Some of the newly posted employees of the public services did buy food from local producers, but many established their own gardens. Besides this, in the short run at least, the expenditure involved in building an office wing is simply much greater than the money spent for food by the staff which may be posted there. The building cooperative therefore faced a much higher level of demand for its services and received greater immediate rewards than did the farming cooperatives.

There was a second major difference between Katofyio and the farming cooperatives. All three cooperatives were, in a sense, the creations of the public sector. But as they developed, Katofyio took advantage of Luapula's position in the major private markets in Zambia, whereas the farming cooperatives, in conformity with development policy in the area, did not. Since the time marketing records have been kept, they have shown that Luapula has exported fish and imported agricultural produce. Katofyio, between building contracts, operated in a way that respected and allowed it to benefit from this position of regional advantage in the national economy. Katofyio simply exported fish and imported processed maize. By contrast, the cooperative farmers specialized in agricultural production in an area that was remote from both the urban demand for their products and the urban sources of their supplies; in so doing, they sought to raise their incomes by engaging in an activity in which Luapula held a comparative disadvantage, rather than advantage, in the national market. When the public sector failed to protect the incomes of the villagers, as it did when building contracts ceased to come in or when agricultural requisites were supplied late or not at all, Katofyio took refuge in the private market forces in Luapula, whereas the farming cooperatives, by remaining in the production of agricultural commodities, suffered from them.

There was a third major difference between Katofyio and the farming cooperatives, and this was the pool of skills upon which the two kinds of cooperatives could draw. The missions in the valley had offered training in the building trades. Carpentry, bricklaying, painting, and preparing mortar were familiar trades to the Kasumpa residents; and many had further developed these skills in town. But cash crop farming was not a familiar skill. The preparation of the land, the time of planting, the spacing of seeds, the application of proper pest controls and fertilizers—few of these skills had been acquired either locally or in town. As the local people said to me, farming was a "new trade." A new enterprise which drew upon the skill of the building trades was therefore based upon a much sounder foundation than one which drew upon the skills of cash crop production.

The fate of the farming cooperatives in Kasumpa therefore demonstrates the major difficulties faced by the government in its attempts to raise village incomes by sponsoring the growth of farming in areas where the market for agricultural produce fails to function. The necessary skills are scarce, the demand for output is low, and when public services fail to function the private market does not cushion agricultural producers. If these considerations suggest that the sponsorship of farming is a risky policy choice, one last comparison between Katofyio and the farming cooperatives suggests that the choice of *cooperative* farming only increases the likelihood of failure. It appears that a key element in the continued functioning of Katofyio was the ability of the officers to establish de facto private rights over collective property. Specifically, the earnings of the cooperative were used to generate a capital good, the truck, which was then used to earn profits in the private market, profits that were treated as private gain and not shared. The farming cooperatives yielded nothing comparable. The land, by law, was held in common; the crops were common property; and the proceeds from sales—what little there were—were divided equally. The officers of the farming cooperatives did not establish property rights over any of the cooperatives' land, capital, or output, and so, unlike the Katofyio officers, they had little incentive to continue working.[29] The officers of Katofyio continued to operate between building contracts; the officers of Chikalamo and Lukungwe quit at the same time as the members. That success was achieved only where private interests eroded the collective constitution of the enterprise suggests the basic weakness of the cooperative form of production.[30]

Peasant Farmers

The formation of village-level cooperatives was one part of the government's rural development program; the promotion of peasant farming was another. As we have noted, with independence, six men and their families separated themselves off from Kasumpa village and set themselves up in farming, joining the four already farming. The farmers too received training and loans from the government and services from the government's tractor units and marketing agency. By producing marketable crops, these villagers attempted to gain cash incomes and so prosper in the rural sector of postindependence Zambia.

Although their incomes were low by comparison with other groups in the nation, by comparison with the cooperative farmers, the individual farmers were doing well. At the time of my research, at least, no individual farmer had gone out of business. Rather, they were still actively planting and they sold the major crops of the Luapula area: maize, groundnuts, bananas, sugarcane, and "European vegetables": cabbages, tomatoes, potatoes, onions, and chard. In the case of maize and groundnuts, they sold their crops to the marketing agency; their fruits and vegetables they sold to the local public institutions—the hospital and the secondary school at Mbereshi Mission and a nearby leprosarium. Some crops, like sugarcane and maize, they marketed in small quantities to the local villagers: to the teachers of the primary school in the village who received monthly paychecks from the government, and to the village brewers who wished to sell sweetened maize beer as a means of earning money. On average, in 1971 the ten Tusha farmers grossed K160 a year; deducting costs and the payments of loan charges to the government, they netted an average of K125 a year. Unlike the members of the farming cooperatives, the individual farmers were thus earning cash incomes from farming.

The problem, however, is that by any other standard these incomes were small. The average annual earnings from urban employment (outside of mining) in 1968 were K640;[31] paid employment in town was thus four times more remunerative than peasant farming in Luapula. More relevant were the pay rates for the lowest-paid occupations in the urban areas; a watchman, for example, earned K360 a year, and a laborer in construction earned K336 in 1968.[32] The low earnings of the Tusha farmers are perhaps most vividly underscored by comparing their earnings with what they could have made from employment in the lowest-paid occupation in Zambia: agricultural labor, where the minimum wage was K.50 per day. Investigations by the Ministry of Rural Development suggest that peasant farming in Luapula requires an average of 57.90 man days per acre per year.[33] Given an average farm size in Tusha of 4.36 acres, this figure implies an average of 252 man days of labor in farming. With average net earnings of K125.80, the farmers could thus have done nearly as well by working for other farmers as they were doing by farming themselves. Their earnings therefore appear low by whatever standard we employ.[34]

The individual farmers were thus doing better than the cooperative farmers; but their incomes were low. Moreover, they shared one of the basic afflictions of the cooperative farmers: an increasing burden of loan debt. By 1972 the Tusha farmers owed an average of K493 to the government credit agency, or roughly three and a half times their average annual net earnings from farming. Most were able to avoid the confiscation of their crops by the marketing agency by selling portions of their produce to local institutions and fellow villagers. But they felt that their position was precarious and they feared bankruptcy, were government to attempt to recover their loans. These fears were reinforced by the government's threats to recover its debts, as illustrated by the following letter:

13 December 1971

To all farmers in Kanyembo

Farmers . . . bring your money here. You know that you have credit of fertilizers and seeds; so that's why I ask you to bring your money. If you do not bring your money, I will ask the government to help us in selling your goods: gardens, houses, and even your live stocks. . . .

> Supervisor in Charge
> Agricultural Finance Company, Ltd.
> Nchelenge District

There are many reasons for the low incomes of the Tusha farmers. Foremost among them appears to be the conduct of the public agencies and the way in which they affected the planning and conduct of farm operations.

As described earlier, the government agencies set up a series of bureaucratic hurdles which producers had to surmount in order to farm successfully. The first of these was the extension worker, whose recommendation had to be gained in order to secure seasonal credit. In the case of the individual farmers his conduct seems to have had a critical effect upon farm incomes.

The extension agent occupied the lowest level in the Department of Agriculture. As he interpreted his role, his objective was to promote agricultural production, not agricultural profits. The agent was aware that Kasumpa was remote from major urban markets; he also knew that farming was a "new trade" in the area. To succeed in raising the level of production in Tusha farms, the extension agent therefore encouraged the farmers to grow maize. His training had taught him that, by comparison with other crops, maize was durable and so could be stored and transported long distances to market. He also had been taught that the skills needed for maize production were simple and easily taught, and that new entrants into farming should therefore begin by growing maize. To fulfill his department's objective of establishing commercial farming in areas where it never existed before—and thus to achieve a distinguished record for himself—the agent therefore conscientiously carried out his department's basic recommendation: that new farmers in remote areas grow maize as their principal crop.[35]

The farmers were aware of the agent's preferences. And their desire to secure loans constituted a strong incentive to abide by them. In order to gain the agent's recommendation the farmers therefore consented to large maize targets and agreed to purchase the relatively expensive hybrid seeds and fertilizers necessary to achieve them.

To a great extent the extension agents were successful in raising maize output in Luapula. As shown by table 7.3, whereas the province had previously imported maize, by 1968 it marketed 22,400 bags over and above its local consumption requirements. And locally Nchelenge District went from virtually a nonproducing district to one that exported maize to the roller mills in the provincial capital.

The government agents thus fulfilled ambitious production targets; indeed, Luapula's record of going from a maize-importing to a maize-exporting area is frequently cited with pride as a major achievement of the new African government.[36] The trouble was that the agricultural extension agents, while maximizing production, were not maximizing profits. As we saw Chapter 6, the price of maize declined over the first several years of independence; and certainly when compared with other agricul-

Table 7.3   Annual Marketed Sale of Maize, by Province (standard bags)

Year	Northwestern Province	Luapula Province	Barotse Province	Total
1964	—	200	—	200
1965	1,100	4,100	300	5,500
1966	1,300	6,800	2,100	10,200
1967	9,900	16,000	5,400	31,300
1968	14,200	22,400	18,600	55,200

Source: Agricultural Rural Marketing Board, "Fifth Annual Report for the Year Ended 31st December, 1968," mimeo. (n.p., n.d.), p. 2.

Note: The Agricultural Rural Marketing Board is not the primary marketing agency in maize in Northern and Eastern provinces; there it is merely a buyer of the surpluses of cooperative marketing agencies, so figures for its purchases in those provinces would provide misleading estimates of the growth of production.

tural commodities maize was a low-priced product. Without high yields over large acreages, it was simply not a very profitable crop. Research conducted by the Ministry of Rural Development in Luapula suggests, for example, that, should producers reserve ten bags for home consumption, and assuming a sales price of K3.50 per bag, producers would have to achieve a yield of nearly 7 bags an acre to *break even* in maize production;[37] the farmers at Tusha had an average yield of 9.11 bags. To gain major profits, large acreages were therefore required; but, in an area where the mechanical services were unreliable and where oxen were not available, large acreages were not possible. The Tusha farmers, for example, worked an average of 4.36 acres per farm. Encouraging the growth of maize therefore encouraged increases in production perhaps, but not in profits.

But the farmers wanted their loans, and by consenting to organize their production around maize they got them. Indeed, reviews of their loan applications revealed that the extension worker, in effect, connived to make sure that they were rewarded for their cooperation. In application after application, he repeatedly recommended the Tusha farmers for loans. He noted that one was a "very hard worker—does not argue with staff. Does not fish; only farms." Another, he stressed, "pays attention to advice. Hardworking. Cooperative." And a third was "interested, keen, eager, and humble to staff."[38] In addition to praising the tractability of the farmers, the extension agent consistently overrated their production capabilities. On average he assumed their acreage to be 8.60, whereas the real figure was 4.36; and he projected maize yields of 10.50 bags per acre, whereas the average yield in 1971–72 (an exceptionally good growing year) was 9.11 bags per acre.[39] The effect, of course, was to make the farmers appear better able to repay their loans than in fact they were. Consequently, the agent was able to reward the farmers with loans for cooperating with his production targets, even while plunging them into debt.

The farmers were aware of what was happening to them. They knew that other crops—fruits and vegetables, for example—fetched a much higher price. The return per acre at 1971 prices and yields was in the area of K73.26 for vegetables and K42.17 for bananas; for maize it was but K35.47. For various reasons, however, the farmers did not alter production patterns so as to take advantage of relative prices and thereby farm more profitably.

The farmers feared the sanctions of the extension agent. Without his recommendation they stood to lose their loans. Moreover, they feared the risks involved in committing themselves to the production of perishables. They would then be limited to producing for the local market, and this market could easily be glutted.[40] The farmers knew that they had little control over the local market and so were vulnerable to the entrance of

new suppliers. In the case of tomatoes, for example, the villagers had
already learned to grow them, and the farmers had lost much of the village
market and a portion of the institutional market as well. Moreover, the
farmers were aware that the school and the hospital wanted to contract
with bulk suppliers. Bulk agreements both simplified their purchasing and
cut transport costs. The school, for example, already purchased some of
its vegetables from a large, United Nations–sponsored cooperative scheme
at the district capital. The U.N. cooperative delivered goods on its own
lorry, whereas the institutions often had to use their own transport in
purchasing goods from the individual farmers. For various reasons the
farmers were therefore reluctant to shift from the production of maize to
the production of higher-priced crops, with the result that their incomes
were lower than they might otherwise have been.[41]

Generalizing from the Kasumpa Experience

The cooperatives had by and large failed; farm incomes were low, and
peasant producers were in debt. And the public services—the tractor
services, rural marketing organizations, and rural credit programs—
operated with abysmal inefficiency. These were the facts of life in Kasumpa, and they constituted important limitations upon its well-being. How
characteristic were these conditions of the more remote districts of Zambia?

It appears that the pattern of the Kasumpa cooperatives was repeated
in many areas of Zambia. Certainly in Luapula, where the cooperative
movement had been enthusiastically received and broadly subscribed, the
number and percentage of failures had been high. Indeed, at the time of
my research, the government was "de-registering" what it termed "moribund" cooperatives in Luapula Province, and its records revealed a broadly distributed state of decline. As the figures in table 7.4 show, over 40
percent of the farming cooperatives formed in Luapula since independence

Table 7.4   Farming Cooperatives, 1971

	Active	*Inactive*	*Moribund*
Mansa	28	14	11
Kawambwa	14	1	9
Mwense	9	4	7
Samfya	23	1	7
Nchelenge	8	4	10
Total	82	24	44

Source: Provincial Co-operative Officer, Mansa, "Annual Report for the Year Ending
31st December 1971," files of the District Co-operative Officer, Nchelenge District
Offices.

were declared inactive or moribund in 1971 by the provincial cooperative officer. Figures from the same source suggest a decline in membership in the farming cooperatives from over 3,000 in 1968 to barely 1,000 in 1971, a decrease of over 60 percent.

This portrait of failure extends beyond Luapula to the national level as well. In a study commissioned by the Ministry of Rural Development, two researchers surveyed the Zambian cooperatives and concluded that "the communal system of . . . farming co-operatives has proved very difficult in all countries where the system has been tried. Zambia is no exception."[42] They also noted: "The low yield per acre [4.6 bags] . . . in combination with the low acreage per member [2.6 acres] means that the production of maize per member in many cases is as low as five to eight bags. This is insufficient . . . even for subsistence needs."[43] By the early 1970s the cooperatives were generally considered a failure, and attempts were being made at the national level to eliminate the inefficient ones and to consolidate the remainder. Under a new national policy, the cooperatives were to be organized in the form of grouped individual farms with common access to central services such as mechanical pools, storage facilities, farm managers, and extension agents.[44] The implementation of this new policy reflects the widespread failure of the old.

The failure of the mechanical services was also a general phenomenon. The provincial cooperative officers in Luapula noted that a full twenty-nine of the sixty-nine tractors posted to the province in 1971 were not working at the year's end. In only two of the five districts were the majority of the tractors in operation; these were Kawambwa and Mansa, which contained the relatively urbanized centers of the province (table 7.5). Failure of mechanical services was a problem prevalent elsewhere in Zambia. Richard Jolly, in his review of the implementation of the pre-independence recommendations of the UN/ECA/FAO–recruited Dudley Seers Commission, notes the breakdown of mechanization services as one

Table 7.5   State of Repair of Tractors, 1971

District	No. of Tractors	No. of Tractors Working	No. of Tractors Not Working
Mansa	25	21	4
Kwambwa	11	8	3
Nchelenge	5	1	4
Samfya	20	8	12
Mwense	7	1	6
Total	68	39	29

Source: Provincial Co-operative Officer, Mansa, "Annual Report for the Year Ending 31st December, 1971," files of the District Co-operative Officer, Nchelenge District Offices.

of the major failures in the national development effort.[45] And G. Olund and J. Russel, in their review of the cooperative program, note the high cost of tractor services and stress that "in certain areas of the country . . . break-even yield points to cover costs [of tractorization] exceed 25 bags [of maize] per acre and even the most excellent farmers could not have hoped to farm properly with mechanized maize cultivation."[46] The result has been the withdrawal of government support for tractor services and attempts to develop oxen-based agriculture. This change in central government policy constitutes a recognition of the failure of the mechanization program, a failure that extended well beyond the boundaries of Kasumpa village.[47]

The indebtedness of the peasant farmers in Kasumpa also appears to have been part of a more general pattern. It is reflected most clearly in the fate of the credit program. In Nchelenge District, the credit agency's failure to make timely loan distributions, which would leave time for proper planting and thus permit sufficient yields to finance loan repayments, constantly bedeviled the peasant farmers. So great did the problem become that the district government appointed a commission of inquiry into the agency in 1971, largely as a means of pressuring it to expedite its services and to reverse the trend of mounting indebtedness among the peasant farmers.[48] In the province as a whole, according to the provincial director of the credit agency, the rate of repayment of the annual distribution of loans was a mere 10 percent; the volume of unpaid obligations to the government, he declared, was "massive" throughout Luapula. A similar picture is revealed at the national level. In a review of the Credit Organization of Zambia, for example, C. S. Lombard and A. H. C. Tweedie estimate that "roughly K2M[illion] per annum is thought to have been disbursed to small farmers and co-operatives. Little data is [sic] available on repayments but it is thought to have varied from virtually zero to about 30 percent in the more successful provinces."[49] The burden of unpaid obligations caused a virtual collapse of the credit organization in 1969. The magnitude of peasant indebtedness is suggested also by the records of the Agricultural Finance Company. In 1970 the Finance Company purchased the Credit Organization of Zambia's outstanding debts, and its records reveal that they totaled K22 million.[50] The low range of the rate of repayment and the vast total of uncollected obligations both imply that rural indebtedness was a widespread phenomenon.

In several critical respects, the fate of the government's rural development program in Kasumpa thus appears to be representative of its plight elsewhere in Zambia. There is another way of assessing the government's program, and the evaluation achieved from this perspective is also informative. On the part of both the government and its constituents in the more remote regions of the country, a major objective of the rural development program was to reverse the pattern of inequality between the more remote and the central regions of the nation. Through government-sponsored attempts to develop cash crop production in the more remote regions, rural dwellers sought to achieve the level of prosperity private market forces had provided for their more favorably located counterparts. But the evidence suggests the persistence of the disparity in the level of well-being between the commercially oriented regions of the line-of-rail provinces and the more remote districts of the nation. There have been two major studies of line-of-rail farming in the postindependence period: one conducted in 1967 by the Food Research Institute of Stanford University and another in 1969 by a research team drawn from the Universities of Nottingham and Zambia. The latter study also contains data on farm incomes off the line of rail. The small sample sizes, the different years in which the observations were made, and the use of differing techniques for measuring the incomes of the farmers make comparisons of the data difficult. And yet the difference between the incomes of the line-of-rail and remote farmers is sufficiently great so as to exceed even high levels of error (see table 7.6).[51] On the basis of these studies as well as impressionistic evidence gained on my own and from discussions with other researchers, I feel confident in asserting that the level of farm incomes in the line-of-rail districts vastly exceeds that in the more remote areas. Further evidence is contained in figures collected from the marketing agency which indicate that the line-of-rail provinces continue to account for over 90 percent of marketed maize production (see table 7.7). And, given the tendency for private markets to operate near the line of rail but not in the more remote areas, it is likely that the figures of the government marketing agency are biased *against* revealing a dominance of the central producers.

It is interesting to examine briefly the reasons for these disparities as suggested in the analyses contained in the Food Research Institute and the joint university studies. The availability of cattle and the use made of cattle

Table 7.6   Average Earnings of Peasant Farmers, by Location

On Line of Rail		*Off Line of Rail*	
Mazabuka Farmers 1967	*Mumbwa Farmers 1969*	*Katete Farmers 1969*	*Tusha Farmers 1971*
Gross Net	Gross Net	Gross Net	Gross Net
K945.30 K507.10	K510.34 K356.42	K188.98 K132.36	K160.25 K125.80
N = 15	N = 67	N = 27	N = 10

Sources: Mazabuka: Kenneth R. M. Anthony and Victor C. Uchendu, *Agricultural Change in Mazabuka District, Zambia*, p. 258; Mumbwa and Katete: Elliott et al., *Agricultural Labour Productivity*, pp. 148, 150; Tusha: author's records.

Table 7.7   Marketed Maize Production, 1964–72 (standard bags)

Year	Central Province	Southern Province	Copperbelt Province	National Total	Line-of-Rail Provinces as % of Total
1964	1,323,900	811,100	3,000	2,251,700	95.0
1965	1,889,200	899,800	3,900	2,899,100	96.3
1966	2,330,300	1,705,600	10,600	4,240,000	95.4
1967	2,326,000	1,680,500	20,100	4,222,700	95.4
1968	1,590,000	1,031,700	15,700	2,908,200	90.7
1969	1,322,000	1,443,600	27,600	3,020,200	92.5
1970	903,200	461,400	6,700	1,490,300	92.0
1971	2,604,400	1,504,200	33,100	4,443,800	93.2
1972	4,196,700	2,115,000	28,700	6,850,600	92.6

Source: Republic of Zambia, Ministry of Rural Development, *Statistical Bulletin, January–March 1973* (Lusaka: Ministry of Rural Development, 1973), p. 9. These figures must be regarded as estimates; note the discrepancy between these totals and those given in table 6.8.

Note: Standard bags equaled 200 pounds in 1964–70, 90 kilograms in 1971–72.

by the line-of-rail farmers is one major reason noted for the superior earnings on the line of rail. Thus, for example, the Food Research Institute study suggests that over 30 percent of the net cash income of the Mazabuka farmers comes directly from cattle sales: "There has been a market for cattle since the arrival of the first European settlers, and farmers are now able to sell their stock to itinerant dealers for resale in the Copper Belt and Lusaka. The sale of cattle . . . forms the second most important source of a farmer's income."[52] In addition to the money gained from cattle sales, the farmers benefit from the increase in agricultural production made possible by the use of cattle. As the authors note, "A characteristic feature of farms in Mazabuka district is the high capital investment in equipment. This includes a wide range of ox-drawn implements. . . . In the last 12 years progressive farmers have acquired increased numbers of ox-drawn implements, particularly cultivators. . . . Only one of the sampled farmers had no ox plough."[53] Having cattle available as a capital input means that the farmers can work larger acreages and achieve higher levels of production. While the authors of the Nottingham University/University of Zambia study pay less attention to cattle sales, they too stress the use of cattle as a primary factor in farm production. They note that in Mumbwa "farmers used over four times as much oxen power as the villagers on their maize and fifteen times as much on their groundnuts."[54] One consequence was that they farmed an average of 22.8 acres, while the villagers farmed 4.9;[55] and, largely as a result, their average annual incomes were nearly four times as great as those of the neighboring villagers.[56]

The Food Research Institute and joint university studies identify yet another major reason for the prosperity of line-of-rail farming: the presence of significant private markets. Insofar as the studies do touch upon the performance of public agencies, they tend to portray them as inefficient and sometimes damaging to farm profits, just as they were in Kasumpa. For example, commenting on the performance of the extension agents, the authors of the joint university study report:

> It is not wholly unfair to say that in the past the tendency has been for the Department of Agriculture in Lusaka to decide, on the basis of field trials and the needs of the economy at large, that certain crops . . . should be grown. The role of the extension service has been to bring every kind of pressure to bear on farmers to grow these crops— including financial pressure, by linking loans to cultivation of certain crops.[57]

The assumption that the crops should be profitable, they conclude, "is belied by practice."[58] The authors comment less critically on the performance of the credit and marketing agencies, reflecting perhaps the better service they provide in the central regions. Nonetheless they do note that, by paying the government price for agricultural products and by deducting loan debts from cash payments to farmers, the marketing service acts to lower farm incomes. The general impression conveyed is that the behavior of the public agencies in the line-of-rail farming community was debilitating to farm incomes, just as I have argued for the case of Kasumpa.

However, there is one major difference between the line of rail and the more remote districts: as the Nottingham University/University of Zambia study shows, the effect upon the farmers of the performance of the public agencies is not nearly so devastating in the line of rail as in Kasumpa. The apparent explanation is the functioning of significant private markets: private suppliers and purchasers compete with the public agencies on the line of rail and the farmers can, and do, take recourse to these competitors in order to avoid the inferior services and lower prices of the public agencies. At a time when the government was lowering the price of maize being offered by its marketing agency, the joint university research team found that "considerable quantities of maize (in some years over a third of the total commercial crop) are sold privately in the Western Province where it commands a substantial premium over the [marketing service's] price at Mumbwa."[59] Further, when the marketing service attempted to deduct loan payments from the proceeds of the sales, they found that "many loanees [did not] market their production through the official buying agency . . . [and] avoid[ed] the stop order [placed on their payments] by arranging to sell privately."[60] In the more remote areas, where private buyers in competitive markets did not exist, the farmers could not protect their incomes by making major sales in the private marketplace.

The study of the Food Research Institute further suggests that many of the line-of-rail farmers purchase their farm inputs from private sources. Because of their access to urban suppliers of these commodities, they can avoid the effects of the late supply and disbursement of farm requisites by the government marketing services which so devastated the more remote farmers.

The presence of cattle and the existence of private markets thus enhanced the incomes from farming on the line of rail. There is a last difference that would help to account for the higher incomes of the more central producers. Given the prospect of higher incomes, the line-of-rail farmers have made larger investments in farming and so can farm more profitably. According to the Food Research Institute study of Mazabuka farmers:

> The potential returns from farming in this area are high and the incentive to adopt innovations correspondingly so. . . . The net return from a maize crop of ten bags per acre was estimated to be about £5, from a 15 bag crop £13, and from a 20 bag crop £21 per acre. Yields of 30 to 40 bags of maize per acre are being obtained by large-scale farmers, and their example continues to provide an added and important stimulus.[61]

These greater yields can be obtained because "farmers have taken a major step towards commercial farming. This is reflected in the amount of purchased inputs used."[62] The authors go on to document the investments made in mechanical shellers and grinders, local water supplies, trained oxen and ox-drawn equipment, fencing, kraals, and storage facilities. And on the basis of a 1955 base-line study of the area, they document a roughly 500 percent increase in yields and a roughly 700 percent increase in farm incomes. Given the year-to-year variability of weather conditions and the differing techniques of the two studies, we must be suspicious of the contrast between the 1955 and the 1967 figures. Nonetheless, we can accept the trend and comprehend how the prospects of profits have called forth greater farm investments in the line-of-rail provinces and therefore higher incomes. The depressed returns to farming in the more remote provinces have not encouraged similar levels of investment, and, undercapitalized as they are, the more remote farmers are left with lower yields and lower incomes.[63]

Other Sources of Income

The intervention of the public sector in Zambia has therefore apparently failed to generate significant rural incomes where the private market failed to function. While the sponsorship of the cooperatives and of the individual farmers represents the core of the government's rural development program, there were, at least in Luapula, other sources of rural income. One of the most important was the fishing industry.

Insofar as the incomes of the Kasumpa villagers were dependent on the prosperity of the fishing industry, they were dependent upon an industry that continued in a state of relative decline. The price of fish was government regulated, and the government was slow to increase prices; from independence until 1967, the producer price of dry fish remained unchanged at 0.11 kwacha a pound and that of fresh fish at 0.03 kwacha a pound. The government did take advantage of the decimalization of the currency in 1967 to "sneak by" an increase to 0.15 kwacha a pound of dried fish and 0.05 kwacha a pound of fresh—rises of 36 and 67 percent respectively. Until March of 1972 the price again remained unchanged.

The price of fish thus increased modestly over the period 1964 to 1972; other prices, however, increased at a much faster rate. The result was that without increases in production the fishermen were able to purchase fewer goods with the proceeds of their sales. If we can assume that the consumption patterns of Luapula fishermen closely resembled those of Southern Province residents, then, on the basis of a study conducted by two economists from the University of Zambia, we can infer that a quantity of fish in 1969 would exchange for 16 percent fewer goods than did the same quantity in 1964. Without increases in production, their real incomes thus decreased about 16 percent over the six-year period.[64]

Most indications are that production from the fishery in fact did not increase and that it possibly declined. Government estimates indicate that, whereas the Lake Mweru/Luapula fishery produced 6,411 short tons of fish in 1964, it produced only 6,293 in 1968. I was unable to locate the figures for 1969; the recorded tonnage for 1970 was, however, 6,168, thus suggesting a lowering level of output from the fishery.[65]

Several major reasons have been put forward for this. One is the fixed structure of producer prices. At fixed prices, when the demand for fish increases, as it has in recent years, the market tends to adjust not through increased domestic production but rather through increased imports from abroad. Moreover, biological factors appear to have limited the output of the fishery. We have already noted the disappearance of the *mpumbu*, a species of fish favored by urban consumers. In later years, particularly in 1963–68, there was a decline in the number of a second popular species, the bream. While the reason for the disappearance of the mpumbu remains a mystery, the decline of the bream appears to be largely a result of the recent low water levels of the fishery.[66]

A third major reason for the decline in production is the postindependence relaxation of regulations prohibiting fishing in the breeding areas and during the spawning season. Only in 1969 did the African government begin to enforce these regulations, and then only after the decline in bream had led local fishermen to appreciate the beneficial effects of regulations.[67] The enforcement of regulations is still sporadic, however, and it appears that the government is unwilling to impose regulations upon the fishermen, who dominate many of the local party units in the area.[68]

Even more important than the decline in the overall production, however, is the absence of any increase in productivity. The technology of the industry has remained static, and with it the productivity of the fishermen. Even though bream are apparently declining in number, other species are abundant; unlike bream, they tend to concentrate further from the shore in the deeper waters of the lake.[69] To work the deeper waters, the fishermen require fairly large and stable boats capable of being mechanically powered; they also require deep-lying nets which can be trawled. Few of the fishermen currently possess this kind of equipment. In a 1969 study of 1,381 fishermen (an estimated 75 percent of the fishing population in the valley), a government economist found that a total of 130, or 10 percent, possessed engines and that only 503, or roughly 37 percent, had boats capable of operating with engines, that is, either plank or fiberglass boats as opposed to canoes.[70]

A minority of the fishermen—somewhere from a tenth to a third, assuming engines could be shared—thus possessed equipment that would enable them to fish away from the shore margins. The remainder, or over 60 percent of the fishermen, did not. Even in the case of this advantaged minority, their situation left much to be desired. Many fishermen were highly critical of the fiberglass boats made available through the fisheries department; they were, they said, "too light and unstable"[71] and therefore dangerous in the open waters. In addition, even when better boats and engines did enable them to work far from shore, the fishermen were frustrated by the inadequate design of their nets. The so-called Nkwazi nets distributed by the fisheries department were, in their words, "too short especially where nets were used in open lake."[72] The limitations of their equipment—equipment of virtually the same kind employed on the lake since the 1950s—meant that the fishermen were unable to offset the adverse shift in prices by increasing their productivity.

The government has attempted to increase the output of the fishery and the productivity of the fishermen. Rather than approaching the problem as one of static technology, however, it has approached the problem as one of marketing. As the director of the Wildlife, Fisheries, and National Parks Department wrote in 1971: "It was felt by the Fisheries Division of the department in 1965, and it is still of the same opinion today, that fish marketing is the controlling factor in fishery development."[73]

To increase the demand for fish and thus the incentives for increased productivity, the government acquired controlling interest in Irwin and Johnson, a South African firm which had hitherto specialized in the importation and sale of frozen foods to the European immigrant community. Reincorporating as Lakes Fisheries of Zambia, Ltd., the company constructed fish-processing plants at the Lake Tanganyika and Luapula/ Lake Mweru fisheries, where it purchased the output of local fishermen. The acquisition of Irwin and Johnson absorbed virtually all the funds earmarked for investment in the development of the fisheries under the First National Development Plan.

When I conducted my research, the Lake Mweru plant had been in operation too short a time to permit a close assessment of its impact on the fishery. Discussion with the fishermen did suggest a fundamental problem, however. Lakes Fisheries confined its purchases to fresh fish only; it simply would not handle dried fish. The primary reason for this policy was the company's heavy investment in refrigeration and storage equipment; the company sought to recover its outlay for these facilities by marketing fish through them. From the fishermen's point of view, the company's policy meant that the government's investments had a small impact on their volume of sales. The vast bulk of the consumers of domestic fish prefer dried to fresh fish, and have for years. This preference is partly a matter of taste and partly because the vast majority of the urban consumers lack freezers in which to store fresh fish. In the absence of refrigeration, fresh fish spoil in hours, whereas dried fish, in the proper conditions, can be kept for days. As a result, the sales volume of fresh fish is low by comparison with that for dried, and the government's investment in Lakes Fisheries therefore seems to have had little impact on the volume of production of the fisheries and thus on the fishermen's level of income.[74]

Through political action in the nationalist period, the villagers had helped to place in power a government that would lay hold of the wealth of the cities and transfer it to the countryside through programs of rural development. The new African government did indeed attempt to upgrade the standard of living in the countryside. By creating credit and marketing agencies, offering mechanical and extension services, and providing skill and capital for the farmers in the more remote regions, the government attempted to support the efforts of villagers to increase their incomes by fulfilling the urban demand for agricultural produce. For a variety of complex reasons, examined in this chapter, the rural development program largely failed to increase the levels of village incomes significantly. It remains to examine the response of the villagers to the failure of the government's program.

8

Migration in Postindependence Zambia

In postindependence Zambia, the geographic distribution of economic activity remained much as it was in the colonial period. From the viewpoint of the inhabitants of the more remote districts, the result was the continued attractiveness of the migratory alternative. The postindependence concentration of resources on the line of rail and the relative failure of attempts to upgrade rural incomes in the more remote areas left unaltered two of the basic disparities influencing the migration decision: differences in the likelihood of obtaining an income and differences in the magnitude of the rewards from income sources.

One inquiry reveals that, of the 532 industrial manufacturing establishments existing in 1969, a full 524 (or 98.5 percent) were in the line-of-rail provinces.[1] As shown in table 8.1, the vast majority of jobs consequently remained confined to that region. While the number of employment opportunities rose from approximately 250,000 in 1963 to 330,000 in 1969, the distribution of these opportunities among the regions of Zambia remained largely unchanged. The result, from the point of view of proto-migrants, was to leave largely unaltered the relative likelihood of obtaining jobs; employment chances could be improved fivefold by moving from areas outside the line of rail to the central regions of the country (see table 8.2).

Not only did the distribution of investments in postindependence Zam-

Table 8.1 Distribution of Employment

	1963		1969	
	Percent of All Jobs	*Percent of Population*	*Percent of All Jobs*	*Percent of Population*
Line of Rail	83.6	43.5	83.9	49.9
Off Line of Rail	16.5	56.6	16.1	50.1

Sources: 1963: Calculated from M. D. Veitch, "Employment and the Labour Force," table 1; 1969: Republic of Zambia, *Second National Development Plan*, p. 172.

160

Table 8.2   Employment and Population

	1963			1969		
	Number Employed	*Population*	*Percent Population Employed*	*Number Employed*	*Population*	*Percent Population Employed*
Line-of-rail provinces						
Copperbelt	119,720	544,200	22.0	144,040	816,000	17.7
Central	59,590	505,500	11.8	97,970	713,000	13.7
Southern	34,750	466,300	7.5	33,310	496,000	6.7
Total	214,060	1,516,000	14.1	275,320	2,025,000	13.6
Other provinces	42,230	1,974,800	2.1	52,980	2,033,000	2.6
Total	256,290	3,490,800	7.3	328,300	4,058,000	8.1

Sources: 1963: Calculated from Veitch, "Employment and the Labour Force," table 1; 1969: *Second National Development Plan,* p.172.

bia influence the distribution of job opportunities; it also affected their value. For the high rate of capital formation apparently led to increases in the productivity of labor, with the result that wages rose (see table 8.3). The sole exception to the trend of productivity increases came in 1966, when the disruption of the Zambian economy occasioned by Rhodesia's rebellion against Great Britain led to declines in labor productivity. It will be noted, however, that average earnings rose in any case, pointing out a second major reason for wage increases in the postindependence period: the power of organized labor. With the coming of independence, the African workers, who like their rural counterparts had high expectations of economic rewards from that event, demanded a redistribution of income to wages. And the newly created African government, sensitive to the demands of its organized urban constituents that they be made better off, permitted the transfer.

Independence brought a last major reason for increased wages: the implementation of programs of African advancement. With independence came the opportunity for Africans to use public power to intervene in private industry so as to modify hiring, training, and promotion practices. The government, through "Zambianization committees," tax allowances for training programs, expenditures on education, and actions of its boards of directors in state industries, achieved an upgrading of the African labor force, an upgrading reflected in higher rates of pay. For all these reasons, the average earnings of African working men rose in the years after independence.[2]

From the point of view of the rural dweller, given the degree of stagnation in the rural areas documented in Chapter 7, the rise in wages increased the attractiveness of the migratory alternative: the vast majority of the available jobs were concentrated in the central districts of the nation and a rise in the value of these jobs increased the expected returns to job seeking in that region. In addition, the factors that increased wages did not operate uniformly throughout the nation. The relative confinement of investments on the line of rail, the operation of trade unions there, and the Zambianization of the commercial and industrial enterprises, most of which were located in that region, tended to increase rates of pay more rapidly on the line of rail than off it. One review of regional wage rates in Zambia indicates that in 1968 the Central and Copperbelt provinces—the industrial and commercial heartland of the nation—had private wage rates of K754 and K954 respectively; elsewhere, only in Luapula and Southern provinces were the average annual money earnings of employees in the private sector in excess of K500; in the other four provinces, the figure ranged as low as K262 per annum.[3] These figures suggest a relationship between wage levels and geographic centrality.

Table 8.3 Employment and Earnings of African Labor

Year	(1) African Employees (× 1,000)	(2) Africans as % of All Employees	(3) Index of Output per Man (1964 = 100)	(4) African Employees' Aver. Annual Earnings (K)	(5) African Employees, Index of Aver. Annual Earnings (1964 = 100)	(6) Consumer Price Index	(7) African Employees' Aver. Real Earnings (K)	(8) African Employees, Index of Aver. Real Earnings (1964 = 100)
1962	231	87	87	302	79.1	101.8	297	81.2
1963	225	87	91	320	83.8	101.3	316	86.3
1964	237	88	100	382	100.0	104.5	366	100.0
1965	263	89	108	428	112.0	113.0	379	103.6
1966	295	91	96	480	125.7	124.5	386	105.5
1967	315	91	106	666	174.4	130.7	510	139.3
1968	325	92	112	789	206.6	144.9	545	149.0

Sources: Column 1: Central Statistical Office, *Employment and Earnings 1966–68*, p. 6. Column 3: Republic of Zambia, Office of the Vice-President, Development Division, *Zambian Manpower*, p. 9; this index is based upon the ratio between total expenditures on the gross domestic product at constant prices (with adjustment for rural household consumption) and the average number of wage and salaried employees during the year. Column 4: Central Statistical Office, *Employment and Earnings 1966–68*, p. 6. Column 6: Central Statistical Office, *Monthly Digest of Statistics* 8, no. 8 (August 1972): 49. This version of the index is for all items, lower income consumption patterns; January 1962 =100.

All of the above refers to income opportunities from employment in firms. Many other opportunities existed, however, and these too rendered the line of rail relatively attractive. The aggregation of persons into the urban areas created opportunities for earnings through such activities as brewing and selling beer, peddling wares in the townships, burning and selling charcoal, tailoring, making medicines and providing health care, and repairing radios and bicycles. With the growth of the paid labor force, the demand for these kinds of services rose as well. Because the providers of these services were often not counted in the rolls of the employed, our portrayal of the disparity in economic opportunities between regions on and off the line of rail in Zambia, based as it is on official figures, underestimates the extent of this disparity as it "really" existed and, my rural interviews convinced me, as it was perceived and experienced by those dwelling in the more remote regions of the nation.[4]

Chapter 7 showed that a gap also exists in the levels of production and earnings from agriculture between the central and more remote portions of the country. The earnings of farmers along the line of rail tend to be at least twice those of farmers located in the more remote districts. And even figures for subsistence-level production suggest that Central and Southern Province villagers grow crops valued, on average, at about 150 percent of the national average for subsistence farm families.[5]

The Migratory Response

One response to this pattern of economic disparities was the wholesale exodus of persons from the more remote rural areas to the more central regions of the nation.[6] To analyze this phenomenon, I will follow the work of Mary Elizabeth Jackman and compare the figures on district-level population reported in the 1963 and 1969 national censuses.[7] In her comparison of the two censuses, Jackman attempted to isolate the percentage of the change in population between 1963 and 1969 that could be attributed to migration. Her method is crude and, unless carefully used, error prone. While I use it, therefore, I do so with some caution.

Essentially, Jackman computed for each district what the population should have been in 1969, given the population of that district in 1963 and the average natural rate of increase for the nation. Thus, for each district, i, she computed an index Y_i, where:

$$Y_i = \frac{\text{Pop.}_i 1969 - (\text{Pop.}_i 1963 + K \times \text{Pop.}_i 1963)}{\text{Pop.}_i 1963} \times 100$$

Given that K is the natural rate of increase of the population of Zambia as a whole, this index can be interpreted as a measure of the percent population change between 1963 and 1969 that can be attributed to migration.[8]

Where in-migration has taken place, this measure is positive; conversely, out-migration yields negative values of this index.

The Direction of Migration

Using this index, we can assess the shifts in Zambia's population over the first several years of independence. Combining the districts into meaningful groupings and comparing the signs and values of Jackman's index, we can compare the average value of Jackman's index for districts classified into urban/rural and line-of-rail/off-line-of-rail categories (see table 8.4).[9] We then find that the populations of the urban and peri-urban districts grew at rates that suggest high levels of in-migration, while the populations of the rural districts grew at rates suggesting a loss of population due to migration. In addition, the line of rail as a whole appears to have attracted migrants, while districts off the line of rail appear to have exported them.

We can also perform an analysis of variance on the values of Jackman's index for the different kinds of districts; the results are shown in table 8.5. For both categorizations—urban vs. rural and line of rail vs. off line of

Table 8.4   Changes in Population, 1963–69

Line-of-Rail Provinces:	*Census of June 1963* (× *1,000*)	*Census of August 1969* (× *1,000*)	*Increase*	*Change Attributable to Migration**
Urban districts	778	1,232	58.4%	+42.2%
Peri-urban districts	143	175	22.4	+ 6.2
Rural districts	594	617	3.9	−12.3
Off-Line-of-Rail Provinces:				
All districts	1,975	2,030	2.8	−13.4%
Total Zambia	3,490	4,054	16.2%	

Sources: Computed from Republic of Zambia, *Monthly Digest of Statistics* 8, no. 8 (August 1972); and Jackman, *Recent Population Movements.*

*Using Jackman's index.

Table 8.5   Analysis of Variance of the Jackman Index

Source of Variance	*Sum of Squares*	*Degrees of Freedom*	*Mean Square*	*F*
Urban-rural	11,912.91	1	11,912.91	92.50
Error	5,280.26	41	128.79	
Total	17,193.17	42		
LOR/NLOR	5,232.66	1	5,232.66	18.02
Error	11,905.79	41	290.39	
Total	17,138.45	42		

Note: LOR = line of rail; NLOR = off line of rail.

rail—the F statistics indicate that the magnitudes of the differences in Jackman's index are highly significant. Were the data generated by chance, the odds would be a hundred to one against obtaining these levels of the F statistic. In addition, when we calculate the value of the ω^2 statistics for the two analysis of variance tables, we obtain values of 0.6929 for the first and 0.3053 for the second. This means that over two-thirds of the variance in the value of the Jackman index for the various districts of Zambia can be accounted for by urban-rural differences and nearly one-third by differences in location with respect to the line of rail.

A last means of assessing the shift of population over the first several years of independence in Zambia is correlation analysis. As indices of the urban nature of the districts, we can utilize measures of the classic characteristics of urban society in central Africa: the density of population, the ratio of men to women, and the percent of the population in cash employment. As indices of the degree to which the districts are rural, we can measure the presence of cattle and plows and the percent of the population involved in agriculture and fishing. We can also measure the distance between the district and the nearest major town on the line of rail. When we correlate the value of these indices for each district in 1963 with the percent population change due to migration between 1963 and 1969, we obtain the coefficients in table 8.6.

Where the sign is positive, this implies that an increase in the value of the index correlates with an increase in population; negative signs imply that districts higher on the index tend to have lost population. The distribution of the signs across the various indices therefore suggests a shift of population from rural to urban districts over the first several years of independence. They also suggest a shift from the more remote districts to the line of rail.

Given the regional disparities in economic opportunities that have been documented in this study, these are the kinds of results we would expect to obtain were rural dwellers making choices in accordance with our notion of how villagers behave.

Table 8.6   Pair-wise Correlation Coefficients with
Jackman Index of Migration

Population density	+.6513*
Male/female ratio	+.6938*
Percent males employed for cash	+.8101*
No. of plows per capita	−.1589
No. of cattle per capita	−.1804
Percent males in agriculture and fishing	−.4008*
Distance to nearest town	−.6194*

*Significant at 0.01 level of confidence, one-tailed test.

The Composition of Migration

Having documented the direction of the flow of migrants in independent Zambia, I now turn, as did the students of preindependence migration, to an analysis of its composition. Given our knowledge of the distribution of economic opportunities and our notion of how migration decisions are made, we have strong expectations about who would choose to leave the rural areas; this section will test these expectations.

As much of the analysis in this section parallels my discussion of migration in the colonial period, I can afford to be brief. Save for the expansion of employment opportunities, the increase in wage rates, and the apparently growing gap between urban and rural income opportunities in the postindependence period, little appears to have changed in the labor market in Zambia. As a result, while we can expect vastly increased levels of migration, we should, by and large, expect the same empirical regularities in the makeup of migrants. The regularities examined are of the same kind as those in the preindependence period; they arise in the demographic characteristics of the migrants and in the characteristics of their areas of origin. Wherever possible, I propose to relate the characteristics noted for districts in 1963 to changes in their population over the intercensal period 1963 to 1969.

DEMOGRAPHIC VARIABLES

Age: As the costs of migration are borne in present time, and as the benefits would have to be deferred for a greater period of time by youths than by young adults, young adults should migrate at a higher rate than youths. In addition, as the net benefits of migration for old people are less than those for young adults—because of the shorter period of possible employment for older persons—the rate of migration should be greater for young adults than for old persons. If our model is valid, given that employment rules for youths did not change with independence, we should expect a significant and negative relationship between the percent population of young adults in the rural districts of Zambia in 1963 and subsequent district-level changes in population.

Sex: There is no indication that the relative employment prospects and earnings of men and women have shifted with independence, nor that their relative economic fortunes in the rural areas have altered. The differential between the rural and urban areas should therefore still be greater for men than for women. As a result, we should expect to find a significant negative relationship between the proportion of men in the population of the various rural districts of Zambia and district-level changes in population during the period 1963–69.[10]

Education: The sole demographic variable that may have been revalued with independence is education. At the time of independence, the supply of indigenous skilled manpower was small; for, as we have seen, educational facilities were concentrated among the expatriates in colonial Zambia, and few Africans possessed high levels of education or training. The postindependence expansion of Zambia's economy generated a strong demand for skilled manpower; because education perforce takes time, the new educational facilities created at independence could only slowly respond to this change in demand. As Richard Jolly states:

> Because of the time lag between providing education and obtaining its benefits, the post-Independence expansion had little impact on the supply of skills to the labour force. Educated job seekers up to 1969 were almost all Zambians who had started their secondary, technical, or university education before Independence. And the number joining the labour force from the secondary schools, let alone completing university or other post-secondary education, did not add more than a few per cent to the total stock of such persons.[11]

The result of the shortfall in supply was a precipitous rise in the price of educated labor. All that I have said about the relative rates of employment creation between the rural and urban areas suggests that this price rise would create a strong differential in the expected streams of income between the two sectors for those with some education. We should therefore expect a strongly negative relationship between measures of education in the rural districts of Zambia in 1963 and changes in population in 1963–69.[12]

AREAS OF ORIGIN

We have argued that rural dwellers choose among alternative ways of seeking the benefits of industrialization. Some choose to enter rural production for the urban consumer market and others choose to migrate to the cities and enter the urban market for labor. These two responses are alternatives because, with the growth of income from cash cropping, there is a smaller differential, if other things remain constant, between urban and rural incomes, and thus less incentive to migrate.[13]

Cattle, Plows, and Peasant Farming: Certain factors, we know, constrain the ability of rural dwellers to gain prosperity by selecting the first alternative. An important determinant of the profitability of peasant farming in Zambia is the presence of cattle. If our reasoning is correct, we should therefore find a significant positive relationship between the number of cattle in the rural districts of Zambia in 1963 and the change in district-level population in 1963–69. As an indication of the degree to which cattle have been incorporated into modern farming practices, we can note the number of plows; and we can hypothesize that there will be a significantly positive relationship between the number of plows in the rural districts in 1963 and subsequent changes in population in 1963–69.

Distance: A second primary determinant of the profitability of rural production is distance from the line of rail. The greater the distance, the lower the profits from cash cropping. We should therefore expect a significant negative relationship between distance to town and changes in district population.

However, as I argued in my discussion of migration in the preindependence period, distance also represents one of the major costs of migration, if only in the form of the cost of travel; following this line of reasoning, as distance increases, rates of migration should decrease. Thus, distance operates both to encourage and to discourage migration, and so we can hypothesize that there will be no significant relationship between the distance of rural districts from town and changes in population.

Indirect Measures of Prosperity: To explore further the relationship between rural well-being and migration, we can take note of other characteristics of the migrants' areas of origin. We can measure the income opportunities in the rural districts in terms of the number of persons working for cash, and we can measure the degree to which persons in the rural areas report seeking employment.[14] Our expectation is that there will be a significant positive relationship between the first variable and changes in district population, while the second variable should bear a significant negative relationship with changes in population. Last, as an index of rural prosperity, we will measure the transformation of rural houses from pole and dagga (i.e., mud and stick) to brick construction; the replacement of pole and dagga with brick has long been recognized as a concomitant of increasing prosperity in rural Zambia; thus, there should be a significant positive relationship between the amount of brick construction and changes in population due to migration.

THE PUBLIC SECTOR

The measures of rural well-being described thus far pertain to private economic activity. As measures of the degree of public investment in the countryside, we can measure the total level of public capital spending in the various rural districts. Also, we will specifically measure the level of public capital spending for the most relevant aspect of rural economic life, agricultural production. It is our expectation that there will be significant positive relationships between these measures of public spending and changes in district-level population.

Table 8.7   Variable Listing

Measure	Source
Dependent variable	
Percent population change due to migration, 1963–69	(1)
Explanatory variables	
Demographic	
Percent population aged 10–14, 1963[a]	(2)
Male/female ratio, 1963[b]	(2)
Percent population with some education, 1963	(2)
Rural prosperity	
Per capita number of cattle, 1963	(3)
Per capita number of plows, 1963	(3)
Distance to nearest town[c]	(4)
Percent persons working for cash, 1963	(2)
Percent persons seeking work, 1963	(2)
Governmental expenditure	
Total per capita capital expenditure, 1963–68	(5)
Total per capita capital expenditure on agriculture, 1963–68	(5)

Sources: (1) Jackman, *Recent Population Movements.* (2) Republic of Zambia, *Final Report of the May/June 1963 Census of Africans* (Lusaka: Central Statistical Office, January 1968). (3) Northern Rhodesia, Department of African Affairs, *Annual Report for the Year 1963.* (4) Republic of Zambia, Ministry of Power, Transport, and Works, *Road Mileage Map of Zambia* (Lusaka: Roads Department, January 1969). (5) Northern Rhodesia, *Estimates of Expenditure (Including the Capital Fund) for the Year[s]1st July 1963 to 30th June 1965* (Lusaka: Government Printer, 1963–1965); and Republic of Zambia, *Estimates of Revenue and Expenditure (Including the Capital Fund and Constitutional and Statutory Expenditure) for the [Appropriate Years]* (Lusaka: Government Printer, 1965–68).

a. This is the cohort of persons who would enter the labor market during the intercensal period; in Zambia, "working age" is considered by public sources to be fifteen years and over.

b. This measure is used instead of percent males as the sex ratio is a classic variable in central African demography, especially in the study of urban migration.

c. To measure the distance to the nearest town, I measured the shortest route between the *boma* of the district and the nearest major urban center on the line of rail. In so doing, I assumed that persons travel by road and not by overland routes, even though the latter may be shorter.

Table 8.7 lists all these measures and notes the sources from which they were taken. Measures for the first two groups of explanatory variables were taken in 1963, so that the conditions in the rural areas in 1963 could be related to changes in population in the subsequent intercensal period (1963–69). In the case of government expenditures, I have had to total the investments over the years 1963 to 1968. Significant investments in the rural areas commenced only at independence; in order to gain enough observations to make possible statistical analysis, I therefore had to use expenditures over several budgetary years.[15] The difficulty with this procedure is that, since we measure public investments and migration over nearly identical time periods, if we do find a positive relationship between the two, the relationship could plausibly be interpreted as reflecting the tendency of the government to invest funds in areas into which people are moving.

This problem of interpretation would indeed be a significant one were we to include urban districts in this analysis; then we certainly could not rule out the possibility, for example, that increased public investments resulted from the flow of persons to town. But we are working with the rural districts, where in every case there is a loss of population due to migration.[16] It therefore makes little sense to interpret a positive relationship between migration and public expenditure as demonstrating the tendency of the government to respond to increases in population. Rather, it would seem more plausible to interpret the positive coefficient as revealing the capacity of public investment to retard losses of population. The nature of the sample therefore reduces the ambiguities created by measuring the dependent and independent variables over roughly similar time spans.

Table 8.8 presents the results of the analysis. Under the heading Equation 1 are the partial regression coefficients and significance tests for each of the variables. Because of intercorrelation among the explanatory variables (see table 8.9) there is a downward bias in the t-statistic; under Equation 2, therefore, are listed the partial coefficients and t-statistics for each of the variables for which the t-statistic in equation 1 was 1.000 or more.[17]

Equation 1 lends support to our hypotheses. In the case of nine of the eleven variables, the signs of the coefficients are in the predicted direction. In the case of six of the eleven variables, the t-statistic of the coefficients is 1.000 or more, suggesting significant relationships between the explanatory variables and changes in population. In the case of distance, we made no prediction regarding the sign of the coefficient; and its lack of significance is a predicted result.

Equation 2 has several interesting properties. First, each of the variables is of the predicted sign and all but one are significant. Second, the R^2 of the equation suggests that the variables account for nearly two-thirds of the variance of the changes in district-level populations over the intercensal period (1963–69).

The coefficients of the several variables are highly suggestive. For example, the coefficient of the education variable suggests that if in 1963 the proportion of a given district's population that had some education was 10 percent higher than that of another, it subsequently declined nearly 7 percent in population over the period 1963–69, other things being

Table 8.8 Estimation Equations for Changes in District Population Due to Migration, 1963–69

	Equation 1		Equation 2	
Variable	Coefficient	t-statistic*	Coefficient	t-statistic*
1. Percent schooled, 1963	−0.5130	−2.043	− 0.6613	−3.625
2. Male/female ratio, 1963	−22.91	−1.262	−33.57	−1.769
3. Cattle per capita, 1963	12.85	2.241	10.55	4.298
4. Brick rooms per capita, 1963	17.93	1.642	16.95	2.036
5. Percent employed for cash, 1963	0.3575	1.612	0.4888	1.747
6. Per capita government capital expenditure on agriculture, 1963–68	5.367	1.134	0.8333	0.5234
7. Total per capita government capital expenditure, 1963–68	−2.151	−0.9549		
8. Percent seeking work, 1963	−0.5122	−0.9497		
9. Distance to town, 1963	0.0109	0.9523		
10. Percent population aged 10–14, 1963	−0.5370	−0.5147		
11. Plows per capita, 1963	−57.24	−0.6833		
Constant	19.88		27.06	
R^2	0.7057		0.6464	
F	3.487 (sig. = 0.025)		6.398 (sig = 0.01)	

*t-statistics above 1.703 are significant at the 0.05 level, those above 2.479, at the 0.01 level, one-tailed test.

Table 8.9   Correlation Matrix for Explanatory Variables

	1	2	3	4	5	6	7	8	9	10	11
1	1.0000	.4643	.4618	.2393	.2151	−.0993	.0567	−.1705	−.2931	.3359	.5334
2		1.0000	.1693	.3129	.5207	−.1853	−.0367	−.3840	−.5307	.3176	.2109
3			1.0000	−.3395	.4462	.1359	.0598	−.1252	−.3609	−.3038	.8901
4				1.0000	−.2505	−.1836	−.0211	−.1400	−.2314	−.1697	−.1747
5					1.0000	−.0304	−.1210	−.2843	−.4314	−.2162	.4357
6						1.0000	.8764	−.1160	−.1343	−.0010	.2476
7							1.0000	−.1243	−.0695	.1161	.1854
8								1.0000	.6085	−.1103	−.2679
9									1.0000	.1581	−.4210
10										1.0000	.3359
11											1.0000

Note: Numbers correspond to variables listed in table 8.8.

equal. Because the sex composition variable is a ratio, it is more difficult to interpret in this manner. Nonetheless, its coefficient does suggest that, as has historically been true in Zambia, migration from the rural districts in the postindependence period was principally an exodus of men to town. As shown by the negative sign of the coefficient, a higher ratio of males to females in a rural district in 1963 led to greater levels of out-migration, other things being equal.[18]

The coefficients for the remainder of the variables, all positive in sign, underline the finding that the greater the prosperity in the rural districts of Zambia the lower the subsequent losses of population. Thus, the coefficient to the employment variable suggests that, even with fewer than 20 percent of the jobs located in the rural areas, those few employment opportunities nonetheless produced significant decreases in the rates of out-migration. Because the number of brick rooms per capita is an indirect measure of prosperity, it is a little more difficult to interpret. Nonetheless, its sign and significance are such as to support the contention that the higher the level of rural prosperity, the lower the level of out-migration. The coefficient for the number of cattle per capita strongly underlines the contention that rural prosperity, especially as based upon the use of cattle, serves to reduce the exodus of the population to town. In support of our interpretation of the role of cattle in reducing out-migration, we can note the relationship of this variable to two other variables: the number of plows per capita and the percent of males deriving incomes from agriculture in the districts in 1963. There is a highly significant relationship between the number of cattle per capita and the per capita number of plows ($r = 0.890$, $t = 9.959$, $df = 26$), and a significant relationship in turn between the number of plows per capita and the percent of males deriving incomes from agriculture ($r = 0.333$, $t = 1.799$, $df = 26$). Decreases in the rate of out-migration in rural districts result both directly from cattle and from the indirect effect of cattle on agricultural employment. The structure of the relationships appears to be as shown in figure 8.1.[19] This structure suggests that, as I have contended, cattle underpin productive farming, with the result that districts with more cattle are better able to retain their populations. The failure of government expenditures on agriculture to increase significantly the level of prosperity in the rural districts of Zambia, discussed in the last chapter, is further underscored by the small and insignificant coefficient for the sixth variable in the equation.[20]

The Character of Migration

As in much of Africa, migration in Zambia during the colonial period

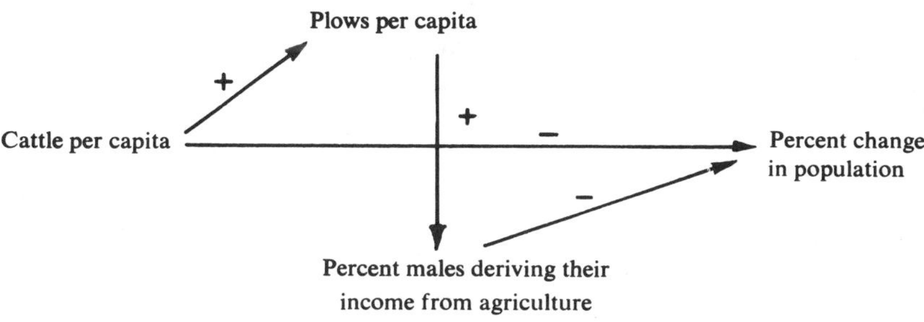

Fig. 8.1

Cattle, Farming, and Migration

was characterized by high family separation, high labor turnover, and close economic and social ties between urbanites and villagers. In this section, we will try to determine the degree to which the character of migration has changed; and, insofar as changes have taken place, we will try to determine if our notion of the migration decision is robust enough to account for them.

Family Separation and Turnover

To a great degree, family separation on the part of urban migrants is a thing of the past in Zambia. In a randomly drawn sample of Rokana mine township and shantytown dwellers I surveyed as part of this study, 478 of the 518, or 93.2 percent, were married with their wives in town; only 21 had never been married, the remainder being widowed or divorced. This predominance of married workers with their wives in town in the present Rokana labor force contrasts strongly with the 46.1 percent who were married with their wives in town in 1947.

Paralleling the decline in family separation is the decline in turnover. While there was a turnover rate of 68.8 percent of the Rokana labor force in 1950, this figure had declined to 8.4 percent in 1965. At least in the mines, high labor turnover, like family separation, appears to have declined with time; and while comparable material on other working populations is not available, no commentary has come to light to suggest that similar trends do not exist elsewhere.[21]

I have argued earlier in this book that family separation and high turnover would be chosen when a worker sought to maximize his income while maintaining contact with his family under conditions where rural-urban income differentials were low. Changes in the rates of family separation and labor force turnover should therefore be responsive to changes in earnings differentials. While data do not exist that would allow us to evaluate this hypothesis directly, it is possible to test a highly imperfect variant of it. Thus, we can relate changes in labor turnover to changes in wage levels for the African employees of the mines (see table 8.10). The results of the time series supports our analysis, for rises in average earnings bear a significant relationship to reductions in turnover.

Also supporting our interpretation is the historical background of the policy of the mines toward the stabilization of African labor. In the early 1950s, the price of African labor rose rapidly on the mines. The main reason for this was the formation of the African Mineworkers' Union. In its very first wage claim, the union demanded 125 shillings per month as a starting wage rate on the mines; the existing rate was 45 shillings, and

Table 8.10   Time Series, Average Earnings and Turnover,
African Mines Labor Force

Year	*Average Annual Turnover* *(in percentages)* Y	*Average Annual Earnings* *(in kwacha)* X
1950	68.8%	K122
1951	70.5	156
1952	60.1	172
1953	52.0	248
1954	47.6	246
1956	27.6	318
1957	33.4	354
1958	42.7	386
1959	27.9	434
1960	30.2	514
1961	22.8	516
1962	17.7	490
1963	9.3	558
1964	8.3	648
1965	8.4%	K718

Sources: Turnover figures: File 5B, African Strength, Year Book Statistics, Copper Industry Service Bureau; and Company Submission, Brown Commission of Inquiry, app. 7. Earnings figures: Republic of Zambia, *Report of the Commission of Inquiry into the Mining Industry, 1966*, p. 159.

Notes:

$Y = 77.64 - 0.1084X$ (-10.00 t-statistic significant at 0.01 level)

$R^2 = 0.8849$ $F = 111.01$, significant at 0.01 level

D.W. $= 1.447$

The figures for 1955 have been eliminated, as the whole labor force of the mines was fired and then rehired in that year in an attempt to break a strike. This resulted in a turnover figure in excess of 100 percent.

the companies were prepared to offer but 60 shillings. No agreement was reached, and, after a massive strike in 1952, an arbitration tribunal settled on 80 shillings.[22] The costs of African labor thus rose dramatically, creating a strong incentive for management to make labor more efficient.

As a step toward recovering the increased costs of labor through increased productivity, the companies sought to reduce the level of turnover in the African labor force. In the words of one of the industry's spokesmen, they sought to promote "long-term employment in industry" on the assumption that reduced turnover "ma[de] for efficiency."[23] The mining companies therefore increased the availability of married housing and encouraged men to bring their families from the villages.[24] Wage increases and reduced turnover have thus gone together in the mines.

Where differences between urban and rural earnings were low, a worker could best maintain contact with his family while maximizing his income by leaving his family in the village and spending about half of his time in each place. Given a high enough differential between urban and rural earnings, the gains to be made by working twelve instead of six months per year at urban labor could offset the loss in rural production incurred by moving his family off the land and the costs of moving it to town. The massive increases in urban wages in the 1950s therefore apparently reduced the necessity for the painful compromise between the objectives of family maintenance and income maximization that had prevailed in earlier periods. The incentive for family separation declined, and with it the rate of turnover.

Social Ties and Resource Flows

Changes also appear to have occurred in the pattern of social and economic ties between villagers and urban dwellers. In particular, the volume of resource flows from the towns to the villages appears to have declined in the postindependence period.

One might expect that simply because families are less frequently separated than they were, say, in the 1930s or 1940s, social linkages

Table 8.11   Mine Township and Shantytown Dwellers Near Rokana Corporation: Most Recent Exchange of Visits with Village

	Last Visit Made to Village	*Last Visitor Received from Village*
Mean	1967. 3	1969. 7
Standard deviation	5.5 years	4.5 years
Mode	1970 (160 cases)	1970 (210 cases)
	N = 518	N = 518

Note: Interviews were conducted in September–October 1971.

Table 8.12   Mine Township and Shantytown Dwellers Near Rokana
Corporation: Most Recent Exchange of News with Village

	News Sent to Village		*News Received from Village*	
	No.	*%*	*No.*	*%*
Never	27	5.2	19	3.7
1971	380	73.4	423	81.7
1970	57	11.0	7	1.4
1969	9	1.7	9	1.7
Prior to 1969	20	3.9	22	4.3
Don't know/does not apply	25	4.8	38	7.4
	518	100.0	518	100.2

Note: Interviews were conducted in September–October 1971.

between town and country would have reduced in number and intensity. As table 8.11 and 8.12 suggest, however, social intercourse between town and village appears to be common, with urban migrants freely exchanging visits and news with their village kin. The frequency of visitation reported in the 1971 Rokana sample in fact bears a striking similarity to that recorded in the sample of Broken Hill residents studied by Godfrey Wilson in 1940. The Rokana residents averaged 3.6 visits home every ten years, while the Broken Hill residents averaged 3 visits home per ten-year period.[25]

Some things have altered, however, the pattern of resource flows being perhaps the most striking among them. Studies of migrants in the colonial period emphasized the contributions of town residents to village kin, especially in terms of personnel and finances. Our data suggest that, at the individual level, these flows have declined.

Given the reduced frequency of family separation, migrants clearly maintain fewer family members in productive undertakings in the village,[26] and, given the concomitant decline in labor turnover, there is a further reduction in the supply of urban manpower to the village economies. Figure 8.2, which can be contrasted to figure 3.4, reveals also that the few who do depart from wage employment on the mines tend no longer to time their departures with the periods of peak labor demand in the villages.

While the changing value of money makes it difficult to compare the level of financial transfers across time, we can nonetheless compare the proportion of earnings transferred by members of our Rokana sample with the proportion remitted by Wilson's sample of residents in Broken Hill. Wilson found that urban workers gave 10.5 percent of their earnings to rural relatives; the figure was 8.7 percent for the married men with wives in town.[27] The Rokana respondents claim to have sent an average of K48 to their rural relatives in the last year, which represents 4.9 percent

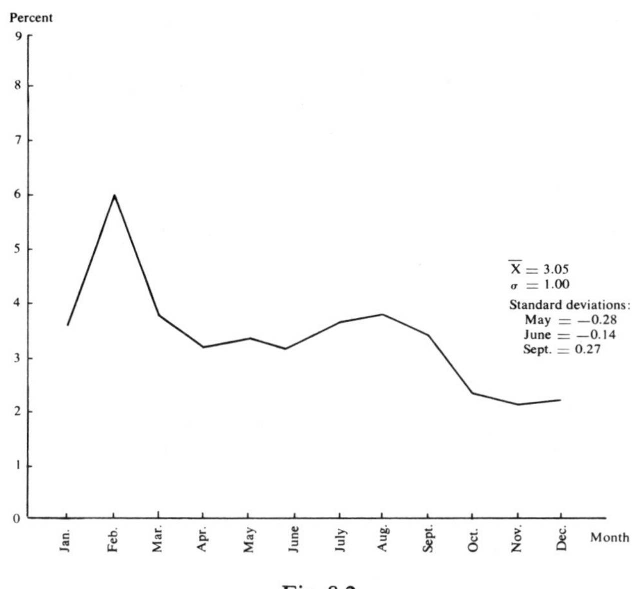

Fig. 8.2

Monthly Turnover, African Labor, Rokana Corporation, 1970
Source: Rokana Corporation, Manpower Services Department, Monthly Reports.

of their average annual earnings; as over 90 percent of the respondents had their wives in town, this figure (4.9%) can best be compared with the 8.7 percent reported by Wilson. Because the data are reported remittances and the prevailing norms favor supporting rural kin, our figures probably overestimate the quantity of money transfers. Reports from the last published urban budget survey in Zambia suggest, however, that a figure of around 4.0 percent is the right order of magnitude.[28]

In my discussion of preindependence Zambia, I interpreted the private transfer of resources to the village areas as attempts by urban residents to secure high future real incomes when they could no longer hold jobs in town. Once jobs were no longer held, there were few other opportunities for wealth in the urban areas. And because gardening in the peri-urban areas was illegal[29] and houses had to be rented, expenses, if only for food and shelter, remained high. High real income during retirement could thus best be realized in the villages, and urban dwellers therefore surrendered a portion of their earnings to the rural areas to preserve claims to land as a way of facilitating their retirement to the countryside. If this interpretation is correct, then, given the apparent decline in resource transfers from the cities by migrants, we should expect to find changes in the potentialities for retirement—changes which rendered a rural retirement less attractive an alternative and which could therefore account for these data. My sample was drawn from the copperbelt, and it is therefore instructive to concentrate on the urban environment of that area.

CHANGES IN THE INCENTIVE FOR RURAL RETIREMENT: GENERAL EVIDENCE

Perhaps one of the most visible changes in postindependence Zambia is in the pattern of urban land use. Over the last several years, people have "invaded" the peri-urban areas on the copperbelt and transformed them in attempts to make a living.

One example is the growth of farming. Farming had not developed on the copperbelt during the colonial period. Political pressure from established producers in Southern Province, George Kay suggests, curtailed the development of European farms in the copperbelt. And as the area was "Crown Land" and therefore leased only to those with large amounts of capital, there were "no real attempts to encourage African farming" in the area.[30] On the contrary, Africans were often forbidden to engage in agriculture near the towns. During the colonial era the police frustrated attempts by Africans to establish peri-urban gardens, treating them as violations of the regulations governing local land use.

As a result of the lack of agricultural development around the copperbelt and the large demand for food by the urban population, "it should [have been] possible and profitable to establish . . . farm units" at the time of independence.[31] And with the transfer of power to the new African government, which was neither beholden to the established European farmers nor willing to enforce the unpopular land-use regulations, Africans came forward to take advantage of the locational advantages for farming. Local workers, organized as cooperatives; retiring miners, operating as individual entrepreneurs; and the wives of workers, attempting to supplement their incomes, all encroached upon the unused lands of the peri-urban areas and set themselves up in farming.[32] Of the few cooperative farms that have succeeded in postindependence Zambia, several are located in the copperbelt.[33] As President Kaunda summed up the nature and significance of the growth of farming in the peri-urban areas:

> There is a tendency to think that the Copperbelt Province is an employee oriented community, that everybody thinks the only way to make a living is to be employed by someone. The increase in the number of small farms and co-operatives shows the advent of a new image. It is an indication of the importance of self-employment as an alternative especially today when industrial jobs tend to be uncertain.[34]

The forests of the area were another underexploited resource. The colonial government had tightly restricted cutting so as to maintain timber reserves for the mines and building trades. With independence the government altered its policy toward the peri-urban forests. Planting new stands so as to replenish the natural reserves, the government allowed higher rates of cutting in existing forests. Many of those who came forward to take advantage of this change in policy sought timber for manufacturing charcoal. The vast majority of the Africans in the city both cook and warm their houses with charcoal; and with the growth of the urban population the demand for charcoal increased dramatically.[35] Either holding licenses from the government, or encroaching illegally upon the forest reserves, the charcoal burners cut trees, fired them, and marketed the finished product in the urban townships. With the changes in policy after independence, and with the growth of the urban population, there thus arose another new opportunity for earning incomes outside of wage employment in the copperbelt area.[36]

With independence, it thus became easier for persons to continue to earn incomes in town after leaving wage employment.[37] It also became less expensive to maintain an urban residence. One of the major costs of remaining in town had been the cost of food; the relaxation of prohibitions on peri-urban agriculture has diminished the necessity for food purchases. Another major cost had been housing; because "unauthorized" houses were liable to be destroyed by the colonial government, the urbanites were compelled to rent houses in the townships, and, upon leaving wage employment, what savings they may have accumulated would have been consumed rapidly by rental payments unless they returned to the villages. In the postindependence period, however, another alternative became available: that of constructing a home in a "shanty" or "squatter" compound.

As any visitor to Zambia over the last several years would surely have noticed, shantytowns have burgeoned around the major urban centers. A study of housing in Lusaka reveals the rapid growth of squatter communities (see table 8.13). One of the major squatter settlements in Lusaka, Kapwepwe compound, was first settled in 1964; by January of 1969, it had

Table 8.13   Resident Population of Lusaka and Environs

	1963	1967
Within city boundaries	16,106	25,806
Peri-urban areas	2,701	27,500
Total	18,807	53,306

Source: Collins, "Urban Housing Policies in Zambia," p. 104.

12,000 residents. Another, Nguluwe compound, was begun in 1966; by February of 1967 over 2,500 people lived in it.[38]

Studies of the squatter townships reveal several things of significance to this analysis. Contrary to popular belief in Zambia, a high percentage of the residents are not unemployed. For example, in Zambia City, a shanty-town on the copperbelt, 71 of the 110 persons surveyed by the Department of Community Development in 1966 were self-employed, most of them being either charcoal burners or farmers who sold their produce in the local urban markets.[39] Moreover, most of the residents, rather than being new arrivals from the rural areas—as most impressionistic commentaries would have it—were in fact longtime city dwellers.[40] Studies of their reasons for moving from the urban townships to the shantytowns reveal motivations that are highly suggestive for our analysis; the residents of Zambia City came to the squatter township for the reasons reported in table 8.14. Finally, the age distribution of the shantytown dwellers tends to be skewed to the older age levels by comparison with those who live in the municipal compounds.[41] One study of change over time reveals that the percentage of total residents comprised by adults over 45 increased from 11 to 25 percent over the period 1963 to 1966, thus suggesting a higher rate of entrance into the squatter compounds by older people than by youths.[42]

These data suggest that persons who leave wage labor in postindependence Zambia tend to remain in town and procure housing in the areas where they need not purchase it. These options did not exist in urban Zambia in the preindependence period to the degree that they exist today. Given the increased opportunity for money from nonwage sources and the greater availability of cheap food and housing in the urban areas, it is reasonable to expect contemporary migrants to find retirement in town a more attractive alternative than did their predecessors. They would there-fore have less incentive to transfer resources to the countryside. And we can thus understand the apparent decline in the contribution of urban residents to the village economies.

CHANGES IN THE INCENTIVE FOR RURAL RETIREMENT: SPECIFIC EVIDENCE
To explore this argument more closely, I conducted a survey of urban

Table 8.14   Reasons for Coming to Zambia City

	No.	%
There is money	46	41.8
Can have houses	47	42.7
Good place to retire/no relatives at home/close to town	17	15.5
	110	100.0

Source: Department of Community Development, Research Unit, *The People of "Zambia City,"* pp. 16–17.

Table 8.15   How Much Thought Have You Given to Retirement?

	No.	%
A lot	250	59.1
A little	53	12.5
Not much at all	115	27.2
No answer	5	1.2
	423	100.0

Source: Rokana sample survey.

Table 8.16   Where Do You Plan to Retire?

	No.	%
In village	370	87.5
In town	36	8.5
In town or village	9	2.1
Don't know	8	1.9
	423	100.0

Source: Rokana sample survey.

dwellers in Kitwe. A systematic random sample was drawn from a list of employees of Rokana Corporation, one of the major mining companies in Zambia, and a random areal sample was drawn from a housing map of the shantytowns adjacent to the mine townships. I have already made use of these data in examining the rates of family separation. These samples also allowed me to investigate the retirement decision more closely and to explore its relationship to the transfer of resources from town to village.

The responses of the Rokana miners when asked how much thought they gave to retirement indicate that retirement is an important consideration for them (see table 8.15). When asked where they plan to retire, the vast majority—nearly 90 percent—replied that they planned to retire to the village (table 8.16). Nearly 90 percent indicated that they had land in the village which would be available to them upon retirement; over 90 percent also indicated that they had relatives who would welcome them upon their return to the village. On the verbal level, therefore, the mine township dwellers conform to the patterns of their preindependence brethren.

When their actual conduct is examined, however, it appears to be at variance with their verbal protestations. I was able to obtain the current addresses of a systematic random sample ($N = 138$) of persons who had left the employ of Rokana Corporation during the period 1966–71. As the addresses were used to mail pension checks,[43] and as the recipients had to present personal identification to claim the checks, it is likely that the addresses were valid indications of actual residential locations. Furthermore, the changes made on the address lists suggest that the former employees made strong efforts to keep them as up to date as possible with

the obvious goal in mind of receiving their pension money. An analysis of
these addresses indicates that 60 percent of the persons leaving employment with the mines over the period 1966–71 were, as of 1971, in town. An
analysis of the change in addresses shows that upon leaving employment
85 of the 138 (62 percent) in fact went back to the rural areas, but that 30
of these persons subsequently returned to town. Not one of the 53 persons
who initially chose to remain in town upon leaving the mines subsequently
moved to the rural areas.[44]

In order to examine the reasons for staying in town instead of returning
to the villages, I surveyed the residents of the shantytowns in the vicinity
of Rokana.[45] The current addresses of the sample of former Rokana
employees strongly suggested that many of them had taken up residence in
these shantytowns, and in fact virtually all the sample of shantytown
dwellers interviewed had previously worked for the mining company.
When asked straight out why they chose to remain in the city rather than
retire to the rural areas, the shantytown residents replied as in table 8.17.

Economic reasons constitute the modal reply to the question. The
importance of economic factors is underlined by data on the employment
status of the shantytown dwellers. The vast majority had urban sources of
income. By far the greatest number (31) were charcoal burners; next came
those who farmed and sold their produce in the urban townships (24 in
number); 14 others were self-employed as herbalists, beer brewers, tailors,
and auto and bicycle repairmen; 17 held jobs.

Table 8.17   Why Did You Remain in Town Instead of Returning to Village?

	No.	%
Economic reasons		
Work available in town	29	30.9
Money in town/none in village	5	5.3
Business in town	6	6.4
Village work too hard	2	2.1
Do not yet have enough money to return to village	5	5.3
Subtotal	47	50.0
Social/cultural reasons		
No relatives in village/all in town	12	12.8
Children in town	5	5.3
Town life better for children	1	1.1
Used to town life	14	14.9
Born in town	3	3.2
Subtotal	35	37.3
Other reasons*	12	12.8
Total	94	100.1

Source: Survey of shantytown dwellers near Rokana.

*I am ill; people in the village do not like me; I have not yet decided to leave the town;
etc.

Table 8.18   Comparative Responses of Shantytown and
Mine Township Residents

	Shantytown Dwellers		*Mine Township Residents*	
Do you have land you can return to in a village?				
	No.	*%*	*No.*	*%*
Yes	64	67.4	380	89.8
No	30	31.6	37	8.7
No answer	1	1.1	6	1.4
Total	95	100.1	423	99.9
Do you have relatives in a village who would welcome you if you returned?				
	No.	*%*	*No.*	*%*
Yes	60	63.2	394	93.1
No	34	35.8	27	6.4
No answer	1	1.1	2	0.5
Total	95	100.1	423	100.0

In interpreting the modal social and cultural responses reported in table
8.18, let us first compare the responses of the shantytown dwellers with
those of the mine employees to several other questionnaire items (table
8.19). In comparing their replies, we should bear in mind that the majority
of the shantytown dwellers have already chosen to maintain an urban
address upon leaving paid employment while the vast majority of the
mineworkers would choose, they state, to return to the village.

During the survey, I asked the shantytown dwellers and the mine
workers whether they had land in the villages and kin who would receive
them upon their return to the rural areas. Access to land is, of course,
mediated to a high degree by family membership; and so it is not surprising
that the shantytown dwellers, who less frequently claim rural relations,
would less frequently claim access to land as well (table 8.18). This pattern
can be interpreted in several ways, and the data do not let us unambigu-

Table 8.19   Indices of Social Ties with Village

	Shantytown Dwellers		*Mine Township Residents*	
Do you ever send news to friends or relatives in the village?				
	No.	*%*	*No.*	*%*
Yes	44	46.3	296	70.0
No	51	53.7	125	29.6
No answer	0	0.0	2	0.4
Total	95	100.0	423	100.0
Last year you heard news from the village:				
Mean response	1963		1968	
Last year you visited your village:				
Mean response	1962		1968	
Last year person from village visited you:				
Mean response	1967		1970	

Table 8.20   Indices of Resource Transfers

| | *Shantytown Dwellers* | | *Mine Township Residents* | |

Have you or have you not ever helped a friend or relative from the village?

	No.	*%*	*No.*	*%*
Yes	32	33.7	335	79.2
No	63	66.3	84	19.9
No answer	0	0.0	4	0.9
Total	95	100.0	423	100.0

Have you ... ever brought a child in from the village for schooling?

	No.	*%*	*No.*	*%*
Yes	29	30.5	206	48.1
No	66	69.5	214	50.6
No answer	0	0.0	3	0.6
Total	95	100.0	423	99.9

Have you ... ever provided school fees for a child in the village?

	No.	*%*	*No.*	*%*
Yes	35	36.8	281	66.4
No	60	63.2	139	32.9
No answer	0	0.0	3	0.6
Total	95	100.0	423	99.9

Have you ... ever sent money to persons in the village?

	No.	*%*	*No.*	*%*
Yes	43	45.3	353	83.5
No	52	54.7	67	15.8
No answer	0	0.0	3	0.7
Total	95	100.0	423	100.0

ously choose among these interpretations. It is, however, compatible with an interpretation based upon our understanding of the decisional behavior of migrants. The shantytown dwellers, who already have decided to remain in town, may lack relatives in the village because they lack the incentive to cultivate ties with rural kin, much less to transfer resources to them. It seems implausible to contend that biologically they lack the same number of kin as the employed mineworkers; but, sociologically, it is plausible that they could have let family bonds atrophy through neglect.[46] Having chosen an urban residence and forsaken a rural retirement—something the employees of the mines have not (yet) done—the shantytown dwellers may have less incentive to foster their relationships with rural kin. The data in tables 8.19 and 8.20 illustrate this relative neglect.

In every case, the differences between the shantytown dwellers and mineworkers are significant at the 0.05 level or above.[47] Not seeking a rural retirement, the shantytown residents, it would appear, remit fewer resources to the rural areas and maintain fewer ties there; and as a result, it can be contended, fewer of them have access to land or to relatives who could help sponsor their reentry into the social and economic life of the village.

The character of urban migration thus appears to have changed in Zambia. Fewer people seem to be returning to the villages, and urban dwellers remit proportionately less to their rural kin.

In this chapter, we have thus explored the increase in value of the urban alternative with independence in Zambia and illustrated the consequences for the pattern and character of rural-urban migration.[48] The next chapter will examine more closely the role of migration in the social and economic life of a particular rural community.

9

Migration from Kasumpa Village

Massive numbers of villagers have sought to take advantage of the expanded opportunities for wealth in the central regions of Zambia and have moved to the line of rail. All that we have said so far has communicated a sense of the gross features of this migration. What we lack is a sense of the finer features of the phenomenon—a feeling of what it means to those who take part in it; of how the decision to migrate is arrived at; and of how migration fits into the social order of local village communities. These details can best be revealed by studying migration in a local setting; and, for this study, this means studying migration from Kasumpa village.

There can be no doubt but that the villagers of Kasumpa appraise the relative economic advantages of life in town and life in the rural areas and that they base migration decisions largely on a consideration of these relative advantages. Evidence for this is contained in my interviews of a sample of household heads in Kasumpa. In these interviews, I probed their perceptions of the advantages and disadvantages of life in the rural areas and towns. What was striking was the frequency with which they couched their responses in economic terms. For example, I asked the household heads whether or not they liked living in town; 26 percent said they did and 64 percent said they did not, with 10 percent offering no opinion. I then asked them why they felt that way; the distribution of replies is shown in table 9.1. All of those who liked the towns did so for economic reasons, and the most common reasons for disliking the towns also had to do with economic factors. The economic basis for appraisals is also disclosed in their evaluation of village life. For example, when I asked the heads of households what they liked most about living in the village, over half of the positive evaluations were based upon economic factors (see table 9.2). When they were asked what they disliked most about life in the village, again, well over half of the negative evaluations

Table 9.1   Why Do You Like (or Dislike) Living in Town?
Responses of Household Heads in Kasumpa Village

	No.	%
Like it because:		
Work, jobs, money available	27	25.7
Dislike it because:		
Like to live independently	4	3.8
Like rural areas	3	2.9
Too much violence/danger in town	3	2.9
Desire to keep family together/		
to support family in the village	8	7.6
Not original home	2	1.9
Too old to work in town	19	18.1
Work is hard to find in town	3	2.9
Life too expensive in town	24	22.9
Have work in rural areas	2	1.9
Don't know/been away too long:	10	9.5
Total	105	100.1

Table 9.2   What Do You Like Most about Living in the Village?
Responses of Household Heads, Kasumpa Village

	No.	%
Can live inexpensively/without		
spending money/with no job/		
even though too old to get a job	55	52.4
Have work here	2	1.9
Can live independently	10	9.5
Can keep the family together here	14	13.3
This is original home	15	14.3
Reputation is here	3	2.9
No one to help me in town	3	2.9
No response/don't know	3	2.9
Total	105	100.1

of the village were based on economic criteria—the absence of employment, the poverty, and the difficulty of work in the countryside (see table 9.3).

That it is the economic advantages of life in town that lead to urban migration is widely recognized in Kasumpa village. It will be recalled, for example, that the chairman of the failing Lukungwe cooperative society threatened to abandon the cooperative and leave for the copperbelt, as cooperative farming was unremunerative; the chairman clearly translated a consideration of relative economic advantage into a consideration of the migration alternative. Similarly, at a meeting I attended, the village headman declaimed: "Why is my village diminishing? Why are there some houses without people? Where are the people going? To the copper-

Table 9.3   What Do You Dislike Most about Living in the Village?
Responses of Household Heads, Kasumpa Village

	No.	*%*
Nothing	63	60.0
No work/money	24	22.9
Standard of living/poverty	5	4.8
Work is hard	2	1.9
Jealousy over money	5	4.8
Personal suffering	6	5.7
Total	105	100.1

belt. To the copperbelt. It is the young people who are to blame. They see here no developments, no chances for money. So they go out to get jobs; and then they call other people to follow them to the towns."[1]

There is also the testimony of the young men themselves—the ones who participate most actively in the flow to town. I held frequent conversations with the youths of Kasumpa village, and I found that their migration plans were firmly based upon their assessment of the relative economic opportunities in the town and the village. As recorded in my notes on one of these discussions with several young men of the village, one young man said:

"My parents have not enough money to feed themselves . . . and I know that my brothers in Ndola and Lusaka, who have jobs, can provide. . . . And so I am leaving. My parents consent to this."

[Another] said: "I see no profit here. The work is very hard. The people have a low standard of living. There is no industry to provide jobs and farming yields no profit."

His friends joined him at this point, saying that even his father's elder brother . . . who works hard as a farmer is still living poorly. "We would prefer to stay," they said, "but then, there is no money here."

There is also objective confirmation of the relationship between rural poverty and emigration. In interviews with the sampled heads of households over the period of my stay in Kasumpa, I carefully attempted to assess their level of cash earnings. Thus, for example, if the household head earned money by selling snuff, I calculated how much snuff he sold, the proceeds from the sales, and the costs that may have been incurred in making and marketing the product. If a respondent reported earning money by chopping and selling poles for roofing, I ascertained the number of trips he made in search of the materials; the number of poles he gathered in each trip; the price at which he sold them; and the costs he incurred, such as the cost of purchasing an ax, were it necessary, or of replacing

Table 9.4 Correlation between Levels of Migration and Average Annual
Cash Earnings from Households in Kasumpa

	Number of *Live Children* *in Town*	*Percent of* *Live Children* *in Town*
Correlation coefficient	–.1915	–.1671
Number of cases	91	91
Level of significance	.035	.057

the tubing on the bicycle used to transport the poles from the bush. On the basis of such calculations, I attempted to estimate the average annual cash earnings of each household head. I also attempted to measure the extent of migration from each household; I found the number of live children in the household who currently resided in town and the percentage of the live children which they represented. The correlations between my estimates of household income and these measures of migration (table 9.4) were such as to indicate that, the poorer the family, the greater the extent of migration from the village to the towns.[2]

Those Who Remain

Thus far I have interpreted migration from Kasumpa as a flight from relative rural poverty. What I want to emphasize at this point, however, is that the benefits from migration are not captured solely by those who move to the more prosperous areas. Migration is also a source of benefits for those who remain behind.

Illustrative of this is that the members of my sample of 105 household heads in Kasumpa reported receiving an average of K20.23 in financial remittances from their children in town during the previous year; not included in this total was the value of articles in kind, such as clothing and household goods. From their sib and the sib of their wives who were abroad in town, the heads of households also reported receiving, on average, an additional K9.40 in cash. Again, this figure does not include the value of gifts in kind and thus underestimates the level of payments received from urban sources.

There is some indication that the cash remittances from the town are used to substitute for cash earnings in the village. Thus, the correlation coefficient for the relationship between the level of remittances and the level of estimated annual cash earnings is -0.1366 (significant at the 0.10 level), indicating that, the poorer the family, the higher the level of remittances received from town. Thus, too, when we relate the average cash income of the households to the level of remittances expressed as a percent of that cash income, we derive a negative and significant correlation coefficient ($r = -0.2370$, $p < 0.012$). This suggests that remittances form a higher percentage of the income of the poor people than they do for the richer ones. In effect, the data suggest remittances from urban kin tend to substitute for locally generated cash.[3]

Cash is only one form of wealth in Kasumpa; there are also real goods and consumer durables, and these too form an important part of the wealth of the village dwellers. In assessing the well-being of the various households in the sample, I therefore attempted to assess their "real goods" holdings. To do so, I developed one index based upon the physical characteristics of their homes. Some contained armchairs with stuffed cushions, a table with a cloth on it, and photographs and calendars on the walls; some even had iron roofs and windows with glass in them. Counting the presence or absence of these characteristics allowed me to construct a measure of prosperity of the head of household which I label the household index. I formed a second index based upon the holdings of income-generating goods. These include bicycles, sewing machines, and grinding wheels. This index I refer to as an ownership score.

I have already noted that remittances from town appear to be used as a substitute for locally generated earnings and so contribute to the upgrading of cash incomes in the village. It also appears that these remittances are used to accumulate goods and so increase real standards of living. Thus, as seen in table 9.5, the correlation coefficients between the value of the remittances from children and sib and the household index are both positive in sign and significant at beyond the 0.01 level. The levels of significance for the correlations between the value of remittances and the ownership score are less impressive, but both are significant at the 0.05 level and both run in the right direction.[4]

The relationship between migration and the accumulation of real goods is underscored by the correlation coefficients in table 9.6, which indicate that, the greater the level of migration from a household, the greater the holdings of real goods (as measured by the household index).

Table 9.5   Correlation between Remittances and Indices of Well-Being

	Value of Remittances from Children	*Value of Remittances from Sib*
Household index		
Correlation coefficient	.2583	.3319
Number of cases	105	105
Level of significance	.004	.001
Ownership score		
Correlation coefficient	.1899	.1677
Number of cases	105	105
Level of significance	.026	.044

Table 9.6　Correlations between Levels of Migration and Household Index

	No. of Live Children	*No. of Live Children in Town*	*No. of Live Children Employed in Town*	*No. of Live Children in Town Remitting Gifts*	*Total Value of Gifts from Children in Town Last Year*
Correlation coefficient	.1119	.1605	.1869	.2011	.2553
Number of cases	105	105	105	105	105
Level of significance	.256	.102	.056	.040	.009

Thus it is clear that migration not only offers an escape from poverty for those who leave but also provides an opportunity for those who stay to increase their incomes. In this chapter, we will continue to concentrate on the fortunes of those who stay, and we will focus on the manner in which they seek private solutions to the problem of rural poverty by utilizing the urban market for labor.

A Human Investment Model

Anthropologists have adopted several major theoretical perspectives that are relevant to this analysis. The first is that, in studying economic relations in peasant societies, it is critical that the scholar view these relations within the context of the social institutions of these societies; for the economic and social relationships, they contend, are inseparable in peasant societies. As Marshall Sahlins states: "Something more is involved than the simple point that economics is functionally related to the social and political arrangements of tribal societies. Economics is not distinguishable from these arrangements. The economy is organized by just such generalized institutions as families and lineages—'embedded' in them."[5] In analyzing the attempts of Kasumpa villagers to secure higher incomes through the urban labor market, we should thus put the family system at the center of our analysis.

The anthropologists have two further points to make and these also influence my conceptualization of the role of the family. The first point is that the family is a dynamic phenomenon, the relationships among its components changing with time. Meyer Fortes, for example, argues that "the developmental factor is intrinsic to domestic organization"; he goes on to illuminate how the allocation of economic and social resources varies among family members—and in particular among generations—with time.[6] The second is that the family is a mutual support system and that, within the context of the family, those who possess resources can reasonably be expected to distribute them to those who do not. Putting the last two points together, the anthropologists obtain one of the classic notions of the family: the family as a system of social security.

This conception is so widespread, at least in the writings on Africa, that is difficult to cite any particularly striking statement of it. Rather, the notion can best be portrayed by describing the kind of family system that appears to underlie much of the literature. Within the family, there are two categories of persons who are being supported: the very young and the very old. Both live off the incomes of the working-age members. The incentive for those of working age to maintain dependents is the recollection that they too were once supported and cared for and that they too have a reasonable expectation of being supported in turn by their children. In Kasumpa village, this conception of the family is regarded as an ideal; this was the way families traditionally worked, the villagers insist, and if a man can manage his affairs competently and can act wisely he can forge this sort of family even today. A man who has achieved such a family is said to have created a family in which there is "good understanding" *(ukumfwana)*. The children feel loved and cared for; the elderly feel secure and wanted; and the man's prosperity and generosity have created an agency from which he too will derive security when his period of dependency arrives.

The lessons of the anthropologists are clear. In analyzing the way in which those who stay in Kasumpa seek to extract economic benefits from the urban market for labor, we should focus on the way the villagers utilize the family system. Also, they seem to admonish us, we should pay particular attention to the intergenerational flow of resources within the family. In so doing, we shall see how the villagers make payments to their children in expectation of future income from these children and thus engage in a form of human investment.[7]

We have already seen that older persons receive money from their children abroad. What is interesting is the degree to which the villagers are explicit about their expectations of support from their migrant children, and the clarity of their perception of their dependence upon it. Thus, when I asked one villager what, if anything, he disliked about life in the village, he replied: "Nothing, for my children support me in many of my problems. If I had no children in the copperbelt, I would suffer. There would be no money even to raise one acre of groundnuts." In response to a later question, he averred: "I cared for my children and now they care for me." Asked about visiting town, he replied with some pride: "I enjoy it, as my children are well employed there. So when I visit I get clothes." This man, like others in Kasumpa, clearly saw his children as an economic resource and perceived his dependence upon them.

To win financial support from the children requires a heavy cash expenditure, however, for several basic reasons. First, the parents seek to retain the affections of their children, and to do this they have to spend money on the possessions that will enable their children to lead an agreeable life in the village. There is a vigorous youth culture in Kasumpa village.[8] As the Kasumpa people state, the social habits of the towns have entered the rural areas; and these habits are expensive. Good clothes, radios and record players, cigarettes, playing cards, and bottled beer—all are material components of the life style of the young, and the youths can and do demand these things so that they can pursue their youthful pleasures. They demand bicycles so that they can visit and socialize after school. They want radios and phonographs. They want striking clothing so that they need not be ashamed in front of their peers and so that they can impress members of the opposite sex with their stylish appearance. They expect to receive pocket money so that they can join their friends at the local store or beer hall and buy drinks and gifts for their girl friends. Many expect their fathers to purchase a separate house for them which they then paint and decorate and occupy. There they can study their lessons, play cards, and entertain. They expect not to have to work in the gardens; after all, what with schooling and homework, they feel that serious inroads have already been made into their leisure time. What the young people expect is to receive an urban standard of living in the rural areas; and if their parents cannot provide it, then they may leave. Quoting once again from my discussions with some of the young men of Kasumpa:

> They all agreed that the thing they do most is to play: football, cards, talking, and looking for girls. They say that the only time they have to work is at plowing time, and then they work in the fields only for a little while. Essentially, though, they have few responsibilities upon them.
> One lad was city bound, and he had a few interesting things to say. He said that he had made overt conditions for staying with his parents. The main one was that his parents provide the things he needs. Most important was clothes. But he also needed money for entertainment, a bicycle, and a record player. But he saw that his parents did not have the money . . . to provide these things. . . . And so he is leaving.

The principal reason that the children are able to demand such a high level of support from their parents is that they represent future income for their parents. As we have seen, the parents place great value on the support they receive from the children once they have grown. Moreover, the children are in a relatively strong bargaining position, because, as members of an extended family, they can conceivably move out of the home of their parents and into the home of their parents' sib. What makes this important is that the extended families spill over from the impoverished rural areas into the relatively prosperous urban sector; many of the parents in Kasumpa have sons and daughters and sisters and brothers who are in town and who draw high incomes there. What the parents may be unwilling or unable to provide, therefore, others can. This serves as an incentive for the parents to spend money on their children, for should their children go elsewhere, then the parents may have lost their children and a major source of their future support. This support will tend to go to those who fulfill the needs of the child when he is a dependent.

Illustrative of this pattern was the life of one of my urban research assistants. A native of Northern Province, the young man now lived with his mother's brother in town. "At home," he told me, "there were no opportunities. I was failing school because I was ashamed for my clothing. The students were laughing at me, and the teachers were angry to find me looking dirty and having no good appearance." When his uncle visited his mother in the village, he was allowed to accompany his uncle to town. "He was good to me. He treated me as his own child and got me clothes and a bicycle. I was not ashamed to go for schooling." His uncle was often questioned, he reports, as to why he should support his sister's child; and his reply was "by supporting him, I am supporting myself. He is a likely one and will be educated and get a good job, and then he will remember our kindnesses. How then is what I am doing for him a loss to me?" The young man, while I knew him, used his pay to purchase a dress for his uncle's wife and shoes for his uncle's children; his parents were mentioned but not financially remembered.

Also pertinent is a conversation I had with an old man in the village who was quite influential in village affairs. He had a reputation for being stingy and inconsiderate of his family; he had married and divorced twice, the reason for both divorces being his unwillingness to share his money with his wife and children. His children had left him and entered the family of his wife's brother, in one case, and his wife's new husband in another. I asked the man about whether he now received support from his children in town, and he replied: "When my son came here, it was not a happy time. He just slept in the house. At light he was gone; mealtimes, he was elsewhere; only after darkness did he come back. We never talked of wise things; his talk was with others. When my son came, he brought me nothing. All the other people have sons who are sending them money. Mine came here and brought no gifts. He doesn't know me." The consensus of others in the village was that the man's stinginess had come back to haunt him. He now ekes out a living by sewing school uniforms. His house is dilapidated, without the appurtenances that grace many other houses in the village. His loss of remittances from grateful children has cost him the ease and prosperity that most men have come to expect in the later years of their lives.

A last illustration of the structure of this situation is the behavior of people who have laid out funds to support the children of others. There was, for example, a senior man in Kasumpa, whom we shall call Joel, who was accused of causing the death of his younger brother Robert through witchcraft. The basis for this accusation was that it was known that Robert had refused to give Joel an expensive and well-crafted rifle which had been sent back to the village by Robert's son, who was a well-paid and rather senior civil servant in one of the national bureaucracies. Joel felt entitled to the gun and had demanded it from Robert, for, as he argued at the time, he had paid for his nephew's education and it was because of this education that the young man was in a position to make such valuable presents. With the death of Robert, this argument became the basis for the accusation of witchcraft. In the minds of the Kasumpa villagers, it appeared credible that a man would murder—or at least be angry enough to cause a death—were he denied access to the earnings of a youth he had supported.

Working-age adults thus spend money on their children, expecting to secure financial returns from these expenditures; and, given the structure of the family and its distribution over areas of varying degrees of wealth, the adults must spend a fairly large amount in order to secure later financial returns. There is one more major reason why the adults make fairly high payments to the youths, and this too is consistent with the notion of investing through the family in other human beings. The reason, adumbrated in the last case described above, is that, since parents seek to gain returns from children by having them migrate to town and remit a portion of their earnings, the parents have an incentive to prepare the children for successful competition in the urban labor markets by trying to give them a proper education. Securing a sufficient education to guarantee remunerative employment can be an expensive enterprise. Not only are there the costs of school itself—at the primary level, amounting mainly to levies for the sports or agricultural clubs; at the secondary level, amounting in colonial times to significant tuition charges—but there are also the costs of uniforms and clothes. These are not trivial costs: clothing is an expensive item, and a uniform for a primary school child can easily cost five kwacha. When the family has several children, the cost of their school clothes becomes a significant item in the total family budget and a major financial undertaking for families whose total average cash earnings are in the neghborhood of K150 per year.[9] Educating children is thus expensive, but it is seen as a major factor influencing the success of the children in the urban labor market, and thus the villagers' ability to use the family to extract benefits from the urban sector. As a result, parents spend money to obtain education for their children.

What I have argued thus far is that Kasumpa villagers appear to have adapted the family to the process of labor migration, and to have done so by emphasizing its qualities as an instrument of human investment. In evaluating this interpretation of the migration behavior of the Kasumpa villagers, we can attempt an indirect test. If my analysis is correct, then as a corollary we should expect less support for migration where alternative forms of investment are available. Where adults can invest their money in things other than children and then draw on these accumulated stocks as a means of supporting themselves in old age, then we should expect lower rates of migration. In many areas of rural Zambia there is such an alternative kind of investment—investment in cattle. Thus we will examine once again the negative relationship between the level of stocks of cattle and the tendency toward out-migration that featured so prominently in the preceding chapter.

I have previously argued that investments in cattle play an important part in raising the profits of agriculture; and I have shown that the impact of cattle in reducing out-migration can in part be accounted for by the relationship between agricultural employment and cattle and plows—two measures of the extent of the commercialization of agricultural production. But it will also be recalled that there remained a relationship between cattle and migration that could not be accounted for by these intervening measures of agricultural commercialization (see fig. 8.1), and it is this remaining linkage that now captures our attention.

The literature on the cattle-holding areas of Zambia suggests that cattle do have a major economic role other than that of aiding farm profits; they serve as a store of value and as a means of gaining interest.[10] As Robin Fielder states, in his analysis of the role of cattle among the Ila of Namwala,

> Ila very often say, "Cattle are our bank." By this . . . they mean a deposit account where their property is saved and where it will increase in value the longer it stays there. Cattle are regarded very much as shares and investments are in capitalist societies. . . . There is no mystery about it at all: the investment is a very sound and highly rational one, and every Ila, educated or otherwise, is imbued with its sense from the time when he herds his father's cattle as a small boy.[11]

Fielder documents the value of cattle investments: "By natural increase alone, in the birth of calves, a man should get an average annual increase of 15 per cent. Add to this the increase in cash value of cattle which has risen 300–400 per cent . . . since 1950, and it will be seen that the cattle owner can expect a 25–30 per cent increase in the cash value of his original herd each year."[12] Then Fielder goes on to describe the uses made of this investment. The cattle are used to capitalize farming in areas where farming is profitable, he clearly reveals; moreover, they can serve as a source of funds to enter other cash-earning activities, such as transport and maize grinding. But cattle are also used in a nonmonetary way—to meet social obligations, such as by paying bride price, meeting funeral obligations, and compensating for social damages. While nonmonetary, Fielder stresses, such social payments are nonetheless economic, in the sense that they are made with the definite expectation of beneficial returns. Indeed, Fielder contends, they are made with the anticipation that these returns will come "increased in value."[13] These social payments can therefore be viewed as an investment; and a significant return on these social investments is kinship support in the senior years of the man's life. As Fielder states, "A man who pays debts and fines for his kin, and who performs other duties which may not involve cattle. . . . builds up what I call 'social credit'. He can hope to be rewarded later by succession to a title and property, and by help from his juniors in his old age."[14]

Evidence collected by Thayer Scudder from the Gwembe Tonga lends further support to this argument. When change in herd size is related to the age of the herd owner, Scudder's data show a tendency for younger men to accumulate cattle and for older men to reduce the size of their holdings; and over the lifetime of the men he has studied for nearly twenty years, Scudder finds them first increasing and then decreasing their holdings of cattle. Scudder's interview materials suggest that the older men deplete their stocks for consumption purposes. Thus, as one respondent told Scudder, when queried as to why he had slaughtered an oxen: "I killed my ox because I myself am grown up. I should eat my cattle before I die."[15]

Expenditures by young adults on cattle therefore serve as a means of securing later returns which will enhance their economic position in the senior years of their lives. As such, these expenditures may compete with those made to enhance the earning capacity of children in their urban marketplace; investments in cattle, in short, may compete with investments in human beings. This helps to explain the highly negative relationship between the per capita stock of cattle and the percent population change due to migration in the rural districts of Zambia, and it also lends credence to our interpretation of migration as a form of human investment among the rural dwellers of Luapula.[16]

The behavior of cattle holders thus gives indirect support for our inter-

Table 9.7 Estimation Equations for Human Investment Model

Dependent variable:	Equation 1 No. of Children in Town		Equation 2 No. of Children Employed in Town		Equation 3 No. of Children Making Remittances from Town		Equation 4 Value of Total Remittances from Town	
	Coefficient	t-statistic	Coefficient	t-statistic	Coefficient	t-statistic	Coefficient	t-statistic
Explanatory variable:								
1. Number of live children	0.3555	5.283[a]	0.2586	4.233[a]	0.1654	3.504[a]	3.228	2.509[a]
2. Children's average age	0.0584	4.317[a]	0.0573	4.666[a]	0.0394	4.155[a]	0.5753	2.225[b]
3. Children's average education	0.4926	1.763[b]	0.4196	1.654[c]	0.3097	1.580[c]	8.161	1.527[c]
4. Estimated annual income	−0.0018	−1.451[c]	−0.0012	−1.076[c]	−0.0014	−1.696[b]	−0.0282	−1.221[c]
Constant term	−2.423		−2.336		−1.529		−22.85	
R^2	0.3919		0.3346		0.2944		0.1685	
F	13.38, $p < .01$		10.44, $p < .01$		8.657, $p < .01$		4.206, $p < .01$	

a. *t*-statistics significant at 0.01 level, one-tailed test.
b. *t*-statistics significant at 0.05 level, one-tailed test.
c. *t*-statistics significant at 0.10 level.

pretation. Fortunately, we are also in a position to make a more direct test of it. If our interpretation is correct, we should be able to make certain predictions about differences in the ability of different kinds of village family units to derive economic benefits from the urban market for labor. The "developmental cycle" hypothesis of the anthropologists clearly suggests that those heads of households who should benefit the most are those whose families are the "most established," in the sense of having produced children and having reared them to an income-earning age. Thus, we should expect that, the greater the number of children and the higher the average age of the children, the greater the returns to the head of household from children in town. The "human investment" interpretation of the developmental cycle of families leads to two further predictions. It suggests that, insofar as education increases the value of persons in the labor market, the greater the effort that was made to educate the children, the greater will be the value of the remittances received from them. The interpretation also suggests that, insofar as past financial sacrifices were made to gain the ability to secure present incomes with less present sacrifice—that is, in effect, to secure an income during retirement—then, the higher the level of remittances from children in the city, the lower will be the level of present cash income secured by working in the village.

Using the data from my research in Kasumpa village, I can directly test the interpretation by testing these predictions. The results of these tests, shown in table 9.7, suggest at least partial support for my hypothesis. The signs of the coefficients for the variables are in the right direction, and the values of the *t*-statistics are above 1.000, most being significant at the conventionally adopted confidence levels (see also table 9.8).

Kasumpa, as we know, lies in the rural hinterland of the nation. Public policies have not led to a significant redistribution of wealth from the towns to the countryside. And so the people of Kasumpa have sought private solutions to the problem of relative rural poverty. They have done so by entering the private market for labor, and by using the most private of all mechanisms—the family—to organize this market and to divert resources from the city to the villages.[17]

Table 9.8 Correlation Coefficients among Explanatory Variables

	1	*2*	*3*	*4*
1	1.0000	−.3787	.4354	−.0234
2		1.0000	−.2527	−.1750
3			1.0000	.1494
4				1.0000

Note: Numbers correspond to variables listed in table 9.7.

10

Political Responses at the Local Level

Thus far we have concentrated on the way in which rural dwellers in postindependence Zambia have sought private solutions to the problem of relative rural poverty by using the markets for produce and labor to lay hold of the wealth of the cities. Nonetheless, like their colonial predecessors, rural dwellers have also engaged in collective action. They have done so in order to gain access to resources which, though generated by urban industry, are allocated not through markets in the countryside but rather by public authorities.

This chapter and the next focus on the politics of the rural areas, making use of two last idealized actors: the politician and the voter. Politicians, we assume, seek to gain and retain office and organize their behavior so as to attain that objective. The way politicians organize their behavior depends in part upon the institutional rules by which offices are assigned in the political system. In Zambia, during the period with which we are concerned, politicians gained office by winning the majority of votes cast in competitive elections. In such an institutional setting, we assume, politicians take stands on issues which they feel will gain them the support of a majority of the electorate and thereby fulfill their objective of winning posts in the political system.

We assume that voters have preferences and evaluate politicians in terms of them. A voter casts his vote for that politician whose stand on the issues corresponds most closely to his own most preferred position.[1] The behavior of the voters and competition among politicians in search of votes thus furnishes the means by which the political system serves the interests of the citizenry. These two chapters will analyze the way in which the villagers acting as citizens seek to manipulate the public authorities in Zambia so as to serve their interests in an enhanced rural well-being. The focus will be on the politics of the rural areas, the dominant forms of rural political behavior, and the impact of rural politics upon Zambia's political system.

Disillusionment with Government

A chief goal of the villagers who took part in the nationalist movement was the attainment of increased incomes. For some of those who were prominent in the nationalist movement, politics did pay off. Following independence the party sought to distribute jobs to those who had been active in the nationalist struggle, and the postindependence expansion of public services in the countryside provided opportunities for it to do so.[2] One constituency official from Kasumpa became an assistant district secretary in the new sub-*boma* which was opened in Mporokoso after independence;* a second now holds a similar job in the Kapalala sub-boma in Samfya. Two party officials nominated themselves for jobs in the marketing and mechanical services. A fifth took part in the virtual rape of the treasury of the Kawambwa Rural Council in which he served as a representative for Kasumpa and surrounding villages. As a rural councillor he joined his colleagues in voting an immediate pay raise for all members of the council right after independence,[3] purchasing "used" communal council property at cut rates,[4] accepting advances on his salary as a form of interest-free loan,[5] and pressuring the council staff to hire his relatives as council laborers.[6] So venal were he and his colleagues that in August of 1966 the government closed the Rural Council, purging it of its offending representatives and staff.

Other party officials did not leave the village for jobs that opened in the public sector after independence; rather, as we have seen earlier, they remained in the village as officers of the new cooperative societies and received literally thousands of kwacha in loans. While the cooperatives have failed to increase the incomes of the rank and file, they have nonetheless, at least in the case of Katofyio, benefited their officers; given that constituency officials hold the majority of the offices in the cooperatives, the result as shown in table 10.1 is the relative enrichment of the nationalist leaders. Analysis of variance reveals significant differences between the estimated annual incomes of the various categories, but the differences in the household indices are not significant.

The ability to gain wealth through politics is largely a thing of the past, however. The rapid postindependence expansion of governmental services in the rural areas is largely over, and the party rarely has an opportunity to

---

*A sub-*boma* is an administrative center which governs a portion of an administrative district. The assistant district secretary in charge of a sub-boma reports to the district secretary at the district headquarters.

Table 10.1   Indices of Income for Members of Cooperative Societies and UNIP

	*Household Index**	*Mean Estimated Annual Income (K)*
Cooperative societies:		
Officeholders	.346	263.10
Ordinary members	.201	111.50
Nonmembers	.211	150.94
United National Independence Party:		
Constituency officials	.417	414.00
Main body officeholders	.216	172.56
Youth wing officeholders	.117	223.80
Ordinary members	.226	122.48
Total population	.221	156.33

*Household index runs from 0.000 to 1.000, with 1.000 being high.

circularize its village branches to solicit applications for new jobs in the public services. Moreover, those who sought benefits as clients of these services and as consumers of their programs have now learned that publicly sponsored efforts to upgrade their standard of living are not working; at the very least, they have learned that these programs are not able to meet their expectations. Many who had turned to political action in hopes of financial improvement have failed to obtain it, and they are now disillusioned with their new African government.

As an example of these attitudes, I quote the remarks of a former chairman of one of the local party branches, who in 1970 resigned the post he had held since the mid-1950s. "I was fed up," he stated, "We were getting nowhere. Many others in the organization had got jobs and I was just sitting idle. For me it had been no worth." For him, politics had not paid off. He no longer works at politics but instead makes baskets, helps build roofs on village houses, and fashions doors and window frames. Not only is this man apathetic, however, he is also resentful. Speaking of the members of Parliament whom he helped put into power, he comments:

> The only reason any member of Parliament comes here is to make campaigns. Other times, they are enjoying themselves with the money we got them. They are eating well; they have big cars. These are from America, and if someone is in it, we can't see him and he just looks blue [from the tinted glass, presumably]. If they see a person walking or on a bicycle, they just chase him off the road and cover him with dust. When a man is fighting for a position, he cooperates with other people. Once in that position, then he is no good. Come time for elections, though, and they will come promising things.

A large percentage of his fellow villagers have undergone an analogous process of disillusionment. Like him, many had sought concrete advantages from the government they helped put into power; of the 105 heads of households sampled in Kasumpa village, 72, or 69 percent, had asked the government for assistance of one kind or another. Table 10.2 reveals the nature of their requests.

Of those who sought betterment from the government, the vast majority failed to obtain it. Only 8 of the 72 villagers who had asked for help felt that they had been given any; the remainder felt that the government had not helped them or that it had given them "the run-around" (see table 10.3).

Like the former branch chairman, many villagers have responded to the failure of the public sector to ameliorate their economic position by becoming cynical about government. While not expressed through mordant references to the American cars of members of Parliament, the cynicism of the villagers nonetheless registers in their responses to several questionnaire items. The sampled household heads were asked whether they agreed or disagreed with two statements: (1) "public officials don't care much what people like you think"; (2) "for the most part, the government serves the interest of only a few and isn't very concerned about the needs of people like yourself." As shown in tables 10.4 and 10.5, over three-fourths agreed with the first statement and over two-thirds with the second.

Table 10.2   Things Requested of Government by Kasumpa Villagers

	No.	%
Loans for:		
Farming or businesses	30	28.6
Purchasing iron roofs for houses	6	5.7
Help with cooperatives	8	7.6
Help with farms	6	5.7
Licenses (for guns, stores)	4	3.8
Reduction in store taxes	5	4.8
Relief from loan debts	3	2.9
Wells for school, village	4	3.8
Jobs	6	5.7
Nothing	33	31.4
	105	100.0

Table 10.3   Result of Requests to Government by Kasumpa Villagers

	No.	%
Helped	8	11.1
Not helped	56	77.8
Got "run-around" from bureaucrats	8	11.1
	72	100.0

Table 10.4   Responses of Kasumpa Village Household Heads to Statement
"Public Officials Don't Care Much What People Like You Think"

	No.	*%*
Agree	82	78.1
Neither agree nor disagree	2	1.9
Disagree	21	20.0
	105	100.0

Table 10.5   Responses of Kasumpa Village Household Heads to Statement
"For the Most Part, the Government Serves the Interests of Only a Few . . ."

	No.	*%*
Agree	75	71.4
Neither agree nor disagree	5	4.8
Disagree	25	23.8
	105	100.0

The hypothesis that the failure of government to give help breeds cynicism is supported in the following cross tabulations. Of those who got help, three-fourths disagreed with the statements that "public officials don't care much about what people like you think," and that the "government serves the interest of only a few . . . "; of those who did not get help, the vast majority agreed with those statements (tables 10.6 and 10.7).[7]

This pattern of disillusionment appeared to be widespread and the Kasumpa villagers did not seem to be atypical in feeling it. The extent of the feeling is suggested in the correspondence between the secretary of the Kawambwa Rural Council and local officials engaged in the registration of voters for the 1966 local government elections. When the secretary asked these officials to seek reasons for the widespread failure of villagers to register for the elections, he obtained some revealing replies. One of

Table 10.6   Relationship between Being Helped by Government and
Cynicism among Kasumpa Villagers

Attitude to statement "Public officials don't care . . ."	*Helped*	*Not Helped*
Agree	1	55
Neither agree nor disagree	1	0
Disagree	6	9
	8	64

Table 10.7   Relationship between Being Helped by Government and
Cynicism among Kasumpa Villagers

Attitude to statement "Government serves interests of only a few . . ."	*Helped*	*Not Helped*
Agree	2	49
Neither agree nor disagree	0	2
Disagree	6	13
	8	64

the registration officials noted, "A few complaints are: We are not given nice jobs, only the tough jobs of ploughing and sweating. Secondly, [the politicians] have failed in their promises. . . . Members of the Rural Council are selfish. And many others."[8] Another wrote:

> I asked them to give me the reasons for their refusal [to register]; these are what they told me:
>
> (a) . . . the local Government . . . has done nothing since Independence.
>
> (b) We cannot register because the Councillors [who] are elected drink too much beer and have no time to speak for people who have elected them.
>
> (c) The Councillors who are in office now take [the] initiative to improve only the areas which have already been improved by the Federal Government and forget the most remote areas which were not improved before.[9]

CRITICISM AND PROTEST

All that we have noted so far bespeaks a disillusionment with the post-independence performance of the government. Attempts at collective improvement through political action have not worked, and the villagers are cynical about the degree to which the government is in fact committed to them and to their well-being. Given that this is so, we must wonder why in Kasumpa and elsewhere in Luapula the governing party continues to survive as a political organization.

UNIP in Kasumpa

Despite widespread disillusionment, UNIP continues to function in Kasumpa village. Evidence of this is the extent to which people seek office in the party. As shown in table 10.8, over one-third of the sampled

Table 10.8   Frequency of UNIP Office Holding among Kasumpa
Village Household Heads

	No.	*%*
Constituency official	3	2.9
Main body		
Officeholder	19	18.1
Committee member	5	4.8
Youth wing		
Officeholder	9	8.6
Committee member	2	1.9
Not an officeholder	67	63.8
	105	100.1

household heads held office in UNIP at the time of my research. As indicated above, in at least one case, persons have voluntarily surrendered office in the party; but this is relatively rare. Twenty-seven percent of the persons in my sample had lost office in UNIP (as shown in table 10.9); but of those only 14 percent voluntarily left office because of political disillusionment (table 10.10). The biggest single reason for leaving office, as shown in table 10.10, was defeat in intraparty elections. Indeed, people continually seek to displace incumbents in the party. In four cases during my stay in the village, new challengers came forward to seize branch-level offices in the party. While I will go into the reasons for this conflict later, I wish to stress here that new candidates, while recognizing that economic opportunity no longer attached to party office holding, still sought posts in UNIP. In every case, they offered as reasons their wish to perform public service in the village and to achieve prominent positions within it.

The party's ability to attract competitors for office is one sign of its continued survival in Kasumpa. Another is its ability to extract financial resources from its members. Once a year the party collects K.50 dues from its members; upon receipt of this money, the party officials affix a stamp in the members' party card. In Kasumpa, 500 such stamps were sold in the fund-raising drive of 1971. One reason for this success was the ability of the party to coerce the members into paying. Party youths, for example, blocked the paths to the river and to the windmill, and women could not collect water without first giving evidence of having paid their dues. But to base the explanation on coercion alone would be to miss the degree to

Table 10.9 Turnover in Office Holding among Household Heads in Kasumpa

Persons who have:	No.	% of Those Who Have Held Office	% of Total Sample
Held and lost office	28	45.2	26.7
Never lost office	34	54.8	32.4
Never held office	43	n.a.	41.0
	105	100.0	100.1

Table 10.10 Reasons for Turnover in Office Holding

Reason	No.	% of Those Who Have Lost Office	% of Total Sample
Moved	6	21.4	5.7
Lost election	13	46.4	12.4
Switched from ANC	2	7.1	1.9
Illness/age	2	7.1	1.9
Job done: won independence	1	3.6	1.0
People disgusted with government	4	14.3	3.8
Does not apply	77	n.a.	73.3
	105	99.9	100.0

which the dues were willingly paid. I never heard expressions of outrage over being compelled to contribute; at worst the levies were seen as a fact of life. So widely accepted was the party's right to exact contributions that UNIP officials were able to sell dues stamps even at funerals in the village. While collecting money for the bereaved, the officials also collected dues for UNIP. No one seemed to find this inappropriate or unwarranted behavior.

I made it a basic part of my research to attempt to explain the continued functioning and acceptance of the party in the impoverished villages of rural Zambia. Most commonly the people I talked with in Kasumpa said that they supported the party because it was *they* who selected its office bearers. Thus, in one branch the membership precipitously and unceremoniously evicted from office two prominent local officials. The impetus for their removal came from the rank and file, who petitioned for—and got—a special branch election. As one UNIP member explained the purge of the two officials, they had "become selfish. They were too rich and lazy. One is always away across the river getting beer and fish to sell in his store. The other [an officeholder in Katofyio] is always away in his lorry. They are working for their own riches now and not for us. They are lazy in their political work. So we turned them out."

In another branch, two other officials lost their posts. Again, the reason given was that the officials had lost interest in political work. They did not go to party meetings, they failed to spread word of political affairs that came down party channels in UNIP, and they failed to seek out and transmit upward the grievances and sentiments of the rank and file. They were replaced by candidates more willing to do these things.

Because of regular and meaningful competitive local elections within the village, the villagers feel that the party officeholders had their interests at heart. For, given competitive elections, the candidates who seek posts in the party have strong incentives to attempt to work for the interests of the villagers. These interests can be subsumed under two general headings. One set I will call "traditional." The other set has to do with the performance of public institutions and involves the problems of rural development. I label these "modern" issues.

Traditional Issues

To a great degree, UNIP even today represents the interests of Kasumpa villagers as against those of their Lunda overlords. The contemporary basis for this division is the split between the villagers and their unpopular headman, Kabeya, who has been "imposed upon Kasumpa by Mwata Kazembe," as the villagers say.

A member of the Lunda aristocracy and a former representative of

Mwata Kazembe in the Kitwe urban court, Kabeya was appointed headman of Kasumpa in 1963 and immediately got into trouble with his new subjects. The fundamental reason for Kabeya's difficulty was that he was a Lunda who was imposed upon the Bemba village by the court of Mwata Kazembe. It would take exceptional political acumen to achieve popularity and acceptance under these circumstances. By all accounts Kabeya's predecessor, Kasumpa, had possessed such exceptional talents, but Kabeya obviously did not. Rather than being able to "learn from everyone—to get wisdom even from a child," as his predecessor was held to do, Kabeya instead acted "proudly and insultingly, lording it over us as if he were a royal chief and we were mere commoners." The facts, of course, were on Kabeya's side; but it was politically damaging for him to remind the people of this.

In hearing cases, Kabeya further damaged his position. For it was held —and I observed directly that this was true—that Kabeya did not let all views emerge; nor did he wait for bases for reconciliation to come forward in his hearings. Rather, claiming a wisdom born of his Lunda ancestry and his experience in the urban courts, Kabeya moved forward to impose findings of fault and to assign blame. Fines and jail sentences rather than reconciliations resulted from Kabeya's adjudications. This too increased his unpopularity; for not only did the people not like having to face the possibility of jail, but they also felt that they were being subjected to an abusive authority, one whom they themselves would not have chosen.

The tension between the Kasumpa villagers and the Lunda political structure was, as we have seen, fundamental and historically persistent, and it had formed the basis for much of the political conflict in the nationalist period. It was therefore natural that the party, insofar as it had championed the interests of the villagers against the Lunda Native Authority, should have become embroiled in this conflict between the villagers and their appointed headman. Rendering UNIP's involvement even more probable was the structure of kin relations within the party at the constituency level.

As I have shown, three Kasumpa residents were constituency-level officials in the party. This group formed a close and cohesive group; they drank together, visited daily, and shared such things as cigarettes, bicycles, radios, and food on a day-to-day basis. In addition, they had close kin relations, and the basis of these relations was the former headman, Kabeya's popular predecessor. Thus, as shown in figure 10.1, Constituency Official No. 1 had married the daughter and firstborn of the former headman; Constituency Official No. 2 was the former headman's grandson and called Constituency Official No. 1 his father; and Constituency Official No. 3 was affinally related to the former headman.[10] Several of the most prominent and influential of the local UNIP leaders were thus kinfolk of the former headman. It was their feeling that Mwata Kazembe should have

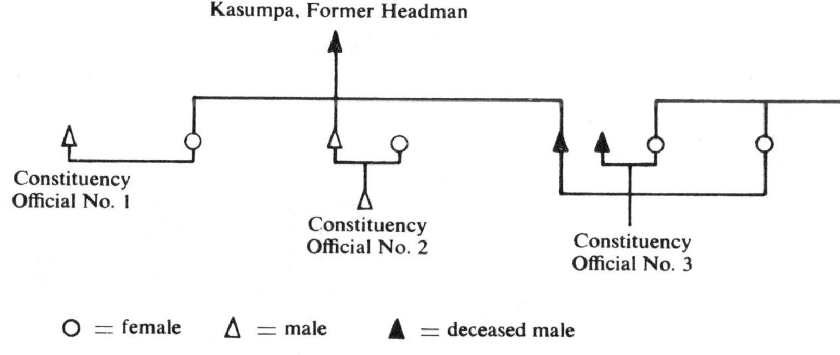

Fig. 10.1

Relationships between Constituency Officials and Former Headman, Kasumpa Village

appointed a lineal descendant of the former headman rather than Kabeya to govern Kasumpa village. Members of the local party elite thus had a direct and personal incentive to oppose Kabeya. And their willingness to perpetuate the opposition of the villagers to the traditional elites in the valley enabled them to gain popularity.

Another major issue was involved in the party's opposition to Kabeya: the issue of witchcraft. This issue was of the utmost importance to every household in the village; for infants and old folk died, and according to traditional beliefs in Kasumpa, with every death there was the possibility of witchcraft. The party officials, with strong competitive incentives to identify with the interest of the people, insisted on calling a witchfinder or *mucapi* to purge the village of witches and so reduce the frequency of deaths in Kasumpa. The headman, as was his obligation under law, refused to countenance or tolerate the making of witchcraft accusations or the divination of witches in the village. Thus, the conflict was joined.

The frequency of deaths in Kasumpa was high. I failed to record the number of funerals that took place in this village of six hundred households during my work there, but it struck me that they took place with oppressive frequency. Indicative, perhaps, is table 10.11, which reveals the relatively high percentage of dead children among the total offspring of the village. When UNIP championed the culturally sanctioned means of reducing the frequency of deaths—in essence, when it attempted to stop the killing—it therefore identified with a centrally important and widespread need in the Kasumpa community. Over the opposition of Kabeya the party officials secured the services of a leading mucapi in the valley.

The UNIP leadership had an even more immediate reason for opposing witchcraft in Kasumpa. They themselves were directly involved in witchcraft cases and Kabeya's opposition to the divination of these cases was thus causing them direct personal harm. One of their colleagues, a man man named Chikabala, had died in January of 1970. He had been one of

Table 10.11   Frequency of Deaths among Children in Kasumpa Village

	Mean	*Standard Deviation*
Number of births per household	7.848	4.463
Number of live children per household	5.505	3.372

the early organizers of the party; indeed, he had assembled the twelve "disciples" for Banda, the first African National Congress organizer in the area. While abjuring further office holding in the party after independence ("My children," he is quoted as saying on 25 October 1964, "my work is done"), he nonetheless remained a revered, honored, and oft consulted senior adviser for those who remained politically active. His death came as a tragic and personal blow. The party leaders sought to divine the reason for his death; Kabeya, as the upholder of the law in Kasumpa, opposed the holding of such proceedings. The village politicians were naturally deeply angered by the actions of the headman.

There was another such witchcraft case, and this case was at the core of the division between the headman and the party at the time of my stay in the village. The case originated within the family of Constituency Official No. 3. Official No. 3 insisted that a mucapi be brought to the village to determine who had caused the death of his mother's brother and to end the witchcraft. Over the opposition of Kabeya, the UNIP leaders contacted a mucapi. They secured a house in the village for him, and the constituency leaders of the youth brigade served as the mucapi's messengers and, on occasion, as his enforcers. The case of Official No. 3 was in fact not resolved. But because a mucapi was brought to Kasumpa, the village was for a time thought to be purged of witches. The party leadership thus had deeply personal reasons for insisting on the termination of witchcraft in the village; and in acting upon these reasons, they opposed the headman and backed popular demands for an "end to dying" in Kasumpa.[11]

The political leaders therefore had personal cause to maintain popular positions on one of the great traditional issues in Kasumpa: the antagonism between the villagers and the Lunda overlordship. In addition the UNIP leaders articulated the position of the villagers in demanding that the government do more for the village and that it alter the performance of public agencies so as to enhance their well-being. We now turn to UNIP's handling of these "modern" issues.

Modern Issues

UNIP used several means to express the people's demands that the government help make them better off. One such means was pressure-group tactics. These involved vocalizing the people's demands to officials of the government, presenting petitions from the villagers, and exerting pressure backed by threats of violence upon employees of the government.

The UNIP leaders lodged numerous petitions with the government. Encounters with officials were relatively frequent, for district-level officers —the district governor, the district secretary, and the agricultural and cooperative officers—attempted to maintain regular contact with the major villages within their domains. Moreover, Kasumpa village is fairly large and accessible and has a history of political significance in the valley. For these reasons, district officials regularly visited the village and the party officials could frequently meet with them.[12]

The encounters with the government officials were often belligerent in tone. The villagers wanted more government services, they wanted them provided more efficiently, and they were not at all reluctant to be frank about these matters. After all, they felt it was they who had put the government into power. As an example of the kind of complaints that they lodged, let me quote from some of the petitions they publicly presented to the district governor when he visited Kasumpa village in January of 1972. The first came from Katofyio I branch of the party and read:

Bwana Governor,

(1) Our well is not working properly. It runs by wind, but the wind here is only in the evening. And its storage tank is small, so by the afternoon it is empty. Then we must drink from the river; but we are downstream from the leprosarium, and we fear illness from there.

(2) Our school needs repairing. The walls are cracked and we fear they will fall on our children.

(3) We want a banana scheme here, so that our people can have employment near the village and our life be improved.

(4) Build us a market. We produce many things but we cannot sell them and they spoil. We need a market where they can be sold.

(5) Rid us of the agricultural assistant here. He does not visit the farms; he gives no loans; he does not fight with NAMBoard and the credit agency to help our families. He is lazy. Take him away.

The second UNIP branch in the village, Katofyio II, continued in the same vein; the secretary read the petition loudly and defiantly, and it stated in part:

NAMBoard is a society which misleads the government. It is saying to the government that the people here do not work hard. That is rubbish. We plant, but we have no markets. That is why our crops are small. Also, they take our produce and they leave us no money. The seeds come too late. Loans are promised, but they do not come; and if they do, they are too late.

Look at us, Mr. Governor. Some of us are dressed in rags. But that does *not* mean we are lazy. It is that we have no employment. Go, Mr.

Governor, and get us schemes; or help our farmers; or mine our minerals. Go and get us jobs.

The third Kasumpa branch, Katofyio III, then presented its petition, which began:

Mr. Governor,

All our people are wanting to get educated and so go to the copperbelt. Our villages are diminishing. But this is because there are no developments here. People would come back from the mines if this place were developed, but the government is not spending money here. Our school is not improved. We need more wells, and the water is diseased. We have no money, for there are no jobs and loans are hard to find. Help us.

Above all, you should help us in the village get money from the land. Make our farmers rich, and we could get jobs there or sell them things. They are failing. They have no market. The tractor comes late. Transport is late. They need loans to hire us for working. Make it so we can stay in our villages, and not go off to become criminals in the towns.

As encounters with government officials go in Kasumpa, these petitions were relatively mild. Other encounters were downright vitriolic, and contained threats of violence. In one case, the agricultural assistant was nearly beaten. He had recommended two farmers for loans but had been informed that they must plant five acres before they could qualify. When he returned to Tusha to measure their gardens, he was met by the farmers and their families, all in a surly mood. They blocked off his path to their gardens and threatened to beat him if he attempted to inspect their fields. When I probed into the feelings of the farmers, they cited the "uselessness of this man." He was felt to be lazy, "not visiting us or advising us. . . . He is much to be beaten. What he does is to force us to farm and to force us to farm, with no loans coming to us; no money coming to us. We get no loans, even though he says he writes recommendations. We end up working to produce crops for the government without getting profits."[13]

Another example is the case of the Kasumpa houses. In 1965, the government constructed a new road in the Luapula valley; to suggest its origins, the government named it Zambia Highway. The government intended to locate the highway inland from Kasumpa, for to locate the road near Kasumpa would require constructing an expensive causeway across the Mbereshi River and the swamps to either side. Through a series of protests, which I will later describe, the Kasumpa people got the government to alter its plan and to cross the Mbereshi (see map 4). In fact, the road then bisected the village; and over twenty houses had to be destroyed to make room for the thoroughfare.

There then arose the question of compensation, and the Kasumpa people, ever eager to extract as much as possible from the public sector, made extravagant claims. It costs roughly K80 to build a four-room house in Kasumpa, including the costs of "traditional" materials and hired labor. None of the affected houses had glass, sheet iron roofs, or any other such expensive appurtenances, and none was particularly large, by all reports, so an average evaluation of K80 per house should have been realistic. The villagers, however, pressed for an average compensation of K196.40, with demands ranging as high as K300. They would not budge in these claims, and the party devoted days to seemingly incessant political lobbying to win concessions on their behalf.

The government had no funds for compensation. The contractor for that part of the road had gone bankrupt—largely because of cost overruns involved in resiting the road in the first place—and none of the departments involved were willing to pay the claims of the villagers. So the villagers, through every means possible, exerted pressure on the government to satisfy their claims. Through their UNIP officials, they brought the matter up with all officers who entered the village. They bicycled and hitchhiked the twenty-five miles to the district headquarters at Nchelenge and "sat in" at the boma offices until the district officials agreed to review their claims. The constituency officials of UNIP placed the matter on the agendas of the district and provincial development committees.[14] And the village politicians began a series of protracted correspondence with the higher level party officials, their member of Parliament, the permanent secretary of the province, and even the State House in Lusaka.[15]

All during this period, the UNIP officials in Kasumpa were under enormous pressure from the villagers; should the compensation not be paid, they feared they might lose their party offices; and they in fact feared worse: they feared for their physical safety. Under pressure from the villagers, they composed the following letter and sent it to the district secretary; after noting and referencing all their previous correspondence, they wrote: "Now we the people with the destroyed homes . . . we are closing the road on the 15th of December 1969. All government cars bearing GRZ [government] plates will not pass unless they pay, so we will get the money to replace the destroyed houses. For the government is not concerned with quiet people, only those who bring violence."[16]

The threat worked; it did not have to be acted upon. Upon receiving a copy of the letter, the district secretary commandeered two policemen armed with rifles and set off for Kasumpa. Stopping first in Mansa to review the case in detail, he went to Kasumpa. There he negotiated down the average claims to K120.00 and then returned to Mansa to locate the funds. "As an old trade unionist," he recalled with some humor, "I know what to do. I yelled, I pounded, and I said: how in hell can you expect me to be able to control my people in my district unless you give me something to take to them. They've come down by 40 percent. Now it's your turn to give."[17] The government gave in. By petition, confrontation, and threats of violence, the UNIP leaders had extracted benefits to which the villagers felt entitled.

Yelling, lobbying, and threatening are but a few of the means used by the party leaders to advance the interests of the villagers. The party leaders also use electoral strategies. They fully realize that in their relationship with the public sector they can exchange votes for public services. And from time to time they have threatened to withhold votes until the level of services was raised.

Perhaps the best example of this kind of behavior again took place in connection with the road. The road was begun in 1965, and the local government elections, the first postindependence test of UNIP's support, were scheduled for August 1966. Had the road been built inland from the village, as the government had planned, and not across the river and swamps beside Kasumpa, as the villagers desired, then the villagers would have had to travel upstream several miles before being able to cross the river to reach the local hospital and secondary school. To serve their people, as noted earlier, the local UNIP officials sought to alter the government's construction plans. They did so by threatening to withhold votes from the government-backed candidates in the 1966 elections. Coining the slogan "No road, no vote," they organized protests throughout all the villages of the Kenyembo-Mofwe area, villages that also stood to gain by a change in the location of the road. As one person recalled:

> We told the government, NO ROAD, NO VOTE. The government had planned to stop the road on the other side of the Mbereshi as they said they didn't have the money to build all the bridges necessary to cross it and the swamps and then to resume construction upstream from Kabelenge. . . . In 1965 we had a big party meeting in Kanyembo and sent a report to the District Officers in Nchelenge. The members of Parliament and party leaders then came and asked for a carte blanche from us to get the road from the government, and we gave it to them.

A similar threat was used to help secure compensation for the houses that had to be destroyed when the road was resited. In June 1969 the government of Zambia held a national referendum, the purpose of which was to empower Parliament to modify certain basic provisions of the constitution. As the opposition felt that authorizing Parliament to modify the constitution was but a prelude to the formation of a one-party state, the referendum was fought on party lines. The government campaigned for votes in the same manner as it did in parliamentary elections. And the local UNIP leaders of Kasumpa used the threat of withholding their votes as a means of altering the behavior of the public officials and of getting them to service their needs. Evidence of this is contained in a memo from the district governor reporting on his tour of Nchelenge district in preparation for the referendum:

> [The] political situation during this period was tense. Wherever the writer visited [in Kanyembo's area] some bad words were spoken . . . and the writer received threatening letters in Chief Kanyembo's area. People from Kasumpa refused to attend the meetings addressed by the writer. And they have a different slogan from our national slogan: no payments, then no vote and no meetings. But the writer did his level best to control the situation and when I explained about the compensation and promised to work hard at it, many people then turned and registered as voters.[18]

"Districtism" and Provincialism

The people of Kasumpa and elsewhere in rural Zambia demand more resources from the public sector, be it in the form of wells, schools, roads, loans, salaries, or payments for produce. And they demand better performance from public agencies. By manipulating their support for local politicians, the people bring intensive pressure to bear upon the public sector at the district and provincial levels. The district and provincial personnel have responded to these pressures by themselves demanding greater resources from the government—resources which they in turn can distribute so as to satisfy the demands of their people—and by demanding the power to determine how these resources should be allocated so as to render the public sector more sensitive and responsive to the preferences of their constituents. These demands for the transfer of resources and power to the district and provincial level, demands based upon the need to resolve the political problems occasioned by the pursuit of wealth through politics in rural Zambia, have, I will argue, helped to lay the foundation for sectionalism in contemporary Zambia.[19]

Demands for Resources

Within Luapula Province, the district-level officials of UNIP and the government compete intensively for greater resources. When the Kasumpa villagers berated the visiting district governor about the need for school repairs, for example, his response was to lobby for a greater allocation for his district from the provincial budget of the Ministry of Education. As he stated:

> The government has given us K4,000 to maintain primary schools in this province. So, when they split the money evenly among the 5 dis-

tricts here, I have money for the repair of one school. I have two education districts in this district; and in this education district alone
I see that the schools in Toka, Mangamu, and Kasumpa badly need
repairs. The parents and local party people are all over me, shouting
about this and fearing for their children when the storms come. So
I go to Mansa, saying we have a special need way up in the valley.[20]

Similar competition takes place over the financing of secondary education.
In a heated debate over the education budget, for example, one district
politician exclaimed, "I would say there is nothing the government has
done in Nchelenge. In Nchelenge District there is only one [secondary]
school. Do you think only one secondary school was what we fought for
and went to prison for?"[21]

Interviews revealed that the district-level officers often competed strenuously for the allocation of new public facilities. For example, in 1968,
a new agricultural research station was approved for the province; as the
Nchelenge district secretary explained it, "At the meetings, we were nearly
at blows. For a while, we were able to argue that here in Nchelenge, we
should have this station. But then, it came down to between Mansa and
Kawambwa—the two places where the farmers are. It was a K100,000
project, and we lost it. But not after a real fight."[22] Similar battles took
place over the location of a tea scheme and the allocation of funds for
new hospital construction.[23] The intensity of this competition is suggested
by one district governor's report to the provincial development committee, the committee of politicians, businessmen, and heads of departments
that meets quarterly to oversee and coordinate public programs in the
province:

> It is disappointing and unbelievable to report . . . that since the [last]
> P[rovincial] D[evelopment] C[ommittee] meeting when we threw in
> our bids for . . . consideration the response is negligible. . . . Of all
> the 9 items [we petitioned for] only [one] item received some support.
> Of the K100,000 bloc vote fund only a nil distribution for Mwense is
> recorded. And from Minor Works allocation totaling K4,000 Mwense
> got the bones to the tune of K100 only.[24]

A similar pattern of competition for governmental expenditures takes
place at the provincial level, as the provincial leaders of Luapula—the
members of Parliament, the provincial cabinet minister, and provincial
heads of departments—seek to gain greater allocations from the central
government and thereby satisfy the demands by the province's citizenry
that the government they put into power make them better off. One example of this competition is a speech by a Luapula M.P. in a district-level
political meeting in March of 1971:

As you know . . . the owners of this province suffered a lot in getting independence. Many suffered, many [went] to prison, and many died. Since independence, the government has done nothing in this province. . . . Before independence we were united together with other provinces, but since then other provinces have wanted [the] lion's share and to eat on their friends' heads. . . . We want government to develop some mines in Luapula Province. In Northern Province, government has established a railway line, . . . so we want government to establish mines in Luapula.[25]

The provincial heads, like their district-level counterparts, compete over concrete projects and expenditure programs. For example, in the First National Development Plan, Luapula was slated to receive a citrus fruit scheme; later, the scheme was transferred to the already agriculturally rich Southern Province. This transfer resulted in the following outburst at the provincial development committee:

The Provincial Agricultural Officer told the committee about the transfer of the citrus scheme to the Southern Province because the area [in Luapula] would not allow for expansion. *The Committee strongly objected to the unilateral proposal and instructed the Provincial Development Officer . . . to take the matter up with the authorities concerned.* The committee said [that] . . . the money involved . . . is a share that rightly belongs to the Luapula.[26]

A similar outburst took place over the location of a proposed cattle-ranching scheme; in this case the conflict was with the Northern Province, and this time the Luapula officials won.[27] On another occasion the dispute involved a teacher training college. As one district governor stated in the meeting of the provincial development committee at which the dispute arose,

He was not happy with the way the Government was treating Luapula Province. He said that a Teachers Training College was a necessity here, and that it was his belief that if Luapula Province did not get a Teachers Training College the Government would find when they next needed votes that Luapula Province would not cooperate. . . . The 1969 programme for this year includes a Teachers Training College for Kitwe [Copperbelt Province]. North Western Province is going to have a Teachers Training College.[28]

Perhaps the item that has most prominently featured in interprovincial competition, however, has been the road between the copperbelt towns and Luapula Province. As I have argued throughout, the remoteness of Luapula from the urban markets has constrained the level of profitability of production and weakened the incentives to invest in the area, by contrast with other regions in Zambia. The provincial-level leaders of the province are aware of this. They realize as well that it is a matter not merely of the distance of the transport routes, but also of their uncertainty: the capricious performance of the Zairian border officials, the deterioration of the existing road under heavy rains, and the delays of unpredictable duration involved in crossing the river make the distance from Luapula to town a greater barrier to market forces than do comparable distances elsewhere in Zambia. The provincial-level politicians and heads of departments therefore coalesce around the demand for a new road for Luapula, one that would bypass the pedicle and connect Luapula to the great north road by linking Serenje district with Samfya (see map 2). This provincial coalition re-forms with every major border incident on the existing road; and it leads Luapula into competition with other provinces. Thus, for example, when Zambian transporters were stranded in the Congo in September of 1968, one observer noted the overwhelming local sentiment that "Zambia [should] reconsider whether the Mukulu Road—planned to link Luapula Province with Serenje—is not more urgently needed than the Solwezi-Chingola Road and the Great North and Great East highways" (in Northern and Eastern Province, respectively).[29] The provincial officials went to Lusaka to lobby with the Ministry of Works to divert funds from these other projects to the development of the Samfya-Serenje road, but their efforts failed.[30] The issue again arose in April 1969. As will be described later, the Luapula provincial elite was at that time involved in a series of maneuvers at the national level—maneuvers that sought to gain them positions of advantage in the national structure of power. To consolidate political support, they again championed the cause of the road, this time through demands lodged in political meetings throughout the province, through statements to the press, and through questions raised in Parliament.[31] As the minister of state for Luapula was quoted as saying at that time: "If we are realistic about developing all provinces in Zambia evenly, let us start at once working on the Samfya-Serenje Road. It is the feeling of everybody in the province that the road is the only answer to overcome the geographical position of the province."[32]

With every major campaign in Luapula demanding the road, the national government made propagandistic gestures in support of its construction. Cabinet ministers, for example, would pose with shovels before the cameras of the press, and the newspapers would publish stories about the road and the government's plan to construct it. The road, however, remains unconstructed.[33] But the pressure for it continues, and this pressure represents continued attempts by the politicians and heads of departments in Luapula to bring greater public-sector benefits to the province by redistributing them, if necessary, from other provinces in Zambia.

Demands for Authority

Not only do the provincial and district officials seek greater quantities of resources from the public sector; they also seek greater control over their allocation. They wish to decentralize authority over public resources so that they can distribute them in a way that is more sensitive to the preferences of their local clientele.

It will be recalled that in January 1969 the government announced a series of measures designed to decentralize the public administration in an attempt to upgrade its rural development program. The president created the post of district governor, made the governors chairmen of the district development committees, and authorized them to coordinate and facilitate the implementation of departmental programs in their areas. In addition, the president appointed ministers of cabinet rank to head the implementation of governmental programs in each of the several provinces and upgraded the head of the civil service in each province to the rank of permanent secretary. The duties of the provincial ministers were roughly equivalent to those of the district governors: they were to coordinate developmental programs and to see that they effectively met the needs of the local citizenry. The impression was thus conveyed that control over public resources was to be placed in the hands of officials at the provincial and district level; and the rationale for this measure was an enhanced regard for the needs of the local populace—those who were supposed to benefit from the extension of governmental programs to the rural areas.[34]

It was the conviction of the district and provincial personnel in Luapula, however, that decentralization was a "sham." Not only did they feel that they did not receive control over public resources; they also felt that their lack of such control was making it difficult for them to respond to the demands of the populace and so retain their popularity and political support. As one provincial official put it in a meeting of the provincial development committee: "Our Government has told us about decentralization of Government'. . . . so as to bring the Government near to the people and have their problems dealt with right at the spot. But yet this has not been a practice at all. Although we have now Provincial Cabinet Ministers and Permanent Secretaries in Provinces, but still matters are referred to Lusaka for final approval, just as it was in the past."[35] At another meeting of the provincial development committee other officials stated:

The Permanent Secretary said that he and his Minister were frequently being frustrated in their efforts by . . . Lusaka. [A district governor] said he agreed with what the Permanent Secretary had said, and added that as he saw it, Lusaka people were spoiling everything and that the Cabinet Minister, Permanent Secretary and Provincial Heads and officers were not able to act in their full capacities within their titles because orders still came from Lusaka. Their titles . . . meant nothing at all, and this was an embarrassing . . . situation.[36]

The crux of the problem of decentralization was that the officials in the "horizontal" components of the governmental administration—the district and provincial officers—had little or no control over the "vertical" departments of government—those specialized programmatic departments which emanated from Lusaka. The area officials had little control over departmental personnel; they could neither hire nor fire members of departments, and in cases of misfeasance or misconduct by departmental personnel they had little power to discipline them, save in consultation with the offenders' departmental superiors.[37] Neither did area officials have control over significant budgetary resources. The 1972 report of the working party on administrative decentralization noted that roughly 90 percent of the 1972 capital budget was for "national" projects, and therefore under the control of the central ministries, and only 10 percent was under the control of the regional heads of government.[38] The result was that local sentiments and priorities, as perceived and articulated at the provincial and district levels, often had little effect on how public resources were allocated or deployed.

With little authority over the personnel or financial resources of public agencies, there was little these officials could do to alter their performance. One result was persistent frustration and repeated demands for authority over departmental personnel. For example, in 1967 the district officials of Mansa had at last got the government to build a new and long-sought-after health facility in their area. But when construction began they were angered to find that the officials from the Ministry of Health who were in charge of constructing the new facility were having to accept design changes imposed upon them by the superiors from Lusaka—design changes which seemed to nullify many of the advantages that had been built into the original proposals. According to the provincial development committee's notes on this issue, the "Committee was very worried that [the] Plan . . . [could] be so varied [by the] Ministry as to bear little resemblance to original thinking. Such procedure completely reverses the original policy where the People's aspirations would be catered for by government. . . . This places an added burden . . . on those who have to keep government policy before the people."[39] The committee went on to demand that in such matters as design the health officials be accountable to their provincial superiors.

Another example of the demands for the devolution of authority is contained in the report of the "commission of inquiry" into the operations of the Agricultural Finance Corporation by the Nchelenge district development committee. One of the primary motivations for this measure was the feeling on the part of local officials that the Agricultural Finance Corporation's officers were totally absorbed in their "departmental" duties and not at all responsive to their district-level counterparts. Given the need for the credit agency to coordinate its operations with other departments involved in the rural development effort, it was felt that the bureaucratic autonomy of the agency was a severe liability to the performance of development programs in the area. As one official summarized the report, "We urged that the officers of this agency attend district development committee meetings, operate in consultation with the agricultural officer and other officials of the Ministry of Rural Development in our district, and come to accept the needs of the farmers of the district as expressed to them by this committee as being as important as the views of their distant superiors. It was the people here who were suffering."[40] The demand for authority is also suggested in the record of a dispute between the marketing service and the provincial officers of Luapula. As recorded in a letter from the permanent secretary of the province to his counterpart in the Ministry of Rural Development:

> I have recently been informed by the Regional Manager of [the] National Agricultural Marketing Board . . . that he has received instructions from his General Manager that he should never go on tour in the accompaniment of any Government Officers without the prior authority obtained from his Head Office . . . [in] Lusaka. It is pathetic that if there is an urgent marketing problem to be solved . . . we must in the first instance seek prior authority from the General Manager . . . in Lusaka.[41]

The frustration over the lack of authority over field personnel has thus led to demands for the devolution of such authority. The provincial and district leaders also seek control over governmental finances. At the time of my work in the area, one of their demands was for the reinstatement of the "bloc vote." The bloc vote was a pool of discretionary funds which could be used to meet unforeseen problems or to relieve "bottlenecks" in local development programs, e.g., by repairing a bridge damaged by unexpectedly high floods in the rainy season or by purchasing an additional lorry when transport problems arose. The local Luapula officials had found the bloc vote extremely useful; several times it had allowed them to resolve unanticipated difficulties and so avoid major delays in the implementation of various governmental programs. They had also found the bloc vote a useful means for compelling the central ministries to make expenditures that had been authorized for the region but which, for some reason, they had delayed in making. The best example of this is provided in the case of the Agricultural Research Station in Luapula. The station had been proposed by the Luapula officials, and had in fact been included in the First National Development Plan. The Ministry of Agriculture had been slow to release funds for its construction, however, and the local officials were upset. In 1969 the provincial development committee therefore devoted K30,000 of its K100,000 annual bloc vote to commence construction of the project: work crews were hired and construction began. With the hiring of over ninety persons, the clearing of the grounds, and the beginning of the foundations, it became politically difficult for the central government to terminate the construction of the research station. This is revealed by a memo in which a representative of the Luapula provincial development committee described his discussions with a ministry official in Lusaka; the minister "said that [the Ministry] had in the face of financial stringency accepted to drop research projects in provinces where work had not commenced but he was strongly opposed to abandoning construction work on the Luapula Research Station where a lot of money had already been spent."[42] By committing local funds to the project, the provincial officials therefore had made it difficult for the national officials to abort a project that had been approved but not funded. They had used funds over which they had formal control to gain influence over the expenditure of funds over which they had no formal control. The bloc vote had therefore enhanced their ability to control patterns of public expenditure.

In this case the provincial officials got what they wanted: the project was continued, and there is now an agricultural research station in Luapula. However, their use of the bloc vote in this manner drew heavy criticism from the central government, which felt that it was losing its ability to direct the expenditure of public funds and to control the purposes for which public resources were to be employed. In 1970, citing "abuse" of the bloc vote, the government therefore terminated it as a part of the budgetary pattern of Zambia. This infuriated the local officials, who demanded its reinstatement. They wanted, and needed, local control over financial resources, and they have not ceased agitating for it.

In their appeals for local control over government personnel and finances, the officials had the support of the province's citizenry. In Kasumpa at least, members of the citizenry were aware that they were being harmed by the degree of centralization of the public administration. Perhaps the most pervasive example of this was the seemingly interminable delays members of the cooperative movements experienced in receiving payments. As I described in Chapter 7, the members of the farming cooperatives faced long bureaucratic delays in receiving pay for work done in stumping and weeding new lands, and the members of the building co-operative had to await official inspection and approval for work done on governmental projects. In both cases the necessity of gaining enough information to convince remote superiors of the validity of the claims for funds delayed the release of these funds, with a resultant decline in the commitment to the cooperatives on the part of their members. Had the local officials had the authority to release the funds, the officers of the cooperatives pointed out, then the problem would not have arisen.

A second example of the village-level impact of the lack of decentralization is that of the feeder road between the Tusha farmers and the main road in the valley. The feeder road was a poor one, thus making marketing a risky business. Private lorries did not dare to employ the road for fear of becoming mired down; and government drivers, while more willing to try to cross the road, often failed to complete the journey and so remained bogged down and idle for days on end. For years the villagers and farmers have demanded the repair of the road; and for years the agricultural officer, the credit officer, and the head of NAMBoard in the area had pressed the government to authorize funds to improve the road. Failing to get money from the departments, this coalition of bureaucrats and local personnel finally got the Provincial Development Committee to authorize bloc-vote money for the road in 1970, but in that very year the bloc vote was rescinded. When the local citizenry heard of this, they were deeply angered. They felt that the government had betrayed them. They also felt that if the local officials, who knew of their needs, had possessed control over the resources to meet these needs, then they would have been better off. The demands by the regional officials that the government give them control over financial resources received a favorable reception on the part of Kasumpa villagers.

In search of higher levels of government services and their more efficient supply, the villagers have thus placed enormous pressures upon local political officials. And these officials, in search of higher levels of political support, have responded to the villagers' demands. The result has been competition among politicians for scarce public resources, rivalries between districts and provinces, and demands for the devolution of power to officials at the regional level. These kinds of behavior have coalesced to form a pattern of political regionalism—a form of politics that characterizes contemporary Zambia and other African nations as well. Rural demands that the government lay hold of the wealth generated by urban industry and distribute it in the countryside so as to make villagers better off have thus helped to transform the nature of politics in postindependence in Zambia.

11

Patterns of Party Conflict

The demands for public amelioration of rural poverty have affected the party system in Zambia, both promoting conflict within the ruling party and intensifying competition between the ruling and opposition parties. As this chapter will show, given the desire of governing politicians to stay in power, the result has been to transform Zambia into the modal form of civilian government in black Africa: the single-party state. Rural poverty, the demand that the state do what private markets have failed to accomplish, the desire of politicians to gain and hold office—these factors, in the context of a competitive party system, impelled the ruling elite to terminate competitive party politics in postindependence Zambia.

Patterns of Intraparty Competition

As we have noted, Zambia attained independence in 1964 under a government formed by the United National Independence Party. The road to governmental office holding was prominence in this party. The major cabinet posts in the new government were held by the dominant figures in UNIP's Central Committee; the presidency and vice-presidency of the government, for example, were occupied respectively by the president and vice president of UNIP.[1] There were thus strong incentives for ambitious politicians to seek prominence in UNIP. In 1967, President Kaunda announced that elections would be held for positions in the Central Committee of UNIP. The result was intense competition for posts in UNIP, as one would expect, given the value attached to these positions.

The details of the subsequent maneuvering are fascinating. Who did what to whom, and why, during the electoral campaign? Such questions deserve full treatment and no doubt will be addressed in future memoirs, biographies, and historical studies written by Zambians themselves. Nonetheless, for our purposes, these details are irrelevant. What is relevant is that the competing politicians formed, as theory would predict, coalitions apparently designed to achieve minimum majorities in the intraparty balloting.[2] The movement toward regional self-assertion described in the last chapter was seized upon by the ambitious politicians at the elite level and the coalitions were formed on a regional basis. These hypotheses are supported by the nature of the winning coalition: that between the Northern and Southern Province candidates. The three Bemba-speaking areas (Northern, Luapula, and Copperbelt) lacked enough votes to win the election: they had 1,900 votes but needed 2,350 to form a majority. Aligning with any other province would have given them this majority; but in the case of either Eastern and Barotse Province the fruits of victory would have had to be shared with four other national politicians, whereas with Southern Province they would have had to be shared with only two. The coalition with the Southern Province could thus gain power at least cost to the Bemba-speaking politicians.[3]

The results of the 1967 election were traumatic. Politicians from the Eastern and Barotse wings of the party found themselves turned out of

Table 11.1   Results of the August 1967 Elections to the UNIP Central Committee

Uncontested	Name	Original Tally	Recounted Votes
President	Kenneth Kaunda		
Chairman	Solomon Kalulu		
Director of publicity	Sikota Wina		
Director of youth	Dingiswayo Banda		
Contested			
Vice-President	Simon Kapwepwe	2,742	2,740
	Reuben Kamanga	2,404	2,010
National secretary	Mainza Chona	2,404	2,393
	Munu Sipalo	1,911	1,210
	Aaron Milner	1,493	1,134
Deputy national secretary			
	Justin Chimba	2,953	2,450
	Humphrey Mulemba	2,314	2,259
National treasurer			
	Elijah Mudenda	2,964	2,962
	Arthur Wina	1,800	1,782
Deputy national treasurer			
	Lewis Changufu	2,893	2,888
	Wesley Nyirenda	1,919	1,868
Deputy national chairman			
	Grey Zulu	2,522	2,674
	Peter Matoka	2,390	2,083
Director of women's brigade			
	Maria Nankolongo	3,270	3,323
	Mukwae Nakatindi	1,436	1,436

Source: Republic of Zambia, *Mulungushi Conference, 1967,* pp. 49–50.

power. The line of succession to the presidency of the republic was shifted from an easterner, Reuben Kamanga, to a Northern Province official, Simon Kapwepwe. And five of the posts on the eleven-member Central Committee were now held by persons from the Northern Province. Almost immediately after the election, the defeated politicians began to consolidate their positions, to bargain with members of the dominant coalition, and to seek its undoing by forging ties with local forces of regional protest.

It was the politicians from the Eastern Province who took the political initiative. Their goal was to undo the result of the intraparty elections and to get back the top posts in the party. To gain popular support, they had to devise an appeal based upon local interests; they therefore sought to relate their electoral fate to the economic fate of the province. To achieve electoral solidarity for their candidacies, they argued that without strong Eastern Province representation in the top posts of the party Eastern Province rural dwellers were losing out in terms of significant development programs. They contended that a majority of the important postindependence development projects were going to the Northern Province, which now dominated the national government: three major projects—the pipeline for oil imports, the planned railway, and the tarring of the major road to the coast—were located in the Northern Province, they pointed out, and this demonstrated that the pattern of public expenditure was linked to the distribution of power. They made these claims in speeches throughout the Eastern Province and in their attempts to forge the "Unity" movement at the local level. So vitriolic were their demands for Eastern Province solidarity and their denunciation of the Northern Province that many Bemba-speaking civil servants posted in the Eastern Province felt endangered and petitioned for evacuation from the area.[4] In their campaigns the Eastern Province politicians thus forged ties between the movements toward provincialism at the national and local levels—ties based upon the politicians' interests in political office holding and the constituents' interests in upgrading their economic standing through increased public expenditures.[5]

The Eastern Province politicians' attempts to "undo" the 1967 elections also involved an intricate and stealthy process of bargaining with members of the dominant coalition. In their maneuvers, the Eastern Province bloc sought to demonstrate to the members of the dominant coalition how poorly they were doing within that coalition and to convince them they could do much better outside it. The two primary targets for these appeals were the politicians from the Copperbelt and Luapula provinces. Neither group had benefited from the 1967 election, for neither had secured posts in the Central Committee; they were therefore susceptible to appeals to turn against the politicians from the Northern Province. For purposes of this study, we will focus on the behavior of one of these target groups: the politicians from Luapula.

The strategy of the Luapula politicians was obvious: to defect to the Eastern Province bloc in exchange for promotions to the national level in UNIP. This strategy was first revealed in the spring of 1969, just after the December 1968 general elections. During the general elections, an irregularity had led to a court ruling that the UNIP candidate in Nchelenge (Kawambwa East Constituency), John Mwanakatwe, was improperly elected; the court called for a rerun of the election. The government decided to hold by-elections in July and UNIP again nominated Mwanakatwe to stand for the parliamentary seat.

Mwanakatwe was from the Northern Province, and his nomination as a candidate from a district in Luapula became a *cause célèbre* among the Luapula politicians. They demanded that a person from Luapula be nominated to stand the election. They argued that Luapula lacked sufficient political representation in the government, and that people of Luapula extraction held fewer offices than did politicians from other provinces. To arouse popular support for their claims, the Luapula members of Parliament toured the townships of the copperbelt and the line of rail, contacting migrants to the urban centers from districts in Luapula; they also toured intensively within the rural districts of Luapula. By so doing they instigated an outpouring of letters, petitions, and telegrams in support of their demand that "the political interests of the province [be] looked after by its own sons and daughters," and that no "outsider be imposed" on the Luapula people.[6]

In seeking popular support for their position, the Luapula politicians used two basic appeals. One was that because Luapula lacked sufficient political representation it was not getting its fair share of government expenditures; as one person put it, "Our members of Parliament told us that since Kapwepwe became vice president and the North had five seats, all the projects were going to the North. We needed more of our people in Parliament."[7] As another appeal they devised and disseminated an "atrocity story." The story contended that Mwanakatwe had chastised the Luapula people for aspiring to assert themselves politically and for demanding industrial and agricultural schemes in their area; Mwanakatwe, the story contended, called the Luapula people *batubula*, or "dumb fishermen," who were "ordained to be ruled by others"[8] and who wouldn't know how to take advantage of alternative economic opportunities even were the government to create them. I attempted to trace this story and found little basis for it. Some political officials in Luapula attributed the remark to Mwanakatwe; others, to Justin Chimba, who was dispatched in 1969 by UNIP's national headquarters to investigate the uproar over Mwanakatwe's nomination;[9] and still others, to Vice-President Kapwepwe, the leader of the Northern Province coalition. All agreed that, when President Kaunda asked an assembled group of provincial and district officials for testimony concerning the remark, no one admitted to having actually been present when it was made. The significance of the story therefore lies not in its veracity. Rather, it lies in the political designs that underlay it. The story was clearly aimed at demonstrating the hauteur and insensitivity of the Northern Province politicians and at severing the bonds of political loyalty between the Luapula constituency and the national-level politicians from the north.

Further evidence of the political maneuvering of the Luapula politicians is contained in a widely circulated petition which they filed with the president of the republic. In it, they indicated that their interests in high office holding had not been served by UNIP.

> We are now more than convinced that . . . our people have not had the benefit of political appointments on the scale enjoyed by those from the Northern Province. . . . In this regard we may mention the appointments to Party leadership on the regional level . . . , politically appointed District Secretaries, District Governors, appointments to foreign missions, membership of the statutory bodies and Government Boards, not to mention appointments in the public service.[10]

To rectify this situation, they put the president on notice that they no longer considered themselves to be adequately represented by the Northern Province delegation that dominated the national offices of UNIP, and they made a thinly veiled plea for membership on the Central Committee.

> Your Excellency, we had the greatest confidence in cross-representation by members from Northern Province. . . . We, in the Luapula Province have learned only by bitterest experience what a grave mistake we have made. . . . Consequently we have regretted how we have lost out by being represented by people from Northern Province. We wish to indicate to Your Excellency that . . . we would be grateful if Your Excellency would grant political recognition and status to our Province in the same way as other Provinces.[11]

To further their campaign for high office, the national officeholders from Luapula spoke out strongly at provincial and district meetings, pointing out the deficiencies in the government programs in their province. They demanded more agricultural training, the revitalization of cooperatives, the building of more numerous and more widely distributed marketing agency depots, higher prices for farm produce, research into better seed types, and more wells.[12] They also demanded and pressed hard in

Parliament for the new road to bypass the pedicle.[13] Luapula, they declared, was suffering; and at one meeting, they demanded "that more attention now be paid to the rural areas. This could be done by freezing some of the capital projects in the urban areas as a means of balancing industrial distribution. The seminar felt that if more industries were created in the rural areas, it would halt the flow of mass immigration into urban areas where jobs are scarce."[14] The forces of provincialism, unleashed by the competition for office at the national level of the party, therefore joined with popular demands at the local level that the government raise the incomes of the village dwellers.

Similar shifts in political loyalty were taking place among another component of the Bemba-speaking coalition: the politicians from the rural areas of the Copperbelt Province, and in particular, from the Lamba/Lenje people of that province. So pronounced did these shifts become that both Luapula and Copperbelt provinces joined in August 1969 with the UNIP representatives from the minority Eastern Province coalition to threaten a motion of no confidence in Simon Kapwepwe, the vice-president of the republic and the leader of the Northern Province coalition. This move precipitated Kapwepwe's resignation from the vice-presidency and led to President Kaunda's dissolution of the UNIP Central Committee that had been elected in 1967. When Kaunda appointed a new interim Central Committee and new cabinet, it was obvious that the strategy of defection had worked. The Eastern Province politicians who had failed to secure posts in 1967—most notably, Nyirenda and Kamanga—were returned to national offices in the party; and, for the first time, the Luapula politicians secured a position in the Central Committee.[15] High office in the party translates into high office in the government, and following the reconstruction of the Central Committee, politicians from Luapula also obtained cabinet rank.[16] From the point of view of the Luapula politicians, their withdrawal from the dominant coalition and their alliance with the Eastern Province politicians had paid off in terms of securing high office. And in the process of the competition for national offices, the rival politicians had aligned with local demands that the government make them better off, and made provincialism a prominent element in the politics of the governing party.[17]

Patterns of Interparty Competition

Thus far we have concentrated on the pattern of regional competition within UNIP, the governing party. We now turn our attention to the pattern of competition between UNIP and opposition parties. The section that follows concentrates on the behavior of rural dwellers within the

UNIP coalition. I contend that, given their political motivations, rural voters would be behaving rationally by withholding votes from the governing party; for it was in their interest to drive up the price of their political loyalty by demanding higher levels of services for a given quantity of votes. Moreover, because UNIP was determined to achieve 100 percent electoral victories, it tended to spend money in the areas of political opposition; rural voters could therefore do better outside UNIP. Both these considerations created an incentive for initially UNIP rural voters to withhold votes from the party and thereby compel the government to purchase their support more dearly.

In addition, I contend, these dynamics at the local level linked up with patterns of conflict at the national level of UNIP. I have indicated that there were winning and losing coalitions at the national level in UNIP, the losing coalition being composed of first the Eastern-Barotse politicians and then the politicians from the Northern Province. In seeking high national posts in Zambia, it was in the interests of the members of these losing coalitions to break away from the governing party and align with opposition parties, in an attempt to form a majority party and secure governmental office. The joining of these forces of political ambition at the elite level and the aspirations for well-being at the local level promoted major shifts in the political loyalty of the rural electorate, and thereby, as we shall see, precipitated the end of party competition in Zambia.

The Barotse Case

The first example of shifts in the political affiliation of major groups of rural voters is drawn from the 1968 general elections, in which one major province, Barotse (now Western; see map 2) shifted from UNIP to ANC (African National Congress). In the 1964 elections, UNIP won every parliamentary seat in Barotse; in 1968, eight of the eleven seats went to ANC.

There were, of course, many reasons for this defection of Barotse from UNIP. Some of these are historical and involve the special position of the Barotse Protectorate in the colonial government, the strains experienced during the integration of the dominant traditional institutions of the province into the administrative structure of Zambia, and, in particular, the late entrance of nationalist political organizers into the Barotse hinterland.[18] While all these factors have been cited as important determinants of the Barotse dissatisfaction with the ruling party in postindependence Zambia, two other major reasons stand out.

The first is the peculiar ill fortune of national-level politicians from Barotse. Soon after independence, two major leaders from Barotse had been expelled from the UNIP cabinet for apparent financial irregularities in the conduct of public business. One of these, Nalumino Mundia, had played a highly prominent role in the nationalist movement and had directed UNIP to its 1964 victory in the independence elections.[19] Later, as we have seen, three of the elite politicians—Munu Sipalo, Arthur Wina, and Princess Mukwae Nakatindi—suffered electoral defeats in the 1967 elections in UNIP. For many politicians from Barotse Province, these defeats confirmed their suspicions that advancement to national office within UNIP was not possible; their chances appeared to be blocked by the dominance of the Northern-Southern Province coalition.

After his dismissal from UNIP, Mundia affiliated with other disaffected politicians and began to organize an opposition party within Barotse Province, called the United Party. Following the defeat of the Barotse candidates in the 1967 Central Committee elections, the United Party began to receive widespread support in Barotse Province. There were many reasons for the Barotse populace to support an opposition party; most prominent among them was their conviction that the UNIP government had failed to bring benefits to Barotse in the postindependence era and, indeed, had done them harm.

Development in Barotse was slow. The Kalahari sands of the region made it difficult to transport supplies and materials from the line of rail to the districts of the province. The sands also made it difficult to surface and upgrade the roads of the area. The particularly low level of initial development in Barotse at the time of independence meant that the province was slow to absorb the expansion of public capital investments following independence. The result of these facts was that few projects reached completion: roads were not constructed, wells not dug, and services not provided. The local citizenry of the area therefore became convinced that the government was doing nothing for them. Thus we note the exasperation in a speech by a UNIP minister, who was attempting to defend the government's performance in the province: "Government had voted £47,000 a long time ago for the tarring of roads in the Mongu [Barotse provincial capital] township. Money had also been voted for the digging of wells in various parts of the province, the construction of staff houses and other projects. But all of these had not been started."[20] Thus we also note the responsiveness of the local populace to the political appeals of politicians who sought to mount an electoral opposition to UNIP. As Moltino quotes the appeals broadcast in one leaflet, the Barotse people had voted UNIP in 1963 and 1964, "and what did [UNIP] give us? What did we get? Nothing. Instead we lost more and more, and we are going to lose more."[21]

Not only did the government appear not to develop Barotse effectively, but it also appeared to cause actual hardship for its population. The case in point was the government's postindependence ban on the recruitment of labor from Barotse for work in the South African gold mines.[22] This decision was in keeping with the general policy of severing economic ties with white South Africa. Whatever the presumed ethical gains from the decision, however, the material costs were high. Much like the rural families of Kasumpa, thousands of households in Barotse derived incomes from their kin "abroad"; and those working-age adults who would otherwise have gone south now remained in the villages, further depressing rural incomes. One Barotse politician noted, "These men were used to getting even £2 a month but now they just roam . . . the villages without anything to do."[23]

The result of the depressed economic situation in Barotse was a willingness to respond to politicians who sought to compete with the government for the support of the Barotse electorate. Mundia's United Party (UP), which sought to mobilize their disaffection, focused overwhelmingly on the economic needs of the Barotse voters. This naturally gave rise to claims that Barotse was secessionist—claims refuted by one opposition leader, who stated: "That is very untrue. What the people in that part of the country wanted is development, full stop."[24] Unfortunately for UP, its fervent attempts to organize led to violent clashes with backers of the government party. In August 1968, supporters of UP assaulted and killed a UNIP regional youth secretary and wounded an assistant provincial minister of state in Copperbelt Province. This led to the banning of the party.[25] The response of those who opposed the government and championed the cause of Barotse prosperity was simple: they switched their support to ANC. Forging a coalition of opposition elements in Zambia, the former leaders of the United Party joined ANC and, as mentioned above, turned UNIP candidates out of eight of the eleven seats in Barotse.[26]

The Aborted Case of Luapula

A second, if more minor, case of electoral opposition took place in Luapula. In this case, electoral shifts were not used to register disaffection with the performance of the government. Rather, the *threats* of such shifts were employed in an attempt to extract greater resources from the government.

We have already noted the willingness of Luapula citizens to withhold votes in protest over the behavior of governmental offices and the conduct of public institutions at the local level. The comments of those unwilling to register in local government elections, the "no road, no vote" protest of the Kasumpa villagers, and the later threat to boycott the 1969 referendum unless compensated for the destroyed houses all suggest the willingness of local villagers to manipulate their major political resource—their votes—so as to increase the level and quality of the services supplied to them by government.

Such manipulations were also utilized in the course of political conflicts at the national level, as in the thinly veiled threat of one provincial leader, protesting the government's failure to construct a teacher training college in Luapula: "[The district governor in Samfya] said that a Teachers Training College was a necessity here, and that it was his belief that if Luapula Province did not get a Teachers Training College, the Government would find when they next needed votes that Luapula Province would not co-operate."[27] It was in the spring of 1971, however, that electoral opposition first became a critical tactic in Luapula. In March of that year, a certain national-level politician threatened to withdraw from the governing coalition and began to organize his supporters in Luapula in preparation for leading them over to the opposition party. His efforts were tactical: he sought to gain high posts for Luapula politicians in the 1971 elections to the Central Committee of UNIP. Only by threatening to defect from the governing party and to take his Luapula followers with him did he apparently feel that he could mount a credible and effective campaign. In effect, he was blackmailing other members of UNIP by threatening to make it a minority party unless his demands were met. As he stated in one speech,

> We want to have the posts of Ministers. . . . To be chosen as a Minister is not easy. . . . They have only chosen two Ministers from this province. . . . Luapula is a big province and cannot have just two Ministers. So when we go to Mulungushi [the place where balloting for Central Committee posts takes place] we want to be elected to top posts in the party. Try to vote for those who will give you all you are asking for in this province.
>
> Others say we are trying to threaten violence. . . . People from Luapula are the bravest people and you are the people who are very interested in getting people in positions in the government. You have the right to this. . . .
>
> We want big changes to take place at Mulungushi. We want to replace even President Kaunda; if he is not working hard for what we want we will replace him. If we fail to get our posts, then we must be ready to be brave and to be prepared to reenter the struggle.[28]

The threats of political opposition and violence are clear in this recorded speech; my interviews suggested that they were even clearer in speeches for which I could locate no written record.

In organizing his supporters, this politician utilized an argument that was of particular interest. As a member of the government, he had served as a high-level political appointee to the provincial administration in Southern Province, the center of ANC support in Zambia; and, he stated, he clearly recalled the extensive development programs mounted by the government in an effort to convert opposition voters to UNIP. He had also been appointed as the cabinet minister for Barotse Province after the government's electoral defeat there in 1968. In his speeches, he recalled the new medical and educational facilities that were built in Barotse after the province's switch to ANC in the 1968 elections; the foreign assistance that was secured after the election in order to build an all-weather road connecting the province with the line of rail; and the new milling, cold storage, and dairy produce facilities that were rushed to completion so as to recover governmental support in that area.[29] In noting these things, this ambitious politician exposed the irrational element in the government's determination to purchase through the provision of public services majority support throughout Zambia and thereby to achieve, through voluntary public choice, a single-party state. Simply stated, given the government's political strategy, it paid to join the opposition. As one local politician recounted in a discussion with me, "He came to Nchelenge . . .with a pile of clothes to give supporters. . . . He told people at the meetings that we were stupid. As a Minister in Mongu [the provincial capital of Barotse] he had seen that the government gave much money to opposition areas, and he had seen this in Namwala [a district in Southern Province] as well. But here, he said, people just follow Kaunda, so why should Kaunda spend money here?"

This attempt to organize a political opposition failed. The police, on orders from the provincial minister, impounded the politician's vehicle and abruptly canceled his speaking engagements. And the president promptly suspended the minister from the government.[30] In the elections to the Central Committee in May of that year, however, three Luapula officials were nominated on the "official slate" of candidates and were elected unopposed.[31] The minister had apparently succeeded in gaining more national posts for Luapula politicians by threatening opposition to the governing party. In that sense, his tactic had worked.

UPP and the End to Party Competition in Zambia

It will be recalled that in August 1969, the UNIP leaders of seven provinces allied to force the resignation of Simon Kapwepwe, the leader of the Northern Province coalition in UNIP, as vice-president of the party and of the government of Zambia. While President Kaunda persuaded

Kapwepwe to withdraw his resignation as vice-president of the republic,[32] he did not refuse his resignation as vice-president of the party. Instead, Kaunda abolished all national posts in the party and replaced the old Central Committee with an interim Executive Committee; to this he appointed several of the previously defeated candidates for Central Committee posts, including Kamanga and Nyirenda, the leaders of the Eastern Province faction. The interim committee was to govern UNIP until the implementation of a new party constitution, one that would furnish a structure for UNIP which hopefully would enable it to mitigate the rivalries and conflicts that had so disrupted its affairs.[33]

The downfall of the Northern Province faction was also marked by the publication in 1970 of the proposals for a new party constitution. The proposals recommended the selection of two persons from each province to serve on the Central Committee; previously, politicians from the Northern Province had held five of the eleven Central Committee posts. In addition, at a later stage of the party reforms, it was proposed that each province have an equal number of votes in the national party elections; previously, the number of votes cast by a province had corresponded to the number of regions within it, and this had given the Northern Province an electoral advantage.[34]

The response of the Northern Province leaders to these attacks upon the institutional basis of their power was much like the response of the Eastern Province politicians to the elections of 1967: they consolidated their coalition—which they named the Committee of 24—and lobbied intensively in opposition to the dominant coalition in UNIP.[35] Perhaps the high point in their campaign came in January of 1971, when members of the Committee of 24 attacked the government for tribalistic practices. John Chisata, in a speech before Parliament, criticized the government for failing to dismiss officeholders formally accused of misuse of public funds; to discipline politicians who made accusations against their colleagues; or to penalize "a top government official" who had been accused of sexual misconduct. This last comment was widely interpreted as referring to the former vice-president of UNIP, whose electoral defeat by Kapwepwe in 1967 had mobilized the Eastern Province against the then dominant Northern Province coalition.[36] Chisata's allegations of "tribalistic favoritism" were quickly supported by another member of the Committee of 24, Justin Chimba.[37]

Despite the apparent attempts to consolidate the Northern Province faction and to disrupt the dominant coalition in UNIP, the constitutional proposals, whose nullification was the primary goal of the Northern Province politicians, were adopted in May 1971. While the first recommendation was not formally incorporated into the party constitution, it was followed in practice; for the new Central Committee, picked in May of 1971, contained at least two persons from each province. The redistribution of votes within the party was formally adopted at the May convention, and this cost the Northern Province its previous electoral advantage. Furthermore, a commission of inquiry was appointed to investigate Chisata's and Chimba's allegations. While it found extensive evidence of financial impropriety among ministers from the Eastern and Southern provinces, it failed to substantiate the contention that the failure to penalize these people was based on a consideration of their tribal membership. In the light of these findings, Justin Chimba was dismissed from his ministerial post in government.[38]

Defeated in the factional in-fighting in UNIP, the Northern Province leaders had but one way of enhancing their chances for high posts in government: withdrawing from UNIP and affiliating with the opposition, thereby achieving a majority position outside UNIP. This they attempted to do. While there had been rumors of a subterranean opposition party for months,[39] Kapwepwe resigned from the government on 21 August 1971 and the next day announced the formation of the United Progressive Party (UPP). Defecting with him were one former minister and three former ministers of state, all from the Northern Province.[40] Within two weeks, Kapwepwe began negotiations for a merger of UPP with ANC, the major opposition party in Zambia.

The new opposition represented a major threat to UNIP. It contained politicians who had been among the important early founders of the nationalist movement: Kapwepwe himself, of course, as well as Justin Chimba and Jameson Chapoloko, early leaders in the antifederation campaign.[41] Because of its heavy Bemba orientation, UPP possessed a political appeal not only in the Northern Province but also in the heavily Bemba Copperbelt Province and the Bemba-speaking Luapula Province. The threat to UNIP's dominance of the copperbelt was particularly strong, given the copperbelt roots of Chisata, Chimba, Chapoloko, Musonda Chambeshi, Robinson Puta, and other prominent members of UPP who had pursued trade union and political careers in that province during the nationalist era.[42] The seriousness of this threat was quickly revealed, as local units of the governing party on the copperbelt split into rival factions and local politicians withdrew from UNIP to form local units of UPP. UNIP fragmented in Ndola, Luanshya, Kitwe, and Mufulira and was seriously disrupted in virtually every copperbelt town.[43]

It is easy to see why the national-level politicians of Northern Province extraction sought to form an opposition party: they wanted higher office, and, having been denied majority support in UNIP, they sought to form a new majority by moving outside it. The question that arises is why they felt that such an opposition party would succeed in Zambia. It is my conviction that the Northern Province politicians perceived that economic grievances were becoming widespread in Zambia and that the government lacked the economic resources to meet the unfulfilled demands of the Zambian citizens.

THE TAKEOVERS OF FOREIGN ENTERPRISES

Many of these grievances arose from the nationalization of various sectors of the economy over the period 1968 to 1970. There were many motivations for these reforms. Some were economic: the desire to maintain foreign exchange reserves or to control inflation by restricting the money supply, for example.[44] But political calculations also underlay them. This is suggested by the timing: each step took place at a peak period of political crisis. The reforms of 19 April 1968 came at the height of the Eastern Province counterattack to the Northern Province victory of 1967. Those of 11 August 1969 came at the time of the displacement of Simon Kapwepwe as vice-president of UNIP. And those of November 1970 came at the time of the controversy over the new party constitution and during the political maneuvering prior to the May 1971 Central Committee elections.

In each case, by announcing new waves of reforms, President Kaunda was able to take the initiative at a time of major political crisis; and each time he was able to gain support by seizing political control over major sectors of the economy, thereby apparently enhancing the government's capacity to allocate economic goods to the people of Zambia. To quote from the president's statement at the time of the reforms of November 1970:

> To Zambian individuals it is important for me to say that the Party through Government has done its part in accordance with the mandate given to it at the last General Elections. We have carried out all the political, economic, social [and] fiscal measures. . . . It is [now] for the people to take advantage of the facilities being created through Government policies. To the people, therefore, we say: Here are opportunities for you to lead a better life. Take up the challenge.[45]

The economic reforms involved virtually every major sector of the economy, but the measures that most directly affected the African population in Zambia involved the retail trades. These reforms affected first the rural areas; then the second-class trading areas of the cities; and then the major downtown retail stores. In each case, they took the same form: the denial of licenses to expatriate traders or, in effect, the compulsory sale of retail enterprises to Zambians.

The initial effect was undoubtedly the strengthening of the United National Independence Party. For it was the job of the local UNIP officials to oversee the reforms in their area by making certain of the citizenship of the purchasers of the stores, preventing price gouging or evasions by the former expatriate proprietors, and distributing the retail centers fairly among competing applicants.[46] For those seeking material benefits, the party thus became a critical avenue for their acquisition. But there also was a second, if delayed, effect: the growth of shortages. Expatriate owners naturally canceled orders and decreased inventories in the face of the termination of their licenses; and many new owners lacked the resources and knowledge to fully provision their establishments.[47] In addition, the number of commercial outlets declined, for, as the reforms reached completion—all sales having to be completed by 1 January 1972—it became obvious that indigenous Zambian citizens lacked the capital to acquire all the stores being put up for sale. During the initial period of the reforms, in Ndola alone, 50 enterprises failed to find new owners; in Kitwe, only 31 of 128 stores were acquired by Zambians; and in Livingstone, only 10.[48] Thus many stores closed, causing layoffs of personnel and inconvenience to customers.

Whereas the short-run effect had been to strengthen government support, the long-run effect was political discontent. By the end of 1971, customers were angered by the decreased number of outlets and the decline in the variety of goods available. The commercial workers, and their union representatives, were outspoken in their fears of layoffs and the uncertainties associated with the changes in management. Most discontented of all, however, were the Zambian businessmen themselves. Many felt the government should have made cheap credit available to help them purchase stores. For lack of such credit, many stores went unsold; and for the businessmen this meant lost opportunities. Those who did succeed in purchasing stores felt that they should have received government credit so as to provision them more fully. And still others, upon beginning their work in the retail trades, found that the government placed stringent restrictions upon imports[49] and forbade them to import from the cheapest sources: South Africa and Rhodesia, Zambia's most industrialized neighbors. The result of these grievances was an increased alienation from the government and a willingness to support opposition parties.

Condemning what it called government mismanagement of the economic reforms, UPP attempted to take advantage of this discontent. Many of its leaders let it be known that they favored the liberalization of trade with the nations of the south. And UPP's local organizers promised increased aid to emergent businessmen if their party attained power. As a result, at least in Kitwe, where I worked during the formation of UPP, the opposition's most vocal and obvious backers were those who had appeared to benefit the most from the economic reforms: the businessmen themselves. In talking with these businessmen, I found that they felt UPP would aid them in getting their businesses on a sound economic footing, something they felt that the UNIP government had not done. They felt that they had been left, as one stated, "to pick UNIP's chestnuts from the fire. The government says: now we have given businesses to Zambians. It tells the people: Don't blame the government if the shops decline. Blame the new businessmen—it's up to them to make the reforms work."[50] The businessmen asserted that it was the economic reforms, more than anything, that had turned them against the government. In this feeling, they were joined by discontented consumers and commercial workers. And the UPP tried to turn this discontent to its advantage in seeking support for its opposition to the government.

THE MINEWORKERS

Another potential member of a UPP coalition against the governing party was the Zambian copper miners. As noted in earlier studies, following independence the government of Zambia had made wage restraint a central tenet of its labor policy and had campaigned intensively for trade union support for this policy.[51] Nowhere was this more true than in the copper mines, where the government did in fact succeed in winning the concerted support of the national level of the Mineworkers' Union for its labor policies. The policies were understandably unpopular at the level of the rank and file, however, and this provided opportunities for dissident leaders to challenge the established leaders of the union and the government.

In 1970–71, the time was particularly ripe for such challenges. As we have noted, a perennial and persistent issue in the mines was the disparity between expatriate and local wages; protests over this disparity had taken place since the 1940s and, on several occasions, had led to major strikes. To remove this issue from the agenda of worker-management relations, the union and the company agreed to establish a unified wage structure throughout the industry. The determining factor in a man's wages was henceforth to be the job he held and not his national background; and, as a preliminary to the implementation of a unified wages structure, the union and management jointly sponsored a comprehensive evaluation and grading of jobs in the copper mines.

From the point of view of the mineworkers, the results of the job evaluation were disappointing. The miners expected that in closing the gap between local and expatriate workers the new wage structure would result in a massive increase in wages. Such was not the case. While wages did increase for most workers, they increased, on average, by only 10 percent, spread over a four-year period. Those who held prominent positions as a result of Zambianization had anticipated the largest increases, for they expected to receive the same wages as their European counterparts; and in this, many were disappointed. Moreover, several hundred miners actually found their jobs downgraded, threatening them with cuts in pay.[52] The result was widespread discontent. As one commentator noted:

> In November 1969, during the evaluation, hundreds of angry miners stormed MUZ [Mineworkers' Union of Zambia] headquarters in Kitwe demanding an explanation of the outcome of the exercise.
>
> Since then, and the time of the introduction of the new wage system, there has been fracas after fracas with threats of a split within MUZ. And communication between the union and the members has become ineffective.
>
> It has become increasingly . . . difficult for MUZ officials to address their members. The only meetings which take place are those for officials at headquarters and branch levels.[53]

This discontent created the opportunity for competing politicians to campaign for the support of the miners. At Rokana and Roan, in particular, prominent miners sought to displace the incumbent leaders of the Mineworkers' Union. Their agitation and opposition to the leadership of the union led to a series of wildcat strikes. In response to these strikes, the government detained several of the dissident leaders,[54] and the minister of labor began an intensive campaign on the copperbelt to get the trade unions and employers to identify the leaders of wildcat strikes, to fire them, and to report their names to the government. Nonetheless, the currents of opposition they organized remained strong in the mining communities, and at both Roan and Rokana strong antiunion factions survived the removal of this leadership.

The UPP sought to promote these dissident factions. Among the top leadership of UPP were several former leaders of the Mineworkers' Union: Robinson Puta, Jameson Chapoloko, Musonda Chambeshi, and John Chisata. Working clandestinely and utilizing their numerous ties with the dissident mineworkers and their spokesmen, the leaders of the UPP hoped to take advantage of currents of dissent in the mine-working community and to gain support for their opposition party.[55]

The Rural Sector

While the political loyalties of the rural sector were deeply divided in Zambia, significant rural discontent existed nonetheless, and the opposition party leaders could plausibly expect to receive support from the aggrieved countryside. Earlier chapters suggested the bases for rural grievances and discontent. Rural incomes were low and were but slowy rising, and the performance of public institutions in the rural areas gave rise to anger and a sense of grievance. At the time of the formation of UPP several specific developments were taking place that dramatized the plight of the rural areas in a particularly vivid fashion.

One was a tightening of rural credit, as the Agricultural Finance Company sought to restrict its loans to farmers who could evidence good prospects for repayment. In and around Kasumpa, for example, a minimum holding of five acres became a prerequisite for receiving credit from the credit agency. This meant that many farmers who had previously received loans no longer qualified for them. The result was cries of protest from the farmers, their supporters in the Department of Agriculture, and the district development committees.[56] Government credit for farming thus became scarce; and many of the farmers, deeply in need of credit if only to generate funds to repay their existing debts to government, found themselves "abandoned" by government. Moreover, as we have seen, after the Olund and Russel report, the government began in 1970 to inspect and evaluate individual cooperatives in Zambia and to liquidate the assets of those they classified as moribund or inoperative. The deregistration of cooperatives, the assessment of the frequency of failures in the cooperative movement, and the totaling up of the costs to government of the training and equipping of the cooperative societies and of the unrecovered loans it had extended to them all attracted widespread comment at that time.[57]

The planning year for the Second National Development Plan was 1971. As part of the planning process, the government reviewed the performance of the economy under the first development plan; and with this review came a heightened awareness of the relative failure of the government's agricultural programs. The government collected extensive background data for the new plan. As part of its efforts it conducted a new census, and the results of the census suggested to many the relative impoverishment of the rural sector, as signified by the influx of people to the towns. Moreover, as part of its planning effort the government attempted to develop new concepts of resource allocation for the rural sector, and one of these attracted widespread public attention. This was the concept of intensive development zones, wherein the government sought to concentrate its resources in restricted areas in the rural sector—areas with the greatest known agricultural potential.[58] As this trend in the government's thinking became known, uneasiness grew over the extent to which the government seemed to be planning to withdraw its support for the vast majority of the rural dwellers in Zambia.[59]

Even if none of these factors had operated, however, 1971 would have been the year in which the "rural problem" captured the attention of many Zambians. For, in July of 1971, the government was compelled to make major purchases of maize from Rhodesia; and to import the maize the government had to violate both the United Nations' sanctions on trade with Rhodesia and its own policy of economic sanctions against that country.[60] These sanctions had for a long time formed the core of Zambia's foreign policy, and the government had spent millions of kwacha in developing alternative import sources and transport routes so as to divert trade away from the rebellious white colony. The violation of these sanctions was therefore a major political embarrassment. In addition, the necessity for maize imports only underlined the government's apparent failure to secure high levels of production from its rural sector; and the government's willingness to spend on the order of K9 per bag for maize from foreign "enemies," while paying only about half that price to domestic producers, naturally gave rise to considerable criticism. This single event, as much as any other, created a presumption of massive failure in the government's rural development program, and therefore made it credible that the political loyalty of the rural electorate could be diverted away from the governing party.

As has always been the case with the formation of parties in Zambia, UPP was slower to organize in the rural areas than it was in the cities. The rural areas are simply more difficult to organize. In addition, because of the protracted intra-UNIP conflicts which had led to the formation of the UPP, the Northern Province leaders of the new party had created many enemies among the political leaders from other provinces; the grievances of these leaders concerning the levels of development in their home areas were therefore not easily transformed into support for the new party. Nonetheless, by the end of September 1971, UPP had posted organizers in the capitals of at least the Bemba-speaking rural provinces, Northern and Luapula; and the party's efforts to attract support in the rural areas soon bore fruit.

Once again, in the Luapula valley, it was Kasumpa village that took the initiative in forming the new party. Two officers of the Katofyio Building Cooperative served as the party's organizers. While in town purchasing building materials, these men visited UPP headquarters in Ndola and received a consignment of pamphlets and membership cards. Once back in Luapula, they secreted these materials and clandestinely began to contact other potential supporters for the new party.

I quizzed these gentlemen closely as to their reasons for supporting UPP. Both had been active in the violence preceding independence, and both had been beaten by the police; but neither had received promotions in the party or jobs in government following independence, and this had embittered them. They had been helped by the government in setting up the cooperative society, however, and they had prospered by comparison with the vast majority of their friends in the village. But in 1971 contracts from the government had ceased coming in; and they had to take recourse to the arduous fish trade to maintain their standard of living. In addition, they had been subject to long and protracted delays in receiving back pay for completed contracts; not only was this frustrating, but it had also caused strained relationships with fellow villagers who had worked for them. The scarcity of contracts and the delays in payment for work completed for the government had led the two men to feel that they were being victimized by the government. Lastly, one had served as a member of the rural council and thus had had an opportunity to assess the government's ability to provide goods and services in his area. He had seen the small quantity of funds available for wells and feeder roads; he had witnessed the scarcity of transport and mechanical equipment that was available to departmental staff; and he had come away convinced of the venality of many of the staff.[61]

These two had participated in the installation of the UNIP government; they had been deeply involved in the new government's attempts to raise incomes in the rural areas; and they had become disillusioned. They therefore began to organize for the opposition, citing the failure of the cooperatives, the plight of the farmers, and the lack of significant development schemes in their area. As one of them stated, in a discussion with a potential convert; "The present government regards us as goats who can just eat the grass. We are suffering. During the struggle they promised us that there would be no more poor people and that we would be rich. It is seven years and we are still poor." Citing in particular the failure of the cooperative societies, he went on to say: "It is now the same as the colonial government. We must turn out the government. Even if we fail, they will have to try to make us happy. Otherwise others will follow us and they will lose power."

The two organizers did succeed in recruiting two other followers in Kasumpa, and they made important converts among some of the more prominent fishermen on Lake Mweru. Nonetheless, they were unable to make an open and concerted effort at organizing opposition sentiment, for reasons that we shall shortly go into.

Limitations on Government Resources

As detailed above, at least three major groups—the new retailers, the miners, and the rural dwellers—possessed genuine grievances and unfulfilled demands for governmental action and these served as an incentive for the entrance of competing political parties.[62] What made the situation particularly dangerous from the government's point of view, however, was the decline of public resources with which to meet these unfulfilled demands.

The government of Zambia, I have argued, can be seen to have continually relied on its ability to command and allocate financial resources as a means of fulfilling demands and thereby gaining political popularity. Several factors, however, made it extremely difficult for the public sector to respond to the threat of UPP in the same manner as it had responded to the enfranchisement of the rural electorate, the 1967 redistribution of power in UNIP, or the incipient defection of the Northern Province faction in 1970. In 1971, the government was no longer in a position to purchase political support.

One reason for this was the decline in 1970 and 1971 of the principal source of public revenues: the mining industry. In June 1970, the price of copper had begun a long and protracted downward slide, one that left it at £411 per ton of electrolytic wirebar at the end of 1971, compared with the 1969 average of £611.[63] In addition, the mining industry experienced a drop in output: from the 1969 high of 720 thousand tons, output dropped to 651 thousand tons in 1971.[64] The principal reason for this decline was the September 1970 mining disaster at Mufulira, an accident that caused scores of deaths and a decline in production from over 7 million tons of ore hoisted per year in 1969 to slightly over 4 million tons of ore hoisted in 1971.[65] By definition, the fall in price and output led to a drop in the value of sales, which slumped from over K660 million in 1970 to approximately K480 million in 1971.[66]

One result of the slump in the copper industry was a decline in government revenues. The industry had paid over K117 million in taxes in 1970; in 1971, it paid in the range of K20 million.[67] Largely as a consequence, total government revenues declined from K432 million in 1970 to approximately K300 million in 1971. A second and equally distressing consequence was an adverse shift in Zambia's balance of payments. From a surplus in current account of K338 million in 1969, Zambia's trade balance declined to a surplus of K86 million in 1970 and then shifted to a deficit of over K100 million in 1971.[68] The deterioration in the balance of payments led in turn to a rapid decline in Zambia's foreign reserves: from K450 million in August of 1970 to an estimated K220 million at the end of 1971.[69]

This decline in government revenues and foreign reserves led to severe restrictions on the level of public expenditure, both because funds were scarce and because of a growing inability to finance the importation of capital goods.[70] In an attempt to counteract these trends, the government began to explore the prospects for large-scale foreign borrowing. It also imposed strict licensing controls on imports and introduced new customs, excise, and income taxes.[71] The last two measures caused widespread public indignation, especially from the new Zambian businessmen, who went so

Table 11.2   The Budget Cut of 1972

	1971 (K million, actual)	1972 (K million, estimated)
Total capital expenditures	187.5	132.7
Total recurrent expenditures, including supplementary estimates	410.1	296.8
Total expenditures	597.6	429.5

Source: Budget Address, *Official Verbatim Report of the Parliamentary Debates of the Fourth Session of the Second National Assembly, 12th January–9th March 1972,* Hansard no. 29, (Lusaka: Government Printer, 1972), pp. 500–37.

far as to accuse the government of causing "economic disaster."[72] Nonetheless, the new taxes and duties could not substitute for the decline in copper revenues, and the government had to impose a 25 percent cut in expenditures for the next budgetary year (see table 11.2). The situation facing the government was perhaps best captured in the words of one commentator in the national press: "The seven fat years are over; are there seven lean years ahead?"[73]

The UPP leaders anticipated this shortfall in the government's capacity to mobilize resources and thereby meet the demands being articulated by broad segments of the populace. Indeed, they made the government's supposed financial mismanagement the center of their propaganda appeals. Thus, for example, in his initial announcement of the formation of UPP, Kapwepwe was quoted as saying:

"The economic situation is nothing but alarming. If . . . we are spending almost K51 million per month in foreign exchange . . . this for sure will land this nation in a . . . crisis," he warned. He explained that the reason for "this senseless expenditure" was due to nothing but carelessness and financial indiscipline in the government. . . .

"I want to state this very strongly that the financial situation is chaotic and we will land this nation in hardships, not to mention mass unemployment . . . " Mr. Kapwepwe said.

"We have even failed to grow maize—as if we had no land and rain. As a result, we have spent K32 million public funds to South Africa and Rhodesia."

Mr. Kapwepwe said he and his colleagues had formed the UPP to see if they could save the country [from] some of those "terrible mistakes."[74]

THE GOVERNMENT'S RESPONSE

A major segment of the ruling coalition had thus withdrawn from UNIP in 1971. As we have seen, this Northern Province faction, in a bid for power, formed an opposition party and concentrated its appeals on those sectors with economic grievances. With ties in the Copperbelt, Luapula, and Northern provinces, and with the potential for an alliance with ANC, which drew strong support from Southern, Central, and Barotse provinces, UPP represented a serious threat to UNIP—a threat which the governing party was no longer able to buy off through the massive infusion of public funds. The response of the government was straightforward: it terminated the era of competitive party politics in Zambia.

The first stage in the government's response was the use of coercion. While UPP must share the blame for the outbreaks of violence that took place after its formation,[75] there can be little doubt but that local UNIP officials organized intimidation and beatings of the followers of the opposition party. During the period when UPP was organizing on the copperbelt, I was conducting research in what had been Kapwepwe's parliamentary constituency. I witnessed many of the steps taken to terminate the activities of the UPP organizers in the mine townships. UNIP youths attacked the organizers for UPP and beat them. They entered their houses, smashed their furniture, ripped up their bedding, and poured water on their food stores.[76] Those UPP supporters who ran shops in the townships found their customers frightened away; in other cases they found that UNIP party workers had locked up their shops and closed their stores, and that the authorities would not intervene to reopen them.[77] Physically intimidated and deprived of their sources of income, the followers of the UPP rapidly dwindled in number.

A second step in the repression of UPP was the initiation in November 1971 of card-checking campaigns. In these campaigns, the UNIP youths organized a program of party-card sales; persons lacking UNIP cards were forced to buy them, and persons discovered possessing UPP cards were in danger of being beaten. In conducting the campaign, the youths encircled markets, bus stops, hospitals, and other public facilities. Marketeers could not sell their goods until they proved that they possessed a UNIP card and held no UPP card, nor could persons board the buses or obtain medical care.[78] One regional secretary was quoted as stating in Ndola, "A UNIP card will definitely be the only passport to buying commodities from shops, markets, bars, and even for boarding trains and buses."[79] Similar tactics were followed in the rural areas, though the relative absence of UPP supporters, at least in Kasumpa village, meant that the level of coercion tended to be lower. Nonetheless, UNIP youths blocked the pathways to the river and to the well, and UNIP cards had to be produced to get water. They checked cards at the village stores. And drivers of automobiles encountered UNIP roadblocks; to pass them, they had to produce party cards or else return to their place of residence and purchase one from the local party officials.

The intimidation of UPP members was not confined to the local level. The central government also mobilized its powers of coercion against the national officers of UPP. Three days after the party's formation, two members of its national executive, Henry Msoni and Zilole Mumba, were seized and detained by the police; and on 20 September 1971 the police seized and detained virtually every major officeholder in UPP, save Simon Kapwepwe.[80] In one fell swoop, the major officeholders in Lusaka, the copperbelt, and Northern Province were seized and put in jail. They were later charged with "organizing the UPP in a manner designed to create tribal conflict in the country" and with having "knowingly or unknowingly assisted in obtaining from governments hostile to Zambia materials, including firearms, and the training of Zambian nationals with the intention to dislodge by unlawful means the legally constituted government."[81] Though not officially banned, UPP was left in tatters.

Needless to say, the arrest and detention of the national party officers had a chilling effect on the local-level supporters of the UPP. In Kasumpa those who supported the party found that their urban contacts were now in prison. Moreover, the uncle of one of the detained UPP organizers lived in the village; and tales of his nephew's arrest and treatment in prison circulated throughout the village, as friends and family members stopped by to bring the uncle up to date on the fate of his kin.

If the arrests had a chilling effect on the UPP organizers, they appeared to have invigorated the UNIP faithful. Thus, for example, the constituency officials from the area telegraphed the state house to say, "(1) While we appreciate naturally your recent action of rounding up some UPP leaders . . . [we] would like you to pack up UPP leader Kapwepwe without delay. (2) Or send him here. [W]e shall involve him in the fishing industry. (3) Give no . . . mercy."[82] The regional secretary urged his constituency officials on: "We should try by all means not to give any chance for any party to penetrate our Region. Each Constituency should form a working machinery and this should be done quickly. . . . Time of talking is now over, it is action, we have to go back to the old 1961 days, vigilance and militance. An enemy is an enemy and he should not be given a chance."[83] In Kasumpa, UNIP branch officials and youths formed small patrols; armed with clubs and spears, they circulated throughout the village at night, being sure that no organizer from UPP was clandestinely meeting with persons in the village. The Katofyio members of UPP had no choice but to withdraw from political activity, to remain quiet, and to leave UNIP supreme and unchallenged.

Following the national purge of UPP, the challenge posed to UNIP was largely over. In December, parliamentary by-elections were held to fill the seats vacated by those who had switched their party membership or who had been detained.[84] The UPP contested five seats: two in the Northern Province, two in Copperbelt Province, and one in the Eastern Province. In only one case—Kapwepwe's challenge for the seat in Mufulira vacated by John Chisata—did UPP emerge victorious. What evidence there is suggests that Kapwepwe gained votes from the traditionally strong ANC contingent in Mufulira, who were in fact instructed by ANC headquarters to vote UPP, and from the major dissident factions in the Mineworkers' Union, which had been strongly courted by John Chisata, former president of the union, while serving as a member of Parliament from Mufulira.[85] The dissident mineworkers also contributed strongly to UPP's challenge in the Rokana mine townships, where their candidate, a former University of Zambia student, polled 20 percent of the votes cast—double the proportion of opposition votes in prior elections in the constituency. Nonetheless the record was clear: UPP won only one of the five seats it contested. Its challenge to UNIP had largely been broken.

The final stage in the abolition of UPP soon followed. Prior to the elections, Wesley Nyirenda, then minister of education, had announced that "the Government will begin working out plans for a one-party state after the . . . by-elections,"[86] and at the height of the balloting the president himself announced the government's decision to institute a one-party state in 1972. Shortly after the election, the government took steps to implement its plans. Following a period of unrest and violence on the copperbelt, the president, on 4 February, announced the banning of UPP and the detention of its leader, Simon Kapwepwe.[87] On the twenty-fifth, the president appointed a commission to formulate constitutional proposals for a single-party state in Zambia. After touring the country taking testimony regarding the appropriate form of the new government,[88] the commission submitted its proposals in October 1972. Following the government's endorsement of the proposals in November, Parliament, on the eighth of December, amended the constitution so as to prohibit all opposition parties and to make UNIP the sole legal party in Zambia.[89] The era of opposition parties was over. It was the end of the era of competitive party politics and the end of the first Republic in Zambia.

In the postindependence period, major sectors of the Zambian electorate had looked to the government to make them better off. This was certainly true of the members of the rural electorate, who sought to gain through politics what they had been unable to achieve through private markets: prosperity and access to the wealth of the towns. As we have seen, it was true of other groups as well. Given competition among politicians for high posts in UNIP, and given competition between UNIP and the political opposition, and in light of the expectations and preferences of their constituents, politicians in the competitive system offered pledges of public services in exchange for votes. And their constituents, who were sophisticated parties to these electoral trades, manipulated as best they could the price of their political allegiance. So long as the government had seemingly inexhaustible resources, it could maintain its dominance in the postindependence game of politics in Zambia, but when its resources became constrained it eliminated the system of competitive party politics. It had become too expensive to remain in power by serving the interests of the rural dwellers and those who behaved like them in the electoral process.

Villagers in search of increased benefits from the government thus contributed to the transformation of the postindependence party system in Zambia. And henceforth, in their search for solutions to the problem of rural poverty in Zambia, they could no longer exploit to their advantage the system of competitive parties. Having been among the most enthusiastic of those who had instigated party competition so as to secure services from the government, the rural dwellers were among those who stood to lose the most from its demise.[90]

12

Rural Responses to Industrialization

Fifty years ago, Zambia was rural and agrarian; today it is urbanized and industrialized to a degree that has been attained by no other nation in black Africa. Within Zambia, the contrast in economic opportunities between the rural and industrial sectors is perhaps as sharply drawn as for any nation in the developing world. In this book I have attempted to account for the transformation of Zambian society and for the pattern of disparate economic opportunities which has resulted. More centrally, I have examined the response of the villages to the precipitate growth of the industrial centers of Zambia.

The villagers of Zambia, I contend, have responded in three major ways. They have sought to benefit from the transformation of their society by exchanging their own resources for money in the urban markets for agricultural produce and industrial labor. They have also sought to gain from the profits of industry by creating political incentives for the government to extract revenues from the industrial sector and to transfer them to the rural areas in the form of public investments. Economic exchanges in the markets for produce and labor and participation in politics have thus characterized the rural response to industrialization in this central African nation.

Besides characterizing the reaction of the villagers to the growth of industry, this study has also examined the relationships among these responses. In one case, the relationship is a simple one: rural prosperity and rural emigration were found to be inversely related. The study isolated the factors that appeared to promote or retard the profitability of agriculture and thereby determine which market response would be chosen. It examined the effect of locational advantages, natural endowments, and the extent and the quality of public investments upon the profitability of farming. Pricing policy, marketing policy, the fate of peasant farmers and the cooperative movement, the role of credit and its method of distribution, and the impact of legislation upon the vesting of rights in land—all these factors have received attention. One general conclusion appeared inescapable: market forces do not penetrate far in Zambia, and the incentives to respond to the growth of urban-industrial centers by engaging in agricultural production decline rapidly with distance from town. Moreover, the public sector appears unable to provide economic services efficiently in areas where the market fails to function. In most rural areas, therefore, to gain access to the wealth of the cities, people emigrate.

Much of the study examined this migratory response of rural dwellers. It found that migration served as an escape from rural poverty. Migration has also served as a means whereby rural dwellers extract wealth from the towns and transfer it to the village communities. The study examined the way in which villagers use the family and kinship system to organize the market for labor and to divert earnings from the more prosperous urban sector. And it documented the decreasing incentive for urban migrants to remit their earnings to rural kin, a weakening that has apparently resulted from the growth of opportunities for postemployment incomes in town and for more prosperous retirements therein.

Cash crop farming and urban migration thus constitute the major market responses to the growth of industry in Zambia, and there is a clear relationship between the two; but what of the relationship between the market and nonmarket responses? The answer to this question, we found, depends upon which market is under discussion. In the market for produce, political participation appears to be complementary to economic behavior; in the market for labor, politics appears to serve as a substitute.

In the next few pages I will elaborate upon these points. In so doing, I hope to place this study in a comparative context and thereby assess its meaning for the general study of peasant politics in the developing areas.

Politics and Migration

In Zambia, as in many developing countries, the urban areas are prosperous while the rural areas are not prosperous to the same degree. To improve their lot, many rural dwellers therefore migrate to the city. But, as we have seen, many others do not. Instead, they remain in the villages and seek to upgrade their standard of living through politics. They seek to compel the government to levy wealth from the towns and distribute it in the countryside in the form of programs of rural development. Politics and migration therefore act as substitute means for benefiting from the wealth of the urban and industrial areas.

They are substitutes, of course, in the trivial sense that once a person has left the countryside he can no longer participate in rural political affairs. But they are substitutes in a more significant sense as well. To the point is

Albert Hirschman's distinction between what he terms "exit"—a market response analogous to migration—and "voice"—a lobbying response analogous to political protest. By Hirschman's reasoning, one of the primary factors determining the response chosen is the person's elasticity of demand for a product. When it is low, then the person will not significantly alter his consumption of the product while it is declining in quality (or increasing in price); rather, he will tend to consume it at former levels while exerting pressure on the supplier to improve its quality (or reduce its price). With regard to village dwellers, we can envisage those who remain in the rural areas as having a low elasticity of demand for rural dwelling; though declining in relative attractiveness by comparison with the city, life in the countryside must continue to be "consumed" by those who are too young, too old, or too poorly educated to exit for the cities. Being unable to leave, they may instead take recourse to politics to upgrade the quality of life in the countryside.[1]

This way of interpreting the relationship between migration and politics may at first seem farfetched, but on closer inspection it appears to be appropriate. It does seem to capture the basis for the politics of despair in impoverished rural communities—communities from which many persons are literally too disadvantaged to escape—and it seems to account for the data presented in other studies. Thus, for example, Audrey Smock, in her comparison of two ethnic unions in the eastern region of Nigeria, notes that the union formed in Mbaise tended to be far more political than the one formed in Abiriba. By contrast with Abiriba, she notes, Mbaise was a far more densely populated rural area and lacked "a trading tradition" by which emigrants could gain wealth in the city and export it to the countryside.[2] Rather than attempting to extract resources from the urban markets, the people of Mbaise instead attempted to extract resources from the government. Similarly, Edward Malefakis, in attempting to explain the rise of peasant anarchism in prerevolutionary Spain, stresses the failure of industrialization in that country. He contrasts Spain's experience with that of Britain and Germany, where industrialization enabled those in search of higher incomes to leave the countryside.[3] Lacking such an alternative, rural dwellers in Spain had instead to engage in politics to increase their incomes; and this was, Malefakis argues, especially true as increases in population led to a decline in average rural incomes and to a growth in the number of landless peasants in Spain. Again, urban migration and rural protest appear as alternatives. Lastly, we can cite Sidney Tarrow's study of rural radicalism in southern Italy, a case study that bears striking parallels to this one. Tarrow notes that the base for rural radicalism lay among those who were unable to take advantage of the expanding industrial market for labor in the north. Instead of migrating, many had to remain behind; and those who remained joined the waves of radical protest that led in the 1950s to the formation of special state agencies to mount massive public investments in the south, both to raise the standard of living and to reduce the level of political protest therein.[4] The pattern of migration (or lack of it), protest, and public intervention in the countryside parallels that reported in this study as well. Tarrow's work, like the others, thus suggests that for those rural dwellers for whom exit is not a viable option political protest can serve as an alternative—a way of compelling the state to divert the wealth of the cities so that villagers may benefit from the opportunities created by the growth of industrialization. Migration and politics appear to serve as alternative responses to the problem of rural poverty.

Politics and Rural Producers

If migration and politics are substitutes, rural production and political protest appear to complement one another. Time and again, studies have shown how rural dwellers, seeking to enhance their incomes by producing goods for sale in the towns, have reverted to politics as a means for attaining their objective. In this instance, the behavior of the Zambian villagers appears to differ significantly from that of others, and the contrasts are instructive.

There have been numerous studies of political action by rural producers who confront the growth of urban markets. One body of literature tends to emphasize the "backwash" effects of the penetration of urban markets into the countryside. Typically, this literature focuses on the fate of rural manufacturers who are unable to compete with the more efficient and better capitalized fabricators in the urban centers. Rural weavers are often a case in point; and the declining fortunes of these producers and others of their ilk have been associated with outbursts of rural protest against encroaching market forces in such diverse areas as France, England, India, and China.[5] This interpretation of rural politics is not particularly helpful in the case of Zambia, however; by the same token, the case study does not contribute much to the literature of this kind; for the growth of the mines and associated industries in central Africa took place in a rural environment in which the level of development simply was much lower than that in the four cases cited above. Rural industries did not exist on a comparable scale, and the passion and force that drove rural protest did not derive in any significant way from a decline in the economic fortunes of established rural producers.[6]

A second major approach relates market behavior to political action through the medium of rural stratification. This literature views peasant protest as a response to the monopoly position of the landed classes. According to this literature, the key to benefiting from the expansion of market opportunities in agriculture is the ability to gain access to land. And, with the penetration of markets into the countryside, the upper classes seek to secure monopoly rights to this productive resource and to use their position to divert the increased earnings to be had from agriculture from the peasant producers to themselves. One result is increased inequality; and another is the banding together of the peasants in an attempt to break up the monopoly position of the landed classes and to lay claim to the profits to be gained from agriculture. Peasant revolutions, land seizures, and land reforms are characteristic outcomes of this pattern of political response to the growth of market opportunities.[7]

A stratification model of rural politics appears to apply in Zambia only along the line of rail. There, as we have seen, with the transformation to freehold tenure, commercial farmers alienated extensive farming areas; and, indeed, the seizure of large farms by highly capitalized farmers made the land issue the dominant issue of indigenous politics in that area. The commercially oriented African villagers could not increase their incomes by expanding their holdings and therefore sought through the nationalist movement to redistribute landholdings to their advantage. Elsewhere, however, it was the fear of the alienation of land rather than its actuality that stirred rural voters. In these more remote areas, which contain the vast majority of the rural dwellers, a stratification model is simply not very useful.

For most areas of Zambia, land has tended to be an abundant factor, and one over which it would be nearly impossible to establish monopoly control. The fact that the mean population density in Zambia even today is in the range of a dozen persons per square mile suggests the extent to which land is freely accessible. Moreover, rights over land tend not to be vested in the ruling classes. For the vast majority of the regions of Zambia, the right to claim land comes with citizenship in a village; and membership can be given, and presumably denied, by a headman. The anthropological literature makes clear, however, that the headman was unlikely to use this power in an exploitative way. For the headmen tended to compete for followers, and the importance of a headman was judged in terms of the number of people he could attract to his village.[8] Where the headman made too many demands on the people, or when he otherwise failed to satisfy their expectations of rural well-being, then his village would tend to fragment, and his people would depart for another village where the headman could better fulfill their needs.[9] Consequently, as George Kay contends, "a District Officer came close to the truth when he observed that the chiefs could not enforce unpopular rules because they feared that their people would abandon them and settle under someone more congenial."[10] Where headmen were unable to enforce unpopular laws, neither could they make major levies of income. The fact that land was abundant, and that headmen were not in a position to set the price of access to it, meant that, despite the increase in the demand for rural products, privileged strata did not arise in the Zambian countryside.[11] The stratification models of peasant politics in the modern era thus do not fare well in the analysis of rural politics in Zambia.[12]

There is a third major model of rural political response to the growth of market opportunities, and this one emphasizes communitarian opposition to individualistic behavior in response to market forces. According to this kind of interpretation, rights to economic resources are vested in the rural community and not in the individual; and resources are distributed in such a way that no member of the community is allowed to be totally bypassed by rising economic fortunes. By the same token, neither is anyone allowed disproportionately to gain. The communal allocation of resources discourages private investment, for it is impossible under such arrangements to gain the full benefit of any augmentation of value that may result from one's labors. And thus, the literature suggests, communitarianism is incongruent with rapid economic growth.

Where demand for rural production is rising, however, market forces provide an incentive to divest the community of control over resources and so increase the chances for private gain. In this way, private-regarding individuals can make greater profits. The conflict is then joined. For the poor, communal institutions guarantee access to the wealth generated by the rise in demand; for the rich or ambitious, communal institutions undercut their ability to gain. Whether in the form of the *kulaks* against the mirs in the Soviet Union; the haciendas against the Indian villages during the era of "liberal reform" in nineteenth-century Latin America; or the lords against the peasants and their demands for access to commons throughout postfeudal Europe, political conflict in the countryside can break out in response to growing chances for wealth from rural production.

At least in the popular literature, African villages are often seen as communities in which resources are vested in collective institutions, be they the lineage, the village, or the tribe. Such a perception apparently underlies the Zambian government's decision to sponsor cooperatives as the chief mechanisms for encouraging commercial crop production in the villages.[13] But when opportunities for private gain become evident, as both Victor Uchendu and Elizabeth Colson have argued, collectivist control of resources appears to be subverted rapidly and easily in contemporary Africa.[14] And the emergence of private rights in property does not appear to have given rise to high degrees of political conflict in the countryside, save in Tanzania, where the government has attempted to promote communal rights to land.[15]

Certainly in this case study we found little place for a communal perspective on the political behavior of villagers. Rather, the villagers appeared to be motivated by a desire for individual gain; and their access to resources appeared to be unconstrained by the vesting of rights in a collectivity. An individualistic model appears to have done better than any alternative I can think of; and this is certainly true in the area of politics, where the issue of communal rights versus individual gain was not joined in Zambia, as apparently it has been in other rural areas of the world.

Three kinds of interpretations have thus been applied toward explaining the political behavior of rural producers when confronted by expanding markets, but only one of them appears to apply in any significant way to the case of Zambia. These models therefore distinguish the Zambian case from others that have been studied, and their general lack of explanatory power encourages us to seek other explanations for why political action should accompany attempts to obtain increased income through the private market for produce.

This case study suggests that we would do well to conceive of village dwellers who derive incomes through private markets as behaving like economic men vis-à-vis the state. Governments tax private incomes and they provide public services. The public services that they provide are often judged not to equal in value the private income surrendered to finance them. Rural producers are as likely to make such assessments as are others; and they are no less likely to engage in political activity when they do. Thus we found that the levying of taxes on rural fishermen, and the failure to compensate in a way that was deemed to have offset in public goods the losses in private income, shaped much of the politic᷍ in the preindependence era. Viewing peasants as economic men also enables us to realize that, like others, they wish to pay less and consume more, and that they are likely to engage in politics to realize these objectives in their relationships with the state. Thus, we found that throughout the contemporary history of the Luapula valley villagers have sought to increase the quantity of goods received from the state and to decrease the price paid for them in the form of taxes. One of the major triumphs of the rural dwellers, after all, was the shifting of the costs of public services from the countryside to the urban industrial areas.[16] In thus viewing rural producers as being, like other people, economic men in their relationship with the state, we can comprehend why they take recourse to the political arena in furtherance of their search for higher incomes.[17]

The state does not affect private incomes solely as a purveyor and financer of public goods, as we have suggested thus far. It also affects private incomes through its attempts to regulate the way in which they are obtained. In agriculture, as elsewhere, the government often regulates private production in such a way that the present incomes of producers are below those they could attain were such regulations not imposed. The result is that voluntary compliance is not achieved, coercion is necessary, and discontent is inevitable. Rural producers are no less prone to discontent under these conditions than are others. And, as we have seen, for the fishermen at least, one result is political protest.

Interpretations like these—ones that see rural producers as behaving as economic men in their relationship with the state—rather than notions of rural decline, rural stratification, or the communal nature of peasants, appear to account best for the rise of political action under conditions of expanded production for the urban market in the countryside of Zambia.[18]

Return to Stratification Theory

Thus far I have given short shrift to one of the major approaches to the study of peasant responses to industrialization, that of stratification analysis. The variant examined was one confined to the rural sector. All that has been written, however, suggests that a model of national stratification—one that includes both the urban and rural sectors—deserves serious attention. For this study has repeatedly documented the large differentials of income between the urban and rural sectors; and much effort has been devoted to exploring the origins of these differentials and to examining their consequences.

Much of the contemporary literature on peasant politics starts with such a differential in mind.[19] The Maoist variant, at least, contends that such a differential is sufficient to establish the peasantry as a distinct class; and the implication for politics is that the peasantry will cohere, rebel, and form the basis for the revolutionary politics of our time. The present case study calls this line of analysis into question. The economic divide between town and country in Zambia is perhaps as distinct as that in any nation; and yet we are hard pressed to find clear instances of collective action on the part of the countryside against the urban centers. Instead, we find the countryside riven with political competition and conflict. Within provinces, district opposes district; and the competition between the rural provinces has been great enough to fragment national parties and to split governing coalitions. Instead of class action in the countryside, we find internal division. This is true in Zambia and, by all reports, it is true throughout much of Africa.

As Marx himself noted, it is difficult for the peasantry to act as a class. Because of the problem of communication between isolated farm settlements, because peasants are numerous, and because they compete on the same side of the markets of greatest importance to them, they encounter great difficulty in organizing a collectivity.[20] As this book has shown, however, although unable to cohere as a political force, the villagers of Zambia do not lack means of registering their preferences in the national political arena. And the effect of the political process as manipulated by the village dwellers has been to transfer wealth from the towns to the countryside and from industry to agriculture, thereby making the regional pattern of inequality less pronounced than it might otherwise be and advancing their collective interests.

The political efforts of the rural dwellers have taken several forms. In some cases, they have taken the form of protest and petition. In others, they have taken the form of electoral defection, as rural dwellers have withdrawn their votes from former political allies and transferred them to the opposition. In still other cases, rural protest has emerged in the shape of sectional alliances. These coalitions have occasionally split the governing party and led to defections to the opposition. Cleavages within the governing elite, the strengthening forces of electoral opposition, and the spread of local dissidence—these phenomena which so often are labeled pathological signs of instability instead appear to mark the normal processes whereby rural dwellers express their wants through political action and vigorously compete for public resources. The Zambian peasants do not act out of a sense of class consciousness, and they appear unable to act as a coherent class; but these signs of political turmoil nonetheless demonstrate their willingness and ability to advance their interests. To paraphrase John Saul, the signs of potential conflict mark a not so "silent class struggle" in Zambia.[21] Given the ferocity of competitive bidding for public resources from the government which characterizes the pattern of politics in Zambia and elsewhere on the continent, such forms of political conflict may well take the place of class conflict as an effective political response to the issues of inequality and resource allocation in developing Africa.

These tactics impose significant costs on governments, however; and many governments are unwilling to pay them. As noted in Chapter 11, through constitutional reform the government of Zambia removed one of the main instruments for registering rural protest and attaining higher levels of public expenditures in the countryside: the competitive party system. In seeking to preserve political stability, the government may have made it more difficult for rural dwellers to alter the regional patterns of relative privilege that characterize the nation. As they have in the past Zambian villagers will continue to choose between private and public solutions to the problem of relative poverty. Either they will resign themselves to their political position and seek private solutions to their economic fate, or they will attempt to devise new forms of political action to compel public measures to enhance their well-being. The way they make this choice will be of central importance to the politics of this developing nation.

Map 1.   Line of Rail in Zambia

Source: Adapted with permission from Mary Elizabeth Jackman, *Recent Population Movements in Zambia*, p. 5.
Note: Names in parentheses are those used in the colonial era.

Map 2.   Districts and Provinces of Zambia

Source: Adapted with permission from Jackman, *Recent Population Movements*, p. 4.

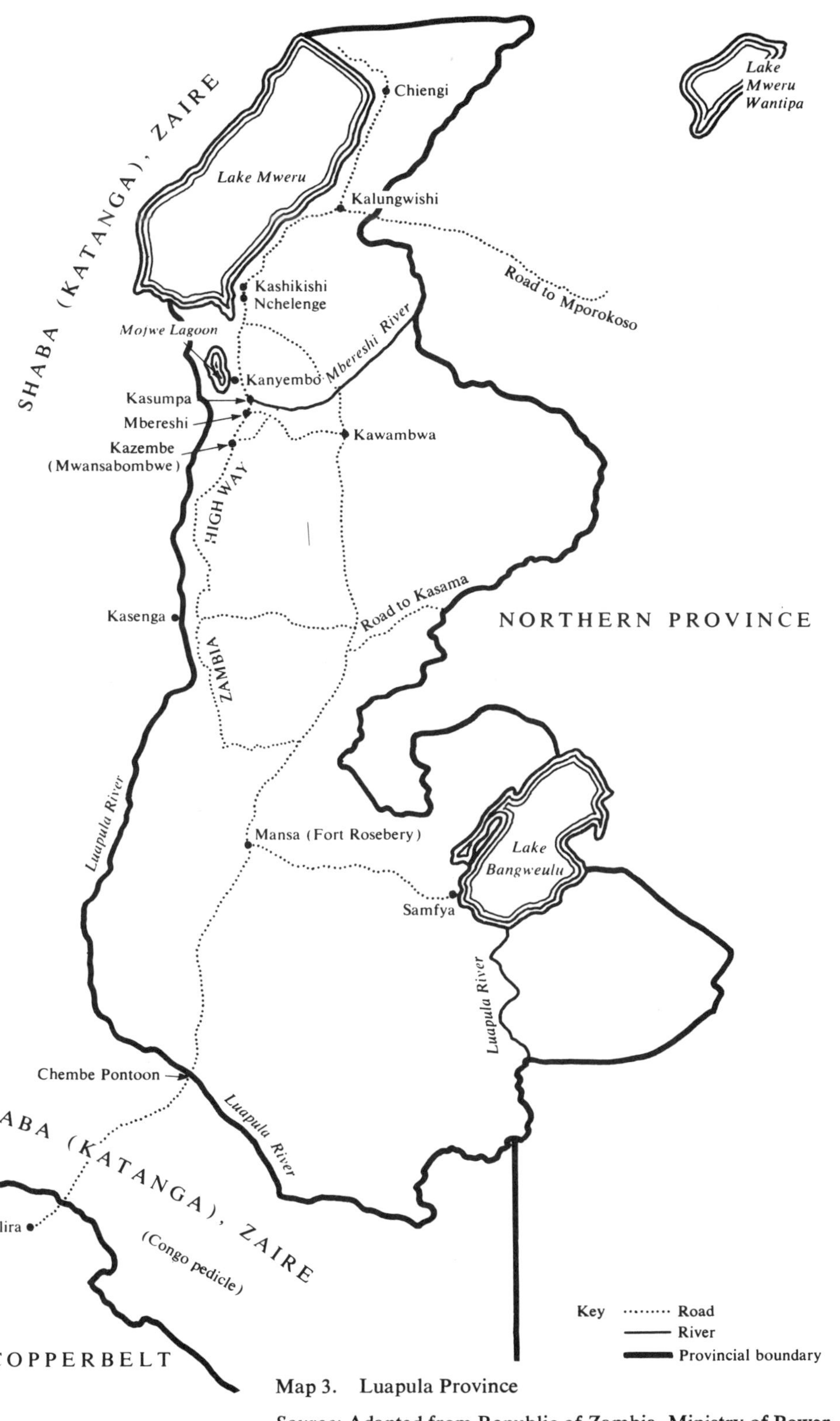

Map 3. Luapula Province

Source: Adapted from Republic of Zambia, Ministry of Power, Transport, and Works, *Road Mileage Map* (Lusaka: Roads Department, January 1969).

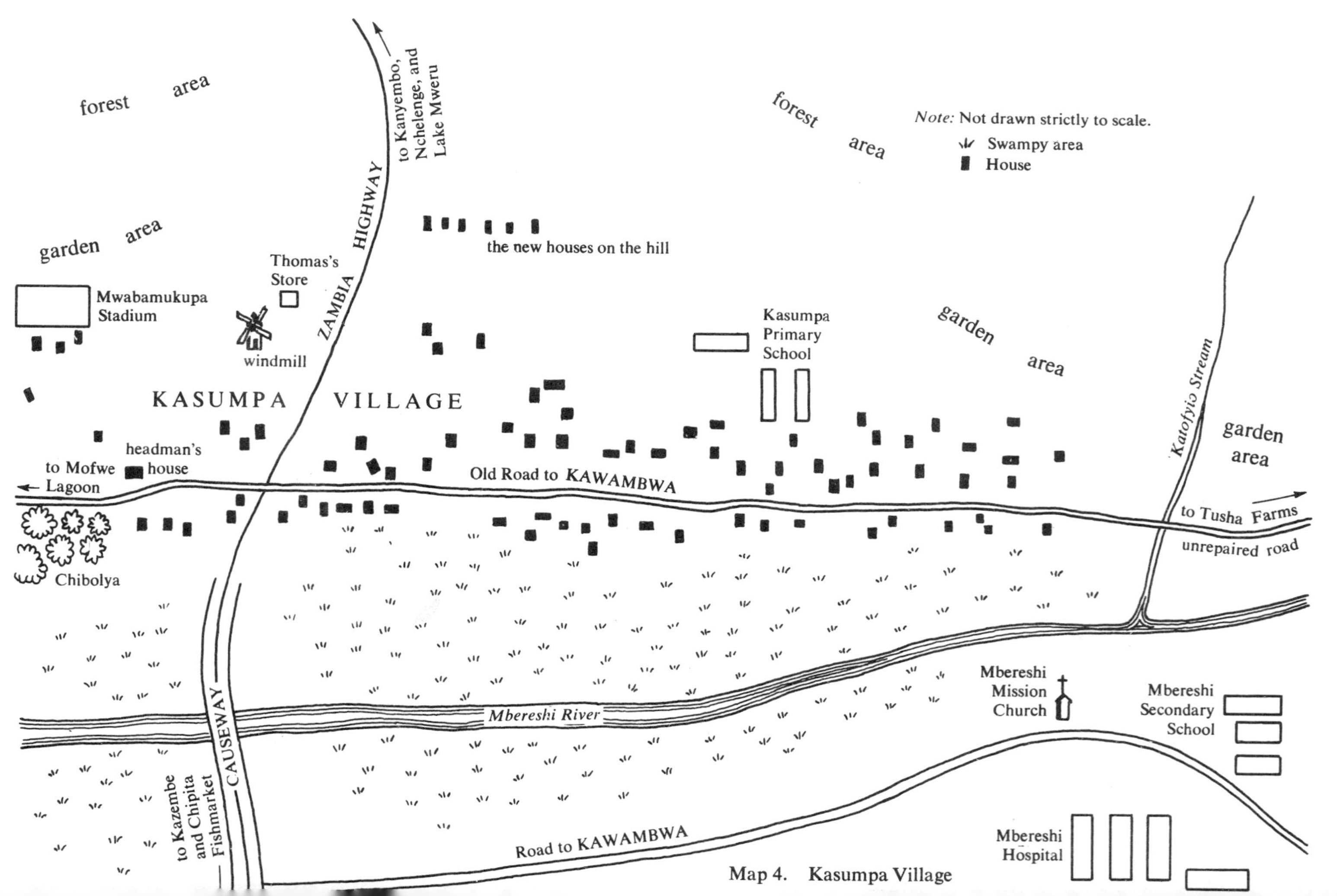

forest area
forest area
Note: Not drawn strictly to scale.
Swampy area
House
to Kanyembo, Nchelenge, and Lake Mweru
ZAMBIA HIGHWAY
garden area
Mwabamukupa Stadium
Thomas's Store
windmill
the new houses on the hill
Kasumpa Primary School
garden area
Kalofyta Stream
garden area
KASUMPA VILLAGE
headman's house
to Mofwe Lagoon
Old Road to KAWAMBWA
to Tusha Farms
unrepaired road
Chibolya
to Kazembe and Chipita Fishmarket
CAUSEWAY
Mbereshi River
Mbereshi Mission Church
Mbereshi Secondary School
Road to KAWAMBWA
Mbereshi Hospital
Map 4. Kasumpa Village

A Note on Research Methods

In selecting and gathering the data for this book, I interpreted the structure of the research problem in terms of three basic dimensions. These dimensions can be labeled: the local scene, the national scene, and time.

These dimensions emerged from my conception of the behavior of rural dwellers. I regarded them as individual choice makers, who were seen as selecting among alternative ways of increasing their well-being. To explain their behavior, I had to account for the relative value of various alternatives that were open to them. And the value of these alternatives had in many instances been set largely by forces outside of their control: central decision makers, residing in the urban-industrial centers of the country, and historical forces—decisions taken in past time, the consequences of which influenced the current value of contemporary alternatives.

Historical Data Sources

History exerted a powerful influence on the behavior of the postindependence residents of Kasumpa village. Thus, for example, the present value of the migratory alternative was influenced by the fact that the villagers resided in the rural hinterland to the great mining centers in central Africa; and an explanation of their migratory behavior therefore required an accounting for the development of the mining industry and the pattern of locational advantages which it engendered in the central African region. As another example of the present power of past events, it became obvious to me that the tendency for Kasumpa villagers to seek income from rural cash crop production clearly required an appreciation of the role of the rural dwellers in the nationalist struggle. For, in installing a government they felt was accountable to them, they developed strong expectations of benefits; in particular, they expected riches from public-sponsored efforts to promote farming in the rural areas. These events—the founding of the mining industry and the nationalist struggle—took place decades ago;

but their effects continue to determine the value of the alternatives open to rural dwellers and to shape and constrain their behavior.

The collection of historical data is a familiar process to most researchers. In the case of central Africa, it is a particularly rich endeavor. Secondary materials of very high quality exist for the region. The work of the old research institutes—the Rhodes-Livingstone Institute and the Rhodes-Livingstone Museum—is of inestimable value for contemporary researchers. Such eminent economic historians as E. A. G. Robinson and Phyllis Deane conducted major studies in the area; and the work of Robert Baldwin remains invaluable. The existence of these secondary sources provides the researcher with rich data which can be ignored only at great peril.[1]

Archival sources also yield material of considerable value. For example, in studying migration, the researcher should be aware that the movement of Africans between town and country was a central issue in the colonial period. The British South Africa Company (BSA) had deliberated ways and means of generating an urban influx from the rural areas. The mines had deliberated on the relative merits of stabilized and temporary work forces in the urban areas. The colonial government worried about the effect of rural depopulation upon the quality of rural life and the governability of the towns. And the rural native authorities strongly reacted to the loss of population and to the effects of urban exposure upon the conduct of their subjects. In these deliberations, data were generated concerning the nature and extent of rural-urban migration and its causes. The BSA record collection, the archives of the mining companies, and the colonial records retained in the National Archives all contain invaluable materials on rural-urban migration. While lacking quantitative materials of any sophistication, records of the native authorities are nonetheless useful on this subject. In particular, the native authorities handled the rural affairs of many urban residents; and the correspondence on these matters is highly informative.

Archival research tends to be conducted in the cities, where the major collections are. Nonetheless, rural sources should not be ignored. Many native authority records that have not been collected by the National Archives are still extant, though decaying; they have either been integrated into the rural council archives or remain, in some instances, in the personal files of the chiefs. I was able to make good use of the Lunda Superior Native Authority records, kept at the Kawambwa Rural Council and in the palace of Mwata Kazembe. Another source is local mission stations. Thus, for example, one reason for the intensity of the migration of persons from Kasumpa village was the skills they had acquired in carpentry and bricklaying; the records of the Mbereshi mission station confirmed the existence of training programs in which these skills were acquired. Lastly, there are fascinating local record collections. Many of the news sheets, records, and correspondence that were part and parcel of the formation of the nationalist movement lie tucked away in trunks and boxes in houses in rural villages. These make valuable reading.

The last local source is, of course, oral history. At several points in my work, this source was extremely useful. One such time was when I was attempting to ascertain the history of Kasumpa village. The village's history was an unusual one and had led to rivalry and conflict with the Lunda Native Authority. This fact appears to have predisposed the villagers to joining the nationalist movement. I gathered the history of the village by taking oral histories from the "old men." Subsequently, by keying the informal praise names used in the oral history to the formal titles of the Lunda chiefs as recorded in a Rhodes-Livingstone Institute publication, and by corroborating the account with that recorded in the district notebooks, I was able to establish fairly hard dates for the narrative and to correct and supplement statements of fact in it. In addition, I was helped by the history narrated by the earlier generation of Kasumpa villagers and recorded at that time by a high school student. Later a schoolteacher and nationalist politician, this gentleman had preserved his handwritten account of the oral history. I had the account typed; one copy I kept, one I gave to him, and a third I placed in the Rhodes-Livingstone Museum.

A second area in which oral history was important was in the record of the nationalist movement. Here the history was a rich one. Indeed, so active did the Kasumpa people claim to have been that I tended to discount their testimony as reflecting more the power of village patriotism than the reality of the past. However, interviews with persons who had worked with the rural police at the time confirmed many of the village tales. And the record of intelligence sources in the colonial police force closely confirmed the reports I gathered. Thus oral history, used in conjunction with such written documents as may be available, provided much information concerning previous critical events whose effects are still experienced in the present.

National Sources

It is fundamentally erroneous to do a "village study" as if there were no significant environment to the village. For, just as past decisions and actions influence the value of alternatives open to local villagers, so do the present-day actions of agents external to the village. The most notable such agency is the government; and an explanation of local behavior must contain in its arguments explanations of the conduct of governmental agencies that so profoundly intrude upon village life.

The sources for such an inquiry are legion; but I found two to be of particular use. One was the records kept by the planning group of the Ministry of Rural Development; the other was the records amassed by the Ministry of Development, Planning, and National Guidance. In both cases, the planning functions undertaken by these agencies led to the compilation of data, reports, and records, and these were of great use. Secondly and most importantly, it so happened that I undertook my work at the time when the Ministry of Development, Planning, and National Guidance was involved in an appraisal of the performance of the national economy under the First National Development Plan. The result was a comprehensive review of all aspects of government policy, and in particular of rural development policy. The reports and documents compiled in this process provided extremely useful research materials.

Not all agencies involved in rural development are under the direct control of the central ministries. Some are parastatal, and access to their records is often more difficult to acquire. Nonetheless, once again, the planning units of these bodies often contain valuable information; and the agencies' participation in the evaluation of the First National Development Plan led to the collection and dissemination of useful research material.

Not all this material is contained in the central ministries. Indeed, much of the material depicting the "real" as opposed to the "intended" performance of the governmental bureaucracies is generated at the local level. In particular, district and provincial development committees deliberate concerning the operations of governmental agencies in the local areas, and their frank and full interchanges yield valuable insight into the conduct of the government bureaus. The minutes, reports, and recommendations of these committees are public documents and can easily be acquired.

Lastly, the annual reports of government bureaucracies often contain useful statistical information. Using this material, I compiled a data bank of indicators concerning each of the administrative districts. These indicators concern such things as the number of cattle and plows, the levels of education, indices of average income, demographic material, and so forth. The indices come in series that span a considerable time period, in some cases several decades. These data, once thoroughly cross-checked, then supported an extensive analysis of the correlates of rural out-migration.

Also available are records of governmental capital expenditures. By carefully tracing over time the funding of particular projects—something that is difficult to do because of the shift of projects and bureaus between ministries; by locating them in specific areas; and by aggregating the resulting amounts over time and over projects, the level of government capital spending for particular districts can be estimated. It is extremely difficult to do this accurately, however; for the budgets of parastatal agencies by districts are often difficult to determine, and the recurrent expenditures of the government tend to be reported by departments or by functions—e.g., salaries, maintenance—and not by region. Nonetheless, capital investments in "new starts" and "completions" can be estimated. These data too were used to account for the level of out-migration from various rural districts and to evaluate the success of the government's rural development programs in curtailing the flight to the cities.

These data were also used to explain voting patterns in Zambia. In particular, I explored the relationship between voting patterns and patterns of public expenditure. To use district-level data for the analysis of voting is difficult, however, as the boundaries of electoral constituencies and administrative districts do not correspond. To circumvent this problem, I reduced the maps of constituencies and districts to the same scale and inscribed them upon transparent overlays. By superimposing the overlays, I was able to pool the two sets of units into a single set of units, these units being defined in terms of the boundaries that delimited matching sets of constituencies and districts. Those boundaries were selected which minimized the loss of data points—that is, aggregated the fewest possible constituencies and/or districts—and maximized the degrees of freedom in the final data set.

Not only did the data enable an analysis of migration and the electoral determinants of patterns of public expenditure; but also they allowed me to determine the level of generality of my local level case study. Thus, I was able to determine whether the local level of public investment was typical or not; I was able to assess whether the correlates of out-migration from Luapula resembled those from other regions (they did); and I was able to discuss the way in which Luapula deviated in important respects from other regions in Zambia. These deviations turned out to be extremely important: the absence of cattle and distance from urban markets, for example, turned out to be a critically important determinant of the low level of farm incomes in the valley. The comparative data on other areas in Zambia thus enabled me to isolate the effect of the particular features on the level of prosperity in Kasumpa village.

Village-Level Data

If the data from historical sources and governmental records must be employed to account for the value of the alternatives between which choices are made at the local level, then data must be gathered from the local level itself to examine the objectives that govern such choices and the manner in which the alternatives are utilized in the attempts to fulfill these objectives. I therefore conducted an intensive study of one village grouping.

As is always the case, the selection of the particular research site was made for reasons of both practicality and suitability for the research objectives. The purpose of my research dictated the selection of an area remote from the line of rail: because of the prosperity of the rural areas in the vicinity of the line of rail, I could best study the response of villagers to relative rural poverty in the more remote districts of the nation. And the attempts by the public sector to rectify the relative poverty brought on by the action of private markets could best be studied in the more remote districts, where large private markets tended not to function. In addition, I wanted to conduct an intensive study. I wanted fine-grained information, in considerable detail; and I wanted to gain as much insight as possible into the subjective state of the rural dwellers. For these reasons, and because of constraints on my time, I preferred to conduct an investigation for a long time in a single small area as opposed to spending many short periods in a variety of research settings. My broader, national data, I felt, would help me to correct the bias inherent in the case study of a single village grouping.

The purposes of my research therefore suggested the selection of a remote village group for proper intensive study. There remained the problem of selection, and here practical considerations became important. The village had to be in an area in which I could speak the language; this meant that the village would have to be in the Copperbelt, Northern, or Luapula Province. It also had to be in an area where I enjoyed the support and confidence of the political officials; and, among these three provinces my best contacts lay among officials in the Luapula area. Lastly, the village had to be in an area where I could feasibly conduct my research. I therefore traveled throughout Luapula, searching for an area where I could find housing, have access to office equipment if need be, and find research assistants. Two such areas were available, both being near mission schools where there were houses, mimeograph equipment, and night classes taught in English at the secondary school level, thus suggesting the availability of research assistants.

At this point, questions of research design once again became critical. Luapula contains two distinct ecologies: one riverine, and the other plateau. Near the river, the villages are densely populated and relatively prosperous; they are involved in the fishing industry, and they tend to have rich soils. On the plateau, water is scarce and soil quality poor; the villages are spread out and thinly populated; and the residents tend to be poor.

I wanted to work in a village area that straddled this ecological divide, and I therefore selected the region about the Mbereshi Mission as my research site. The question of which particular village to study in that region was largely resolved in terms of the reception I received over the first several weeks of my research. For largely accidental reasons, my work in Kasumpa went much better than my work elsewhere. And it then again became a matter of carefully assessing the ways in which Kasumpa village differed from other villages in the area so as to correct the research bias inherent in that fact. My work in the records of the district headquarters; my continued association with persons in villages that I did not intensively study; my contacts with other researchers; and my work in the files of the national bureaucracies helped me to correct for the bias resulting from my selection of this particular village grouping.

In conducting my village studies, I employed two basic methods: participant observation and survey research. The techniques complemented each other in several ways. For one, anthropological methods suggested the basic hypotheses for this research. Through participant observation, I came to appreciate the extent of out-migration; I also came to know the families of Kasumpa and to understand the ways in which they used and coped with the migration process. I also got to know the farmers, both peasant and cooperative. They forcefully registered their frustration and grievances; and, seeing me as a possible communication link with their government, they made certain that I understood both the level and nature of their dissatisfaction. I was also taught the history of the village—its origins in the valley and its role in the nationalist period. Migration, farming, and politics—these subjects repeatedly cropped up in my conversations with the villagers. In these conversations, the subjects of poverty and the desire for gain continually arose; and the role of politics as a means of seeking material betterment was continually emphasized, as were the people's past sacrifices, the promises of the new government, and the frustrations with governmental performance.

On the basis of these experiences, I designed a series of unstructured interviews. Mapping the village on numbered graph paper and consulting a table of random numbers, I selected a random sample of households for intensive investigation. In a series of roughly hour-long, semistructured interviews with each household head, I collected life histories: place and date of birth, education, migration history, work history, and such. I then investigated the sources and amounts of cash income and gained a portrait for each man of his economic cycle: when he did what, at what period in the year, and the amount of his costs and revenues from each activity. These economic data became a permanent and critical part of my data files.

Several months later, I reinterviewed my sample. In these interviews, I collected some information that I had previously gathered in the first round; I did this to test the validity of my data. The main purpose of the second round was to collect new information, however, and to do so in a careful, thorough, and systematic manner. One area I intensively investigated was rural-urban migration. Thus, I gathered information regarding the children and sib of the interviewee, and in particular their residential, educational, and employment histories. I solicited the political history of each respondent—his past political involvement and office holding and his present political activities. I also examined his history of involvement with various governmental programs—the cooperatives, the marketing services, the credit agency, and so forth—and his response to his experiences as a client of the government. Lastly, I sought information that would allow me to assess the villagers' involvement with the outside world as it took place through means other than those of the party, the bureaucracy, and the family. For example, I investigated their involvement with mass media and with various change agents, such as the local teachers, ministers, and so on. The obvious relative insignificance of these influences upon local behavior, as revealed by my subsequent analysis of these data, gave me a sense of conviction in my principal hypotheses.

The structured interviews were long—over one and a half hours. In only one case did I have any difficulty in completing the interview. The early use of participant observation, I feel, contributed to the success of the survey techniques. I was known; I was a familiar figure; and the respondents had learned that I was not in the village to spy upon them, to organize opposition parties, or otherwise to cause trouble. I now lived in the village and had become part of their social lives; and so information flowed more freely between them and me, making interviews less onerous. In addition, through participant observation, I had become more attuned to the thinking of the villagers and to the way in which they expressed themselves; few of the questions therefore jarred them or appeared ridiculous or off base. Because of my earlier experiences, most of the questions therefore "worked" and the interviews went smoothly.

In addition to the survey research I conducted in the village, I also carried out a series of case studies. Some of these focused on the founding of local institutions: the political party and the cooperative societies, for example. Others focused on particular disputes between the government and the village: the dispute over the siting of the roads, the threatened formation of an opposition party, and the conflicts between the marketing services and the farmers are cases in point. Others involved internal conflicts in the village—witchcraft and court cases, by and large. All of these provided data that were extremely valuable in understanding how the villagers actually behaved. And, in at least the second kind of case study,

I was able to check and cross-check the details of the cases through government records, and so assess the validity of the material I had secured.

The material I gathered at the local level I then used to show how the rural dwellers, responding to the alternatives created for them by past events and by the intervention of outside sources, sought to fulfill their desires for greater material well-being.

Notes

INTRODUCTION

1. Peter R. Gould, "Research Strategies for Rural Spatial Planning," p. 281.

2. The notion of income maximization has been employed in selected instances throughout the literature on the responses of rural dwellers to the rise of industry; and it appears to have served quite ably as a basis for explanations. This is most clearly the case in agriculture. Recent general works on peasant production indicate that it is misleading to interpret their agricultural practices in terms of such notions as a high leisure preference, a high consumption preference, or conservatism and tradition-bound behavior. These works also suggest that peasants organize their production practices so as to achieve efficiencies, and that, where prices rise and profits are to be made, peasants will increase their output in much the same way as the "rational producers" of the "modern" nations of the world. The classic work in this vein is Theodore W. Schultz, *Transforming Traditional Agriculture*. Based on their research, both William O. Jones and Victor C. Uchendu contend that the economic behavior of African rural producers can best be seen as rational behavior, little constrained by traditional cultures and institutions. Empirical studies of the supply schedules of African cash croppers appear to support the contention of Jones and Uchendu; and, even closer to the subjects of this study, empirical studies of peasant producers in Zambia itself reveal that the tendency for African maize growers to behave as income maximizers is at least as strong as that of their European counterparts. See William O. Jones, "Economic Man in Africa"; Victor C. Uchendu, "The Impact of Changing Agricultural Technology on African Land Tenure," and "Socioeconomic and Cultural Determinants of Rural Change in East and West Africa"; and Marvin P. Miracle, *Maize in Tropical Africa*, pp. 255–57. See also such studies as P. T. Bauer and B. S. Yamey, "A Case Study of Response to Price in an Underdeveloped Country"; Merrill J. Bateman, *Cocoa in the Ghanian Economy: An Econometric Model*; and Robert M. Stern, "The Determinants of Cocoa Supply in West Africa."

Similar findings emerge from the study of rural emigration. Thus, for example, Pamela Brigg, in a comprehensive survey of empirical studies of rural-urban migration conducted in all regions of the developing world, finds that economic motivations appear to be the major reason for migration from the countryside to town. Joseph Gugler, in a review of the literature on African rural-urban migration in particular, similarly concludes that "economic factors are of major importance." Indeed, the very fact that migration and labor migration have rarely been distinguished in the literature in Africa suggests the importance of economic choice to this phenomenon, and the relevance of income maximization models to explanations of it. See Pamela Brigg, "A Survey of Case Studies on Migration to Urban Areas"; and Joseph Gugler, "On the Theory of Rural-Urban Migration," p. 155.

In the studies of the politics of rural dwellers, several findings suggest that an explanation based upon economic motivations would capture much of the reality of peasant political behavior. For one, in North America at least, economic motivations seem to shape much of the political behavior of farming populations. Historical studies have long emphasized the agrarian-commercial divide that formed perhaps the central political cleavage of the United States at the time of its own "nation building." See Joseph Charles, *The Origins of the American Party System*; William Nisbet Chambers, *Political Parties in a New Nation*; and the materials contained in Jackson Turner Main, *Political Parties before the Constitution*. More recently, the authors of the most sustained and sophisticated series of analyses of American voting behavior found it necessary to put aside their social-psychological perspective and to consider seriously the economic basis of voting behavior when they attempted to explicate the farm vote in contemporary American elections. See Angus Campbell, Philip E. Converse, Warren E. Miller, and Donald E. Stokes, *The American Voter*, abridged ed., ch. 13, pp. 210–30. For a more general analysis of the economic basis of political action, see Gerald H. Kramer, "Short-Term Fluctuations in U.S. Voting Behavior, 1896–1964," and the commentaries on this paper appearing in the "Papers and Proceedings of the Eighty-fifth Annual Meeting of the American Economics Association, Toronto, Ontario, December 28–30, 1972," published in the *American Economic Review* 63, no. 2 (May 1973): 160–80. Few groups in North America, it seems, so readily seek political avenues toward economic goals as do rural producers; and at least in North America no other group has gained such apparent success in obtaining "radical" solutions to the problems of the marketplace. The classic study of this is Seymour Martin Lipset, *Agrarian Socialism*; see also Grant McConnell, *Private Power and American Democracy* (New York: Vintage Books, 1970). The economic basis of political action also appears to characterize rural politics outside North America. The spate of recent writings on peasant radicalism repeatedly and unblushingly takes recourse to explanations based upon economic motivations. And while these studies differ in their designation of the sufficient conditions for outbreaks of peasant rebellions, they nonetheless return again and again to the desire of rural populations to enhance their incomes as the necessary condition for peasant unrest and rural rebellion. Examples are: Gerrit Huizer, *The Revolutionary Potential of Peasants in Latin America*; the contributions in Henry A. Landsberger, *Latin American Peasant Movements*; and Rodolfo Stavenhagen, ed., *Agrarian Problems and Peasant Movements in Latin America*. Perhaps the most explicit analysis of peasant rebellion in rational-choice terms is Nathan Leites and Charles Wolf, Jr., *Rebellion and Authority: An Analytic Essay on Insurgent Conflicts*.

A study based on the notion of income maximization may be one dimensional. Clearly, however, it may be justifiably so, given the above evidence that the approach is appropriate to the topics of investigation. There are, however, certain risks involved in such a radical simplification. Particularly in areas changing as rapidly as central Africa, such a study risks losing a sense of the complexity of the people of that region. Certainly, where change has been so rapid, men cannot be as one dimensional as they will herein appear. New values and old must coexist; and confusion and ambiguity, not purposeful behavior based on narrow goals, must at times characterize the behavior of people in change. By postulating that the actors in the drama of rapid change behave merely to make themselves better off—to choose more income rather than less—is to lose sensitivity to these possibilities for richness and complexity. The answer to this problem is simple intellectual honesty. When my interpretation becomes forced or strained, I therefore show where the paradigm of income maximization appears to fail and where other principles of behavior appear to take over.

3. There is some debate as to whether African village populations consist of peasants or not. For purposes of this study, I will refer to them as peasants because, like peasants elsewhere, they are intimately linked into markets and market relationships that extend beyond the villages in which they reside and because they are subordinate elements in political hierarchies that range from their local communities to the national centers. I agree with Lloyd A. Fallers, however, who denies that African rural dwellers have the sense of inherent cultural inferiority that is presumably possessed by peasants elsewhere. For relevant discussions, see John S. Saul and Roger Woods, "African Peasantries"; Jack Goody, "Feudalism in Africa?"; and Lloyd A. Fallers, "Are African Cultivators to Be Called 'Peasants'?"

4. See T. W. Schultz, "New Evidence on Farmer Responses to Economic Opportunities from the Early Agrarian History of Western Europe." See also the contributions in E. L. Jones, ed., *Agriculture and Economic Growth in England, 1650–1815.*

5. Maurice Dobb, *Soviet Economic Development since 1917*; and Naum Jasny, *The Socialized Agriculture of the USSR.* See also Sula Benet, trans. and ed., *The Village of Variatino*; Jerome Blum, *Lord and Peasant in Russia*; R. P. Dore, "Agricultural Improvement in Japan, 1870–1900"; Thomas C. Smith, *The Agrarian Origins of Modern Japan*; and William W. Lockwood, *The Economic Development of Japan.*

6. Symptomatic of this attention are the journal *Rural Africana*, the research monographs published by the Food Research Institute of Stanford University, the Land Tenure Center of the University of Wisconsin, the African rural employment network of Michigan State University, and the diffusion-of-innovations research project of Michigan State University. See also such books as William Allan, *The African Husbandman*; Guy Hunter, *Modernizing Peasant Societies*; René Dumont, *False Start in Africa*; and John D. de Wilde et al., *Experiences with Agricultural Development in Tropical Africa.* Others are listed in the Bibliography.

7. See E. G. Ravenstein, "On the Laws of Migration"; Arthur Redford, *Labour Migration in England*; and relevant sections from Phyllis Deane and W. A. Cole, *British Economic Growth, 1688–1959.* See also J. D. Chambers, "Enclosure and Labour Supply in the Industrial Revolution."

8. Perhaps the clearest statement of this is Evgeniĭ Alekseevich Preobrazhenskiĭ, *The New Economics.*

9. The literature on this topic is too voluminous to cite. For references see the bibliographic studies by William J. and Judith L. Hanna, *Urban Dynamics in*

Black Africa; and Brigg, "Migration to Urban Areas." See also the relevant sections of Robin J. Pryor, *Internal Migration and Urbanisation*.

10. E. J. Hobsbawm, *Primitive Rebels*.

11. In the United States, the Whiskey Rebellion was a protest by Pennsylvania farmers against the fiscal policies of the Federalist regime as developed and implemented by Alexander Hamilton. See the discussion in Charles, *Origins of the American Party System*. For Japan, see Hugh Borton, *Peasant Uprisings in Japan of the Tokugawa Period*; and the relevant sections of Barrington Moore, Jr., *Social Origins of Dictatorship and Democracy*. For a discussion of peasant resistance to collectivization, see the relevant sections of Jasny, *Socialized Agriculture of the USSR*.

12. Thus, for example, Moore, in his *Social Origins of Dictatorship and Democracy*, hypothesizes that modernization results in communist forms of government where the dominant modernizing elite attains power through peasant revolution. Also note the peasant focus of such essays on contemporary revolutions as Régis Debray, *Revolution in the Revolution?*; the writings in Norman Miller and Roderick Aya, eds., *National Liberation*; Eric R. Wolf, *Peasant Wars of the Twentieth Century*; and Joel Migdal, *Peasants, Politics, and Revolution*. More directly addressed to circumstances in Africa is Frantz Fanon, *The Wretched of the Earth*.

13. Indicative of this is the dominant thesis of the early writings on African nationalism which saw nationalist movements as essentially urban phenomena. The clearest statement of this perspective is in Thomas L. Hodgkin, *Nationalism in Colonial Africa*.

14. Peasant protest has been examined in West Africa in such works as Martin Kilson's study of Sierra Leone, *Political Change in a West African State*; Aristide R. Zolberg's *One-Party Government in the Ivory Coast*; Dennis Austin's *Politics in Ghana*; and Willard Johnson's "The *Union Des Populations du Cameroun* in Rebellion." For discussions of rural rebellion in Zaire, see such works as Renée C. Fox, Willy De Craemer, and Jean-Marie Ribeaucourt, " 'The Second Independence': A Case Study of the Kwilu Rebellion in the Congo"; Herbert F. Weiss, *Political Protest in the Congo*; and Crawford Young, "Domestic Violence in Africa: The Congo." Perhaps the most celebrated example of rural rebellion in contemporary Africa is the Mau Mau rebellion; and the most important single study of Mau Mau is that of Carl G. Rosberg, Jr., and John Nottingham, *The Myth of "Mau Mau."* For an important general review of this literature see John S. Saul, "On African Populism."

15. See, for example, Moore, *Social Origins of Dictatorship and Democracy;* and the more recent work by Migdal, *Peasants, Politics, and Revolution*.

16. This relationship is portrayed in Daniel Lerner, *The Passing of Traditional Society,* and Karl W. Deutsch, "Social Mobilization and Political Development."

In the early stages of the literature, social and economic modernization was related to the growth of participation in the form of nationalist protest. More recently it has been related to the growth of participation in the form of politically "destabilizing" forces such as sectionalism or revolutionary protest. Contrast, for example, Deutsch's *Nationalism and Social Communication* with Samuel P. Huntington, *Political Order in Changing Societies*.

17. Kingsley Davis and Hilda Hertz Golden, "Urbanisation and the Develop-

ment of Pre-Industrial Areas," *Economic Development and Cultural Change* 3 (1954/55): 20, as quoted in Helmuth Heisler, *Urbanisation and the Government of Migration*, p. 2.

18. For comparative materials, see the references in note 14 above. For relevant materials on rural Zambia, see Henry S. Meebelo, *Reaction to Colonialism;* and Thomas Rasmussen, "The Popular Basis of Anti-Colonial Protest."

19. I have attempted to review and synthesize these studies in Robert H. Bates, "Ethnic Competition and Modernization in Contemporary Africa." Also, see Frank W. Holmquist, "Toward a Political Theory of Rural Self-Help Development in Africa."

20. As George Dalton has written:
Nowadays, new opportunities for income growth, new modes of production, and new cultural achievement are frequently provided by . . . agencies and facilities which link the village to the region and nation by creating whole new sets of economic and cultural transactions. . . . The . . . anthropologists who were in the field before 1950 studied [villages] at a time when the regions and nations of which they were a part were relatively static. . . . They are no longer so. With an end to semi-isolation comes . . . development from above. . . .

If [we] are to understand the causes and consequences of change in the rural community [we] must enlarge [our] studies these days to include the region and the nation whose policies, activities, and personnel now impinge on the local community in unprecedented ways and with unprecedented frequency. [George Dalton, "Introduction," in *Economic Development and Social Change: The Modernization of Village Communities,* ed. George Dalton, pp. 12, 15]

CHAPTER 1

1. See, for example, the discussions contained in Richard Hall, *Zambia*; W. V. Brelsford, *The Tribes of Zambia*; and Eric Stokes and Richard Brown, eds., *The Zambesian Past: Studies in Central African History*. Since writing this chapter, I have come across some of the recent papers of Peter H. Lary, which seem to provide the best history of the nineteenth-century political and military affairs in the valley. See, for example, his "Aspects of Luapula Society and History in the Later Nineteenth Century" (paper presented to the Department of Political and Administrative Studies Seminar, University of Zambia, August 1973).

2. For comparative information, see Elizabeth Colson and Max Gluckman, eds., *Seven Tribes of British Central Africa.*

3. See, for example, Sir R. F. Burton, *The Lands of Cazembe,* and A. C. P. Gamitto, *King Kazembe*, which is a translation by Ian Cunnison of a report first published in 1854.

4. Toward this end, Mwata Kazembe XIV published the official Lunda history, *Ifikolwe Fyandi na Bantu Bandi.* Insight into the political basis for this effort in historiography is contained in the preface to Ian Cunnison, *Central Bantu Historical Texts, II*, which is a translation of Mwata Kazembe XIV, *Ifikolwe Fyandi.*

5. Perhaps the most succinct discussions of the motivations of the explorers are contained in Prosser Gifford, "The Framework for a Nation," pp. 40–45;

L. H. Gann, *A History of Northern Rhodesia*, pp. 15–35; and Robert I. Rotberg, *The Rise of Nationalism in Central Africa*, pp. 1–26. See also Ian Cunnison, "Kazembe and the Portuguese, 1798–1832," and "Kazembe and the Arabs to 1870"; A. H. Quiggin, *Trade Routes, Trade and Currency in East Africa*, Occasional Papers of the Rhodes-Livingstone Museum no. 5 (Livingstone: Rhodes-Livingstone Museum, 1949).

6. The most vivid descriptions of these levies are contained in Gamitto, *King Kazembe*, vol. 2, ch. 1.

7. I use as my primary sources for the history of the Bemba entrance into the valley oral histories taken from Mr. Chitente and Mr. Wapyanmbwa, elders in Kasumpa village. I also rely upon notes taken at the funeral of Mr. Chimfwembe of Kasumpa village, who had inherited the title of Mwabamukupa, and at the ceremonies during which his successor was chosen. Finally, I possess a copy of a manuscript written by a former local schoolteacher and African National Congress organizing secretary, Mr. Willy Chishimba, who is a resident of Kasumpa village. Transcribed while Mr. Chishimba was a secondary school student, this manuscript records the oral tradition of the Bemba entry into the valley as narrated by the elders of Kasumpa village; I have deposited a copy in the collection of the National Museum in Livingstone. As oral tradition uses names for the Kazembes that are not widely known (e.g., Mwata Mbanga for Kanyembo Ntemena), I have had to key the oral tradition to the standard histories of the Lunda through the list of praise names recorded by Jacques Chileya Chiwale in *Central Bantu Historical Texts, III.* See also Republic of Zambia, National Archives, *Calendars of the District Notebooks (Luapula Province) 1797–1963*, 1: 13, 23.

8. The best accounts of the BSA in central Africa are included in Gifford, "Framework for a Nation"; Gann, *History of Northern Rhodesia;* and Rotberg, *Rise of Nationalism.* See also Michael Gelfand, *Northern Rhodesia in the Days of the Charter*; Kenneth Bradley, *Copper Venture;* and Francis L. Coleman, *The Northern Rhodesia Copperbelt, 1899–1962*, pp. 1–5. For discussions of events in the Luapula valley, see W. Lammond, "The Luapula Valley"; and E. Averay Jones, "Memories of Abandoned Bomas—No. 6: Kalungwishi."

9. The oral histories reveal further motivations for this action. For one, Kanyembo Ntemena's successor was not personally indebted to Mwabamukupa, as Ntemena had been. Second, at the orders of Kanyembo Ntemena, Mwabamukupa had intercepted and slain a prince who had committed adultery with one of Kanyembo's wives; this prince was the brother of the new Kazembe, who therefore bore a personal grievance against Mwabamukupa.

10. Ian G. Cunnison discusses this new policy of installing members of the royal lineage as territorial chiefs in his book *The Luapula Peoples of Northern Rhodesia*, p. 167. Kazembe's first selection was Chiboshi. After Chiboshi proved unsatisfactory, he created the subchieftaincy of Kanyembo.

11. The other is Chilindi village, outside the Mbereshi Mission. The special circumstances surrounding the headmanship of Chilindi date back to the time when the missionaries divested themselves of direct administrative and judicial responsibility over the affairs of their converts.

CHAPTER 2

1. As the London manager of the chartered company stated in a memo-

randum of 1910: "The problem of Northern Rhodesia is not a colonization problem. It is the problem of how best to develop a great estate on scientific lines so that it may be made to yield the maximum profit to its owner." Quoted by Peter Slinn, "The Legacy of the British South Africa Company," p. 26.

2. J. Austen Bancroft, *Mining in Northern Rhodesia*, p. 52.

3. Ibid., p. 73. See also the discussion in E. A. G. Robinson, "The Economic Problem," pp. 139–55; and Slinn's "British South Africa Company," pp. 31–33.

4. Prosser Gifford, "The Framework for a Nation," pp. 241–44.

5. Robert E. Baldwin, *Economic Development and Export Growth*, p. 33. See also L. H. Gann, *A History of Northern Rhodesia*, pp. 205–7; and Kenneth Bradley, *Copper Venture*, pp. 79–93. Also to be noted is the cost advantage enjoyed by the central African producers. The Rhodesian copper mines in 1933 could deliver blister copper to the European market at 3.5 cents a pound; by contrast, the lowest cost United States producer, Kennecott, incurred *domestic* costs of 7.9 cents a pound. Rhodesian copper was therefore in a good position to penetrate the international trade in copper after the depression—something it rapidly did, thereby helping to fragment the international cartel which had sought to control the market on behalf of established producers. See Gifford, "Framework for a Nation," p. 256 ff.; and Robinson, "Economic Problem."

6. The development of the territory's railways is discussed in Gann, *History of Northern Rhodesia;* Baldwin, *Economic Development;* and R. M. Bostock, "The Transport Sector." Of these sources, the last was the most useful to me. See also Edwin. T. Haefele and Eleanor B. Steinberg, *Government Controls on Transport.*

7. Baldwin, *Economic Development*, p. 38.

8. Ibid., p. 40.

9. Northern Rhodesia, *Report on the Census of Population of Northern Rhodesia Held on 15th October, 1946*, p. 12.

10. Republic of Zambia, *Census of Production 1965 and 1966*, p. 41.

11. Northern Rhodesia, *Report on the Census*, p. 71; and M. D. Veitch, "Employment and the Labour Force, Regional Analysis" (typescript, author's collection, July 21, 1970), table 1.

12. Phyllis Deane, *Colonial Social Accounting*, pp. 63–64.

13. Robinson, "Economic Problem," p. 186.

14. Quoted by John A. Hellen, *Rural Economic Development in Zambia*, p. 79, from J. H. Wellington, "Some Geographical Aspects of the Peopling of Africa," *South African Journal of Science* 34 (1937): 29–60.

15. The most recent source uncovered during my research indicates that about one-half of the territory of Zambia is infested with tsetse. The cost of clearing the fly from one square mile of land was given as between £1,500 and £3,000; to this initial expenditure must be added an additional £800 for residual insecticide. See Hellen, *Rural Economic Development*, pp. 118–20.

16. Hellen notes that, "at its peak, Fort Jameson was the home of some two hundred and fifty farmers." By 1954, he suggests, there were "no more than twenty-five farmers." He concludes: "The most recent reports [1967] tell how the area was completely abandoned by European farmers. . . . In 1962 a scheme was inaugurated by the Northern Rhodesian and Federal Governments which enabled the Europeans to voluntarily resettle on a farm-for-farm exchange basis either on the line of rail or at Mkushi in the Central Province. . . . Despite good local soil the Fort Jameson farmers were always faced by geographical isolation. . . . Were Lusaka . . . not in reality so distant the history of settle-

ment in the area might have been strikingly different" (*Rural Economic Development*, p. 175). George Kay discusses the high costs of marketing in the Eastern Province and its effect on farm incomes in his article "Agricultural Progress in Zambia's Eastern Province."

17. Baldwin, *Economic Development*, p. 141. See also R. W. Dean, "Changes in Farming over the Past Fifty Years."

18. For a discussion of land policy, see Gann, *History of Northern Rhodesia*, pp. 136–38, 215–24, 372–73. While similar tenure arrangements were implemented in small areas in the Northwestern and Northern provinces, the lack of demand for output and the costs of marketing in those areas led to the failure to establish commercialized agriculture. Extensive freehold alienation was permitted in the Eastern Province, but again commercialized farming largely failed in that area. See Hellen, *Rural Economic Development*, p. 175.

19. See, for example, her essay "Migration in Africa: Trends and Possibilities"; see also Colson, *Life among the Cattle-Owning Plateau Tonga*. For a review of the development of line-of-rail cash cropping among Africans see Kenneth R. M. Anthony and Victor C. Uchendu, *Agricultural Change in Mazabuka District*, esp. pp. 222–26. At this point it should also be noted that the development of African cash cropping was artificially restricted by the exclusion of African producers from access to the best soils on the line of rail and by the attempts of European farmers to prevent Africans from entering production so as to keep their farm wages low. This discriminatory treatment of African producers nonetheless failed to prevent the rise of African peasant farmers in the Southern and Central provinces; and it is the success of the African peasant farmers in this area, in contrast with their failure elsewhere, that I attempt to explain in this section. Thus my analysis tends to downplay discriminatory treatment.

20. Gann, *History of Northern Rhodesia*, p. 285 ff.

21. Hellen, *Rural Economic Development*, p. 131.

22. William Allan, "African Land Usage," p. 17.

23. W. Allan, Max Gluckman, D. U. Peters, and C. G. Trapnell, *Land Holding and Land Usage among the Plateau Tonga of Mazabuka District*, p. 166. See also H. Vaux, "Unusual Aspects of Native Land Tenure in the Mazabuka District." The urban wage figures are taken from Deane, *Colonial Social Accounting*, p. 251.

24. Hellen, *Rural Economic Development*, pp. 186, 191.

25. Comparative historical data indicate that the principal problem in Luapula is one of marketing and not quality of soil, methods of production, etc. For when a major transport route was developed through the area to supply the north-eastern front during World War I, the valley farmers produced abundantly for the market created by the war. Thus Gifford notes: "The large tribes, like the Lunda of the Luapula under Chief Kazembe, often did an outstanding job of supply. [It was reported] that Luapula District would transport between April and November 1916 to Abercorn and Kasama at least 1,500,000 lbs. of food—of this 1,270,000 lbs. will be purchased in the Kawambwa-Fort Rosebery-Chiengi sub-Districts. . . . The remarkable fact of the war years in Northern Rhodesia is the response of subsistence agriculture to additional incentives" ("Framework for a Nation," pp. 169–70). For descriptions of the agricultural potential of the area, see William Allan, *The African Husbandman*, pp. 140–43; Marvin P. Miracle, *Agriculture in the Congo Basin*, pp. 125–26; and C. G. Trapnell, *The Soils, Vegetation and Agriculture of North-Eastern Rhodesia*, p. 26 ff. All three of these studies concur on the quality of the valley soils near the river.

26. Hellen, *Rural Economic Development*, p. 218 ff. Also J. Moffat Thomson,

Report on the Native Fishing Industry; and Ian G. Cunnison, *The Luapula Peoples of Northern Rhodesia*, p. 9.

27. Northern Rhodesia, Department of African Affairs, *Annual Report for the Year 1951*, p. 14. See also W. Lammond, "The Luapula Valley"; Denis Paine, "Lake Mweru, Its Fish and Fishing Industry"; and S. Williams, "The Mweru-Luapula Fisheries."

28. Cunnison, *Luapula Peoples,* p. 13.

29. Northern Rhodesia, Department of African Affairs, *Annual Report for the Year 1949*, p. 21. See also G. Fryer, "Mwamfuli's Village: The New Fulcrum of the Bangweulu Fish Trade"; and interview notes in the author's collection with Mrs. Luka Mumba, the Chisakula brothers, Mr. Kapapula, and Mrs. Chilongo, all prominent Luapula businessmen who were deeply involved in the fish trade.

30. Northern Rhodesia, Department of Native Affairs, *Annual Report for the Year 1929*, p. 6.

31. Ibid., *Annual Report for the Year 1931*, p. 1.

32. Cunnison, *Luapula Peoples*, p. 25.

33. Ibid., p. 2.

34. Northern Rhodesia, Department of African Affairs, *Annual Report for the Year 1948*, p. 11.

35. One of the reasons I selected this village for study was that its economy is based on both agriculture and fishing. It thus reflects, in one research site, the two major kinds of economies characteristic of Luapula as a whole.

36. Albert O. Hirschman, *Journeys toward Progress*, p. 36 (his italics). In the case of the developing areas, this effect may be rare, given the initially low levels of development; for there may be a long list of projects, each of which could offer very high returns to investment expenditures. Increased revenues may therefore be absorbed by high-return investment opportunities, and the areas that offer lower rates of return may continue to be ignored. I am indebted to Lance Davis for this point. As a general statement, it is no doubt true, but in recent times the great affluence of the copper mines and the resultant expansion of government revenues makes it less germane to this case than to other developing nations.

37. Memorandum by Sir Lawrence Wallace, December 1920, cited in Gifford, "Framework for a Nation," pp. 183–85. Bradley indicates that the losses to the company in the Northern Rhodesian territories were averaging about £130,000 a year by 1924 (*Copper Venture*, p. 27).

38. This policy orientation is best summarized in Helmuth Heisler, *Urbanization and the Government of Migration*, esp. pp. 1–13. For an excellent study of the relative supply of public services in the central and peripheral areas of Zambia, see Dennis Lee Dresang, "The Zambia Civil Service."

39. The best discussion of this is in Elena L. Berger, *Labour, Race and Colonial Rule*, p. 20 ff.

40. Deane, *Colonial Social Accounting*, p. 36; Gifford, "Framework for a Nation," pp. 276–79; Gann, *History of Northern Rhodesia*, pp. 392–94. Berger notes that the revenues rose from £4.3 million in 1947 to £11.9 million in 1950. See Berger, p. 8. See also Peter Slinn, "British South Africa Company," pp. 42–43.

41. Northern Rhodesia, *Ten-Year Development Plan for Northern Rhodesia as Approved by Legislative Council on 11th February 1947*.

42. See Northern Rhodesia, Development Commissioner, *Recent Advances in the Northern and Luapula Provinces of Northern Rhodesia, Being a Report on Intensive Rural Development*; and Northern Rhodesia, *Report on Intensive Rural*

*Development in the Northern and Luapula Provinces of Northern Rhodesia, 1957–
1961*. As stated in the first of these documents, the government was troubled by
conditions in these areas which had led to "an ever-increasing drift of population,
men, women, and children to Copperbelt and Railway Belt towns. . . . The
contribution to the general prosperity which these [migrants] were making
through their participation in industry was not adequately reflected in their
homeland" (*Recent Advances*, p. 3).

43. See, for example, Gann, *History of Northern Rhodesia*, passim; Robert I.
Rotberg, *The Rise of Nationalism in Central Africa*, ch. 4, 9, 10; and David C.
Mulford, *Zambia*, ch. 1 and 2.

44. Mulford, *Zambia*, pp. 10–13; idem, *The Northern Rhodesia General Election*, pp. 1–6; and Margaret Rouse Bates, "UNIP in Postindependence Zambia."

45. Under the electoral laws of the territory in effect until 1957, only 11
Africans qualified to vote out of an electorate of 20,000 voters. See Mulford,
Northern Rhodesia General Election, p. 4.

46. Rotberg notes: "When he opened its first session, the acting governor of
Northern Rhodesia explained that the members of the African Representative
Council should seek primarily to advise the governor of the Protectorate on
matters directly affecting their constituents. He spoke grandly of their responsibilities:

> It is not your function to make the laws of the land . . . nor is it your func-
> tion to administer those laws . . . but you will have a hand in the shaping
> of those laws which affect Africans and it is for that reason that certain draft
> legislation will be submitted to you . . . for any comments and advice you
> wish to give. . . . The Governor is not bound to accept your advice. . . .
> [Rotberg, *Rise of Nationalism*, pp. 207–08]

On the limitation of political activity by African associations, Rotberg notes
the following reaction by the governor, Sir James Crawford Maxwell, to the
criticism emanating from the Livingstone Welfare Society: "The governor . . .
demanded that his subordinates forbid criticism. . . . He reprimanded them
orally, and cautioned the secretary of the association: 'His Excellency does not
want government officials to be criticized again. The tone of . . . the speeches is
noted with regret' " (p. 126). Rotberg also notes that the welfare societies were
explicitly forbidden to organize in the rural areas (p. 132).

47. These figures are computed from Northern Rhodesia, *Approved Estimates
of the Development Fund, 1954–1955* (Lusaka: Government Printer, 1954), p. 3;
and Baldwin, *Economic Development*, pp. 194–95. See also Dresang, "Zambia
Civil Service," p. 52.

48. Berger, *Labour, Race and Colonial Rule*, p. 8.

49. Baldwin, *Economic Development*, p. 196.

50. Ibid., pp. 194–95.

51. Ibid., p. 201.

52. Gann, *History of Northern Rhodesia*, p. 373. For more thorough discussions of this very complex subject, see Elizabeth Colson, "The Impact of the
Colonial Period on the Definition of Land Rights"; and C. M. N. White, "A
Survey of African Land Tenure in Northern Rhodesia." See also other works by
these authors listed in the Bibliography. Discussions with observers indicate that
especially in the areas of profitable farming there has been a common-law transition to individual tenure; but this has yet to be legitimated either by statute or by
a major court ruling. The most concise and thorough discussion of agricultural

policy in the colonial period, and one I have drawn on throughout, is S. M. Makings, *Agricultural Change in Northern Rhodesia/Zambia.*

53. Quoted from the annual report of the Department of Agriculture, in Hellen, *Rural Economic Development*, pp. 129–30.

54. An exception were the farmers in the peasant farming scheme (see n. 56, below). Even at its height, however, the scheme involved a mere 2,565 farmers, or less than 1 percent of the farm families in the rural areas. For a discussion see James Hadfield, *Report on the Peasant Farming Survey.*

55. Hellen, *Rural Economic Development*, pp. 140–41. For an assessment of the scheme, see A. M. M. Rees, "An Economic Survey of Plateau Tonga Improved Farmers," *Bulletin of the Department of Agriculture, Northern Rhodesia*, no. 14 (1958).

56. Again, the areas of commercial production in the Eastern Province were an exception. Also, it may be countered, the above-mentioned peasant farming scheme was an important exception. However, the scheme was small: in 1955 it involved a mere 651 farm families, and in 1961 only 2,565 farmers, or less than 1 percent of the farm families. Even in the case of this small set of highly privileged small-scale farmers, the government was able to do little to upgrade their economic standing in comparison with that of persons in the urban and industrial areas. Thus James Hadfield, in his evaluation of this scheme, reported: "Sales per acre of main crops grown are very low. Only 2.6 bags of maize and 1.8 bags of groundnuts were sold from each acre of . . . crops grown. Though Peasant Farmers have taken some steps up the ladder from subsistence agriculture, in this respect they have not taken very many" (*Peasant Farming Survey*, p. 17). He went on to note: "A distressingly large number of Peasant Farm incomes are low . . . about 34 percent were under £25. This is clearly a serious state of affairs. In this Territory, in 1962, an average African male worker in town earned about £120 a year; an average African mine-worker gets over £250 a year, and mine wages are still rising rapidly" (ibid., p. 24).

57. Baldwin, *Economic Development*, p. 157.

58. The official price was the price at which government facilities would purchase maize and at which the government would buy maize from officially sponsored peasant farmers and (occasional) cooperative societies in these remoter regions (see note 56). See James Hadfield, *The Marketing of African Agricultural Produce in Northern Rhodesia*, Agricultural Bulletin no. 18 (Lusaka: Government Printer, n.d.); and Bastiaan de Gaay Fortman, "Zambia's Markets: Problems and Opportunities."

59. For example, in 1960, approximately 25,000 bags of maize had to be imported into the province (Hellen, *Rural Economic Development*, p. 216). While the government made a modest attempt at establishing peasant farmers in the province, the program enrolled a total of 86 farmers at its height, or less than 0.5 percent of all the improved farmers in the territory; at the time, the province contained over 10 percent of the total population. Almost all these improved farmers were located either in Fort Rosebery District or in Mushota, outside of Kawambwa; the program had little impact at all in the valley.

60. See Northern Rhodesia, Development Commissioner, *Recent Advances*, and Northern Rhodesia, *Report on Intensive Rural Development*. Any reader of the administrative reports from this area over this period will appreciate the strength of the government's interest in making these investments so as to strengthen the financial position of the "native authorities" in these areas. The native authorities collected revenues from the fish trade in the form of net, boat,

and motor taxes, as well as levies from the traders. See the discussion in Chapter 5.

61. A list of the projects undertaken is contained in Northern Rhodesia, *Report on Intensive Rural Development*.

62. Northern Rhodesia, Department of African Affairs, *Annual Report for the Year 1948* (Lusaka: Government Printer, 1949), p. 11.

CHAPTER 3

1. Stated so baldly, this conception of the behavior of villagers appears rather obvious. But it can be broken down to reveal the full range of considerations entering the migration decision.

To begin with, villagers appraise the magnitudes of the urban and rural income streams. Second, they evaluate the costs of obtaining them. To gain rural earnings, villagers must pay such costs as leisure foregone, the costs of implements, and the costs of hiring labor, if only in the form of support payments for dependents who may work in their fields. So too, to obtain the stream of future income from urban employment, the village dweller must pay the costs of migrating. Travel, the loss of income while searching for a job, and the psychic costs of severance from the village and adjustment to urban living—these costs must be paid in order to lay claim to earnings from the urban sector. Third, there are the uncertainties attached to the two income streams. In the rural sector, such factors as blights, variability in rainfall, ill health, or predation can radically alter the earnings from agriculture. On the other hand, the urban labor market is risky as well; to a greater or lesser degree, it is unknown to the village dweller, and there is always the possibility of unemployment. Finally, there is the factor of time. The magnitude of costs and benefits looms larger for village dwellers, as for most people, the sooner they occur. For purposes of this study, it is useful to assume that villagers tend to discount future costs and earnings at a "very high" rate, if only because they are poor. In any case, we will assume that, like most people, they prefer to receive income in present time and to pay costs later.

This argument can be formalized rather simply and in a way that enhances rather than obfuscates its presentation. Let E be the real value of earnings; those from the rural sector can be labeled E_r and those from the urban areas E_u. Let P be the probability of gaining earnings and C the costs of obtaining them. As both the rural and urban alternatives represent streams of future earnings, we need to calculate earnings over time; t will stand for time, its value running up to n in units of one year. Moreover, as these future earnings are being evaluated in present time, we will need a discount rate, i. For we must assume that, like all people, villagers have a preference for temporally proximate earnings and place a higher value on tomorrow's earnings than those to be gained ten years hence.

Letting V be the expected value, the prospective migrant will evaluate the urban alternative by:

$$V_u = \sum_{t=0}^{n} [P \cdot E_u - C]/(1 + i)^t.$$

Similarly, he will appraise the rural alternative as:

$$V_r = \sum_{t=0}^{n} [P \cdot E_r - C]/(1 + i)^t.$$

A necessary condition of rural-urban migration is that $V_u - V_r > 0$. Let D

represent the magnitude of the differential $V_u - V_r$; evaluating D only over its positive values, the likelihood that a villager will migrate will increase with the magnitude of this differential. The rate of migration from any given area, we assume, is a function of the magnitude of this motivating differential.

This formulation is derived from Michael P. Todaro, "A Model of Labor Mignation and Urban Unemployment in Less Developed Countries." As background, see also Theodore W. Schultz, "Reflections on Investment in Man"; and Larry A. Sjaastad, "The Costs and Returns of Human Migration." For a defense of the importance of economic considerations in African migration see Joseph Gugler, "On the Theory of Rural-Urban Migration." For an important commentary on the pitfalls facing those doing empirical work on migration, see J. B. Knight, "Measuring Urban-Rural Income Differentials."

Lance Davis in a personal communication stresses that human investment models of migration imply that the rates of migration should be sensitive to the interest rate. As I will argue in later chapters, when urban dwellers did gain access to banks and pension schemes, the rate of investment in rural retirement and thus in return migration did appear to be affected by the interest rate in financial markets; such access is a relatively recent phenomenon, however, and is totally absent in most rural areas. I will also argue that those rural dwellers who do have access to investment opportunities that yield interest, such as cattle herds, have less incentive to invest in migration and lower rates of migration.

2. Kenneth Bradley, *Copper Venture,* p. 55. The materials in this section are drawn largely from this book and from Prosser Gifford, "The Framework for a Nation"; J. Austen Bancroft, *Mining in Northern Rhodesia;* Francis L. Coleman, *The Northern Rhodesia Copperbelt;* and Alan Drysdall, "Prospecting and Mining Activity."

3. The company was entitled to 30 percent of the stock of any mining concern operating in Southern Rhodesia. See Gifford, "Framework for a Nation," p. 122.

4. The Director's Report of the British South Africa Company for the two years ending 31 March 1900 stated: "The supply of labour [in Southern Rhodesia] has been even worse and less reliable than before. The favourable position occupied by the native in this territory is such as to render it unnecessary for him to improve his material condition" (quoted in Gifford, p. 124). As Gifford goes on to comment, the settlers stated that "African labor couldn't be paid much, because it was worth little, produced little, and cared less" (p. 127). Consequently, "the alternative to raising wages was to increase the reservoir of employees, drawing upon areas where opportunities were fewer and the population larger. By 1921 over 64% of the Africans in employment in Southern Rhodesia came from outside its boundaries" (ibid., p. 128). See also Giovanni Arrighi, "Labor Supplies in Historical Perspective: A Study of the Proletarianization of the African Peasantry in Rhodesia," in Giovanni Arrighi and John S. Saul, *Essays on the Political Economy of Africa.*

5. Gifford, p. 138. See also Charles W. Coulter, "The Sociological Problem," p. 56.

6. Gifford refers to this tax as a "punitive tax on subsistence" (p. 138). Rotberg notes the early policy of burning the huts of tax defaulters, and the later change from hut burning to imprisonment as a means of punishment. In 1933, he notes, 7,589 persons were imprisoned as tax defaulters (Robert I. Rotberg, *The Rise of Nationalism in Central Africa,* p. 47).

7. Rotberg, p. 42.

8. Gifford, pp. 125–26.

9. John A. Hellen, *Rural Economic Development in Zambia,* p. 101. At this point, Hellen is relying on material drawn from P. Scott, "Migrant Labour in Southern Rhodesia," *Geographical Review* 44, no. 1 (1954): 29–48. Perhaps the best discussions of labor recruitment are Coulter, "Sociological Problem"; Helmuth Heisler, *Urbanisation and the Government of Migration;* and J. Clyde Mitchell, "Wage Labour and African Population Movements in Central Africa." See also Prothero's "Foreign Migrant Labour for South Africa."

10. Gerald L. Caplan, *The Elites of Barotseland, 1878–1969,* pp. 87–88.

11. Gifford, "Framework for a Nation," pp. 203–7. See also the anonymously published article "Alfred Sharpe's Travels in the Northern Province and Katanga," *Northern Rhodesia Journal* 3, no. 3 (1957): 210–19.

12. Bruce Fetter, "Immigrants to Elisabethville," p. 23. See also J. E. Stephenson, "R. W. Yule: An Appreciation"; Val Gielgud, "Some Reminiscences of George Grey," *Northern Rhodesia Journal* 3, no. 2 (1956): 146–53; and Heisler, *Urbanisation,* p. 40.

13. Fetter, "Immigrants," p. 24. It should be noted that the flow to the mines was interrupted in 1907–8 by the outbreak of sleeping sickness in the valley and the consequent imposition of a quarantine in the area. The border with the Congo was officially sealed until 1922, though the evidence strongly suggests that restrictions were effectively lifted in 1909 (see Gifford, "Framework for a Nation," p. 154).

14. Gifford, pp. 179–80, n.

15. Fetter, "Immigrants," p. 27.

16. E. A. G. Robinson, "The Economic Problem," p. 169. This figure is the wage paid to underground labor; for surface workers the figure would be 17s. 6d.

17. Elena L. Berger, *Labour, Race and Colonial Rule,* p. 13.

18. William J. Barber, *The Economy of British Central Africa,* p. 198.

19. The growth of the expected value of the urban alternative was apparently coupled with a shift in tastes, as rural dwellers came to desire new goods and commodities. Unable to satisfy these new wants with earnings from rural production, many entered the urban market for labor. As a result, the voluntary search for labor became sufficiently great that the major employers terminated their payments to the labor recruitment agencies. See Peter Harries-Jones, "The Tribes in the Towns," p. 125; Mitchell, "Wage Labour," p. 205; and Heisler, *Urbanisation,* p. 46 ff.

20. J. Clyde Mitchell, "Some Theoretical Approaches to the Sociological Interpretation of Labour Circulation," pp. 81–82. Also see Mitchell's review article "The Causes of Labour Migration," and his "Factors Motivating Migration from Rural Areas." The best general review of the comparative findings in the demographic correlates of migration is probably Harley L. Browning's "Migrant Selectivity and the Growth of Large Cities in Developing Societies."

21. Godfrey Wilson, *An Essay on the Economics of Detribalization in Northern Rhodesia,* pts. 1–2; Merran McCulloch, *A Social Survey of the African Population of Livingstone;* J. Clyde Mitchell, *African Urbanization in Ndola and Luanshya;* and David G. Bettison, *Numerical Data on African Dwellers in Lusaka, Northern Rhodesia.*

22. See McCulloch, *Social Survey,* p. 15.

23. See, for example, William Watson, *Tribal Cohesion in a Money Economy*, p. 70; Isaac Schapera, *Migrant Labour and Tribal Life*, p. 39 ff.; John C. Caldwell, *African Rural-Urban Migration,* p. 58; Michael Banton, *West African City,* p. 48 ff.; Patrick O. Ohadike, *Some Demographic Measurements for Africans in Zambia,* p. 14; and Bruce Herrick, "Urbanization and Urban Migration in Latin America." See also the empirical findings summarized in William J. Hanna and Judith L. Hanna, *Urban Dynamics in Black Africa.*

24. This is not, of course, the case where the youth's income is that of the working adults, that is, where the youths are dependents. It could be argued that men were offered more jobs because they were more prone to migrate. This argument makes little sense to me. I cannot plausibly see the mines offering underground work to women, the railways hiring women to lay tracks, and so forth. It makes more sense to me to see the differential rates of migration as resulting from differential bids for labor.

25. Northern Rhodesia, *Report on the Census of Population of Northern Rhodesia Held on 15th October, 1946,* p. 119. There is little reason to believe that men and women would supply labor at different rates under similar circumstances; rather, the cause for differential employment rates appears to lie in the structure of the demand for labor.

26. Bettison, *Numerical Data,* p. 84.

27. The tacit rule was that if you "civilize a woman, you civilize a family," as one missionary put it to me. In 1946, the employment rate of women in agriculture was twice the average rate of female employment in all industrial sectors (4.7 percent and 2.4 percent, respectively), and the rate in mission work was nearly three times the average rate (Northern Rhodesia, *Report on the Census of Population,* p. 119).

28. Phyllis Deane, *Colonial Social Accounting,* p. 27.

29. P. H. Gulliver, "Nyakyusa Labour Migration," p. 48. Also emphasizing the sex-selectivity of migration is the analysis by Ohadike of the 1963 census, which reveals that the "rural male/female ratio at 90 was in favour of more females than males as opposed to 106 and 128 respectively for the [commercial] farm and the urban area" (Ohadike, *Demographic Measurements,* p. 16). Moreover, George Kay reports: "A District Commissioner at Mpika collected an account of absenteeism amongst women as well as men in 1960. This exercise showed that whereas 6,891 men (55 percent of the total adult male population) were absent from their village homes, only 2,144 women (19 percent of all adult females) were away" (George Kay, *A Social Geography of Zambia,* pp. 80–81).

30. See, for example, Ralph E. Beals, Mildred B. Levy, and Leon N. Moses, "Rationality and Migration in Ghana"; Caldwell, *African Rural-Urban Migration;* Herrick, "Urban Migration in Latin America"; and Michael J. Greenwood, "An Analysis of the Determinants of Geographic Labor Mobility in the United States." See also Mildred B. Levy and Walter J. Wadycki, "Education and the Decision to Migrate."

31. Gulliver, "Nyakyusa Labour Migration," p. 58.

32. One notable study that makes use of a sophisticated variant of this approach is Daniel Lerner, *The Passing of Traditional Society.*

33. Kay, *Social Geography*, p. 80.

34. Ibid.

35. For an analysis of the relative rural versus urban impact of the mission

programs, see John V. Taylor and Dorothea Lehmann, *Christians of the Copperbelt;* and J. E. Gardiner, "Missions," in *Zambia in Maps,* ed. D. Hywel Davies. See also Peter Bolink, *Towards Church Union in Zambia.*

36. Kay, *Social Geography,* p. 73.

37. Bettison, *Numerical Data,* p. 75. Given that both education and employment were essentially first- or at most second-generational phenomena at this time, it is doubtful that richer people were purchasing more education; such classlike phenomena had yet to develop significantly among Zambian Africans at that time.

38. McCulloch, *Social Survey,* p. 40.

39. Ibid., p. 42.

40. The argument that positive returns to education are stronger for urban employment than they are for rural sources of income is "perhaps . . . valid for much of Africa," in the words of Stephen Heyneman. As he states:

There appears to be small measurable monetary incentive to send a child to school if he is to remain in the rural areas. Returns to primary education in Kenyan urban areas average 11 % above that of rural areas, while returns to urban secondary education averaged 30 % more. Though education was associated with an increase in a landowner's crop production of £23 per year, since a fifteen year old had less than a 30 % chance of becoming a landowner by age 27, most private incentive for primary and secondary education in Kenya must be perceived as non-agricultural in nature. [Stephen P. Heyneman, "Fallacies in Educational Economics," p. 33]

41. J. Clyde Mitchell, "The Distribution of African Labour by Area of Origin on the Coppermines of Northern Rhodesia," p. 34. For a further analysis of the role of distance, see Mitchell's "Wage Labour," and his "Distance, Transportation, and Urban Involvement in Zambia."

42. Harries-Jones, "Tribes in the Towns," p. 130.

43. Bettison, *Numerical Data,* p. 65.

44. McCulloch, *Social Survey,* p. 28. Lance Davis, in a personal communication, argues that the line of rail might serve as an iso-cost area, so that once it is entered, any place on the line of rail could be attained for insignificant costs. The data from this earlier period strongly suggest, however, that this is not the case; for, if it were, the proportion of persons from different rural areas to be found in each of the major line-of-rail centers should be equal to their relative proportions in the population as a whole.

45. Harries-Jones, "Tribes in the Towns," p. 134; and Bettison, *Numerical Data,* pp. 68–69.

46. McCulloch, *Social Survey,* p. 44.

47. Harries-Jones, "Tribes in the Towns," pp. 125–27; and Patrick O. Ohadike, *Development of and Factors in the Employment of African Migrants in the Copper Mines of Zambia, 1940–66,* pp. 9–14. For a fuller discussion, see the next section of this chapter and the references cited therein.

48. Elizabeth Colson, "Migration in Africa: Trends and Possibilities," p. 111.

49. W. Allan, Max Gluckman, D. U. Peters, and C. G. Trapnell, *Land Holding and Land Usage among the Plateau Tonga of Mazabuka District,* p. 162.

50. Colson, "Migration in Africa," p. 111.

51. Allan et al., *Land Holding and Land Usage,* p. 160.

52. R. R. Kuczynski, *Demographic Survey of the British Colonial Empire,* 2:

468. The data for this year, and the tax roll data for the years up to and including 1934, are the only population data from administrative sources which this careful demographer was willing to accept as valid.

53. McCulloch, *Social Survey,* p. 26.

54. Cited in Allan et al., *Land Holding and Land Usage,* p. 160.

55. Kay, *Social Geography,* p. 78.

56. Harries-Jones, "Tribes in the Towns," pp. 125–27; and Ohadike, *African Migrants,* pp. 9–14.

57. Ohadike, *Employment of African Migrants,* pp. 7–8.

58. Ian G. Cunnison, *The Luapula Peoples of Northern Rhodesia,* p. 44.

59. Ibid., p. 47.

60. The use of migration as an alternative source of income to agricultural production was perhaps best portrayed by E. A. G. Robinson: "Having nothing else to sell, the Native has sold himself" ("Economic Problem," p. 135).

61. Wilson, *Economics of Detribalization,* pt. 1, p. 59.

62. McCulloch *Social Survey,* p. 20.

63. Wilson, pt. 1, p. 59.

64. Figures from Copper Industry Service Bureau, File 5B, African Strength, Year Book Statistics; and from Rokana Corporation, Manpower Services Department, Monthly Reports.

65. L. H. Gann, *A History of Northern Rhodesia,* p. 363. Data from 1938 indicate that in excess of 43% of the mineworkers at Mufulira, Roan, and Rokana had been in service for less than six months; see Major G. St. J. Orde Browne, *Labour Conditions in Northern Rhodesia* (London: His Majesty's Stationery Office, 1938). Harries-Jones, writing of an earlier period, notes: "In 1927, of the 1,000 African employees at the Roan, 80 percent, were single men. Average length of service was three months and the average labour turnover was 300 percent" ("Tribes in the Towns," p. 125).

66. Bettison, *Numerical Data,* p. 28; and Mitchell, *African Urbanization,* p. 6.

67. For example, Bettison, pp. 51–59.

68. Wilson, *Economics of Detribalization,* pt. 1, p. 59.

69. Mitchell, *African Urbanization,* p. 6.

70. Wilson, pt. 1, p. 43.

71. George Kay, "Sources and Uses of Cash in Some Ushi Villages."

72. Thus, E. A. G. Robinson writes: "Northern Rhodesia, when the demand for labour at the mines increased, attempted to restrict the flow of labour out of the country. The agent who recruited labour for the Congo mines was informed that the number of men he might recruit would be gradually reduced. The Rhodesian Native Labour Bureau, which recruited for Southern Rhodesian employers, was limited progressively to a much lower figure than the average of previous years" ("Economic Problem," p. 160).

73. As Robinson stated: "In the early stages the mines recruited individually, and, as was inevitable, in competition to some extent with each other. . . . This state of affairs was unsatisfactory . . . and . . . the mines joined together in March 1930 to form the Native Labour Association" which recruited for all the mines by offering uniform wages and conditions of service to all prospective laborers (ibid).

74. The depression led to a reduction of over 30 percent in wages at the mines (from 17s. 6d. to 12s. 6d. per thirty working days for surface workers); after the 1940 strikes wages rose, but not to the predepression level (the comparable figure was 15s. after 1940). See Berger, *Labour, Race and Colonial Rule,* pp. 48, 56.

75. Barber, *Economy of British Central Africa,* pp. 204–7.

76. Robert E. Baldwin, *Economic Development and Export Growth,* pp. 134–37. It is interesting to note that Walter Elkan finds that those who can combine farm and wage incomes and who can do so in the urban areas are the most permanent urban dwellers: ironically, the proletarians of his study are those urban workers who live on neighboring farms. See Walter Elkan, *Migrants and Proletarians.*

77. The most generous pensions were paid by the mines, where a pension of at most £72 per year was paid in 1959. The pension was purposely designed to be large enough to provide a comfortable rural retirement but not so large as to make possible a comfortable retirement in town. See Baldwin, *Economic Development,* pp. 138–39.

78. Kay, *Social Geography,* pp. 74, 91–92; Robert I. Rotberg, *The Rise of Nationalism in Central Africa,* pp. 130–31. See, for example, the discussion by John Collins. The government, he contends, favored tied housing for Africans—housing that was rented by employees and could be occupied only so long as the African retained his job—as it both made the collection of rents easier and prevented permanent settlement in town. In addition, zoning requirements prevented Africans from constructing their own houses, for the minimum value of permitted houses was high; expensive standards of construction were maintained; and the cost of surveying and registering land for leasing purposes was very high as well. John Collins, "The Evolution of Urban Housing Policies in Zambia with Particular Reference to Lusaka," pp. 14–24.

79. See Bettison, *Numerical Data,* p. 107; and Kay, *Social Geography,* pp. 93–94. See also C. E. Duff, ed., *First Report on a Regional Survey of the Copperbelt, 1959* (Lusaka: Government Printer, 1960).

80. J. van Velsen, "Labour Migration as a Positive Factor in the Continuity of Tonga Tribal Society," p. 233. Note also the commentary on a series of discussions on the subject of rural land rights held at Munali Secondary School in the mid-1950s: "There was concensus among all Africans who spoke in this discussion that it was necessary for the town worker to have . . . a foothold in the country as . . . a place to retire to in times of poverty and other frustrations of African town life. No speaker wanted rural land rights as a matter of principle, only as a matter of expediency" (*Present Interrelations in Central African Rural and Urban Life,* ed. R. J. Apthorpe, pp. vii–viii).

81. Berger, *Labour, Race and Colonial Rule,* pp. 36–37. In the terms applied to this set of issues in the literature on Zambia, by resisting the stabilization of labor the government, out of regard for its philosophy of indirect rule, sought also to prevent the detribalization of the native population. See also Heisler, *Urbanisation,* for a review of official policy toward the stabilization of labor.

CHAPTER 4

1. The standard sources for the history of the nationalist period are: L. H. Gann, *A History of Northern Rhodesia;* J. W. Davidson, *The Northern Rhodesian Legislative Council;* Robert I. Rotberg, *The Rise of Nationalism in Central Africa;* and David C. Mulford, *Zambia.* See also the relevant sections of Margaret R. Bates, "UNIP in Postindependence Zambia."

2. The relevant portion of the Passfield Memorandum reads: "The interests of the African natives must be paramount, and . . . if, and when, those interests and the interests of the immigrant races should conflict, the former should prevail." Obviously this statement of British colonial policy was threatening to

the European settler community. Quoted from Davidson, *Northern Rhodesian Legislative Council*, p. 69.

3. Rotberg, *Rise of Nationalism*, p. 112.

4. For the reaction of the British government to the results of this election, see Gann, *History of Northern Rhodesia*, pp. 397–402.

5. United Kingdom Government, *Central African Territories: Report of the Conference on Closer Association*, Cmd. 8233 (London: His Majesty's Stationery Office, 1951).

6. United Kingdom Government, *Draft Federal Scheme for Central African Federation*, Cmd. 8573 (London: His Majesty's Stationery Office, 1952).

7. See the discussion in Colin Leys, " 'Partnership' as the Dismantling of the Colour Bar," pp. 98–109. As is noted in that chapter, the expansion of the Federal Assembly in 1957 further diluted the effectiveness of its African representatives.

8. Rotberg, *Rise of Nationalism*, p. 202.

9. Ibid., p. 212.

10. United Kingdom Government, *Central African Territories*.

11. A. L. Epstein, *Politics in an Urban African Community*, p. 160.

12. Gann, *History of Northern Rhodesia,* p. 424.

13. Mulford, *Zambia*, p. 194.

14. Ibid., p. 198.

15. For detailed treatments of these elections, see Mulford, *Zambia;* and Margaret R. Bates, "UNIP in Postindependence Zambia."

16. See, for example, George Bennett, *Kenya: A Political History, The Colonial Period* (London: Oxford University Press, 1963); and George Bennett and Carl G. Rosberg, *The Kenyatta Election: Kenya, 1960–1961* (London: Oxford University Press, for the Institute of Commonwealth Studies, 1961).

17. For an earlier attempt to address these questions, see Thomas Rasmussen, "The Popular Basis of Anti-Colonial Protest."

18. Quoted from Epstein, *Politics in an Urban African Community*, p. 104.

19. Ibid.

20. Elena L. Berger, *Labour, Race and Colonial Rule*, p. 45.

21. Ibid., pp. 45–46.

22. See the discussions in ibid., and in Robert H. Bates, *Unions, Parties, and Political Development*.

23. See the discussions in Rotberg, *Rise of Nationalism*, pp. 265–78; and Epstein, *Politics in an Urban African Community*, pp. 171–80. See also Colin Leys, " 'Partnership,' "; and Wittington K. Sikalumbi, "The Circumstances Which Gave Rise to the Banning of the Zambia African Congress of Northern Rhodesia" (unpublished manuscript), which contains an interesting history of this earlier period as well. The question arises as to why new retailers did not enter the market so as to fulfill the demands of Africans. The main reason appears to be that licensing boards were dominated by European politicians who had a stake in restricting entry (out of a regard for the interests of existing retailers) and in preserving market discrimination (out of a regard for the prejudices of the European consumers); aligned with these politicians were the colonial officials, who sought to restrict entry to highly capitalized retailers who could afford the equipment (e.g., cold storage facilities) that would protect urban health standards.

24. Epstein, *Politics in an Urban African Community*, p. 168.

25. The economic basis for participation in the nationalist movement is also

indicated by the hawkers' subsequent behavior. According to Esptein, "following . . . the new opportunities opened up by the changed policy of the Municipal Board, the hawkers saw little further advantage in their attachment to the branch [of ANC], which they promptly abandoned *en masse* . . . " (ibid., p. 171).

26. William J. Barber, "Federation and the Distribution of Economic Benefits," pp. 90–91.

27. See, for example, "Northern Rhodesia Is Facing the Problem of Unemployment and Poor Services for Africans," in UNIP, Luapula Division, *Newsletter*, n.p., n.d.; and "Open Letter, Divisional Secretary to All Chiefs, Luapula Province," in UNIP, Luapula Division, *Newsletter* (January 1961). Both describe in some detail the reasons for the loss of funds from the territory under the federal agreements.

28. As stated by one observer,

Congress adopted the bold policy of sending out organizers to tour the reserves and hold meetings there. These organizers sought to impress on the villagers the need for unity and to convince the chiefs of the need for collaboration in a common purpose.

The response was immediate and enthusiastic; by and large, both chiefs and villagers accepted the Congress line. The warmth of the response was something of a surprise to all concerned, not least to the Administration. Most of the Congress organizers were educated urban Africans not immediately concerned with tribal affairs and therefore considered not to be the type likely to affect the opinions of "conservative" peasants. [William Watson, "The Social Background," p. 155]

29. George Kay, *A Social Geography of Zambia,* p. 76.

30. Gann, *History of Northern Rhodesia*, p. 107.

31. Quoted in Rotberg, *Rise of Nationalism*, pp. 111–12.

32. "Circular to All Party Branches, Luapula Division," from Acting Divissional Treasurer, S.C. Kaushi, mimeo. (n.p., n.d.), from the files of a branch official, Kasumpa village.

33. "Circular to All Party Branches, Luapula Division," from Divisional Publicity Secretary, M. M. Lumande, mimeo. (n.p., n.d.), from the files of a branch official, Kasumpa village.

34. The most important such lobbyist was Dauti Yamba, a Luanshya school teacher who was also the founding president of the Federation of Welfare Societies and later a leading official in the African National Congress. Yamba regularly transmitted to Mwata Kazembe the minutes of the urban welfare societies in Kitwe and Luanshya as well as the minutes of political meetings on the copperbelt. His correspondence from Salisbury, where he served as a member of the Federal Assembly, constitutes a moving indictment of racial policies in Rhodesia. These letters are to be found in the Palace Files of Mwata Kazembe in Mwansabombwe and in the following Lunda Native Authority files, now held by the Kawambwa Rural Council: AFN/2, CUS/2, ADM/10, and INF/2/1. For further discussion of the relationship between urban migration and rural protest in the nationalist period, see Rasmussen, "Popular Basis of Anti-Colonial Protest."

35. Elder Kafuti Kasembe, Ndola African Location, to Mwata Kazembe, Mwansabombwe, 10 February 1952, from file AFN/2, Kawambwa Rural Council.

36. Mwata Kazembe, Mwansabombwe, to Elder Kafuti Kasembe, Ndola African Location, 29 February 1952, from file AFN/2, Kawambwa Rural Council.

37. For an important general discussion of the land issue in African politics, see Robert I. Rotberg, "The Rise of African Nationalism."

38. Rotberg, *Rise of Nationalism,* pp. 126–28.

39. W. Allan, Max Gluckman, D. U. Peters, and C. G. Trapnell, *Land Holding and Land Usage among the Plateau Tonga of Mazabuka District.* See also Gann, *History of Northern Rhodesia,* pp. 306–7.

40. Gann, p. 425. See also the discussion in Rasmussen, "Popular Basis of Anti-Colonial Protest."

41. The depth of the resentment generated by the mission's alienation of land is also revealed in the report of a surveyor who in 1962 delimited the lands to be returned by the missionaries to native tenure. His activities were at first vigorously opposed by local party officials, who misunderstood his purpose and feared further "encroachments on [village] gardens." His report also suggests the strength of the desire for further lands, for when he succeeded in convincing the party officials of what he was doing he was then subjected to their demands for "land where to settle. . . . I told [them] to apply to the . . . Native Authority." These reports are contained in Agricultural Councillor to District Commissioner, Kawambwa, 27 June 1962, Palace Files, LAN/2.

42. At that time, the 215,000 white settlers in Southern Rhodesia comprised an estimated 7.6 percent of the territory's population. See Watson, "Social Background," p. 146.

43. Gann, discussing the evidence before the Bledisloe Commission in *History of Northern Rhodesia,* p. 275.

44. Ibid., p. 407.

45. See, for example, the interview with John Chishimba, 11 November 1971, author's collection.

46. For a similar argument, see Watson, "The Social Background," pp. 138–47.

CHAPTER 5

1. See, for example, the requests by the commanding officer of the Luapula Division of the police to make wholesale arrests in Kasumpa village, noted in the Record of a Meeting Held at Government House on 13 July 1960, S/S 108/4/01, Mulford Collection. See also the requests by the native authority for government support in "removing the subversive elements in Kasumpa Village" ("Monthly Intelligence Report," September 1959, DG/58/4/01, Mulford Collection).

2. Prior to moving it to Kawambwa and thence to Fort Rosebery. See Special Branch Report to Administrative Secretary, 22 September 1959, S/S 108/4/01, Mulford Collection, and "Monthly Intelligence Report," January 1960, S/S 108/4/01, Mulford Collection.

3. Northern Rhodesia, Department of African Affairs, *Annual Report for the Year 1953,* p. 26.

4. Northern Rhodesia, Department of African Affairs, *Annual Report for the Year 1956,* p. 28.

5. L. H. Gann, *A History of Northern Rhodesia,* pp. 229, 292.

6. See Northern Rhodesia, *Report of the Financial Relationship Committee.* See also Mwata Kanyembo VI, "The Lunda Kingdom and Its Civil Government" typescript (1963), Palace Files, Mwansabombwe.

7. Northern Rhodesia, Department of African Affairs, *Annual Report for the Year 1956,* p. 29. See also Lunda Native Authority, "Estimates," 1954–64, in the files of the Kawambwa Rural Council.

8. Northern Rhodesia, Department of African Affairs, *Annual Report for the Year 1954,* p. 4.

9. "Annual Report," District Officer, Kawambwa, to Chief Secretary, Lusaka, 1949, ADM/1, Kawambwa Rural Council.

10. The central origin of the agricultural policy perhaps accounts for its inappropriateness to the Luapula valley. The policy may have been relevant to the plateau, where famine was in fact a periodic problem; but it was of little relevance to the valley, where famine rarely was a problem, with the exception of the area governed by Chief Kashiba.

11. Edward Muhango to District Commissioner, 28 March 1963, in AFN/7/4/1, Kawambwa District Commissioner, Mufulira Archives.

12. District Commissioner to Mwata Kazembe, 29 March 1963, in AFN/7/4/1, Kawambwa District Commissioner, Mufulira Archives.

13. District Commissioner to Secretary Councillor, Lunda Native Authority, 5 January 1962, in AFN/7/4/1, Kawambwa District Commissioner, Mufulira Archives.

14. See correspondence throughout November of 1955 between the District Commissioner of Kawambwa and Mwata Kazembe, in CON/1, Kawambwa Rural Council.

15. See, for example, District Commissioner, Kawambwa, to Senior Chief Kazembe, 11 February 1956, in ADM/10, Kawambwa Rural Council.

16. District Commissioner, Kawambwa, to Mwata Kazembe, 23 March 1963, in AFN/7/4/1, Kawambwa District Commissioner, Mufulira Archives.

17. Other studies have emphasized the opposition of the mass-based nationalist movements to the native authorities in British colonial Africa, but in most of these other studies the emphasis has been on the class antagonisms between the chiefs and the people. Thus, Martin Kilson argues that in Sierra Leone the chiefs utilized their political positions to achieve control over land, labor, and tribute and thereby to appropriate the gains to be made from the rise in cash crop production (Kilson, *Political Change in a West African State*). This led, he contends, to the generation of nationalist opposition to the chiefs and the native authorities. Dennis Austin presents a similar argument for the rise of "youth brigades" in the Ashanti areas of Ghana (Austin, *Politics in Ghana, 1946–1960*). And Gerald Caplan, in his analysis of the Barotse area of Zambia, notes the growing gap between the incomes of those in the native authority and those of the masses—a gap which derived from payments made by the British South Africa Company to the native authority for mining concessions in Zambia (Caplan, *The Elites of Barotseland, 1878–1969*). In the case of Luapula, however, there appeared to be very little class antagonism underlying rural protest in the nationalist period, and very little private appropriation of profits from "cash cropping" through the control of political agencies. Rather, the antagonism between the people and the native authority largely arose, as I shall argue,

over the issues of the relative size of the public and private share of the wealth to be gained from fishing and the nature of public regulation of private enterprise in the industry.

18. Crane Brinton, in his analysis of European revolutions, writes: "It is interesting to note . . . that they all had in common a financial origin, all began as protests against taxation" (*The Anatomy of Revolution*, 3d ed., p. 36).

19. See, for example, M. M. Lumande, "Europeans Have Separated Us," in UNIP, Luapula Division, *Newsletter* (n.p., n.d.).

20. Interviews with former employees of the native authority revealed the depth of their fear of having to make levies in the valley during this period; and former messengers and revenue collectors still speak of the relief they felt when they resigned from the service of the native authority and no longer had to face the protests and violence that the party leaders organized against them.

21. Northern Rhodesia, Department of African Affairs, *Annual Report for the Year 1953,* p. 40. Regulations of rural enterprise stimulated the formation of nationalist movements all over Africa. For example, Austin describes the outbreak of nationalist agitation against government regulations designed to stop the spread of swollen shoot disease in the cocoa industry in his *Politics in Ghana.* Göran Hydén detected a similar basis for the formation of local party units in the West Lake district of Tanganyika (*Political Development in Rural Tanzania*).

22. Secretary, African National Congress, Kasumpa Village, to District Commissioner, Kawambwa, 10 December 1956, in CON/1, Kawambwa Rural Council.

23. Report of the Lunda Agricultural Assistant to the Lunda Chief Councillor, 29 July 1957, in LNA/AGR/4, Palace Files.

24. See the commentary on the "marked effect on the cost of living" in the Luapula valley created by the imposition of the federal tariffs contained in Northern Rhodesia, Department of African Affairs, *Annual Report for the Year 1955,* p. 36. William J. Barber, on p. 141 of *The Economy of British Central Africa,* places the date of the tariff revisions at 1957; but my evidence indicates that it was two years earlier.

25. Provincial Commissioner to Chief Secretary, 13 January 1960, in DG/58/4/01, Mulford Collection.

26. Northern Rhodesia, Department of African Affairs, *Annual Report for the Year 1960,* p. 25.

27. Ibid., p. 32.

28. Ibid.

29. Ibid.

30. Fresh fish equivalents. One pound of dried fish is assumed to equal four pounds of fresh fish.

31. Northern Rhodesia, Department of African Affairs, *Annual Report for the Year 1958,* p. 31. See also Northern Rhodesia, *Report on Intensive Rural Development in the Northern and Luapula Provinces of Northern Rhodesia, 1957–1961,* p. 33. The reports seem to indicate that the disruption in the market organization, at least in the short term, was responsible for the decline in sales; it is also possible that urban consumers, when given the chance to consume according to their own tastes, reduced their consumption of fish in favor of other commodities.

32. Because of the violence, the Greek traders in Kasenga abandoned their stores, ice plant, and transport fleet and fled for safety across the river to Northern Rhodesia.

33. Central Statistical Office, *Fisheries Statistics (Natural Waters) 1968*, table 1.1. See also Northern Rhodesia, *Report on Intensive Rural Development*, p. 33.

34. Northern Rhodesia, Department of African Affairs, *Annual Report for the Year 1962*, p. iii; and Joint Fisheries Research Organization to District Commissioner, Kawambwa, in FIS/2, Kawambwa Rural Council.

35. The quantity figures are from Central Statistical Office, *Fisheries Statistics (Natural Waters) 1968*, table 1.1. The price figures (which assume a price of 1 shilling per pound) are taken from the "Mweru/Luapula Fisheries, Annual Report for the Year 1961," mimeo. (1962), p. 1, from Lunda Native Authority File FIS/5, Kawambwa Rural Council.

36. James C. Davies, "Toward a Theory of Revolution"; Ted Robert Gurr, *Why Men Rebel;* Ivo K. Feierabend and Rosalind L. Feierabend, "Agressive Behaviors within Polities, 1948–1962"; Mancur Olson, Jr., "Rapid Growth as a Destabilizing Factor"; and Gilbert Merkx, "Economics and History in the Study of Rebellions: The Argentine Case," in *Political Development and Change: A Policy Approach*, ed. Garry D. Brewer and Ronald D. Brunner.

37. See the petition to the Lunda Native Authority contained in file LNA/LAN/2, Kawambwa Rural Council; and Northern Rhodesia, Department of African Affairs, *Annual Report for the Year 1960*, p. 32.

38. Fisheries Councillor of the Lunda Native Authority, "Annual Report for 1960," 20 January 1961, FIS/5, Kawambwa Rural Council.

39. "Mweru/Luapula Fisheries, Annual Report for the Year 1961," mimeo. (1962), pp. 1–2, from Lunda Native Authority file FIS/5, Kawambwa Rural Council.

40. See the materials in the Lunda Native Authority files FIS/2, FIS/5, and FIS/6 in the Kawambwa Rural Council.

41. For a published discussion of this, see David C. Mulford, *Zambia,* pp. 71–74. See also the materials on the failure of the tours of African National Congress leaders in the Luapula valley contained in "Biographical Note on Harry Nkumbula," S/S 201/05, Mulford Collection. The accounts contained in these references corroborate what my informants had told me: that the failure of the ANC leaders to organize actively at the village level in the valley led to a precipitate decline of the party's support in the area.

42. Quotation from interview with Mama Katie Kakusa, 17 May 1972, who served as one of the principal ANC, ZANC, and UNIP organizers in Kawambwa District. In fact, she ran the party almost single-handedly during the period when the male ZANC organizers were in jail. See also the interview notes with Conrad Chisanga, 14 March 1972, and Chola Bwalya, 17 May 1972, author's collection.

43. Interviews with Sunday Mwamba, 30 November 1971; Edward Kaputo, 1 November 1971; Bancom Kabungo, 11 December 1971; and John Chishimba, 11 December 1971, author's collection. See also the files of the Welfare and Education Councillor, Lunda Native Authority, held by the Kawamba Rural Council.

44. Special Branch Report to Administrative Secretary, 22 September 1959, in S/S 108/4/01, Mulford Collection. See also my interview with Katie Kakusa, 17 May 1972.

45. Mulford, *Zambia,* pp. 106–28.

46. See, for example, "Where We Came from and Where We Are Now," Circular to All Party Units, Luapula Division, by D. E. Mulenshi, Deputy Divisional Secretary, mimeo. (n.p.,n.d.), author's collection, which reports in detail

on the status of the constitutional negotiations in February 1961. See also the detailed treatment of the splits within the British delegation at the negotiations contained in "Have No Confidence in the British Government," Circular to All Party Units, Luapula Division, by D. E. Mulenshi, Deputy Divisional Secretary, mimeo. (n.p., n.d.), author's collection.

47. Telegram from Katofyio I, II, III (Kasumpa Village UNIP branches) to UNIP Delegation, c/o Colonial Secretary, London, 19 December 1960, files of Kasumpa Party officials.

48. Telegram from Katofyio I, II, III (Kasumpa Village UNIP branches) to Bwana Kaunda, c/o Colonial Secretary, London, 5 January 1961, files of Kasumpa Party officials.

49. See the discussion in Robert I. Rotberg, *The Rise of Nationalism in Central Africa,* p. 312; and Mulford, *Zambia,* p. 194.

50. Report of Mr. S. M. Mununga, Member of the Legislative Council for Luapula Constituency, 11 October 1961, pp. 2–3, in POL/40, Kawambwa Rural Council.

51. *Northern News,* 22 August 1961.

52. *Northern News,* 23 August 1961.

53. With self-government in Zambia, the payment of the head tax stopped entirely. There is evidence, however, that the decline in tax payments had paralleled the de facto shift in political power. Thus, a colonial government report notes a 39 percent decrease in tax payments in Luapula Province from 1960 to 1962. The report goes on to state that the "fall off in tax payments in Northern and Luapula Province was very serious. . . . Native Authorities in the area were nearly bankrupt and were cutting back on staff. An interesting feature of this was that tax payments by people from these areas who were living somewhere else had fallen off just as much as those of people resident there. . . . [Therefore] payment of tax could not be said to be related . . . to the economic condition of the tax payers" (Record of Discussions between Kaunda and the Chief Secretary, 4 October 1962, S/S 108/014, Mulford Collection).

54. Assistant Natural Resources Councillor to Natural Resources Councillor, Lunda Native Authority, 2 February 1963, FIS/2, Kawambwa Rural Council.

55. Fisheries Officer to Lunda Native Authority Councillors, 9 March 1964, FIS/6, Kawambwa Rural Council.

56. See the Minutes of the Lunda Tribal Council, 14 November 1963, Palace Files, Mwansabombwe, p. 2.

With reference to the proposed sacking of employees of the council, it was revealed by the acting secretary councillor that "not only [were the] Councillors . . . in favor of sacking of Departmental [employees] but [they] were also making indirect applications for employment in the Native Authority." From Acting Secretary Councillor to Mwata Kazembe, 17 December 1963, AFN/PAL/16, Palace Files, Mwansabombwe.

Though it may alarm some to read this, there can be little question but that the desire to gain employment and remuneration in the public service was a major goal of many of the nationalist leaders. It is important that this was so, for the payoffs attached to the positions of leadership helped to furnish an incentive for the leaders to organize the movement to provide the indivisible benefits of independence to the population as a whole. Indeed, Mancur Olson's analysis of collective action suggests that, without such special inducements, it is doubtful whether persons would have forged an organization to meet the collective needs of the residents of the valley (Mancur Olson, Jr., *The Logic of Collective Action*).

Olson also argues that coercion may be necessary in forging a collective movement in order to exclude from it, and from the benefits it may provide, those who wish to gain these benefits without paying the costs; were many people able to do this, he argues, there would be little incentive for anyone to contribute to these costs, and the movement would fail. Though I was unable to gain much detail, it was clear that ZANC and UNIP did put pressure upon those who were unwilling to make financial contributions to the party by purchasing membership cards, or who were unwilling to attend meetings, vote in party elections, or otherwise devote time to the party's affairs. In particular, the Jehovah's Witnesses in Luapula—like Jehovah's Witnesses elsewhere—denied the legitimacy of the party's efforts to seek secular power and thus were unwilling to engage in political activities during the nationalist period. Enraged that these people would nonetheless benefit from their labors, party leaders in some regions organized attacks on the members of this denomination with as much vehemence as they organized their campaigns against the colonial government. The periodic clashes between the party and the Witnesses were major events in some areas of the province. They were however not particularly important around Kasumpa and I therefore have few details with which to illustrate this conflict. Nonetheless, the fact that the clashes did take place, in addition to the fact that the party leaders did benefit directly and privately, helps to illustrate how the structure of incentives may have operated to transform the collective desire for a new government into an organized effort to achieve that objective.

57. Minutes of the Lunda Tribal Council, 14 November 1963, Palace Files, Mwansabombwe, p. 4.

58. Ibid., p. 5–9.

59. Ibid., p. 10.

60. Ibid.

61. Ibid., p. 12.

62. Interviews with Joseph Kapupili, 11 December 1971, and Albert Katei, 3 November 1971.

63. The demand orientation of the rural dwellers for government investments is similarly noted in Hydén's *Political Development in Rural Tanzania*, p. 165 ff. The relationship between the volume of demands and the level of taxation in West Africa is described by W. Arthur Lewis, who writes: "The African villager has now come to take it for granted that the central government will provide water, schools, hospital service, roads, and even electricity free, or at highly subsidized rates. If decentralization were in vogue, the village could be told that it could have as much . . . water or electricity as it is willing to pay for out of village taxes. . . . The clear connection between taxation and the quantity of service would both check demand and increase the willingness to pay taxes" (W. Arthur Lewis, *Politics in West Africa*, p. 54).

64. Tour Report 1/62, District Officer (Seconded) Northern Rhodesia Police Headquarters, 17–23 January 1962, in DG/58/4/01, Mulford Collection.

CHAPTER 6

1. Out of a total of £26.98 million in direct taxes, the copper companies paid £25.29 million. See Federation of Rhodesia and Nyasaland, *Report of the Commissioner of Taxes for the Year Ending 30 June 1963*. If other sources of taxes are considered—mineral royalties and customs and excise duties, for example—the relative contribution of the mining companies to the public treasury becomes

even greater. Rural-urban public investment patterns in Zambia are discussed in Donald Rothchild, "Rural-Urban Inequities and Resource Allocation in Zambia."

2. Central Statistical Office, *Census of Production 1965 and 1966*, p. 41.

3. See the discussion in Charles Harvey, "Tax Reform in the Mining Industry."

4. For a general discussion of budgetary strategies under conditions of low redundancy, see Naomi Caiden and Aaron Wildavsky, *Planning and Budgeting in Poor Countries.*

The colonial government had maximized the expected value of its revenues by accumulating surpluses. But it appears that the enfranchisement of a highly vocal constituency with great expectations of the public sector, as well as the increase in revenues at the time of independence, led to ways of maximizing expected revenues that were based upon strategies of spending and not of accumulation. See the discussion of the aims and objectives of the First National Development Plan in Republic of Zambia, *Second National Development Plan, January, 1972–December, 1976*, p. 1. See also United Nations, Economic Commission for Africa, Food and Agriculture Organization, *Report of the UN/ECA/FAO Economic Survey Mission on the Economic Development of Zambia* (Ndola: Falcon Press, 1964), pp. 13–14.

Another reason for wanting to diversify is that the reserves of copper are of course finite, and that, unless other industries are created, there will be no economic base for the government to tax when the reserves are depleted. As Alan Drysdall writes, "The total copper content of the Copperbelt reserves is approximately 26 million short tons, i.e., 12.5 percent of the world's total reserves . . . as recently estimated by the U.S. Bureau of Mines. However, these figures are no cause for complacency: at the present rate of production and without allowing for such factors as mining losses and dilution, the Copperbelt's reserves . . . only guarantee an average life of some 22 years" (Alan Drysdall, "Prospecting and Mining Activity," p. 73).

For an analysis of the relationship between variations in export earnings (overwhelmingly from copper) and variations in the gross national product in Zambia, see Alistair Young, *Industrial-Diversification in Zambia*, pp. 75–78.

5. Perhaps the best overall discussion of this policy is contained in Young, *Industrial Diversification in Zambia.* A strategy of diversification which seeks to form domestic sources for inputs into a leading sector leaves the economy still strongly tied to the fortunes of that dominant sector. Nonetheless, given limited resources, it is likely that the most efficient means of developing new economic activities is to take advantage of the demand for goods from the leading sector. Presumably, the new enterprises will market to other consumers as well and so develop markets independent of the leading sector.

6. Robert E. Baldwin, *Economic Development and Export Growth*, p. 37.

7. Republic of Zambia, *Second National Development Plan*, pp. 19–20.

8. Ibid., p. 20. This source reveals that the number of establishments in the metal-working group rose from 98 to 171 in the first planning period. See also Norman Kessel, "Mining and the Factors Constraining Economic Development"; Michael Faber, "The Development of the Manufacturing Sector"; and A. Young, "Patterns of Development in Zambian Manufacturing Industry since Independence," and *Industrial Diversification in Zambia*, ch. 7.

9. See Kessel, "Factors Constraining Economic Development," p. 260; and

Kim Border's analogous analysis of Republic of Zambia, *National Accounts and Input-Output Tables, 1969*, in the author's collection.

10. Some readers may argue that the adoption of tax holidays and a tax credit system by the government of Zambia is inconsistent with my contention that governments seek to maximize the present value of their expected revenues. My model, however, is one of government allocations; and, I contend, governments *spend* so as to maximize the present value of their expected revenues. That governments should adopt tax holidays and tax write-offs and surrender present revenues in expectation of greater future returns is thus consistent with my model. For descriptions of these governmental measures, see C. R. M. Harvey, "The Fiscal System"; and Charles Harvey, "Tax Reform in the Mining Industry." See also Young, *Industrial Diversification in Zambia*, pp. 183–87.

11. This was one of the major effects of the first set of economic reforms according to Mark Bostock in his "The Background to Participation."

12. Callum Christie, "The Construction Sector," in *Constraints on the Economic Development of Zambia*, ed. Charles Elliott, p. 306.

13. Dennis Lee Dresang, "The Zambia Civil Service," p. 120.

14. Calculated from Central Statistical Office, *Monthly Digest of Statistics* 8, no. 8 (August 1972): 57.

15. Ibid., p. 56.

16. Charles Harvey, "The Control of Inflation in a Very Open Economy," p. 45.

17. Calculated from Republic of Zambia, *Financial Report for the Year Ended 31st December 1869*, pp. 7–9. In making this calculation, I have omitted the earnings from the copper export tax, to preserve comparability. The export tax was imposed in 1966 essentially as a windfall tax on high copper prices. It was levied at 40 percent of the price of copper in excess of £300 per ton; below that price, the tax did not operate. As a windfall tax it was not a permanent part of the fiscal structure.

Including this tax, the revenues from the copper industry in 1969—the most prosperous year on record up to that time—comprised 58 percent of all government tax earnings.

18. The best discussion of this is contained in Richard Hall, *The High Price of Principles*. See also Peter Slinn, "The Legacy of the British South Africa Company," p. 48.

19. For the export tax, see n. 17 above. A good review of the sources of public revenues is C. R. M. Harvey, "Fiscal System."

20. Republic of Zambia, *Estimates of Revenue and Expenditure for the Year 1st July 1965 to 30th June 1966*, p. 7.

21. Perhaps the best introduction to the philosophy of Humanism are the articles and speeches contained in Bastiaan de Gaay Fortman, ed., *After Mulungushi*.

22. Dr. K. D. Kaunda, *Humanism in Zambia and a Guide to Its Implementation*, p. 31.

23. C. Stephen Lombard, *The Growth of Co-operatives in Zambia*, p. 18.

24. The local mission had taught masonry, carpentry, and other kinds of construction skills and had offered "training on the job" in the process of developing the mission facilities.

25. Lombard, *Growth of Co-operatives*, p. 18. That local UNIP leaders reaped the rewards of independence by founding the cooperative societies is further

confirmed by data from Serenje District, where thirteen of the fourteen agricultural cooperatives were founded by UNIP constituency and branch leaders. Ian Scott, "The Functions of the Local Level Party since Independence," p. 22.

26. "Director of Co-operative Societies to All Provincial Co-operative Officers," Mechanization Circular 19/67, 20th November 1967, from the files of the District Co-operative Officer, Nchelenge District Offices.

27. Lombard, *Growth of Co-operatives*, p. 19.

28. See the memo "Development of Agriculture, Rules and Regulations," in Lunda Native Authority file AGR/3, held by the Kawambwa Rural Council.

29. C. G. Trapnell, *The Soils, Vegetation and Agriculture of North-Eastern Rhodesia*, p. 26.

30. C. R. M. Harvey, "Financial Constraints on Zambia Development," pp. 139–40. See also Sheridan Johns, "Para-statal Bodies in Zambia: Problems and Prospects."

31. Quoted in NAMBoard, "A Short History of the Rural Marketing Department" (paper submitted to the Agricultural and Natural Resources Committee for the Second National Development Plan, 1971), p. 5. Another treatment of the history of this organization is contained in Johns, "Para-statal Bodies in Zambia."

32. See, for example, K. D. Kaunda, *Zambia's Guideline for the Next Decade*.

33. Kenneth David Kaunda, "Address at the Opening of the First Session of the Second National Assembly, 22 January 1969," in Republic of Zambia, *Official Verbatim Report of the Debates of the First Session of the Second National Assembly, 21st January–23rd April 1969*, Hansard no. 17 (Lusaka: Government Printer, 1969), pp. 41–42.

34. It was estimated that, for the prices as fixed at this period, the break-even point of the average rural marketing depot was when the volume of produce at that depot reached 4,000 bags. On the line of rail, this volume could be met by 50 or fewer farmers. In the more remote districts, like Nchelenge, there were fewer than 300 farmers and they were spread out over the entire district; altogether they marketed, in 1968, a mere 2,500 bags. The scale of output was thus so low that it was virtually impossible for the marketing service's depot to cover its costs. See the discussion in *Farming in Zambia*, October 1968, p. 11.

35. While in principle well advised, this measure was, at least initially, a failure, for the plant was subject to paralyzing mechanical problems. It was built in such a way that the nitrates corroded much of the equipment; and for much of its early existence it was inoperative. NAMBoard thereupon became a monopoly importer of fertilizer.

36. In Luapula Province in 1967, the Credit Organization of Zambia gave out £139,920 in seasonal agricultural loans and recovered £1,759 in repayments on those loans, or about 1 percent (Minutes of the Provincial Development Committee Held from 4th–5th January 1968, p. 9, in ADM/5/1, vol. 2, Nchelenge District Offices). Presumably, more repayments could be expected after the harvest, ending in May of that year; the figures recorded are for 1 January–31 December 1967, the accounting year. Sheridan Johns notes that "in a belated report covering . . . August, 1967, to June, 1968, COZ revealed that only 25% of the loans made to non-commercial farmers had been recovered" (Johns, "Para-statal Bodies in Zambia," p. 230, n.).

37. See the discussion in *Commercial Farming*, October 1968, pp. 21–23.

38. Thayer Scudder, in comments on this section of my study, stresses an important additional problem: the uniform and indiscriminate promotion of maize production throughout the rural areas was insensitive to ecological variations. From an economic viewpoint, this of course amounted to promoting a misallocation of resources by failing to take advantage of the opportunities for regional specialization.

39. See the discussion contained in Department of Agriculture, *Review of the Operations of the Agricultural Marketing Committee during the Year Ending 30th June 1965.*

40. Central Statistical Office, *Monthly Digest of Statistics* 8, no. 8, (August 1972): 59.

41. See, for example, the forecasts contained in Stephen Goodman, "The Foreign Exchange Constraint."

42. While food, beverages, and oils and fats remained a fairly constant percentage of the total import bill between 1964 and 1969—about 12 percent—by 1969 the total value of imported agricultural commodities (K35.5 million) was over two-thirds of the sales value of marketed domestic production. The opportunities for import substitution were thus great. To defend its capacity to make capital imports and thereby to expand and diversify its domestic revenue base, the government sought to expand domestic agricultural production. For this reason too, the government began in 1968 to manipulate domestic prices. See Central Statistical Office, *Monthly Digest of Statistics* 8, no. 8, (August 1972): 19. See also C. S. Lombard and A. H. C. Tweedie, *Agriculture in Zambia since Independence*, p. 88. The value of imported cereals and starches, principally maize, was K8.7 million, while the value of the domestic harvest of maize was K8.9 million in 1969 (ibid.).

43. See *Zambian Commercial Farming,* May 1971, p. 10.

44. *Central African Mail,* 19 February 1965, p. 1. From the collection of Margaret Rouse Bates, henceforth referred to as the MRB collection.

45. In 1964 only the main roll seats were counted and not those reserved for the upper roll, i.e., largely European, electorate. During the first years after independence, ten upper roll constituencies were maintained which were restricted to an essentially European electorate. The idea behind this constitutional arrangement was to insure the representation of the Europeans' interests in Parliament and thus ease the tensions arising in the European community from the shift to African self-government.

46. *Zambia News,* 10 March 1968, p. 3; *Central African Mail,* 7 February 1964, MRB collection. See also Thomas Rasmussen, "Political Competition and One-Party Dominance in Zambia"; and Robert Molteno and Ian Scott, "The 1968 General Election and the Political System."

47. *Central African Mail,* 19 February 1965, p. 1, from MRB collection.

48. *Zambia News,* 7 February 1965, p. 6, MRB collection.

49. Zambia Information Services, Press Release 319/66 (18 February 1966), MRB collection. The speech was being made in Mumbwa.

50. *Zambia News,* 7 February 1964, p. 2, MRB collection.

51. To perform this analysis, district maps were fitted to maps of similar scale representing electoral constituencies. The voting data could then be related to variations in various measures reported by the several departments of the government. When the boundaries were not coterminous, higher levels of aggregation

were used; in each case the level of aggregation selected was the lowest level at which a correspondence between the administrative and electoral boundaries could be achieved.

52. The matrix of correlation coefficients for the explanatory variables is shown in the table below. The high degree of multicolinearity in these measures causes a downward bias in the t-statistic. These effects thus encourage us to take low values of the t-statistic more seriously than we would in cases where multicolinearity effects are absent.

Correlation Coefficients between Explanatory Variables

	1	*2*	*3*
1	1.000	0.8816	0.7648
2		1.0000	0.7936
3			1.0000

Notes: 1 = plows per capita, 1963
            2 = cattle per capita, 1963
            3 = percent registered voters voting ANC, 1964

CHAPTER 7

1. From interviews with the treasurer of the cooperative.

2. Some comparative wage rates may offer a perspective on these figures. According to 1969 data, the national average wage rate for carpenters was K69.4 per month and for bricklayers K53.1 per month (Central Statistical Office, *Survey of Occupations 1969*, p. 35). According to the *Statistical Year-Book 1970*, the average monthly earnings of laborers in construction were K28.0 (Central Statistical Office, *Statistical Year-Book 1970*, p. 47). The lowest-paid occupation, according to these sources, was that of the hired laborers on farms, and they earned a wage comparable to that of the laborers in Katofyio, K14.4 per month (Central Statistical Office, *Survey of Occupations 1969*, p. 14).

One of the major problems with the wage rates offered by Katofyio appears to have been that they were not high enough to compensate for the loss of subsistence production. The cooperative worked throughout the valley and the members were sometimes absent from the village for weeks at a time; these absences sometimes overlapped with planting and harvesting times. As a result, villagers were reluctant to accept employment again with the cooperative when new contracts came through. In response to this problem, the officers of the cooperative began to hire workers at the contract sites. But this practice led to criticism from the government that the cooperative was now functioning as a contractor and not as a cooperative, and the government was considering reviewing Katofyio's legal standing as a cooperative, and thus its eligibility for loans and services from public sources (interview with Co-operative Officer, 3 May 1972; and "Annual Report of the District Co-operative Officer," 30 November 1971, pp. 3–4, in the files of the Department of Co-operatives, Nchelenge District Offices).

3. One member, a skilled carpenter, had earned K34.00 for a month's work, but because he had had to wait nine months for his money he became disillusioned and withdrew from Katofyio. As he put it, "I saw it was a difficult thing, for you can spend months without pay. . . . I feel that I can do better working

for myself, even though I get less money" (interview, 1 December 1971).

4. This account of the trip, as well as the financial assessment of it, is drawn from field notes taken while accompanying the Katofyio officers.

5. Thus, for example, by breaking a drum of petrol, purchased for K20, into 10 tins and exchanging each tin for 40 fish, they could get approximately 400 fish per drum. Assuming that each fish weighed one pound when dried and so fetched 0.22 kwacha when sold at the copperbelt, the officers realized K88.00, or a profit of K68.00 for the exchange, not counting transport costs.

6. This story of the disparate economic fortunes of the leaders and the rank and file of the cooperative finds parallels throughout East Africa. See, for example, John S. Saul, "Marketing Cooperatives in a Developing Country: The Tanzanian Case"; and the contributions of Nelson Kasfir, Gören Hydén, and O. Okereke in *Co-operatives and Rural Development in East Africa*, ed. Carl Gösta Widstrand. For some West African examples, see Robert Johnston, "Cooperatives and Agricultural Production in Sierra Leone"; and Marvin P. Miracle and Ann Seidman, "Cooperatives in Ghana, 1951–1965."

7. See Minute of the District Co-operative Officer, 3/8/68, in Co-operative Unions, General, file of the Department of Co-operatives, Nchelenge District Offices.

8. See the "Quarterly Report of the District Co-operative Officer, Nchelenge," March 1968, in the files of the Department of Co-operatives, Nchelenge District Offices.

9. What records are available suggest, for example, that Chikalamo, in 1967 alone, received K300 in maintenance allowances for the members, K240 as a stumping subsidy, and K669.63 as a seasonal loan to cover the costs of tractor hire, fertilizers, and seeds. From materials contained in the files of the Secretary, Chikalamo Farming Co-operative, Kasumpa village.

10. According to the credit officer, the cooperative would have had to farm at least fifty acres with yields of not less than fifteen bags an acre of maize and three bags an acre of groundnuts and beans to meet these loan payments. These were the estimated production levels that were used to justify the loans that were made to the cooperative; fewer acres or lower yields would lead to earning levels insufficient to repay the loan. From the cooperatives' loan application, contained in file NE/70/S of the Agricultural Finance Corporation, Nchelenge District Offices.

11. Report, 19/2/72, in file NE/70/S of the Agricultural Finance Corporation, Nchelenge District Offices. See also District Co-operative Officer, Nchelenge, "1st Quarterly Report," 30 March 1972, from the files of the Department of Co-operatives, Nchelenge District Offices, and District Co-operative Officer, Nchelenge, "Annual Report," 30 November 1971, pp. 2–3, from the files of the Department of Co-operatives, Nchelenge District Offices.

12. By 1968 their loan debts already amounted to over K6,000. From Co-operative Officer, Kawambwa, to Chairman of All Co-operative Unions, 7 August 1968, in Co-operative Union, General, files of the District Co-operative Officer, Nchelenge District Offices.

13. Computed from NAMBoard, Nchelenge District, Distribution and Buying Program, 1970. Files of NAMBoard District Depot, Nchelenge.

14. The recommended planting date for maize in the area is 1–21 November; for groundnuts, it is 1–22 December. This information is from District Agricultural Officer to Nchelenge District Development Committee, 3 March 1970, file ADM/4/6, vol. 2, Nchelenge District Offices.

15. See, for example, Co-operative Officer, Mechanization, to District Co-

operative Officers, Kawambwa, Nchelenge, Mwense, 30 September 1970, in Co-operative Unions, General, files of the District Co-operative Officer, Nchelenge District Offices.

16. Agricultural Rural Marketing Board, *Fifth Annual Report of the Agricultural Rural Marketing Board for the Year Ended 31st December 1968*, p. 12.

17. De Vries, in his discussion of the 1968/69 survey of village producers, indicates that this is a general problem facing attempts to deliver services at the village level: "The survey counted 24,443 villages—an average size of 85 people. Indeed, 13,673 have 50 or less inhabitants, and only 127 villages have 450 or more" (E. de Vries, "The Importance of Traditional Agriculture in Zambia," p. 2).

A detailed study of government services in Serenje District makes the same point: "Although a population of about 50,000 is generally considered to be a reasonable number for maintaining a comprehensive organization, the fact that the number is scattered in tiny clusters of about twenty people over virtually the whole district makes it extremely difficult to provide services of any kind in a reasonably efficient way" (R. C. E. Kapteyn and C. R. Emery, *Research Project on Administration for Rural Development*, p. 25).

Such problems have recently led to a policy of concentrating public investments in "intensive development zones." See Republic of Zambia, *Second National Development Plan, January 1972-December 1976*, p. 65.

18. Provincial Co-operative Officer, Mansa, "Annual Report for the Year Ending 31st December 1971," from the files of the District Co-operative Officer, Nchelenge District Offices.

19. One variant of these statments is that what the villagers really want is not to be farmers, cooperative or otherwise, but to be paid employees of the government. There is some truth to this, for then the villagers would have an income and would not have to wait until a future and risky harvest to obtain it; many of the villagers would be pleased with such an arrangement.

There is also a cultural reason for this preference. Many of the villagers have worked in town, and their image of an economic activity is one of wage employment. When they demand that the government give them ways of earning an income, many are in fact demanding chances for wage employment, be it in agriculture or elsewhere.

For a description of similar kinds of attitudes on the part of villagers in Tanzania, see Clyde R. Ingle, *From Village to State in Tanzania*, p. 51. See also Ingle's description of a rural development bureaucracy which apparently, like the bureaucracy in Zambia, placed more emphasis on production than profits and so failed to create incentives appropriate to the attainment of its own goals (ibid., p. 60 ff.).

20. Provincial Co-operative Officer to Co-operative Assistant, Kawambwa, 5 March 1970, in file Co-operative Unions, General, District Co-operative Officer, Nchelenge District Offices.

21. Chairman of Lukungwe Farming Co-operative to District Co-operative Officer, Kawambwa, 26 June 1966, in file Co-operative Unions, General, District Co-operative Officer, Nchelenge District Offices.

22. Chairman of Lukungwe Farming Co-operative to the Farm Manager, Kwambwa, 25 April 1968, in file Co-operative Unions, General, District Co-operative Officer, Nchelenge District Offices. The hyperbole is notable: there is no jungle in Zambia.

23. Provincial Co-operatives Officer to Secretary, Lukungwe Farming Co-operative, 20 June 1968, in file Co-operative Unions, General, District Co-operative Officer, Nchelenge District Offices.

24. Minutes of a Meeting [of the Officers of Lukungwe Farming Co-operative] Sent to the District Co-operative Officer, Nchelenge, 23 February 1969, in file Co-operative Unions, General, District Co-operative Officer, Nchelenge District Offices.

25. Minutes of a Meeting [of the officers of Lukungwe Farming Co-operative] Sent to the District Co-operative Officer, Nchelenge, 28 July 1969, in file Co-operative Unions, General, Nchelenge District Offices.

26. Interview, 22 November 1971.

27. Interview, 5 November 1971.

28. Interview, 22 February 1972.

29. The officers of the farming cooperatives did, at the end, seize and sell the stock of fertilizers and pocket the proceeds. But, these stocks, unlike the Katofyio lorry, were liquidated in one act and could not yield income over an extended period of time.

30. Commenting on this section, Thayer Scudder contended that the range of considerations going into farming—in terms of the selection of inputs, the use of appropriate production techniques, and the adaptation to the local ecology—is simply more complex than that underlying construction and the building trades. This makes it more difficult to initiate new agricultural programs.

It should be noted here that the government's image of the villager tends to be one in which community-centered, as opposed to self-interested, behavior is the norm; and the cooperatives were chosen as a primary mechanism for increasing village production in order to take advantage of this supposed communitarian tendency (see, for example, Dr. Kenneth David Kaunda, *Humanism in Zambia and a Guide to Its Implementation*, pp. 28–29). One of my key points is that an individualistic conception of villagers appears to capture much of their behavior; and that, insofar as this is true, it is prima facie evidence that the government's policy is based upon a misconception of the behavior of villagers and so rests on precarious foundations. For similar tendencies on the part of Tanzanian villagers, who resisted the formation of public goods without the payment of private rewards, see Ingle, *From Village to State in Tanzania*, p. 163 ff.

31. Republic of Zambia, Cabinet Office, *Report to the Government of Zambia on Incomes, Wages and Prices in Zambia*, p. 9.

32. Central Statistical Office, *Statistical Year-Book 1970*, p. 47.

33. See Ministry of Rural Development, Land Use Services Division, *Farm Budgeting Handbook, Luapula Province*, p. 8.

34. The question naturally arises: why stay in farming? The reason appears to be that these independent farmers, on average, were in their late forties; and the income stream they would obtain by remaining in farming most likely exceeded the income stream they could reasonably expect to obtain from wage employment, taking into account the probability of getting a job and the costs of finding one. In fact, the K125.80 was regarded by some farmers as a satisfactory retirement income; that Tusha derives from the Bemba word *ukutusha*—to rest or retire—is relevant here.

35. This tendency on the part of extension agents was reported also by C. M. Elliott et al. in their study of farming in Katete and Mumbwa. As they note, "It is not wholly unfair to say that in the past the tendency has been for the Department of Agriculture in Lusaka to decide . . . that certain crops . . . should be grown. The role of the extension service has been to bring every kind of pressure to bear on farmers to grow these crops—including financial pressure, by linking loans to the cultivation of certain crops" (C. M. Elliott, J. E. Bessell, R. A. J. Roberts, and N. Vanzetti, *Some Determinants of Agricultural Labour Productivity in Zambia*, p. 74).

36. See, for example, Mr. R. C. Kamanga, Minister of Rural Development, "Opening Address by the Minister of Rural Development, Mansa Agricultural Show," Background no. 54, 1971, Zambia Information Services (16 July 1971), p. 2; and President Kenneth Kaunda, "*Take up the Challenge*," p. 27.

37. Because it assumes that the farmers place no value on their labor, this calculation underestimates the break-even point. Calculated from Ministry of Rural Development, Land Use Service Division, *Farm Budgeting Handbook*, pp. 8–10.

38. From notes made by the extension agent on loan applications contained in the files of the Agricultural Finance Company, Nchelenge District Offices.

39. Ibid.

40. One farmer—not in Kasumpa—had become rich from farming. He planted a very small percentage of his land in maize; and by irrigating the rest he was able to grow vegetables and market them in almost every season.

Tactical behavior may have been rational in this market, for with only ten farmers and a small market, each farmer could perceive the impact on price of one farmer's production. I still do not understand, however, why so many remained out of production for the local market, thereby letting others gain the profits to be made from the production of perishable commodities.

41. For a description of the U.N.–sponsored scheme in Kawambwa, called the Pambashe Famers' Union, see E. G. Nadeau, "A Comparison of Two Farmers' Co-operative Unions in Northern Zambia." Nadeau notes that, besides the factor of external aid, a primary reason for the success of the Pambashe Farmers' Union was that the U.N. management "shift[ed] the production emphasis from low income per acre crops, such as maize, and from perishable vegetables to potatoes and onions which provide high incomes per acre and can . . . withstand the trip to the copperbelt market" (ibid., p. 12).

42. G. Olund and J. Russel, *Survey of Farming Co-operatives*, p. 26.

43. Ibid., p. 2.

44. See, for example, the discussion in Republic of Zambia, *Second National Development Plan*, pp. 81–82. See also C. Stephen Lombard, *The Growth of Co-operatives in Zambia, 1914-71*, p. 28.

45. Richard Jolly, "The Seers Report in Retrospect," p. 21.

46. Olund and Russel, *Survey of Farming Co-operatives*, p. 27.

47. President K. D. Kaunda, "Address at the Opening of Seminar on Rural Development, Held in Lusaka on 23rd March 1970," Background 24/1970, Zambia Information Services, p. 5. The failure of mechanization schemes in Africa is widespread. See, for example, René Dumont, *False Start in Africa*, 2d ed., ch. 4; and a review of the most notable of the mechanization failures: S. Herbert Frankel, "The Kongwa Experiment: Lessons of the East African Groundnut Scheme," in *Readings in Economic Development and Administration in Tanzania*, ed. Hadley E. Smith, pp. 326–34.

48. See the "Report on the Findings of the Commission of Inquiry Conducted from 23rd to 24th July 1971," contained in the files of NAMBoard, Nchelenge District Depot. The record of the deliberations of the District Development Committee that led to the forming of the Commission of Inquiry notes, "The farmers . . . complained bitterly that loans are paid very late . . . after the cultivation period. In the same way seeds and all farming requisites are issued to farms late by [the marketing agency] and thus no farmer makes good use of his loan." The session then grew so unruly that the chairman moved to set up the Commission of Inquiry. See Minutes of the Nchelenge District Development Committee, 5 March 1971, p. 6, in file ADM/4/6, vol. 2, Nchelenge District

Offices. See also the report District Agricultural Offices to Nchelenge District Development Committee, 3 March 1970, in ADM/4/6, vol. 2, Nchelenge District Offices.

For a similar criticism of the performance of this agency in Northern Province, see Nadeau, "Two Farmers' Co-operative Unions," pp. 9–10.

49. C. S. Lombard and A. H. C. Tweedie, *Agriculture in Zambia since Independence*, p. 78.

50. Ibid. For comparative material from Kenya on the functioning of agricultural credit, see J. Vasthoff, *Small Farm Credit and Development*. Vasthoff emphasizes the low rate of loan repayment on pages 36–40. An interesting, if alarming, response of a government credit agency to similar patterns of defaults on small farm loans occurred in Mexico, where the credit agency took over the management of debtor farms in order to increase their profits and thereby reduce their loan debts. See the interesting discussion in Charles W. Anderson, "Bankers as Revolutionaries," p. 172 ff. See also Charles T. Nisbet, "Supervised Credit Programs for Small Farmers in Chile," *Inter-American Economic Affairs* 21, no. 2 (autumn 1967): 37–54.

51. It is interesting to note that, in the opinion of the authors of the Nottingham University/University of Zambia study, the figures for Katete District suggest that the Katete farmers could have done better, given the level of their skills, in wage employment; as we have seen, such also was the case with the Tusha farmers. In fact, even had the Katate farmers devoted their entire acreages to the production of the highest-priced crop, they could have earned more from wage labor than from farming at current prices for produce and labor. Elliott et al., *Agricultural Labour Productivity*, p. 129.

52. Kenneth R. M. Anthony and Victor C. Uchendu, *Agricultural Change in Mazabuka District, Zambia*, p. 259.

53. Ibid., p. 252.

54. Elliott et al., *Agricultural Labour Productivity*, p. 15.

55. Ibid., p. 12.

56. Ibid., pp. 147–48.

57. Ibid., p. 74.

58. Ibid.

59. Ibid., p. 3.

60. Ibid., p. 88.

61. Anthony and Uchendu, *Agricultural Change*, pp. 259–60.

62. Ibid., p. 257.

63. Throughout this analysis, I have concentrated on maize and not on other crops. I have done so because of the overwhelming emphasis placed on maize production by the government and because of the central importance of maize in the peasant cash economy. My picture would have been more optimistic had I focused on poultry, cotton, or pig production, where significant increases in production have taken place and where producers off the line of rail have contributed to the growth in production. See Lombard and Tweedie, *Agriculture in Zambia since Independence*.

64. Fabian J. M. Maimbo and James Fry, "An Investigation into the Change in the Terms of Trade between the Rural and Urban Sectors of Zambia," p. 108. The fishermen themselves, of course, have been intensely aware of the shifting prices. Thus, the notes from a seminar of fishermen in March 1972 record the fishermen as saying: "Since independence the country has passed through many changes, changes that have seen the raising of prices on consumer goods. Unfortunately, the poor fisherman still remains stuck to his 5n [0.05 kwacha] per lb.

of fresh and 15n [0.15 kwacha] per lb. of dried fish. . . . The price of a bag of mealie meal has gone up from K3.00 to K4.13 since independence. Although members [of the meeting] could not suggest what the new price would be, they however unanimously agreed that prices be raised to catch up with changing times." From "Notes on a Fisheries Seminar, 14–15th March 1972," in file DEV/7 of the Provincial Fisheries Officer, Provincial Offices, Mansa.

65. Figures from Central Statistical Office, *Fisheries Statistics (Natural Waters) 1968*, table 1.1; and personal communication, Provincial Officer, Department of Fisheries, 10 June 1971.

66. Department of Game and Fisheries, Fisheries Training Centre, "Preliminary Report on Lake Mweru Fishery," 28 April 1970, in file FSH/5 of the Fisheries Officer, Nchelenge District Offices.

67. See, for example, the correspondence between Senior Chief Mununga and the Fisheries Officer, Nchelenge, 6 October 1969 and 15 October 1969, in file FSH/5 of the Fisheries Officer, Nchelenge District Offices.

68. Interview with several of the leading fishermen in Kashikishi, 18 February 1972. See also the letter from fishermen to the District Secretary, Kashombwe, Congo (L) and to the Fisheries Officer, 18 April 1971, in file FSH/5, Nchelenge District Offices.

69. See, for example, Department of Game and Fisheries, Fisheries Training Centre, "Preliminary Report on Lake Mweru Fishery," 28 April 1970, pp. 3–4, in file FSH/5 of the Fisheries Officer, Nchelenge District Offices.

70. The results of the survey are contained in S. K. Mayowe, "Mweru/Luapula Fishery: Commercial Fishing Survey," 8 September 1969, in file FSH/5, Fisheries Officer, Nchelenge District Offices.

71. Complaint registered in the Minutes, Fisheries Seminar, 16 August 1971, p. 2, as reported to me in a personal communication from the Provincial Fisheries Officer, Mansa, 14 June 1972.

72. Ibid., p. 1.

73. Director, Wildlife, Fisheries, and National Parks Department, to the Permanent Secretary, Ministry of Land and Natural Resources, 15 February 1971, personal communication.

74. This analysis is drawn from interviews with executives in Lakes Fisheries of Zambia, 6 October 1971; and from Department of Fisheries, "A Tentative Programme for Fisheries in the Second National Development Plan," second draft of a working paper presented to the Agricultural and Natural Resources Committee for the Second National Development Plan. One report of the income of fishermen in 1966 examined the "cash surplus" of owners of plank boats with and without engines, and of owners of canoes. If boats and engines are assumed to depreciate over an expected life of five years and two and one-half years respectively, and nets over a life of two years, the surplus amounts to K11 per week for the owners of plank boats with engines, K7.00 per week for the owners of plank boats without engines, and K2.70 per week for the owners of canoes. See D. M. F. Beatty, "Cash Surplus of Fishing Units on Lake Mweru, 1966," typescript (1968), from the files of the Provincial Fisheries Officer, Mansa. My interviews in the fish camps suggested that most fishermen expected to make five trips per month to the fish markets during the rainy season. They expected to sell approximately 75 pounds of dried fish at K.15 per pound on each trip, or to make roughly K56.25 a month. What the actual profits were, as opposed to the gross revenues, I was unable to calculate.

CHAPTER 8

1. Republic of Zambia, *Second National Development Plan, January, 1972–December, 1976*, p. 172.

2. There is much debate over the Zambianization programs, with serious accusations leveled at their supposed "tokenism." These accusations focus on the managerial power given high-level African employees rather than on their salaries, so my point still stands. See Michael Burawoy, *The Colour of Class on the Copper Mines*. A review of the period of the First National Development Plan states, "in 1964, the average wage of an expatriate was about nine times that of an African, whereas in 1970, it was about six times . . . " (*Second National Development Plan*, p. 10).

The major documents pertaining to wages policy in this period are Republic of Zambia, Cabinet Office, *Report to the Government of Zambia on Incomes, Wages, and Prices in Zambia*; and Republic of Zambia, Office of the Vice President, Development Division, *Zambian Manpower*.

3. Central Statistical Office, *Employment and Earnings, 1966–68*, p. 45.

4. See, for example, the following comment in the so-called Turner Report:
In a "squatter compound" in Mongu, I was given the results of a detailed income and expenditure survey. This showed that, although probably about a fifth of the adult men had no employment, average *cash* income per head was more than K75 per year; reported income was drawn from unskilled or casual labour, from petty trade, and particularly from the unlicensed brewing of beer and spirits. This income compares with the K30 per head which was estimated . . . to be earned by the local peasant farmers—and of which very little was in cash. [Cabinet Office, *Incomes, Wages, and Prices in Zambia*, p. 13]

5. E. de Vries, "The Importance of Traditional Agriculture in Zambia," p. 5.

6. Much of the following discussion is based on an analysis developed with the assistance of Bruce Bennett. For an expanded and modified analysis, see Robert H. Bates and Bruce W. Bennett, "Determinants of the Rural Exodus in Zambia."

7. See Mary Elizabeth Jackman, *Recent Population Movements in Zambia*.

8. As the birthrate is assumed to be constant and so is absorbed into the constant terms in our regression equations, what is in fact being accounted for by these equations is the percent change in district-level populations between the two censuses. These changes are then interpreted as changes due to migration.

The value of K used by Jackman is 16.2 percent. Use of this constant introduces several kinds of possible errors, each of which Bennett and I have sought to avoid. First, the figure itself could be wrong; but, because we tend to rely on regression analysis in this study of migration, this is not critical. For the effect of the constant is absorbed into the constant of the regression equation; and the analysis tends to focus on the values of the coefficients and not of the intercept term. Second, the figure is a national figure and so assumes that the natural rate of increase of the population is uniform across the districts of Zambia. I do not know to what extent this assumption is erroneous, but data from a generation ago suggest regional variations in fertility, and it is more plausible to assume that these differences have persisted rather than disappeared. See J. Clyde Mitchell, "Differential Fertility amongst Urban Africans in Zambia." This source of error would be critical if a similar pattern of differences existed among the independent variables as well, but in no case is it apparent that the independent variables vary along the northeastern axis in Zambia—the axis of fertility differences detected by Mitchell—and so this source of error should not influence our results.

There is a third problem with the Jackman index: its failure to distinguish between domestic and international migration. As Patrick Ohadike points out, both African and European immigrants from abroad tend to settle in the line-of-rail districts. Much of our analysis ignores these districts, however, and examines the exodus of persons from the more remote areas. See Patrick O. Ohadike, *Some Demographic Measurements for Africans in Zambia.*

9. Line-of-rail districts are all those districts in the Copperbelt, Southern, and Central provinces. The urban districts are Kabwe, Lusaka, Livingstone, Kitwe, Ndola, Luanshya, Kalulushi, Chililabombwe, Chingola, and Mufulira. The peri-urban districts are Ndola Rural and Kabwe Rural. Due to changes in district boundaries between the two censuses, Lusaka Rural and Urban had to be combined in order to preserve comparability in the results. Similarly, the 1969 figures for Mwense and Nchelenge had to be summed with those of Kawambwa, as the first two districts had not been separated from Kawambwa in 1963.

10. Data for 1969 indicate that employed Zambian males earn, per month, K46.5 in basic wages, while employed Zambian females earn K59.7 (Republic of Zambia, Central Statistical Office, *Survey of Occupations 1969*, p. 41). But 70 percent of the working-age males in town are "working," according to the 1969 census, as compared with only 14 percent of the working-age females; in the rural areas the rates are 50 percent and 13 percent respectively (Central Statistical Office, *Census of Population and Housing 1969*, p. B55). Thus, the expected value of job seeking is still higher for men than for women.

11. Richard Jolly, "The Skilled Manpower Constraint," p. 39. Jolly also states that there came "dramatic increases in demand, the result of a considerable expansion in the economy. . . . This expansion was fuelled by unprecedented increases in government revenue and foreign exchange which grew three or four times in as many years" (p. 23).

12. Suggesting the effect of educational scarcity on wage rates is that the wage differential between those with degrees and those with "0" level qualifications in Zambia was over £700 per annum in 1965 whereas in England in 1965 it was less than £400, and in India in 1961 it was a little over £100 (ibid., p. 43). See also John C. Caldwell, *African Rural-Urban Migration*, p. 60; and Michael J. Greenwood, "An Analysis of the Determinants of Geographic Labor Mobility in the United States."

13. The inverse relationship between the growth of peasant farming and the supply of urban labor from the countryside was noted by the colonial government in Uganda. As Walter Elkan notes: "In the district of West Nile, the introduction of cotton on a quite modest scale in 1925 had an immediately adverse effect on labour recruitment. The Government was anxious to maintain the supply to Buganda and the Eastern Province from other districts and refused to encourage a further extension of cotton growing in the West Nile, until such time as labour difficulties in the more central districts because less acute" (Walter Elkan, *Migrants and Proletarians*, pp. 34–35).

The pattern also characterizes the different courses of development of the two Indian villages of Dalena and Wangala as analyzed by T. Scarlett Epstein in her classic study *Economic Development and Social Change in South India.* See also Epstein's follow-up study, *South India: Yesterday, Today, and Tomorrow;* and T.

Paul Schultz's study of Colombia, where measures of rural earnings relate inversely to rates of out-migration (T. Paul Schultz, "Internal Migration").

Elsewhere in Africa, we find for Malawi that rural resource deprivation leads to higher levels of out-migration (Margaret Read, "Migrant Labour in Africa and Its Effects on Tribal Life," p. 610). And for Tanganyika, we find that the Chagga and Sukuma, who specialize in cash crop production, have lower rates of rural emigration than do other tribes in the territory (A. W. Southall, "Population Movements in East Africa," p. 169).

14. These measures, when expressed as percents of the population, do not add to unity, simply because many rural dwellers are subsistence producers.

15. In the preindependence years of low rural expenditures, in any one year, many rural areas failed to receive any capital expenditures at all.

16. This analysis concentrates solely on the rural districts; the ten urban and two peri-urban districts are removed from the sample, as are the three rural districts that have received large numbers of refugees from the Angola war: Solwezi, Senanga, and Kaoma.

17. Bennett and I experimented with different ways of representing the variables and their interrelations; these experiments could in general be termed tests of the degree to which linear specifications were warranted by the data. For example, I thought it plausible in the case of the sex ratio that it might be the degree of imbalance in the ratio that related to out-migration. That is, where either men or women were in excess, then the area might "export" people. The relationship between the sex ratio and migration could therefore be quadratic. We found, however, that a quadratic estimate of the relationship between this measure of "demographic imbalance" and migration did not improve the estimates in a significant manner.

We also examined the possibility of nonlinear effects due to multiplicative relationships among the independent variables. For example, we entertained the possibility that distance could have an accelerating effect on the relationship between, for example, the number of cattle per capita and the reduction of out-migration; that is, the effect of cattle upon out-migration might be stronger the further the district from town. However, we were not able to detect significant relationships of this kind with the distance variable. We probed for similar kinds of relationships with a measure of population density. In particular we sought to determine whether, when farming intensified in areas of high population density, it may have produced out-migration, whereas the intensification of farming in areas of low population density may have discouraged out-migration. Using the number of cattle per capita as an index of farming, we found no effect of this kind that was statistically significant. Using the number of plows per capita as the index, however, we found the following:

$$Y_i = -13.54 + 155.0(x_1) - 3.425(x_2)$$
$$(2.426) \qquad (-1.506)$$

The t-ratios are given in parentheses. The first is significant at the 0.05 level and the second at 0.10 with a one-tailed test. F-ratio: 3.176, nearly significant at the 0.05 level. $R = 0.4501$; $R^2 = 0.2026$.

Y_i = the percentage change in the population of any district i due to migration over the period 1963–69

x_1 = the number of plows per capita, 1963

x_2 = the number of plows per capita in 1963, multiplied by the population density

Several things are notable about this equation. The first is that the t-ratios are not significant at the levels of confidence within which I operate in the rest of this chapter. This notwithstanding, the equation is exceedingly interesting. For, as one would expect, the greater the intensity of farming as measured by this index, the greater the stability of the rural population; indeed, immigration takes place as farming increases. However, this relationship completely reverses under conditions of high population density. Under conditions of high population density, intensification of farming drives people off the land. Nonetheless, because the introduction of population density in this form into the more complex equations did not meet the standards of significance conventionally observed, I did not incorporate multiplicative treatments of the density variable into the subsequent analysis.

18. This is at variance with Jackman's argument. Noting that one of the major effects of postindependence migration has been to even up the sex ratio throughout Zambia, Jackman implies that women now migrate at a higher rate than men. See Jackman, *Recent Population Movements*, pp. 16–26. See also the data in Patrick O. Ohadike, "Urbanization, Migration and Migrants in Zambia: A Survey of Patterns, Variations and Change in Lusaka" (paper presented to the International African Institute, Eleventh International African Seminar, in Association with the University of Zambia, Lusaka, September 1972). Ohadike's data reveal the same correlates of migration as does this analysis but demonstrate an upsurge of female migration into Lusaka (pp. 7–9, 16, 18). It is interesting to note that the education variable emerges as a strong correlate of migration in Ohadike's analysis.

19. To test for this structure, Bennett and I have determined: (1) there is a significant relationship between "cattle" and "migration," controlling for the other two variables; (2) there is no relationship between the number of plow per capita and the percentage change in population due to migration when agricultural employment is controlled; and (3) the relationship between cattle and agricultural employment drops to zero when the number of plows per capita is controlled.

20. In another analysis, expenditures on rural health facilities were found to decrease the rates of rural out-migration significantly (Bates and Bennett, "Rural Exodus in Zambia"). Nonetheless, the coefficient was small, indicating that, other things being equal, the government would have to spend a great deal to produce a moderate decline in rural out-migration (1 kwacha per capita in 1963–68 to secure 3.4 percent less out-migration).

Two other points should be registered before leaving the analysis of the national level data. The first is my total exasperation at being unable to test directly the major hypothesis: that rural dwellers respond to the difference in the expected value of income alternatives in deciding whether to migrate. The major reason this hypothesis could not be tested is the total absence of district-level measures of average incomes. I therefore heartily concur with Bruce Herrick, who decries the "lack of comparable [income] data by which to measure, however roughly, the income alternatives facing potential migrants. This gap in the desirable data is one of the first which should be filled by any future research in this area" (Bruce Herrick, *Urban Migration and Economic Development in Chile*, p. 102). As a very rough formulation of a direct test of our hypothesis, however, Bennett and I calculated the effect on out-migration of the degree to which a person would increase the possibility of finding employment by moving from the rural to the urban areas. The results are as follows:

$$Y_i = 1.2870 - 0.4068(P_u - P_i)$$
$$(-1.431)$$

where:

Y_i = the estimated change in population of district i due to migration, 1963–69

P_i = the probability of cash employment in district i, as measured by the percentage of males in cash employment in the district in 1963

P_u = the mean probability of cash employment in the urban sector, as measured by the mean percentage of males in cash employment in the ten urban districts in 1963

The sign of the coefficient is as predicted, and the coefficient is nearly statistically significant. However, as wage employment represents but one of the possible income opportunities, and as the variable can not be weighted by the level of earning so as to estimate the differential in the expected value of earnings in the two sectors, this is not a direct test of the hypothesis. See also Greenwood, "Geographic Labor Mobility."

21. There is evidence of similar trends in East Africa. See William M. Vogel, *Is Labor Migration of Decreasing Significance in the Economies of East Africa?* For a discussion of the changing character of migration in Zambia that makes many of the points made here, though using a different data base, see Helmuth Heisler, "The Pattern of Migration in Zambia." A basic point at issue between Heisler's article and my analysis is his contention that cash-cropping is *not* a significant retardant of migratory flows.

22. The wage rate was actually computed in terms of shillings per ticket, or 30 working days. For a discussion of these events, see Elena L. Berger, *Labour, Race and Colonial Rule*, pp. 120–23. See also Robert E. Baldwin, *Economic Development and Export Growth*, pp. 136–40. The figures computed by P. K. Lomas indicate that the minimum total monthly remuneration of the lowest-paid African surface workers on the mines rose by 457 percent during the period 1949–56; for underground workers, the comparable figure is 392 percent. See his article "African Trade Unions on the Copperbelt," p. 120.

23. Sir Ronald L. Prain, "The Stabilization of Labour in the Rhodesian Copperbelt," in idem, *Selected Papers, 1953–1957*, 1:101.

24. Back in the 1930s the relationship between family separation and the tendency to remain in the labor force was noted by Charles W. Coulter, who observed: "At the Roan Antelope, with a force of 1839, the married men employed remain an average of 20.25 months; the single men, 9.79 months" (Charles W. Coulter, "The Sociological Problem," p. 61, n.). See also the analysis of turnover by Baldwin, who finds that changes in the stability of the mines' labor force most closely correlate with changes in the proportion of the work force who are married (Baldwin, *Economic Development*, pp. 125–30).

25. Godfrey Wilson, *An Essay on the Economics of Detribalization in Northern Rhodesia*, pt. 1, p. 59.

26. David G. Bettison detected a significant decrease in the percent of children

maintained in the countryside by the residents of Lusaka over the period 1954–57, save among the residents of the poorest townships. See his *Numerical Data on African Dwellers in Lusaka, Northern Rhodesia,* p. 28.

27. Wilson, *Economics of Detribalization,* pt. 1, p. 61.

28. See Helmuth Heisler, *Urbanisation and the Government of Migration,* p. 16. A total of 76.5 percent of the respondents report sending money in the last year, with the mean number of remittances per respondent being 1.6 per year. The quantity of the remittances is positively related to income; but as a percent of income the quantity declines with the wealth of the respondent: richer urban dwellers send proportionately less than do those with lower earnings.

For comparative material, see David Jacobson, *Itinerant Townsmen,* pp. 46–47. Jacobson finds precisely the same pattern; his "elite" sample tended to send slightly more remittances than did the "nonelite" sample, but where the nonelite remitted over 20 percent of their incomes the elite remitted between 2 and 4 percent of theirs.

29. Robert Rotberg notes: "Members of the Choma and Lusaka [welfare] associations separately requested the right to farm plots of agricultural land outside the confines of their urban townships. Africans who already called themselves 'detribalized' wanted these allotments both in order to grow food for themselves and for sale. . . . But, a member of the Choma association asked, 'do you think the government will ever agree for a black man to have a piece of land near the township?' The questioner doubted correctly" (Robert I. Rotberg, *The Rise of Nationalism in Central Africa,* p. 129). For a discussion of urban land use and housing policy, and the changes with independence, see Department of Town and Country Planning, *Development Planning and Research Unit, Low Cost Residential Development in Lusaka.*

See also Bettison, *Numerical Data,* p. 107; George Kay, *A Social Geography of Zambia,* pp. 93–94; and C. E. Duff, ed., *First Report on a Regional Survey of the Copperbelt, 1959.*

For supporting material on the difficulties of retirement in town in the colonial era, see Northern Rhodesia, *Social Security in Northern Rhodesia, Part II: The Protection of Old Age;* Northern Rhodesia, *Final Report of the Commission of Inquiry into the Cost of Living;* A. Lynn Saffrey, *A Report on Some Aspects of African Living Conditions on the Copperbelt of Northern Rhodesia.*

30. Kay, *Social Geography,* p. 93.

31. Ibid., p. 94.

32. Kay writes that "a study of the cultivated zone around Ndola . . . noted that the area involved increased from 3.5 square miles in 1947 to about 11.5 square miles in 1954. . . . Cultivation is undertaken mostly by residents in towns, but there is a tendency for temporary homes to appear among the gardens" (Kay, *Social Geography,* p. 96).

33. Perhaps the most impressive of these are the Kafulafuta and Kafubu cooperative schemes. See President K. D. Kaunda, "Speech at the Copperbelt Agricultural Show on June 4, 1971," p. 2 ff.

34. Ibid., p. 1.

35. For a discussion of the charcoal trade, see Louis James Mihalyi, "Charcoal from the Zambian Forests."

36. The economic reforms of 1968, which will be discussed in later chapters, created a third opportunity for gaining an income in town from sources other than wages: that of becoming a businessman. When the government terminated

in April of 1968 the licenses of expatriate businessmen trading in the "second class," i.e., non-downtown, retail areas, it compelled them in effect to sell out to native Zambians. By banning the highly capitalized expatriate retailers from trading in the second-class areas, it left these markets open to the entrance of indigenous traders. One study of African businessmen in Kapwepwe Compound, a Lusaka shantytown, found that 40 percent had opened shop since the economic reforms of 1968 and over 90 percent had entered business after independence. See Andrew A. Beveridge and Anthony R. Oberschall, "African Urban Retailers."

37. As noted in Chapter 3, n. 1, Lance Davis has argued in a personal communication that insofar as migration is a form of investment, as I have contended, then the rate of migration should be a function of the interest rate. In discussing migration from the rural areas, I have argued that, because of the absence of financial markets in the villages, the rate of migration is not, by and large, influenced by the rate of interest in financial markets. I will argue in the next chapter, however, that where there is an effective rate of interest for nonfinancial investments—as in the case of cattle, which reproduce—then the rate of migration does decline. In the urban areas, however, financial institutions do exist; and their yields appear to reduce the incentive to invest in return migration. Thus, for example, when asked how they are preparing for their retirement, the mineworkers gave the answers shown in the table below. The miners thus do attempt to secure future incomes through personal savings and the use of pension schemes, and these investment must, to some degree, compete with remittances as a means for securing a high future real income.

What Steps Have You Taken to Prepare for Your Retirement?
Responses of Mineworkers

	No.	%
Saving money/pension	72	17.0
Building a store/have a business	9	2.1
Preparing a farm	67	15.8
Planning a business	138	32.7
Building a house	6	1.4
Will just return home	26	6.2
Don't know	11	2.6
No answer/other	9	2.1
Not applicable*	85	20.1
Total	423	100.0

Source: Rokana sample survey.
*Not thinking about retirement.

38. John Collins, "The Evolution of Urban Housing Policies in Zambia with Particular Reference to Lusaka," pp. 109–10. See also Department of Town and Country Planning, Development Planning and Research Unit, *Low Cost Residential Development in Lusaka,* p. 19 ff.; and idem, *Mwaziona: A Study of an Unofficial Housing Area,* pp. 14, 17.

39. Department of Community Development, Research Unit, *The People of "Zambia City,"* p. 12; and Department of Town and Country Planning, Development Planning and Research Unit, *Mwaziona,* p. 52.

40. See for example Department of Community Development, Research Unit, *A Socio-Economic Survey of Kalingalinga*, p. 17; and idem, *Ground Floor to Development: A Survey of Nguluwe Compound*, pp. 2–3, 11. See also Department of Town and Country Planning, Development Planning and Research Unit, *Mwaziona*, p. 47 ff.

41. See the reports of the Research Unit of the Department of Community Development listed above. In the surveys I ran in and about the mine townships of Rokana, I found that the residents of the squatter townships had first settled in town, on the mean, in 1944; the comparable year for the residents of the mine townships was 1953. A similar differential in the mean year of settlement in town between shantytown and non-shantytown dwellers was apparently evident in the colonial period. Thus Bettison notes in his study of Lusaka: "It appears . . . that the unauthorized compounds contain a generally older proportion of the population than [do the other] suburbs" (*Numerical Data*, p. 38). He also writes: "Of a sample of 1970 occupied males some 155 or 8 percent stated that they were self-employed. Almost half of these were found to be resident in the Unauthorized [i.e., shanty] Compounds" (ibid., p. 84).

42. Department of Community Development, *People of "Zambia City,"* p. 9. To be noted is that this portrait goes a long way toward revising the picture popularly held of shantytown dwellers in the third world. The popular image of these townships is that the residents are destitute and shiftless and that life there is disorganized and chaotic. I find instead that the residents are economically active and stable, in the sense of having resided for a long period in the city, and that the townships are highly organized, both politically and socially. These data thus contribute to the revision of the assessment of shantytown life that has been made by such studies as William Mangin, ed., *Peasants in Cities*; and Joan M. Nelson, *Migrants, Urban Poverty, and Instability in Developing Nations*. See also Marc Howard Ross's study of a squatter compound in Nairobi: *The Political Integration of Urban Squatters*. For a similar argument based on a survey of Luangwa, one of the shantytowns I sampled for this work, see Abel Pandawa, "Life in a Squatter Community."

43. The payments from the pension fund were made in installments over a period of several years.

44. These findings support Leonard Plotnicov's skeptical view of the verbally expressed rural retirement intentions of urban dwellers in Nigeria. See his "Nigerians: The Dream is Unfulfilled."

45. The towns surveyed were Mulenga Farms, Zambia Township, and Luangwa Township. For an anthropological study of Luangwa, see Pandawa, "Life in a Squatter Community."

46. The sole biological factor that may be relevant is age. The shantytown dwellers, being older, may have fewer kin in the rural areas and so less incentive to remit resources to the rural areas or to maintain social ties there. To test this alternative explanation, I constructed tables 8.18–8.20 while controlling for age, and the differences remained significant and in the same direction, even with age controlled.

47. In the case of the discrete data, a χ^2 test was applied after eliminating the category of "no answer," where the expected cell sizes were small; for the data involving means and variances, I applied a one-way analysis of variance.

48. The following tables present a comparison of some of my data with that of Wilson and Mitchell from an earlier period. It is important to note the different definitions used in the second table.

Total Length of Residence Away from Rural Areas

	RACM 1951	Other Luanshya 1951	Ndola 1951	Broken Hill 1940	Rokana 1971
5 yrs. or less	35.2%	40.6%	33.0%	31.9%	1.9%
Over 5 yrs.	64.8	59.4	67.0	68.1	11.5
Over 10 yrs.	40.5	42.2	45.8	46.0	22.0
Over 15 yrs.	19.6	23.1	24.3	28.6	15.8
Over 20 yrs	10.6	11.6	13.6	18.5	17.9
Over 25 yrs.	2.4 %	4.6 %	4.6 %	15.7 %	30.9 %
Sample size	1,519	468	767	644	423

Sources: Rokana figures are from my own survey, computed from responses to the question: "In what year did you settle in town?" All other figures are from J. Clyde Mitchell, "Urbanization, Detribalization, and Stabilization in Southern Africa," p. 703.

Migrant Status of African Males

Status	RACM 1951	Other Luanshya 1951	Ndola 1951	Broken Hill 1940	Rokana 1971
Labor migrant	54.5%	53.3%	54.7%	55.5%	21.0%
Temporarily stabilized	39.0	38.8	32.6	37.9	74.5
Permanently stabilized	6.5%	7.9%	12.7%	6.6%	4.5%
Sample size	1,519	468	767	644	423

Source: Rokana figures are from my own survey (see note below). All others are from Mitchell, "Urbanization, Detribalization, and Stabilization in Southern Africa," p. 708.

Note: In estimating the migrant status of Rokana employees, I used the following de-definitions:

Permanently stabilized: Born in town, will retire in town; does not maintain even the most common ties with village (i.e., sending money or news).

Labor migrant: Born in village, will retire in village; maintains the least frequently observed ties with village (e.g., helped a villager find a job; gave room or board to a job seeker from village).

Temporarily stabilized: All others.

CHAPTER 9

1. In what was surely one of the most disturbing encounters in my research, I was witness to an impassioned dispute between a sick wife and her husband. In loud and abusive terms, the woman blamed her illness and misfortune on her husband's inability to earn money in the village and demanded that he go to town. He argued that he was too old to get employment there, and she cried back: "You could become a thief *[sakaliongo]* and support me in that way." He protested that the shame would be too great. The man won out and the family did not emigrate; but their sense of poverty had compelled them at least to consider the alternative, and in a particularly grim fashion.

2. This pattern conforms to that found by Joseph Lopreato in his study of a rural village in Southern Italy. Lopreato found that migrants from the village

tended to emanate from the lower socioeconomic strata of the village (although not the very lowest, who could not afford the costs of migration). See Joseph Lopreato, *Peasants No More*, p. 209 ff.

3. The relationship between total income and the percentage of income from remittances remains significant and negative even when we control for the fact that poorer families have more children in town. In a comparative study of cash incomes in five villages in Luapula in the late 1950s, George Kay found a similar pattern: remittances formed the highest percentage of cash incomes in the poorest village. Remittances constituted 53.8 percent of the total income in the poorest village; in the richest, remittances composed 5.5 percent of the total income. In Kasumpa, the mean level is 37.6 percent. See George Kay, "Sources and Uses of Cash in Some Ushi Villages."

4. A similar finding is reported by Lopreato, who notes that the earnings from migration form a significant basis for the social and economic upgrading of households in a village in southern Italy. See Lopreato, *Peasants No More*, p. 216 ff. Also relevant is the work of George Foster, who reports that Mexican villagers use remittances from kin who are located in the economy external to the village to upgrade their standard of living—something they are unable to do through the exploitation of local resources. See George M. Foster, *Tzintzuntzan*, pp. 286–87.

5. Marshall Sahlins, "Tribal Economics," p. 43.

6. Meyer Fortes, "Introduction," in *The Developmental Cycle in Domestic Groups*, ed. Jack Goody, p. 3. See also Robert F. Gray and P. H. Gulliver, eds., *The Family Estate in Africa*. Polly Hill, in her book *Rural Hausa*, takes strong exception to this view, calling it "rigid and deterministic" (p. 57); but her data tend to show a fairly strong relationship between wealth and positions in the life cycle, although her commentaries focus on variations in wealth unexplainable by positions in the life cycle (p. 78 ff.).

7. In analyzing the economic role of the family, I realize that we are isolating but one component in a complex social situation in which feelings of loyalty, tenderness, and affection are fully as important as considerations of self-interest. My isolation of the material component of family relationships is an act of abstraction, not cynicism, on my part, for I recognize that these other factors are also important. Considerations of personal advantage clearly did exist, however: dissent, conflict, and even violence within families revealed this. Moreover, they were important determinants of much of the behavior in which I was interested. In isolating the role of material factors within the family and assessing their importance, I am therefore attempting to examine a significant feature of family life; I am trying to be faithful to what I observed; and I am in no way attempting to slight the altruistic and self-sacrificing behavior I also observed. For a provocative presentation of a model of the kind I present here, see Paul A. Samuelson, "An Exact Consumption-Loan Model of Interest with or without the Social Contrivance of Money." An excellent general treatment of the peasants' use of the family in coping with social change is given by Joel S. Migdal in "The Role of the Family in Relation to the Tension of Societal Change." The role of the family in facilitating migration has been widely studied, though not commonly from the perspective taken here. In the literature on United States migration, for example, see the so-called Beech Creek studies of Appalachia reported in James S. Brown, Harry K. Schwarzweller, and J. J. Mangalam, "Kentucky Mountain Migration and the Stem Family"; and Harry K. Schwarzweller and

John F. Seggar, "Kinship Involvement." For an example in the literature on Japan, see Ezra F. Vogel, "Kinship Structure, Migration to the City, and Modernization." Andrei Simić discusses the subject in his study of urban migration in Yugoslavia, *The Peasant Urbanites.* For Indonesia, see the article by Edward M. Bruner, which emphasizes human investment aspects of the phenomenon: "Medan: The Role of Kinship in an Indonesian City." For a Latin American case, see E. A. Wilkening, João Bosco Pinto, and José Pastore, "Role of the Extended Family in Migration and Adaptation in Brazil."

8. Writing about Luapula in the colonial period, John Taylor and Dorothea Lehmann noted: "The boys lived a most free and happy life in their small world. During the school holidays they could be seen together in neighborhood groups all day, amusing themselves, playing football, quarrelling, walking along the road singing, sitting in little groups to play with the spinning tops, and once making . . . a musical instrument on which they took turns to play." (John V. Taylor and Dorothea Lehmann, *Christians of the Copperbelt*, p. 70).

9. For a discussion of these costs, see the feature article "Do Uniforms Mean Misery?" in the *Times of Zambia*, 29 June 1972.

10. The best papers on this are: Robin J. Fielder, "The Role of Cattle in the Ila Economy," and "The Significance of the Accumulation of Wealth in Subsistence Economies." See also Elizabeth Colson, "The Role of Cattle among the Plateau Tonga of Mazabuka District."

11. Fielder, "Role of Cattle," p. 351.

12. Ibid., p. 352.

13. Ibid.

14. Ibid.

15. Thayer Scudder, personal communication. Robin Fielder, in a personal communication, pointed out that, among the Ila, persons try to accumulate large enough herds that they can consume from them without a decline in herd size.

16. This interpretation of the low rate of migration from cattle-bearing areas may also be relevant to the reinterpretation of the so-called cattle complex, a term used to describe the reluctant response to modern opportunities among cattle-keeping persons in Africa. In particular, it may help to explain the failure of pastoralist adults to educate their children and to encourage them to seek entrance into modern occupations in the urban sector. As Fielder writes, "Anthropologists have misnamed the 'cattle complex,' to suggest cultures where the people's economic concern is overlaid by mystical and ritual devotion to their stock, and by the desire to accumulate merely for prestige. . . . I want to put the case that 'traditional' cattle owners have very rational economic justification for behaving as they do" ("Role of Cattle," p. 351).

See also P. H. Gulliver's reinterpretation of the conservative behavior of the pastoral Masai in his "The Conservative Commitment in Northern Tanzania."

17. Several further comments should be made. Equation 4 in table 9.7 can be read as suggesting that the addition of one child to the family leads to an increase in the annual cash inflow from the city of 3.2 kwacha; the addition of one more year of average education for the children adds 8 kwacha a year in remittances; and so forth. The coefficients in the other three equations can be interpreted in a similar manner; but the units are such that the conclusions would then read the "number of children who . . . " rather than the "number of kwacha which . . . "

The results suggest that it is indeed reasonable for the parents to spend money on their children in the ways noted in this chapter. Assume, for example, that a year's education costs K20 in direct school expenses, plus an additional K20 for an allowance that allows the child to "make a good appearance" at school, as one informant expressed it; the total outlay for an additional year's schooling would then be K40. But, according to the estimates in table 9.7, an additional year's schooling should result in an additional K8 per annum in remittances. Assuming a work life of 26 years (age 20 to 45) and a discount rate of 0.05, the returns to this additional year would be valued at approximately K120; if earnings are discounted at 0.08 per year, the returns are then in the neighborhood of K90. In either case, the expenditure appears justified, in the absence of more profitable uses for the money.

In evaluating these results, the low R^2 should be noted and stressed. Obviously migration is a complex phenomenon. While the results are significant, in the sense that they cannot be plausibly attributed to chance, the linear equations account for a relatively small percentage of the variations in the migration behavior of Kasumpa households. Important factors which I did not take into account, and so did not measure and include in the equations, are obviously at work here. Whatever the cause, at best we account for but two-fifths of the variance; the major part remains unexplained.

Lastly, I should caution that I am here interpreting observations made at one point in time in terms of an argument about processes that take place over time. Naturally, I never saw a child who at age eleven received new clothing from his father mature to age thirty-five and then mail his father some money; rather, from observations made at one specific time, I inferred that this kind of process was taking place. Such interpretations should, of course, be based on data gathered from repeated observations over time. I hope to return to Kasumpa to make such observations.

CHAPTER 10

1. This formulation, of course, draws on the perspective of Anthony Downs as presented in *An Economic Theory of Democracy*. For a critique see Brian M. Barry, *Sociologists, Economists and Democracy*. For a discussion of more recent materials, see William H. Riker and Peter C. Ordeshook, *An Introduction to Political Theory*. One of the few analysts to apply this approach, in any variant, to Africa is W. Arthur Lewis, who assumes directly that "throughout history a personal love of power has been the prime motive of politicians," and who goes on to develop the implications of that assumption for West Africa (W. Arthur Lewis, *Politics in West Africa*, p. 30 ff. See also David R. Smock and Audry C. Smock, *Cultural and Political Aspects of Rural Transformation*, p. 134 ff.; and the study of education services contained in Henry Bienen, *Kenya*, p.49 ff.

2. See the circular from the Regional Secretary to all Branch Leaders, Chienge Region, 7 May 1965, from file NC/CR/2, Nchelenge District Offices, which reads in part (translated from Chibemba): "I want all Branches to do the work I am going to give you. Try to write all the names of those with some education who have not been employed. . . . I want all these names without wasting time. . . . I want these names in a short time. . . . Work hard in the party because people are being chosen from the party where their labor is examined for good vacancies; people who can get good recommendations from the party can be given good jobs."

An examination of the correspondence regarding staffing in the Kawambwa Rural Council shows that letters of recommendation from the party are a necessary, if not a sufficient, factor in obtaining public service employment in Luapula. See, for example, the Secretary, Kawambwa Rural Council, to the Regional Publicity Secretary, UNIP, Kawambwa Region, 8 December 1965, file KRC/ADM/2 of the Kawambwa Rural Council.

3. The councillors were given a £5 a month subsistence allowance while on council duties. In voting themselves a raise, they contended that "councillors worked hard during the struggle. . . . Most lost their employment and some were dismissed from schools. We . . . therefore . . . request the Ministry of Local Government to consider the increase [to £25] very seriously. Our education is also needed if the Ministry could assist financially." From Minutes of the 1st Kawambwa Rural District Council Finance Committee, 25–30 January 1965, p. 3, file ANF/27, Kawambwa Rural Council.

4. See the letter from the Provincial Local Government Officer to the Secretary, Kawambwa Rural Council, 4 April 1966 (file KRC/HQ/FIN/4, Kawambwa Rural Council), which reads in part: "I refer to the minutes of the Finance Committee Meeting held on 24 February, 1969. Paragraph 15 of these minutes represents a most unusual approach. I am pleased to see that tenders were called for in selling the lorry but I cannot understand why the highest offer was not accepted. . . . As a result of this irresponsible decision the Council has lost £100." The lorry was sold to a councillor who had set himself up as a contractor; the bulk of his contracts were with the council, for whom he built and maintained public roads.

See also the sales reported in Minutes of the 8th Meeting of the Finance Committee of the Kawambwa Rural Council, 6 September 1965, file ANF/27, Kawambwa Rural Council.

5. The pervasiveness of this behavior is revealed on page 3 of the letter from the Permanent Secretary of the Ministry of Local Government and Housing to the Provincial Local Government Officer, Fort Rosebery, 8 April 1965, and in his letter to the Sub-treasurer, Kawambwa Rural Council, 8 April 1965, file FIN/4/2/1, Kawambwa Rural Council. The national-level bureaucrats in the Ministry of Local Government attempted to block all further salary payments until such advances were paid back in full.

6. One way in which this was done was to place contracts for council projects with relatives. The result was that "the rates for . . . contracts had been excessive and that in some cases very little money had actually been spent on the [contracted works]" (Provincial Local Government Officer to Chairman, Kawambwa Rural Council, 17 May 1966, file ADM/2, vol. 3, Kawambwa Rural Council).

See also the letters of protest written by a revenue collector who felt that a newly elected councillor was attempting to replace him with a relative (file ADM/2, vol. 3, Kawambwa Rural Council).

7. Because of the small value of some of the expected cell frequencies, significance tests are invalid in the case of these tables. Similar analyses for villagers in Tanzania are presented by Gören Hydén in his study *Political Development in Rural Tanzania*, p. 207 ff.; and Clyde R. Ingle, *From Village to State in Tanzania*, p. 156. Guy Hunter, like many others, sees in the growth of cynicism the decline and weakening of governing parties. As will be seen, I do not agree; rather, like Hydén, I see in it the basis for the transformation of these parties into pressure

groups vis-à-vis the governing administration, the mediating factor being intra-party competition among the local-level politicians. See Guy Hunter, *Modernizing Peasant Societies*, p. 76 ff.

8. Registering Officer . . . to the Secretary, Kawambwa Rural Council, 25 April 1966, file KRC/LOC/Ele/123, Kawambwa Rural Council.

9. Registering Officer . . to the Returning Officer, Kawambwa, 25 April 1966, file KRC/LOC/Ele/123, Kawambwa Rural Council.

10. The marriage of Constituency Official No. 1 was tragically barren. But Constituency Official No. 2 loaned one of his children to his "father" so that he might have company in his home and so that his wife might have help about the house and in the gardens. Similarly, the children of Constituency Official No. 3 helped Constituency Official No. 1. And, as was well known in the village, Constituency Officials No. 2 and 3 were inseparable friends. Besides socializing together, they ran a bicycle repair service together; and they collaborated in a much celebrated witchcraft case, to be detailed below. That two of the three leaders who joined the issue of village opposition to the Lunda overlords should themselves be Lunda calls into question my formulation of this issue. However, the issue was not one of opposition to Lunda dominance, per se; rather, it was opposition to the manner in which such domination was exercised. The villagers wanted to choose their own headman, even if it was from the ranks of the ruling Lunda families.

11. As the case that brought the mucapi to Kasumpa is of central importance to the politics of Kasumpa, I will describe it here. The petitioner in this case was Constituency Official No. 3; the precipitating event was the death of David, his mother's brother, from snake bite; and the target of the accusations was MC, his grandmother's brother, i.e., his great uncle. The genealogical relations of the disputants are shown in the figure.

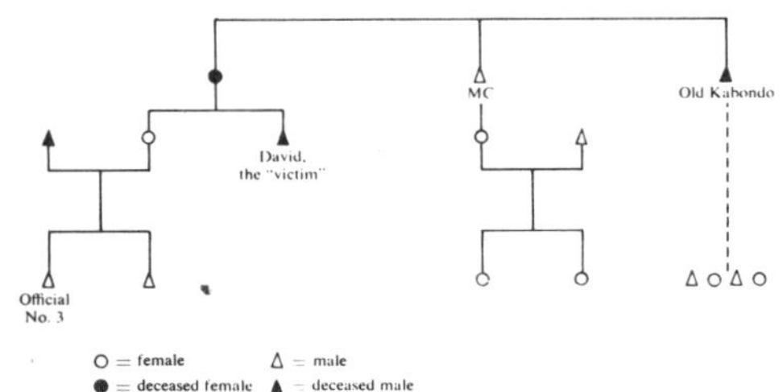

Relationships between Parties to Witchcraft Dispute

To understand this case, several things should be noted. First, MC was not a popular figure in the village; Official No. 3 was. Official No. 3 had been a central figure in the twelve years of nationalist agitation; he was a man of no pretentions with a deep personal knowledge of all the families in the village and with an endearing willingness to talk and banter with all. Despite being a party official, he paid attention to and vocally identified with the villagers' dissatisfaction with the government; he was, indeed, the government's most earnest critic in Kasumpa. For all of these reasons, the people of Kasumpa loved him. By contrast, MC was unpopular. He was an abrupt and abrasive man, who frequently quarreled with other persons in the village.

Shortly before the death of David, MC had been involved in a court case with several of the other villagers. MC had insisted on having his gardens near the village, and the goats of several families had browsed in them. By customary law, the owners of the goats were liable for the damages they had caused to MC's crops; but the feeling of most people was that MC should have located his gardens further from the village in the first place and so have avoided becoming embroiled in a dispute with his fellow villagers. That MC actually stood on his rights—which appeared to most to be merely technicalities in this case—and pressed suits for damages in the courts only further alienated him from the village community. It was against this MC that Official No. 3 lodged his witchcraft accusation.

The question arises: why should Official No. 3 have pressed on with the witchcraft case? He deeply loved his uncle and wanted justice done; but then by all accounts he also used to love MC, and they had often visited and socialized together. So feelings of affection cannot have been the basis for his behavior. Another consideration and this I feel is most important, is that by pressing this accusation Official No. 3 could gain control over the family of which he, MC, and the now deceased David were a part. Returning to the diagram, we can see that, of the older generation in this family, only MC survives. It should also be noted that Official N. 3 has inherited the name of old Kabondo, as well as the custody of his children; thus, were MC discredited, Official No. 3 would effectively move into the senior position in the family. In the case of this family, the rewards associated with holding the senior position were substantial. The children of old Kabondo, for example, are now completing their schooling on the copperbelt—the expenses, including K32 for a typing course, having been paid by Official No. 3—and their earnings from urban employment are expected to be high. In addition, MC's grandchildren had been supported in their schooling by Official N. 3 and by his brother; and, in the culminating point of this case, these two benefactors wrote MC's grandchildren presenting the accusations against MC and urging them to remember instead "those who are living here peacefully in the village and who cared for you when you were in schooling." To gain the senior position vis-à-vis the children of the family by successfully discrediting MC would therefore yield potential financial advantage. There is, in addition, a third factor: the potential for gaining a headmanship. The headmanship of a neighboring village is inherited within this family. Official No. 3, because of his political prominence and broad popularity, stands a good chance of being selected for this post. He does in fact desire it and has pledged as one of his "campaign promises" to rid the village of witches. It would be useful to his cause to demonstrate this commitment by pressing witchcraft cases in Kasumpa; and to do so while simultaneously discrediting the possibly superior claims to the headmanship of a genealogical elder would obviously improve his chances even more.

12. Even when the officials did not come to Kasumpa village, they were nonetheless accessible, for party officials could easily go to them. Kasumpa is but seven miles from Kanyembo (see map 3), and politicians from Kasumpa staff the party's constituency offices there three days each week. The magistrate's court, the office of the agricultural assistant, and the tractor station are in Kanyembo; and touring officers stop there to make contact with the staff of these organizations, Chief Kanyembo, and the constituency officials themselves. The Kasumpa politicians therefore have ready access to their district-level superiors.

In my questionnaire, I asked three questions derived from the classical index of political cynicism. I have already reported the distribution of responses to the first two items, which asked whether the respondents agreed or disagreed with the statements (1) "public officials don't care much what persons like you think," and (2) "for the most part, the government serves the interests of only a few and isn't very concerned about the needs of persons like yourself." As we have seen (tables

10.4 and 10.5), over 70 percent of the respondents gave answers that could be construed as reflecting political cynicism. In responding to the third statement— "people like you don't have any say about what the government does"— over a third reported that they did have some say; the majority of these, however, felt that while they did have some say, the government did not listen. Communication per se thus did not appear to be a problem; rather, the problem seemed to be one of governmental responsiveness, or lack of it, to what the people said.

13. Field notes, 26 February 1972.

14. See, for example, Minutes of the 2nd Provincial Development Committee Meeting for Luapula Province Held at Nchelenge on 26 November 1970, p. 8, file ADM/5/1, vol. 2, Nchelenge District Offices.

15. Copies of this correspondence are held in General File, COM/3/2, Nchelenge District Offices.

16. UNIP political officials, Kasumpa Village, to the Provincial Road Engineer, 29 November 1969, c.c. State Minister, Mansa; Chief Mwata Kazembe, Mwansabombwe; District Secretary and District Governor, Nchelenge; Secretary General, State House, Lusaka. From General File, COM/3/2, Nchelenge District Offices.

17. Interview, 18 April 1972.

18. District Governor, "Tour Report and Report on Registration of Voters from 17th November 1969–12th December 1969," p. 1, file Elections (General) LP/ADM/14/1, Nchelenge District Offices.

19. For a similar interpretation of the growth of district consciousness, see Frank W. Holmquist, "Toward a Political Theory of Rural Self-Help Development in Africa"; and Holmquist's chapter "Implementing Rural Development Projects," in *Development Administration*, ed. Göran Hydén. See also Henry Bienen's interpretation of ethnic politics in Kenya in *Kenya*, p. 131 ff.; and the interpretation of rural development programs in Nigeria in Smock and Smock, *Rural Transformation*, p. 134 ff. I have attempted to draw together and synthesize studies of sectional politics in Robert H. Bates, "Ethnic Competition and Modernization in Contemporary Africa."

20. Interview, 10 March 1972.

21. Minutes of the Chiengi Regional Conference, 25 March 1971, p. 2, files of the Nchelenge District Offices.

22. Interview, 18 April 1972.

23. Interview, 5 November 1971.

24. Mwense District Development Committee, Resolutions to Be Presented to Next Provincial Development Committee, 2 August 1970, by District Governor, Mwense (n.d.), files of the Nchelenge District Offices.

25. Minutes of the Chiengi Regional Conference, 25 March 1971, p. 1, files of the Nchelenge District Offices.

26. Minutes of the Provincial Development Committee Held in the Conference Room at Mansa from 26–27 April 1968, p. 11, file ADM/5/1, vol. 2, Nchelenge District Offices.

27. Minutes of Luapula Province Development Committee, Meeting at Fort Rosebery on 5 January 1967, p. 3, file ADM/5/1, vol. 2, Nchelenge District Offices.

28. Minutes of the Provincial Development Committee Meeting Held on the 23 June 1969 at the Catholic Hall, p. 13, file ADM/5/1, vol. 3, Nchelenge District Offices.

29. *Times of Zambia*, 22 September 1968.

30. See the Provincial Development Officer, Tour Report on Visit to Lusaka,

4 November 1968, in file Prov. L 28, in the Office of National Development and Planning.

31. See *Times of Zambia*, 18 July 1969; and *Official Verbatim Report of the Debates of the First Session (Resumed) of the Second National Assembly, 1st July–18th July 1969*, Hansard no. 18, (Lusaka: Government Printer, 1969), pp. 9–12.

32. M. Ngalande," Luapula Province: Political Report on the Implementation of Humanism in Zambia" (report presented to the National Council of the United National Independence Party, November 1968), p. 2, quoted in Robert Molteno, "Cleavage and Conflict in Zambian Politics," p. 73.

33. There are several reasons for this. Luapula does in fact possess a relatively high-quality all-weather road connecting it with the towns; Barotse, by contrast, does not. Moreover, the Great North Road was the major route to the coastal ports and carried a major portion of Zambia's imports and exports; the road to Luapula did not. These considerations governed the allocation of the government's road budget and lowered the priority of the Luapula route. Third, it was the government's assessment that the new road would be immensely expensive. As it would pass through the swampy regions of the Lake Bangweulu area, the road would require the construction of causeways and drainage facilities, and this, in the estimation of the government's engineers, would make it "the most expensive stretch of road ever built in Zambia (twice as much as some sections of the Great North Road)" (Permanent Secretary, Development Division, Minute to Minister of State, 18 April 1969, file Prov. L 38, Office of National Development and Planning). Moreover, the government evaluated the benefits from the road as being highly uncertain. Over the proposed Serenje-Samfya route, the distance from Mansa to the copperbelt would be 365 miles, as compared with 130 miles over the existing route. One government official summarized his reaction by saying, "We must . . . compare on the one hand a capital cost of K4.2 m. plus a journey nearly three times as long . . . and on the other hand a relatively good and short route with the attendant difficulties caused by Congolese officials" (ibid.).

34. Among the responsibilities assigned to the district governors, for example, were "to ensure the successful implementation of development programmes within the District" and "to ensure the efficiency of all Government Departments" (Cabinet Office, 7 June 1971, to all District Governors). A Cabinet Office memorandum defined the objectives of governmental decentralization as follows:

The principal objectives of His Excellency's administrative reforms are: (i) to ensure as far as possible direct contact between the Cabinet, as the central policy-making body of the Government, and the people in the provinces and districts whose well-being must be the main objective of all Government activity, with the aim of accelerating development of the rural areas;
(ii) to revive the village as a basic unit . . . in the rural areas and make it an effective unit for development . . .
(iv) to ensure that the Government's development plans are implemented vigorously by increasing productivity through co-operatives and by encouraging village industry. . . . [Cabinet Office Circular no. 24 of 1970, 1 May 1970]

35. Minutes of a Meeting of the Provincial Development Committee Held on

16 February 1970 in the Community Hall, Mansa, p. 8, file ADM/5/1, vol. 2, Nchelenge District Offices.

36. Minutes of the Provincial Development Committee Held on 23 June 1969 at the Catholic Hall, p. 6, file ADM/5/1, vol. 3, Nchelenge District Offices.

37. Republic of Zambia, Cabinet Office, *Report of the Working Party Appointed to Review the System of Decentralized Administration*, p. 41. For parallel studies of the need for coordination in developmental administration, see the contributions of Göran Hydén, Robert Jackson, and David Leonard in *Development Administration*, ed. Hydén et al. See also Bienen, *Kenya*, pp. 25–65.

38. Cabinet Office, *Report of the Working Party*, p. 64. My own interviews with budgetary officials in Lusaka confirmed the same percentage distributions for the 1970 and 1971 budgets.

39. Minutes of Luapula Provincial Development Committee, Meeting at Fort Rosebery on 5 January 1967, p. 10, file ADM/5/1, vol. 2, Nchelenge District Offices.

40. Interview, 7 March 1972.

41. Permanent Secretary, Luapula Province, to Permanent Secretary, Ministry of Rural Development, 10 November 1969, file Prov. L31, Office of National Development and Planning.

42. Luapula Development Officer, Tour Report on the Lusaka Trip (3–7 February 1969), 11 February 1969, file Prov. L 22, Office of National Development and Planning.

CHAPTER 11

1. This, like other statements in this book, is an oversimplification, of course. For Kaunda went to great lengths to expedite the rise to governmental office fo "new faces" in politics—technically trained personnel who had remained outside the struggle for independence. Nonetheless, it is a measure of the importance of the party as a means for achieving high governmental office that Kaunda should have had to work so hard to place these people in office. For a description of his efforts, see his own account in Kenneth Kaunda, *A Humanist in Africa:* the study by David C. Mulford, *Zambia: The Politics of Independence, 1957–1964*; and in particular Margaret Rouse Bates, "UNIP in Postindependence Zambia."

2. For details of these elections, see Republic of Zambia, *Mulungushi Conference, 1967*. See also Robert I. Rotberg, "Tribalism and Politics in Zambia"; and William H. Riker, *The Theory of Political Coalitions*.

3. To comprehend this analysis, two other kinds of information must be considered. The first is the distribution of votes in the election. This distribution was based on the number of party regions in each province, with each region receiving 100 votes (see table). The other is the provincial background of the candidates:

Distribution of UNIP Regions by Province

Province	*No. of Regions*
Northern Province	7
Luapula Province	4
Copperbelt (Western) Province	8
Eastern Province	5
Southern Province	7
Central Province	6
Western (Barotse) Province	5
Northwestern Province	5

Note: Each region cast 100 votes.

Province:	Candidates:
Northern	Kaunda, Kapwepwe, Chimba, Changufu, Nankolongo
Northwestern	Mulemba, Matoka
Eastern	Banda, Kamanga, Nyirenda, Zulu
Barotse (Western)	Sikota and Arthur Wina, Sipalo, Nakatindi
Central	Kalulu
Western (Copperbelt)	Milner
Southern	Chona, Mudenda

(Taken from Margaret Rouse Bates, "UNIP in Postindependence Zambia," ch. 6.) The question then arises: Why did the Northern Province faction not ally with Northwestern, Central, or Western instead of with Southern Province? There were but two candidates from the Southern and just one from the Central and Western Provinces. One explanation is that there were seven regions in the south and only five in the northwest, so that more support, in terms of votes, could be gained for the same price, in terms of top positions, from Southern Province. Central Province was already a member of the coalition and there was some uncertainty as to the solidarity of the Copperbelt delegation; this heightened the attractiveness of the seven-region delegation. Last, because UNIP had weak indigenous roots in the south, many of the Southern Province delegates to the convention were in fact persons from Northern Province who had been dispatched to Southern Province to serve as organizers there; and they could be counted on to vote for the Northern Province candidates.

4. Interviews with former civil servants in the area, 10 December 1967 and 8 March 1972.

5. The Eastern Province leaders brought these claims before the February 1968 meeting of the UNIP National Council. In protest President Kaunda resigned, because, in his words, "I was upset by the tribal and provincial approach to our national problems"; a few hours later, he rescinded his resignation. See the *Zambia Mail*, 14 February 1968. For details, see also William Tordoff and Robert Molteno, "Introduction," p. 26, and Robert Molteno, "Cleavage and Conflict in Zambian Politics."

6. Statement published in the *Times of Zambia*, 18 July 1969.

7. Interview with local politicians in Kawambwa, 2 December 1971.

8. One public citation of this story is contained in the *Times of Zambia*, July 18, 1969. *Batubula* is a derogatory word for fisherman. Loosely translated, it connotes someone who soaks his buttocks in the water.

9. See *Times of Zambia*, 15 July 1969.

10. Members of Parliament to His Excellency, Dr. K. D. Kaunda, President of the Republic of Zambia, 21 August 1969, p. 3, files of the Kawambwa District Council.

11. Ibid., p. 5.

12. See, for example Minutes of the Proceedings of the First Territorial Seminar on Political Education Convened by the Political Committee of the Central Committee of the United National Independence Party, 22 February 1969, file SOC/3/2, vol. 2, Kawambwa Rural Council. See also the "blue print for rural development" which was advocated by the politicians of Luapula in May 1970; it is described in an article in *Times of Zambia*, 17 May 1970.

13. See *Official Verbatim Report of the Debates of the First Session (Resumed) of the Second National Assembly, 1st July–18 July 1969*, Hansard no. 18 (Lusaka: Government Printer, 1969), pp. 9–12.

14. Minutes of the Proceedings of the First Territorial Seminar, p. 4.

15. Wilson Chakulya was promoted to a Central Committee post.

16. Wilson Chakulya, who had already held a post in the cabinet; Sylvester Chisembele; and Alex Shapi.

17. Should the reader feel that my analysis of the relationship between the quest for office, the demands for rural development, and the rise of provincialism be overdrawn, let him note the following speech by a Luapula minister, made as part of a campaign for support in the 1971 elections to the UNIP Central Committee:

My respected men: Many things are failing to be done because the government has chosen only two ministers from this province and we are failing in our challenges to those many people chosen as ministers from other provinces. We have no chance of opposing what the Cabinet has decided. . . . From 1964 to 1968, there was no minister chosen from this province, and that is why there was no development here. . . . People from Northern Province had all the posts in government at independence. They did nothing for other provinces; they did everything in their province. . . . There are five cabinet ministers from Northern Province and 2 from Luapula. There are 14 Ministers of State from Northern Province and only 2 from Luapula Province. There are 14 governors from Northern Province and only about 6 from Luapula Province. Government has not chosen anyone from Luapula to go and be an ambassador.

He then demanded support for Luapula politicians in the upcoming Central Committee elections and threatened withdrawal from UNIP if this campaign for greater Luapula representation failed (Minutes of Chiengi Regional Conference, 25 March 1971, from Nchelenge District Offices).

18. For background to the Barotse defection, see the discussions contained in Mulford, *Zambia*; Gerald L. Caplan, *The Elites of Barotseland*; and Molteno, "Cleavage and Conflict." See also two articles by Martin Meredith, "End of the Old Feudal Government," *Times of Zambia*, 17 September 1965; and "The Slow Consent," *Times of Zambia*, 22 September 1965, from the collection of Margaret Rouse Bates (henceforth referred to as MRB collection).

19. See *Zambia News*, 30 January 1966; *Zambia Mail*, 4 February 1966 (MRB collection). For subsequent defections from UNIP on the part of Barotse politicians, see the case of Dickson Chikulo, *Zambia News*, 20 March 1966; reports in the *Zambia Mail*, 22 April 1966; and Zambia Information Services, Press Release no. 791/66, 3 May 1966 (MRB collection).

20. *Zambia Mail*, 3 September 1965 (MRB collection).

21. Quoted from "Political Orbit" (a political leaflet that supported the United Party) by Molteno in "Cleavage and Conflict," pp. 73–74.

22. See Caplan, *Elites of Barotseland*, p. 214.

23. *Zambia Mail*, 7 November 1967 (MRB collection).

24. Quoted in Molteno, "Cleavage and Conflict," p. 74.

25. See *Zambia Mail*, 16 August 1968; *Times of Zambia*, 15 and 16 August 1968 (MRB collection).

26. For an account of the election, see Ian Scott and Robert Molteno, "The Zambian General Elections."

27. Minutes of the Provincial Development Committee Meeting Held on the

23 June 1969 at the Catholic Hall, p. 13, file ADM/5/1, vol. 3, Nchelenge District Offices.

28. Cabinet Minister for the Western Province to Chiengi Regional Conference, 25 March 1971, pp. 2–4, the files of the Nchelenge District Offices, translated from Bemba.

29. Interviews, 24 October 1971 and 5 April 1972.

30. Zambia Information Services, Press Release no. 74/71, 19 April 1971.

31. *Zambia Daily Mail*, 11 May 1971.

32. Explicitly until the completion of his three-year term. With the expiration of that period in 1970, President Kaunda nominated Mainza Chona to serve as vice-president.

33. For a discussion of these events, see Tordoff and Molteno, "Introduction," and William Tordoff and Ian Scott, "Political Parties: Structures and Policies."

34. See note 3 and table above for the distribution of regions and votes among the several provinces.

35. The Committee of 24 consisted of three representatives from each of the UNIP regions in the province; by this time, there were eight party regions in the province,

36. See *Times of Zambia*, 22 January 1971, and *Zambia Daily Mail*, 18 and 22 January 1971. The *Times of Zambia* 19 February 1971, reported Chisata as naming Reuben Kamanga specifically in making this charge.

37. *Times of Zambia*, 26 January 1971.

38. Chisata had already been dropped from the government because of his involvement in an assault case on the copperbelt. See the *Times of Zambia*, 4 June 1971; and Republic of Zamiba, *Report of the Commission of Inquiry into the Allegations Made by Mr. Justin Chimba and Mr. John Chisata.*

39. See, for example, the story on the "Lusaka Militants," *Zambia Daily Mail*, 20 January 1971; and the accusations against Maselino Bwembya, *Zambia Daily Mail*, 8 February and 7 April 1971.

40. Also in the UPP Executive Committee were three Eastern Province persons: Henry Msoni, Ray Banda, and Zilole Mumba. As the *Times of Zambia* stated: "Mr. Kapwepwe included them to give his movement a 'national' character which it would have lacked had all the executive members originated from Northern Province" (*Times of Zambia*, 29 August 1971). The former minister was Justin Chimba. The former ministers of state were John Chisata (Ministry of Labour and Social Services), Victor Ng'andu (Ministry of Rural Development), and Jameson Chapoloko (Ministry of Health). Another member of the Executive Committee, Musonda Chambeshi, had formerly been a district governor and a member of the UNIP Central Committee. All of these national-level political figures were from the Northern Province; no national-level figures defected to UPP from any of the other provinces in Zambia (see *Zambia Daily Mail*, 23 August 1971).

41. See Robert H. Bates, *Unions, Parties, and Political Development in Zambia*; and Robert I. Rotberg, *The Rise of Nationalism in Central Africa*, p. 234.

42. For details on the earlier careers of these persons, see Bates, *Unions, Parties, and Political Development*; and A. L. Epstein, *Politics in an Urban African Community*.

43. I was conducting research in Kitwe at the time of the formation of UPP, and I can attest to the fragmentation of the UNIP party branches in at least the mine townships in that area. See also the press report on "witchhunts" for UPP

supporters within UNIP in the *Zambia Daily Mail*, 3 August 1971; and stories on defections to UPP from UNIP on the copperbelt in *Times of Zambia*, 17 September and 18 November 1971; and in *Zambia Daily Mail*, 24 August 1971.

44. See the analysis in Charles Harvey, "Economic Independence," in *Economic Independence and Zambian Copper: A Case Study of Foreign Investment*, ed. Mark Bostock and Charles Harvey, pp. 3–22.

45. President Kenneth D. Kaunda, *"Take Up the Challenge"*, p. 68.

46. For discussions of this, see Gerry G. Chabwera, "Rural Local Government in Lundazi." For a discussion of the organization of the takeovers in Lusaka, see *Times of Zambia, Business Review*, 27 August 1971.

47. For a discussion of some of these issues, see Anthony Oberschall, "African Businessmen in Rural Zambia," draft chapter, forthcoming; and Andrew Alan Beveridge, "Converts to Capitalism," and "Economic Independence, Indigenization, and the African Businessman."

48. *Times of Zambia*, 21 November 1971; 23 and 24 December 1971.

49. At this time, the government had imposed severe restrictions on imports to conserve dwindling reserves of foreign currencies; this is discussed below.

50. Interview, 3 September 1971.

51. Bates, *Unions, Parties, and Political Development*. See also Anirudha Gupta, "Trade Unionism and Politics on the Copperbelt," in *Politics in Zambia*, ed. Tordoff, pp. 288–319.

52. See *Times of Zambia, Business Review*, 10 September 1971.

53. Ibid. Other features of the agreement also drew bitter criticism. To curtail absenteeism after pay day, the companies and union agreed to permit the companies to disallow two days of sick pay for miners reporting in sick at the end of the month. And to increase the productivity of the labor force, the company and union agreed to accelerate the retirement of senior, unskilled miners, so as to make way for younger men. See "Memorandum of Agreement between Nchanga Consolidated Copper Mines Limited, Roan Consolidated Mines Limited, and the Mine Workers Union of Zambia, 7 September 1970" (author's collection), pp. 10–14.

54. *Times of Zambia*, 26 May 1971; *Zambia Daily Mail*, 21 October 1971. See also the discussion in James Fry, "Issues in Wage Determination," draft chapter for a forthcoming volume on wages and income policy in Africa.

55. One report noted that

> dissident miners, angered by the Government's roundup of rebel leaders earlier this year, had pledged their support for the new party, called the United Progressive Party. This was revealed . . . by informed sources who said that before the reports that UPP had been formed in Luanshya, there had been secret movements among the miners' dissident groups. The sources said that the rebel miners had promised the organizers of the new party that they would back it "financially or otherwise." The sources added that dissidents had been able to persuade some loyal miners, who had sympathised with their cause in the early stages of the war against the Mineworkers' Union leadership, to canvass for support on behalf of the new party. [*Zambia Daily Mail*, 2 August 1971]

56. See, for example, the outburst from the Mansa district development committee over the cutback in rural credit, reported in the *Times of Zambia*, 29 July 1971.

57. See, for example, the feature article in the *Times of Zambia, Business Review*, 10 September 1971.

58. In the area around Kasumpa village, Mushota was selected as the intensive development zone. This was the area where the peasant farming scheme had been implemented by the colonial government in the federal era and where the United Nations maintains a large, prosperous, and mechanized farming scheme. In essence, by concentrating its resources, the government has chosen to spend public funds where farming is already developed and to write off, relatively speaking, areas like Kasumpa, where farming represents a "new trade." The implications for the spread of inequality in Luapula, and elsewhere in Zambia, are obvious.

59. An interesting commentary on this topic was made by the governor of the Bank of Zambia, which handled the accounts of the various public agencies involved in the rural development effort. In March 1972 he announced that the Agricultural Finance Company had fully drawn its account and had no further funds for rural credit; in making this disclosure he said:

> There was a tendency in Zambia for huge subsidies and grants to Government-sponsored institutions and organizations. While this happened, little attention was paid to hard-headed business assessment, which led us into a situation where many a para-statal organization was a bottomless pit of banking credit. The public's money was being lent to organizations incapable of using it profitably or productively to the community's benefit. The governor said it was unethical to set up such organizations and then make them behave as if they had no commercial functions to perform "or merely as extended tentacles of government control or employment exchanges for inefficient verandah boys." [*Times of Zambia*, 19 March 1972]

Attitudes like his, which emphasized the efficient and rational use of limited public resources, naturally favored the shift of government funds out of subsistence agriculture areas and into productive, commercially viable ones. The governor was acutely aware of this, and on several occasions he publicly urged the government in effect to write off the more remote districts of Zambia and to devote its resources to the development of the line of rail. See, for example, Valentine Musakanya, "Where to Spend Our Scarce Resources," pp. z18–z20.

60. For a background to these policies, see Richard Hall, *The High Price of Principles*. For accounts of the maize importation, see *Times of Zambia, Business Review*, 30 July 1971, 10 and 24 September 1971.

61. He ceased attending council meetings out of a sense of futility and disgust. He never stopped petitioning to receive his council stipend, however.

62. It should be noted that there were other groups which supported UPP. In Kitwe, where I worked at the time of the party's formation, the mayor and former mayors supported the party; they had been appointed to their posts by Kapwepwe while he was a UNIP minister. The party also received the support of the Mutima wa Jesu religious sect, for reasons that are unknown to me; and it maintained close contact with the Lenshina followers who had fled the Zambian armed forces and lived just across the border in Zaire. Another important group was the "dead wood" that had been purged from UNIP—personnel that had been displaced from UNIP office in favor of younger and better educated officeholders. Fortunately for UNIP, many of these people, as one expressed it

to me, "had been given good jobs in the state industries as political appointees. We feel we are doing well there and so don't want to go with UPP" (interview with former Chingola Regional Secretary, 15 September 1971). Not all his fellows felt this way, however; and these ex-officeholders in UNIP were important leaders for UPP in the copperbelt area.

In the Rokana mine townships, persons who had lost out in recent branch elections tended to defect to the opposition party. A last group that was important were the university students. During a major upheaval at the university, Kapwepwe had vigorously opposed the government's decision to close it. His support won him converts in his break with the government; one of the students who left the university to work for UPP became the party's provincial organizer in Luapula.

63. Figures from Mindeco, *Mindeco Mining Year Book 1971* (Kitwe: Copper Industry Service Bureau, 1972), p. 33.

64. Ibid., p. 23.

65. Ibid., p. 26.

66. Ibid., p. 31. See also the article in the *Times of Zambia*, 31 July 1971.

67. Interviews, Ministry of Finance, 8 May 1972. See also Mindeco, *Year Book*, p. 30.

68. Republic of Zambia, *Monthly Digest of Statistics* 8, no. 8 (August 1972): 58. The figures for 1970 and 1971 were still provisional.

69. Ministry of Finance, *Economic Report 1971*, p. 34.

70. For the first time, Zambia began to attempt to finance its development programs through significant foreign borrowing. To finance projects for the second development program, for example, the government negotiated a K10 million loan from the United Nations Development Program. See *Zambia Daily Mail*, 10 July 1972; *Times of Zambia*, 11 July 1972.

71. See the Budget Address in the *Official Verbatim Report of the Parliamentary Debates of the Fourth Session of the Second National Assembly, 12th January–9th March, 1972*, Hansard no. 29 (Lusaka: Government Printer, 1972), pp. 500–535. See also *Times of Zambia*, 2 January 1972.

72. Quote from the Lusaka Chamber of Commerce, in *Times of Zambia*, 8 June 1972.

73. Title of editorial in *Times of Zambia*, 8 December 1971.

74. *Zambia Daily Mail*, 23 August 1971.

75. See, for example, the reports of the beating of the UNIP regional secretary, Vincent Mulenga, in Ndola in the *Zambia Daily Mail* and the *Times of Zambia*, 24 January 1972.

76. The beatings took place after the youth regional secretary for Kitwe had received a message from Freedom House, the national UNIP headquarters, which he took as indicating the "UPP was to be destroyed, even the little children," as he put it to me. The Kitwe police arrested those responsible for the beatings and pressed charges against them in court. For a report, see *Times of Zambia*, 22 September 1971. They also interrogated all the UNIP officials who may have given the orders for the beatings. Later, the head of the police in Kitwe was transferred.

77. Field notes, 5 September 1971. The township council ratified the acts of the party workers and kept the stores closed. They revoked the trading licenses of the UPP store owners and demanded that they evacuate their council houses.

For similar incidents in other towns, see the report in the *Times of Zambia*, 7 September 1971.

78. In Kitwe, the police did intervene, forcefully, to preserve free access to the hospitals. See also *Zambia Daily Mail*, 6 December 1971.

79. *Times of Zambia*, 23 November 1971. See also the stories in the *Times of Zambia* for 10, 22, and 30 November 1971.

80. *Times of Zambia* and *Zambia Daily Mail*, 21 September 1971.

81. The charges were published in the *Zambia Daily Mail*, 4 October 1971. On 13 September 1971 it was announced that the East German trade mission had been closed in Zambia (*Times of Zambia*, 13 September 1971); later, it was charged that South Africa and Portugal had been the sources of foreign assistance to UPP. See the series of articles in the *Zambia Daily Mail*, 14–16 December 1971.

82. Telegram, 24 September 1971, file LP/SOC3/2, vol. 4, Nchelenge District Offices.

83. Regional Secretary to All Constituency Secretaries, Nchelenge, 10 November 1971, file LP/SOC/3/2, vol. 4, Nchelenge District Offices.

84. When a member of Parliament shifts from one party to another in Zambia, he must run again for his parliamentary seat.

85. See the discussion in Cherry Gertzel, Kasuka Mutukwa, Ian Scott, and Malcolm Wallis, "Zambia's Final Experience of Inter-Party Elections."

86. *Zambia Daily Mail*, 8 December 1971.

87. Background no. 6, 1972, Zambia Information Services (4 February 1972).

88. The president and vice-president of the African National Congress were offered seats on the commission but refused to fill them. The appointment of the commission was announced in Background no. 5, 1972, Zambian Information Services (1 March 1972).

89. See *Daily Parliamentary Debates, No. 31 d., Friday 8th December 1972, Official Verbatim Report of the Debates of the Fourth Session (Resumed) of the Second National Assembly.* Members of the opposition in Parliament were allowed to keep their seats until the dissolution of Parliament and the holding of the first elections under the new constitution.

90. The end of party competition did not mean the end of political competition. Indeed, in the December 1973 elections, the first to be held under the one-party constitution, candidates competed in many constituencies where elections had previously gone uncontested. For, under the new constitution, local units of UNIP, in conjunction with the national officers of the party, certified for each seat two to three UNIP candidates, who then competed for parliamentary posts under the same party label; in many areas where UNIP certified rival candidates, ANC had not previously contested parliamentary seats. In my opinion, this competition between candidates is not as meaningful as competition between parties, however. For in voting for a candidate under the new constitution, which expanded Parliament to 125 seats, the voter is influencing the selection of a person who represents 1/125 of a potential policy decision at the national level. Under the old system, the voter was selecting a person who was a member of a coalition that could control over one-half of the parliamentary votes and thus decisively affect government policy. As a result, the expected returns to voting were stronger under the old constitution, which may account for the decline in turnout from 77 percent of the registered voters in the last election under the old constitution to 39 percent in the first election under the new one.

CHAPTER 12

1. See Albert O. Hirschman, *Exit, Voice, and Loyalty.* Hirschman's analysis is applied by John M. Orbell and Toru Uno in "A Theory of Neighborhood Problem Solving."

2. Audrey C. Smock, *Ibo Politics*, p. 82.

3. Edward E. Malefakis, *Agrarian Reform and Peasant Revolution in Spain.*

4. Sidney G. Tarrow, *Peasant Communism in Southern Italy.*

5. See, for example, Charles Tilly, *The Vendée;* and Arthur Redford, *Labour Migration in England*, p. 35 ff. The destruction of India's textile industry is noted in Beatrice Pitney Lamb, *India*, p. 71 ff; and the decimation of local handicrafts, and of the economic fortunes of those who fabricated them, in China is discussed in Eric R. Wolf, *Peasant Wars of the Twentieth Century*, p. 131 ff.

6. Like all such statements, this must be qualified. Thus, for example, I clearly recall the bitterness and anger of the village blacksmith of Kasumpa, who told how he and his father before him had been put out of business by the British South Africa Company which, because of its monopoly rights to minerals in Northern Rhodesia, had forbade the extraction or smelting of mineral ores. Nonetheless, while locally important, blacksmithing was not a widespread trade in the territory; nor do the blacksmiths seem to have been prominent in the nationalist movement, even in Kasumpa.

7. The growth of the latifundia and of rural inequality with the commercialization of agriculture is discussed in Wolf, *Peasant Wars of the Twentieth Century*, passim; and an excellent local case study of the phenomenon is given in Paul Friedrich, *Agrarian Revolt in a Mexican Village.* Perhaps the most intensive investigation of rural stratification is in the literature from Latin America. In particular, see Solon Barraclough, ed., *Agrarian Structure in Latin America*; Ernest Feder, *The Rape of the Peasantry*; and Rodolfo Stavenhangen, ed., *Agrarian Problems and Peasant Movements in Latin America.* For a discussion of the income distribution effects of various land tenure relationships, see L. S. Shapley and Martin Shubik, "Ownership and the Production Function"; and for a general assessment of the political consequences see Bruce M. Russett, "Inequality and Instability." See also Joel S. Migdal, *Peasants, Politics and Revolution*, p. 134 ff.

8. See the discussions contained in the symposium Max Gluckman, J. C. Mitchell, and J. A. Barnes, "The Village Headman in British Central Africa," *Africa* 9, no. 2 (April 1949): 89–107.

9. The basis for the fragmentation of villages and the transfer of populations among them received intensive attention from the anthropologists of the colonial period. See, for example, Victor W. Turner, *Schism and Continuity in an African Society* (Manchester: Manchester University Press, 1957).

10. George Kay, *Social Aspects of Village Regrouping in Zambia* (Lusaka: Institute for Social Research, University of Zambia, 1967), p. 14.

11. The failure of political elites in the rural areas to transform their positions of power into positions of disproportionate wealth caught the attention of anthropologists in the area. See, for example, the notion of the distributive chief propounded by Schapera. Chiefs seeking followers, he contends, had to compete in generosity and so gave up wealth for political position. See I. Schapera, "Economic Changes in South African Native Life." For an application of this theory to Zambia, see Max Gluckman, *Economy of the Central Barotse Plain*,

Rhodes-Livingstone Papers, no. 7 (Livingstone: Rhodes-Livingstone Institute, 1941). The one area where the chiefs did prosper was in Barotse; but this resulted not from the exploitation of land for agricultural purposes but from stipends from the government. See Gerald L. Caplan, *The Elites of Barotseland.*

12. Again, to some extent, this statement must be modified. As I have argued, the interrelations between the indigenous and settler farming populations on the line of rail during the colonial era could be conceived of in these terms; and such may be the case again in the present era, with the acquisition of farms by modern bureaucrats and businessmen and by the mining companies. Again, however, for Zambia as a whole, I feel that the rural stratification model of agrarian political behavior is inapplicable. For discussions of the applicability of the inequality model to African rural politics in general, see W. Arthur Lewis, *Politics in West Africa*, p. 38; and Jack Goody, "Feudalism in Africa?" For specific attempts to apply such a model, see Martin Kilson, *Political Change in a West African State*; and Lucy C. Behrman, *Muslim Brotherhoods and Politics in Senegal.*

13. See, for example, Kenneth David Kaunda, *Humanism in Zambia and a Guide to Its Implementation*, p. 28 ff.

14. See, for example, Victor C. Uchendu, "The Impact of Changing Agricultural Technology on African Land Tenure"; and Elizabeth Colson, "The Impact of the Colonial Period on the Definition of Land Rights."

15. In Tanzania, where the state has attempted to institutionalize communal land rights, it has alienated many of the more prosperous emergent farmers. For a discussion, see the essays contained in Carl Gösta Widstrand, ed., *Co-operatives and Rural Development in East Africa*; and especially the critique of the communalistic assumptions of the government about villagers contained in S. E. Migot-Adholla's chapter "Traditional Society and Co-operatives," ibid., pp. 17–37. See also the analysis of "Operation Dodoma" contained in Frances Hill, *Mobilization and Participation in Tanzania*, forthcoming; and John S. Saul, "African Socialism in One Country: Tanzania," in Giovanni Arrighi and John S. Saul, *Essays on the Political Economy of Africa*, pp. 237–335.

The issue briefly arose in an explosive manner in Kenya, where it formed part of the debate between the Odinga and Mboya wings of KANU. For a discussion, see Cherry Gertzel, *The Politics of Independent Kenya*; John W. Harbeson, *Nation-Building in Kenya*; and Colin Leys, *Underdevelopment in Kenya.*

16. In his essay on West African politics, Arthur Lewis comments:

The African villager has now come to take for granted that the central government will provide water, schools, hospital services, roads and even electricity free, or at highly subsidized rates. If decentralization were in vogue, the village could be told that it could have as much subsidized water or electricity as it is willing to pay for out of village taxes, and demands would not so grossly exceed available finances. The clear connection between taxation and quantity of service would both check demand and increase the willingness to pay taxes. [Lewis, *Politics in West Africa*, p. 54]

17. For a preliminary, and in some ways misguided, statement of this kind of behavior, see James M. Buchanan, *Public Finance in Democratic Process.*

18. For another analysis of rural political behavior in much these same terms, see Göran Hydén, *Political Development in Rural Tanzania*, p. 165 ff.

19. See, for example, the references in note 7 to this chapter.

20. Marx makes these points in his famous passage in "The Eighteenth

Brumaire of Louis Boneparte." See the excerpts quoted in Karl Marx, "Peasantry as a Class." Marx's own assessment of the difficulty of class action by peasants is revived as a general critique of stratification theory by Mancur Olson, Jr. in his *The Logic of Collective Action.*

21. Saul, "African Socialism in One Country."

A NOTE ON RESEARCH METHODS

1. University of Zambia, Institute for Social Research, *A Complete List of the Publications of the Former Rhodes-Livingstone Institute* (Lusaka: Institute for Social Research of the University of Zambia, 1966); Phyllis Deane, *Colonial Social Accounting*; Robert E. Baldwin, *Economic Development and Export Growth*; E. A. G. Robinson, "The Economic Problem."

Selected Bibliography

The Bibliography is organized in the following manner:

I. Bibliographies
II. Comparative Literature
   A. Non-African
   B. On Africa
   C. On Migration
III. Materials on Zambia
   A. General
   B. On Luapula
   C. On the Growth of the Line of Rail
   D. On Agriculture
   E. On Migration
   F. On Politics
IV. Official Publications
   A. Great Britain
   B. Federation of Rhodesia and Nyasaland
   C. Northern Rhodesia
   D. Republic of Zambia
V. Files Consulted
   A. National Level
   B. Local Level
VI. Newspapers

I. Bibliographies

Brigg, Pamela. "A Survey of Case Studies on Migration to Urban Areas." Draft report. International Bank for Reconstruction and Development, 25 January 1971.

Byerlee, Derek. *Research on Migration in Africa: Past, Present and Future.* African Rural Employment Paper, no. 2. East Lansing: Department of Agricultural Economics, Michigan State University, September 1972.

Dejene, Tekola, and Smith, Scott E. *Experiences in Rural Development: A Se-*

lected, *Annotated Bibliography of Planning, Implementing, and Evaluating Rural Development in Africa.* Washington, D. C.: Overseas Liaison Committee of the American Council on Education, August 1973.

Graves, Nancy B., and Graves, Theodore P. "Adaptive Strategies in Urban Migration." In *Annual Review of Anthropology*, edited by Bernard J. Siegel, Alan R. Beals, and Stephen A. Tyler, pp. 117–51. Palo Alto, Cal.: Annual Reviews, 1974.

Hanna, William John, and Hanna, Judith Lynne. *Urban Dynamics in Black Africa.* Chicago and New York: Aldine-Atherton, 1971.

Land Tenure Center Library. *Rural Development in Africa: A Bibliography.* Madison, Wis.: Land Tenure Center Library, March 1971.

Pryor, Robin J. *Internal Migration and Urbanisation: An Introduction and Bibliography.* Monograph Series, no. 2. Townsville, Australia: Department of Geography, James Cook University of North Queensland, 1971.

II. Comparative Literature

A. Non-African

Almond, Gabriel A.; Flanagan, Scott C.; and Mundt, Robert J.; eds. *Crisis, Choice, and Change: Historical Studies of Political Development.* Boston: Little, Brown, 1973.

Anderson, Charles W. "Bankers as Revolutionaries: Politics and Development Banking in Mexico." In *The Political Economy of Mexico*, edited by William P. Glade, Jr., and Charles W. Anderson, pp. 103–85. Madison: University of Wisconsin Press, 1963.

Apter, David Ernest. *Choice and the Politics of Allocation: A Developmental Theory.* New Haven: Yale University Press, 1971.

Barraclough, Solon Lovett, ed. *Agrarian Structure in Latin America: A Resume of the CIDA Land Tenure Studies of Argentina, Brazil, Chile, Colombia, Ecuador, Guatemala, Peru.* Lexington, Mass.: Lexington Books, 1973.

Barry, Brian M. *Sociologists, Economists and Democracy.* London: Collier-Macmillan, 1970.

Benet, Sula, trans. and ed. *The Village of Variatino: An Ethnographic Study of a Russian Village from before the Revolution to the Present.* Garden City, N. Y.: Anchor Books, 1970.

Blum, Jerome. *Lord and Peasant in Russia, from the Ninth to the Nineteenth Century.* Princeton: Princeton University Press, 1961.

Borton, Hugh. *Peasant Uprisings in Japan of the Tokugawa Period.* Tokyo: Asiatic Society of Japan, 1938.

Brewer, Garry D., and Brunner, Ronald D., eds. *Political Development and Change: A Policy Approach.* New York: Free Press, 1975.

Brinton, Clarence Crane. *The Anatomy of Revolution.* 3d ed. New York: Vintage Books, 1965.

Brunner, Ronald D., and Brewer, Garry D. *Organized Complexity: Empirical Theories of Political Development.* New York: Free Press, 1971.

Buchanan, James M. *Public Finance in Democratic Process: Fiscal Institutions and Individual Choice*. Chapel Hill: University of North Carolina Press, 1976.

Caiden, Naomi, and Wildavsky, Aaron. *Planning and Budgeting in Poor Countries*. New York: John Wiley and Sons, 1974.

Campbell, Angus; Converse, Philip E.; Miller, Warren E.; and Stokes, Donald E. *The American Voter*. Abr. ed. New York: John Wiley and Sons, 1964.

Chambers, J. D. "Enclosure and Labour Supply in the Industrial Revolution." In *Agriculture and Economic Growth in England, 1650–1815*, edited by Eric L. Jones, pp. 94–127. London: Methuen, 1967.

Chambers, William Nisbet. *Political Parties in a New Nation: The American Experience, 1776–1809*. New York: Oxford University Press, 1963.

Charles, Joseph. *The Origins of the American Party System: Three Essays*. Williamsburg, Va.: Institute of Early American History and Culture, 1956.

Dalton, George, ed. *Economic Development and Social Change: The Modernization of Village Communities*. Garden City, N. Y.: Natural History Press, for the American Museum of Natural History, 1971.

Davies, James Chowning. "Toward a Theory of Revolution." *American Sociological Review* 27, no. 1 (February 1962): 5–19.

————, ed. *When Men Revolt and Why: A Reader in Political Violence and Revolution*. New York: Free Press, 1971.

Deane, Phyllis, and Cole, W. A. *British Economic Growth, 1688–1959: Trends and Structure*. 2d ed. Cambridge: At the University Press, 1967.

Debray, Régis. *Revolution in the Revolution? Armed Struggle and Political Struggle in Latin America*. Translated by Bobbye Ortiz. New York: Grove Press, 1967.

Deutsch, Karl Wolfgang. *Nationalism and Social Communication: An Inquiry into the Foundations of Nationality*. Cambridge: M.I.T. Press, 1953.

————. "Social Mobilization and Political Development." *American Political Science Review* 55, no. 3 (September 1961): 493–514.

Dew, Edward. *Politics in the Altiplano: The Dynamics of Change in Rural Peru*. Austin: University of Texas Press, for the Institute of Latin American Studies, 1969.

Dobb, Maurice Herbert. *Soviet Economic Development since 1917*. New York: International Publishers, 1948.

Dore, R. P. "Agricultural Improvement in Japan, 1870–1900." In *Agrarian Change and Economic Development: The Historical Problems*, edited by Eric L. Jones and S. J. Woolf, pp. 95–122. London: Methuen, 1969.

Downs, Anthony. *An Economic Theory of Democracy*. New York: Harper and Row, 1957.

Easton, David. "An Approach to the Analysis of Political Systems." *World Politics* 9, no. 3 (April 1957): 383–400.

————. *The Political System: An Inquiry into the State of Political Science*. New York: Alfred A. Knopf, 1953.

————. *A Systems Analysis of Political Life*. New York: John Wiley and Sons, 1965.

Epstein, Trude Scarlett. *Capitalism, Primitive and Modern: Some Aspects of Tolai*

Economic Growth. Canberra: Australian National University Press, 1968.

————. *Economic Development and Social Change in South India*. Manchester: Manchester University Press, 1962.

————. *South India, Yesterday, Today, and Tomorrow: Mysore Villages Revisited*. New York: Holmes and Meier, 1973.

Feder, Ernest. *The Rape of the Peasantry: Latin America's Land Holding System*. Garden City, N. Y.: Anchor Books, 1971.

Feierabend, Ivo K., and Feierabend, Rosalind L. "Aggressive Behaviors within Polities, 1948–1962: A Cross-National Study." In *When Men Revolt and Why: A Reader in Political Violence and Revolution*, edited by James Chowning Davies, pp. 229–49. New York: Free Press, 1971.

Foster, George M[cClelland]. *Tzintzuntzan: Mexican Peasants in a Changing World*. Boston: Little, Brown, 1967.

Friedrich, Paul. *Agrarian Revolt in a Mexican Village*. Englewood Cliffs, N. J.: Prentice-Hall, 1970.

Glade, William P., Jr., and Anderson, Charles W., eds. *The Political Economy of Mexico*. Madison: University of Wisconsin Press, 1968.

Goody, Jack, ed. *The Developmental Cycle in Domestic Groups*. Cambridge Papers in Social Anthropology, no. 1. Cambridge: At the University Press, 1958.

Gurr, Ted Robert. *Why Men Rebel*. Princeton: Princeton University Press, 1970.

Hayek, Friedrich August von, ed. *Capitalism and the Historians*. Chicago: University of Chicago Press, 1963.

Hirschman, Albert O. *Exit, Voice, and Loyalty: Responses to Decline in Firms, Organizations, and States*. Cambridge: Harvard University Press, 1970.

————. *Journeys toward Progress: Studies of Economic Policy-Making in Latin America*. New York: Twentieth Century Fund, 1963.

Hobsbawm, Eric J. *Primitive Rebels: Studies in Archaic Forms of Social Movement in the Nineteenth and Twentieth Centuries*. New York: W. W. Norton, 1959.

Hodder, B. W. *Economic Development in the Tropics*. London: Methuen, 1968.

Huizer, Gerrit. *The Revolutionary Potential of Peasants in Latin America*. Lexington, Mass.: Lexington Books, 1972.

Huntington, Samuel P. *Political Order in Changing Societies*. New Haven: Yale University Press, 1968.

Hutchinson, Sir Joseph Burtt. *Farming and Food Supply: The Interdependence of Countryside and Town*. Cambridge: At the University Press, 1972.

Ilchman, Warren F[rederick], and Uphoff, Norman Thomas. *The Political Economy of Change*. Berkeley and Los Angeles: University of California Press, 1969.

Jasny, Naum. *The Socialized Agriculture of the USSR: Plans and Performance*. Stanford: Stanford University Press, 1949.

Johnson, Chalmers A. *Peasant Nationalism and Communist Power: The Emergence of Revolutionary China, 1937–1945*. Stanford: Stanford University Press, 1962.

Jones, Eric L., ed. *Agriculture and Economic Growth in England, 1650–1815.* London: Methuen, 1967.

———, and Woolf, S. J., ed. *Agrarian Change and Economic Development: The Historical Problems.* London: Methuen, 1969.

Kramer, Gerald H. "Short-Term Fluctuations in U. S. Voting Behavior, 1896–1964." *American Political Science Review* 65, no. 1 (March 1971): 131–43.

Lamb, Beatrice Pitney. *India: A World in Transition.* 3d ed. New York: Praeger Publishers, 1968.

Landsberger, Henry A., ed. *Latin American Peasant Movements.* Ithaca, N. Y.: Cornell University Press, 1969.

Leites, Nathan, and Wolf, Charles, Jr. *Rebellion and Authority: An Analytic Essay on Insurgent Conflicts.* Chicago: Markham, 1970.

Lerner, Daniel. *The Passing of Traditional Society: Modernizing the Middle East.* Glencoe, Ill.: Free Press, 1958.

Lipset, Seymour Martin. *Agrarian Socialism: The Cooperative Commonwealth Federation in Saskatchewan, A Study in Political Sociology.* Berkeley and Los Angeles: University of California Press, 1950.

Lockwood, William Wirt. *The Economic Development of Japan: Growth and Structural Change, 1868–1938.* Princeton: Princeton University Press, 1954.

Main, Jackson Turner. *Political Parties before the Constitution.* Chapel Hill: University of North Carolina Press, 1973.

Malefakis, Edward E. *Agrarian Reform and Peasant Revolution in Spain Origins of the Civil War.* New Haven: Yale University Press, 1970.

Mangin, William, ed. *Peasants in Cities: Readings in the Anthropology of Urbanization.* Boston: Houghton Mifflin, 1970.

Marx, Karl. "Peasantry as a Class." In *Peasants and Peasant Societies: Selected Readings,* edited by Teodor Shanin, pp. 229–37. Harmondsworth, Eng.: Penguin Books, 1971.

Migdal, Joel S. *Peasants, Politics, and Revolution: Pressures toward Political and Social Change in the Third World.* Princeton: Princeton University Press, 1974.

———. "The Role of the Family in Relation to the Tension of Societal Change." *International Journal of Group Tensions* 4 (June 1974): 184–207.

Miller, Norman, and Aya, Roderick, eds. *National Liberation: Revolution in the Third World.* New York: Free Press, 1971.

Moore, Barrington, Jr. *Social Origins of Dictatorship and Democracy: Lord and Peasant in the Making of the Modern World.* Boston: Beacon Press, 1966.

Moreno, Francisco José, and Mitrani, Barbara. *Conflict and Violence in Latin American Politics: A Book of Readings.* New York: Thomas Y. Crowell, 1971.

Nelson, Joan M. *Migrants, Urban Poverty, and Instability in Developing Nations.* Occasional Papers in International Affairs, no. 22. Cambridge: Center for International Affairs, Harvard University, September 1969.

Olson, Mancur, Jr. *The Logic of Collective Action: Public Goods and the Theory of Groups.* Cambridge: Harvard University Press, 1965.

———. "Rapid Growth as a Destabilizing Force." *Journal of Economic History* 23, no. 4 (December 1963): 529–52.

Petras, James F., and Merino, Hugo Zemelman. *Peasants in Revolt: A Chilean*

Case Study, 1965–1971. Austin: University of Texas Press, for the Institute of Latin American Studies, 1972.

Powell, John Duncan. *Political Mobilization of the Venezuelan Peasant*. Cambridge: Harvard University Press, 1971.

Preobrazhenskiĭ, Evgeniĭ Alekseevich. *The New Economics*. Translated by Brian Pearce. Oxford: Clarendon Press, 1965.

Riker, William H. *The Theory of Political Coalitions*. New Haven: Yale University Press, 1962.

————, and Ordeshook, Peter C. *An Introduction to Positive Political Theory*. Englewood Cliffs, N. J.: Prentice-Hall, 1973.

Robinson, Ronald, and Johnston, Peter, eds. *Prospects for Employment Opportunities in the Nineteen-Seventies: Papers and Impressions of the Seventh Cambridge Conference on Development Problems, 13th to 24th September 1970 at Jesus College*. London: His Majesty's Stationery Office, 1971.

Rogers, Everett M., and Svenning, Lynne. *Modernization among Peasants: The Impact of Communication*. New York: Holt, Rinehart and Winston, 1969.

Russett, Bruce M. "Inequality and Instability: The Relation of Land Tenure to Politics." *World Politics* 16, no. 3 (April 1964): 442–54.

Sahlins, Marshall. "Tribal Economics." In *Economic Development and Social Change: The Modernization of Village Communities*, edited by George Dalton, pp. 43–61. Garden City, N. Y.: Natural History Press, for the American Museum of Natural History, 1971.

Samuelson, Paul A. "An Exact Consumption-Loan Model of Interest with or without the Social Contrivance of Money." *Journal of Political Economy* 66, no. 6 (December 1958): 467–82.

Schultz, Theodore William. "New Evidence on Farmer Responses to Economic Opportunities from the Early Agrarian History of Western Europe." In *Subsistence Agriculture and Economic Development*, edited by Clifton R. Wharton, Jr., pp. 105–10. Chicago: Aldine, 1969.

————. *Transforming Traditional Agriculture*. New Haven: Yale University Press, 1964.

Scitovsky, Tibor. *Welfare and Competition*. Rev. ed. Homewood, Ill.: Richard D. Irwin, 1971.

Shanin, Teodor, ed. *Peasants and Peasant Societies: Selected Readings*. Harmondsworth, Eng.: Penguin Books, 1971.

Shapely, L. S., and Shubik, Martin. "Ownership and the Production Function." *Quarterly Journal of Economics* 81, no. 1 (February 1967): 88–111.

Smith, Thomas Carlyle. *The Agrarian Origins of Modern Japan*. Stanford: Stanford University Press, 1959.

Stavenhagen, Rodolfo, ed. *Agrarian Problems and Peasant Movements in Latin America*. Garden City, N. Y.: Doubleday, 1970.

Tarrow, Sidney G. *Peasant Communism in Southern Italy*. New Haven: Yale University Press, 1967.

Thorbecke, Erik, ed. *The Role of Agriculture in Economic Development*. New York: National Bureau of Economic Research, 1969.

Tilly, Charles. *The Vendée: A Sociological Analysis of the Counterrevolution of 1793*. Cambridge: Harvard University Press, 1964.

Tocqueville, Alexis de. *The Ancien Regime and the French Revolution*. Translated by Stuart Gilbert. Manchester: Fontana Library, 1966.

Tullis, F. LaMond. *Lord and Peasant in Peru: A Paradigm of Political and Social Change*. Cambridge: Harvard University Press, 1970.

Uphoff, Norman T., and Ilchman, Warren F., eds. *The Political Economy of Development: Theoretical and Empirical Contributions*. Berkeley and Los Angeles: University of California Press, 1972.

Verba, Sidney, and Nye, Norman H. *Participation in America: Political Democracy and Social Equality*. New York: Harper and Row, 1972.

Wallerstein, Immanuel. *The Modern World System: Capitalist Agriculture and the Origins of the World-Economy in the Sixteenth Century*. New York: Academic Press, 1974.

Wharton, Clifton R., Jr., ed. *Subsistence Agriculture and Economic Development*. Chicago: Aldine, 1969.

Wolf, Eric R[obert]. *Peasants*. Englewood Cliffs, N. J.: Prentice-Hall, 1966.

———. *Peasant Wars of the Twentieth Century*. New York: Harper and Row, 1969.

Worsley, Peter, ed. *Two Blades of Grass: Rural Cooperatives in Agricultural Modernization*. Manchester: Manchester University Press, 1971.

B. On Africa

Allan, William. *The African Husbandman*. New York: Barnes and Noble, 1965.

Arrighi, Giovanni, and Saul, John S. *Essays on the Political Economy of Africa*. New York and London: Monthly Review Press, 1973.

Austin, Dennis. *Politics in Ghana, 1946–1960*. London: Oxford University Press, 1964.

Bateman, Merrill Joseph. *Cocoa in the Ghanaian Economy: An Econometric Model*. Amsterdam: North-Holland, 1966.

Bates, Robert H. "Ethnic Competition and Modernization in Contemporary Africa." *Comparative Political Studies* 6, no. 4 (Jaunary 1974): 457–84.

Bauer, P. T., and Yamey, B. S. "A Case Study of Response to Price in an Underdeveloped Country." *Economic Journal* 69, no. 276 (December 1959): 800–805.

Behrman, Lucy C. *Muslim Brotherhoods and Politics in Senegal*. Cambridge: Harvard University Press, 1970.

Bienen, Henry. *Kenya: The Politics of Participation and Control*. Princeton: Princeton University Press, 1974.

Clayton, Eric S. *Agrarian Development in Peasant Economies: Some Lessons from Kenya*. Oxford: Pergamon Press, 1964.

Colson, Elizabeth. "The Impact of the Colonial Period on the Definition of Land Rights." In *Profiles of Change: African Society and Colonial Rule*, edited by Victor Witter Turner, pp. 193–215. Cambridge: At the University Press, 1971.

deWilde, John C[harles]; McLoughlin, Peter F. M.; Guinard, André; Scudder, Thayer; and Maubouché, Robert. *Experiences with Agricultural Development in Tropical Africa*. 2 vols. Baltimore: Johns Hopkins Press, for the International Bank for Reconstruction and Development, 1967.

Dumont, René. *False Start in Africa*. 2d ed., rev. Translated by Phyllis Nauts Ott. New York: Frederick A. Praeger, 1969.

Elliott, C. M. "Agriculture and Economic Development in Africa: Theory and Experience, 1880–1914." In *Agrarian Change and Economic Development: The Historical Problems*, edited by Eric L. Jones and S. J. Wolf, pp. 123–50. London: Methuen, 1969.

Fallers, Lloyd A. "Are African Cultivators to Be Called 'Peasants'?" In *Economic Development and Social Change: The Modernization of Village Communities*, edited by George Dalton, pp. 169–77. Garden City, N. Y.: Natural History Press, for the American Museum of Natural History, 1971.

Fanon, Frantz. *The Wretched of the Earth*. Translated by Constance Farrington. New York: Grove Press, 1965.

Foster, Philip J. *Education and Social Change in Ghana*. Chicago: University of Chicago Press, 1965.

Fox, Renée C.; De Craemer, Willy; and Ribeaucourt, Jean-Marie. " 'The Second Independence': A Case Study of the Kwilu Rebellion in the Congo." *Comparative Studies in Society and History* 8 (October 1965): 78–109.

Gertzel, Cherry [J.] *The Politics of Independent Kenya: 1963–8*. Nairobi: East African Publishing House, 1970.

Goody, Jack. "Feudalism in Africa?" In *Economic Development and Social Change: The Modernization of Village Communities,* edited by George Dalton, pp. 148–68. Garden City, N. Y.: Natural History Press, for the American Museum of Natural History, 1971.

Gray, Robert F., and Gulliver, P. H., eds. *The Family Estate in Africa: Studies in the Role of Property in Family Structure and Lineage Continuity*. Boston: Boston University Press, 1964.

Gulliver, P. H. "The Conservative Commitment in Northern Tanzania: The Arusha and Masai." In *Tradition and Transition in East Africa: Studies of the Tribal Element in the Modern Era*, edited by P. H. Gulliver, pp. 223–42. Berkeley and Los Angeles: University of California Press, 1969.

Harbeson, John [Willis]. *Nation-Building in Kenya: The Role of Land Reform*. Evanston, Ill.: Northwestern University Press, 1973.

Hill, Frances. *Mobilization and Participation in Tanzania*. Forthcoming.

Hill, Polly. *Rural Hausa: A Village and a Setting*. Cambridge: At the University Press, 1972.

Hodgkin, Thomas Lionel. *Nationalism in Colonial Africa*. London: Frederick Muller, 1956.

Holmquist, Frank W. "Toward a Political Theory of Rural Self-Help Development in Africa." *Rural Africana*, no. 18 (fall 1972): 60–79.

Hunter, Guy. *Modernizing Peasant Societies: A Comparative Study in Asia and Africa*. London: Oxford University Press, for the Institute of Race Relations, 1969.

Hydén, Göran. *Political Development in Rural Tanzania*. Nairobi: East African Publishing House, 1969.

————; Jackson, Robert; and Okumu, John; eds. *Development Administration: The Kenyan Experience*. Nairobi: Oxford University Press, 1970.

Ingle, Clyde R[eid]. *From Village to State in Tanzania: The Politics of Rural Development*. Ithaca, N. Y.: Cornell University Press, 1972.

Johnson, Willard. "The *Union Des Populations du Cameroun* in Rebellion: The Integrative Backlash of Insurgency." In *Protest and Power in Black Africa*, edited by Robert I. Rotberg and Ali A. Mazrui, pp. 671–92. New York: Oxford University Press, 1970.

Johnston, Robert. "Cooperatives and Agricultural Production in Sierra Leone." *Rural Africana*, no. 8 (spring 1969): 47–57.

Jones, William O. "Economic Man in Africa." *Food Research Institute Studies* 1, no. 2 (May 1960): 107–34.

————. *Manioc in Africa*. Stanford: Stanford University Press, 1959.

Kaneda, Hiromitsu, and Johnston, Bruce F. "Urban Food Expenditure Patterns in Tropical Africa." *Food Research Institute Studies* 2, no. 3 (November 1961): 229–75.

Kilson, Martin. *Political Change in a West African State: A Study of the Modernization Process in Sierra Leone*. Cambridge: Harvard University Press, 1966.

Lewis, W[illiam] Arthur. *Politics in West Africa*. New York: Oxford University Press, 1965.

Leys, Colin. *Underdevelopment in Kenya: The Political Economy of Neo-Colonialism, 1964–1971*. Berkeley and Los Angeles: University of California Press, 1974.

McKelvey, John J., Jr. *Man against Tsetse: Struggle for Africa*. Ithaca, N. Y.: Cornell University Press, 1973.

Makings, S. M. *Agricultural Problems of Developing Countries in Africa*. Nairobi: Oxford University Press, 1967.

Miracle, Marvin P. *Agriculture in the Congo Basin: Tradition and Change in African Rural Economies*. Madison: University of Wisconsin Press, 1967.

————. *Maize in Tropical Africa*. Madison: University of Wisconsin Press, 1966.

————, and Seidman, Ann. "Cooperatives in Ghana, 1951–1965." *African Urban Notes* 5, no. 3 (fall 1970): 59–94.

Morrison, Donald George; Mitchell, Robert Cameron; Paden, John Naber; and Stevenson, Hugh Michael. *Black Africa: A Comparative Handbook*. New York: Free Press, 1972.

————, and Stevenson, Hugh Michael. "Integration and Instability: Patterns of African Political Development." *American Political Science Review* 66, no. 3 (September 1972): 902–27.

Rosberg, Carl G[ustav], Jr., and Nottingham, John. *The Myth of "Mau Mau": Nationalism in Kenya*. New York: Frederick A. Praeger, 1966.

Ross, Marc Howard. *The Political Integration of Urban Squatters*. Evanston, Ill.: Northwestern University Press, 1973.

Rotberg, Robert I. "The Rise of African Nationalism: The Case of East and Central Africa." *World Politics* 15, no. 1 (October 1962): 75–90.

Saul, John S. "On African Populism." In *Essays on the Political Economy of Africa*, by Giovanni Arrighi and John S. Saul, pp. 152–79. New York and London: Monthly Review Press, 1973.

————. "Marketing Cooperatives in a Developing Country: The Tanzanian Case." In *Two Blades of Grass: Rural Cooperatives in Agricultural Modernization*, edited by Peter Worsley, pp. 347–70. Manchester: Manchester University Press, 1971.

————, and Woods, Roger. "African Peasantries." In *Peasants and Peasant Societies: Selected Readings*, edited by Teodor Shanin, pp. 103–14. Harmondsworth, Eng.: Penguin Books, 1971.

Schapera, I. "Economic Changes in South African Native Life." In *Tribal and Peasant Economies: Readings in Economic Anthropology*, edited by George Dalton, pp. 136–54. Garden City, N. Y.: Natural History Press, for the American Museum of Natural History, 1967.

Sklar, Richard L. "Political Science and National Integration—A Radical Approach." *Journal of Modern African Studies* 5, no. 1 (May 1967): 1–11.

Smith, Hadley E., ed. *Readings on Economic Development and Administration in Tanzania.* London: Oxford University Press, for the Institute of Public Administration, University College, Dar es Salaam, 1966.

Smock, Audrey C. *Ibo Politics: The Role of Ethnic Unions in Eastern Nigeria.* Cambridge: Harvard University Press, 1971.

Smock, David R., and Smock, Audrey C. *Cultural and Political Aspects of Rural Transformation: A Case Study of Eastern Nigeria.* New York: Praeger Publishers, 1972.

Stern, Robert M. "The Determinants of Cocoa Supply in West Africa." In *African Primary Products and International Trade*, edited by I. G. Stewart and H. W. Ord, pp. 65–82. Edinburgh: Edinburgh University Press, 1965.

Uchendu, Victor C. "The Impact of Changing Agricultural Technology on African Land Tenure." *Journal of the Developing Areas* 4, no. 4 (July 1970): 477–86.

————. "Socioeconomic and Cultural Determinants of Rural Change in East and West Africa." *Food Research Institute Studies in Agricultural Economics, Trade, and Development* 8, no. 3 (1968): 225–42.

————. "Some Issues in African Land Tenure." *Tropical Africa* 44, no. 2 (April 1967): 91–101.

Vastoff, Josef. *Small Farm Credit and Development: Some Experiences in East Africa with Special Reference to Kenya.* New York: Humanities Press, 1968.

Weiss, Herbert F. *Political Protest in the Congo: The Parti Solidaire African during the Independence Struggle.* Princeton: Princeton University Press, 1967.

Widstrand, Carl Gösta, ed. *Co-operatives and Rural Development in East Africa.* New York: African Publishing Corp., 1970.

Young, Crawford. "Domestic Violence in Africa: The Congo." In *Issues of Political Development*, by Charles W. Anderson, Fred R. von der Mehden, and Crawford Young, pp. 120–42. Englewood Cliffs, N. J.: Prentice-Hall, 1967.

Zolberg, Aristide, R. *One-Party Government in the Ivory Coast.* Princeton: Princeton University Press, 1964.

C. On Migration

Banton, Michael P. *West African City: A Study of Tribal Life in Freetown.* London: Oxford University Press, 1957.

Beals, Ralph E.; Levy, Mildred B; and Moses, Leon N. "Rationality and Migration in Ghana." *Review of Economics and Statistics* 49, no. 4 (November 1967): 480–86.

Becker, Gary S[tanley]. *Human Capital: A Theoretical and Empirical Analysis, with Special Reference to Education.* New York: National Bureau of Economic Research, 1964.

————. "Investment in Human Capital: A Theoretical Analysis." *Journal of Political Economy* 70, no. 5, pt. 2 (suppl., October 1962): 9–49.

Berg, Elliot J. "Backward-Sloping Labor Supply Functions in Dual Economies—The Africa Case." In *Social Change: The Colonial Situation,* edited by Immanuel Maurice Wallerstein, pp. 114–36. New York: John Wiley and Sons, 1966.

Berry, Sara S. "The Marketing of Migrant Labor Services in African Cities: A Relatively Unexplored Topic." *African Urban Notes* 5, no. 3 (fall 1970): 144–53.

Brown, James S.; Schwarzweller, Harry K.; and Mangalam, J. F. J. "Kentucky Mountain Migration and the Stem Family: An American Variation on a Theme by LePlay." *Rural Sociology* 28 (March 1963): 48–69.

Browning, Harley L. "Migrant Selectivity and the Growth of Large Cities in Developing Societies." In *Rapid Population Growth: Consequences and Policy Implications,* edited by Study Committee, Office of the Foreign Secretary, National Academy of Sciences, pp. 273–314. Baltimore and London: Johns Hopkins University Press, 1971.

Bruner, Edward M. "Medan: The Role of Kinship in an Indonesian City." In *Peasants in Cities: Readings in the Anthropology of Urbanization,* edited by William Mangin, pp. 122–34. Boston: Houghton Mifflin, 1970.

Byerlee, Derek, and Eicher, Carl K. *Rural Employment, Migration, and Economic Development: Theoretical Issues and Empirical Evidence from Africa.* African Rural Employment Paper no. 1. East Lansing: Department of Agricultural Economics, Michigan State University, September 1972.

Caldwell, John C[harles]. *African Rural-Urban Migration: The Movement to Ghana's Towns.* New York: Columbia University Press, 1969.

Elkan, Walter. *Migrants and Proletarians: Urban Labour in the Economic Development of Uganda.* London: Oxford University Press, for the East African Institute of Social Research, 1960.

Greenwood, Michael J. "An Analysis of the Determinants of Geographic Labor Mobility in the United States." *Review of Economics and Statistics* 51, no. 2 (May 1969): 189–94.

Gugler, Joseph. "On the Theory of Rural-Urban Migration: The Case of Subsaharan Africa." In *Migration,* Sociological Studies 2, edited by J[ohn] A[rcher] Jackson, pp. 134–55. Cambridge: At the University Press, 1969.

Harris, John R., and Todaro, Michael P. "Wages, Industrial Employment and Labour Productivity: The Kenyan Experience." *Eastern Africa Economic Review* 1, no. 1 (June 1969): 29–64.

Herrick, Bruce H. "Urbanization and Urban Migration in Latin America: An Economist's View." In *Latin American Urban Research*, edited by Francine F. Rabinovitz and Felicity M. Trueblood, pp. 71–81. Beverly Hills: Sage Publications, 1971.

————. *Urban Migration and Economic Development in Chile*. Cambridge: M.I.T. Press, 1966.

Heyneman, Stephen P. "Fallacies in Educational Economics: Some Heresies Relevant to African Planning." *Manpower and Unemployment Research in Africa* 5, no. 1 (April 1972): 31–37.

Jacobson, David. *Itinerant Townsmen: Friendship and Social Order in Urban Uganda*. Menlo Park, Cal.: Cummings, 1973.

Johnson, George E. "The Structure of Rural-Urban Migration Models." *Eastern Africa Economic Review* 3, no. 1 (June 1971): 21–28.

Knight, Gregory C. *Ecology and Change: Rural Modernization in an African Community*. New York: Academic Press, 1974.

Knight, John B. "Measuring Urban-Rural Income Differentials." Paper presented to the Conference on Urban Unemployment in Africa, Institute of Development Studies, University of Sussex, 12–16 September 1971.

————. "Rural-Urban Income Comparisons and Migration in Ghana." *Bulletin of the Oxford Institute of Economics and Statistics* (May 1972): 199–228.

Kuznets, Simon Smith; Thomas, Dorothy Swaine; et al. *Population Redistribution and Economic Growth: United States, 1870–1950*. Philadelphia: American Philosophical Society, 1957.

Levy, Mildred B., and Wadycki, Walter J. "Education and the Decision to Migrate: An Econometric Analysis of Migration in Venezuela." *Econometrica* 42, no. 2 (March 1974): 377–88.

Lopreato, Joseph. *Peasants No More: Social Class and Social Change in an Underdeveloped Society*. San Francisco: Chandler, 1967.

O'Brien, Rita Cruise. "Unemployment, the Family and Class Formation in Africa." *Manpower and Unemployment Research in Africa* 6, no. 2 (November 1973): 47–59.

Okun, Bernard, and Richardson, Richard W. "Regional Income Inequality and Internal Population Migration." *Economic Development and Cultural Change* 9, no. 2 (January 1961): 128–43.

Orbell, John M., and Uno, Toru. "A Theory of Neighborhood Problem Solving: Political Action *vs.* Residential Mobility." *American Political Science Review* 66, no. 2 (June 1972): 471–89.

Plotnicov, Leonard. "Nigerians: The Dream is Unfulfilled." In *Peasants in Cities: Readings in the Anthropology of Urbanization*, edited by William Mangin, pp. 170–74. Boston: Houghton Mifflin, 1970.

Ravenstein, E. G. "On the Laws of Migration," pts. 1 and 2. *Journal of the Statistical Society* 48 (June 1885): 167–227; and 52 (June 1889): 241–305.

Read, Margaret. "Migrant Labour in Africa and Its Effects on Tribal Life." *International Labour Review* 45 (1942): 605–31.

Redford, Arthur. *Labour Migration in England, 1800–1850.* Manchester: Manchester University Press, 1926.

Sahota, Gian S. "An Economic Analysis of Internal Migration in Brazil." *Journal of Political Economy* 76, no. 2 (March/April 1968): 218–45.

Schapera, Isaac. *Migrant Labour and Tribal Life: A Study of Conditions in Bechuanaland Protectorate.* London: Oxford University Press, 1947.

Schultz, T. Paul. "Internal Migration: A Quantitative Study of Rural-Urban Migration in Colombia." In *Structural Change in a Developing Economy: Colombia's Problems and Prospects,* by Richard R. Nelson, T. Paul Schultz, and Robert L. Slighton, pp. 45–76. Princeton: Princeton University Press, 1971.

Schultz, Theodore W. "Reflections on Investment in Man." *Journal of Political Economy* 70, no. 5, pt. 2 (suppl., October 1962): 1–8.

Scudder, Thayer. "The Economic Basis of Egyptian Nubian Labor Migration." In *Contemporary Egyptian Nubia,* vol. 1, edited by Robert A[lan] Fernea, pp. 100–141. New Haven: Human Relations Area Files, 1966.

Schwarzweller, Harry K., and Seggar, John F. "Kinship Involvement: A Factor in the Adjustment of Rural Migrants." *Journal of Marriage and the Family* 29, no. 4 (November 1967): 662–71.

Simić, Andrei. *The Peasant Urbanites: A Study of Rural-Urban Mobility in Serbia.* New York: Seminar Press, 1973.

Sjaastad, Larry A. "The Costs and Returns of Human Migration." *Journal of Political Economy* 70, no. 5, pt. 2 (suppl., October 1962): 80–93.

Southall, A. W. "Population Movements in East Africa." In *Essays on African Population,* edited by Kenneth Michael Barbour and R. M. Prothero, pp. 157–92. New York: Frederick A. Praeger, 1961.

Stiglitz, Joseph E. "Rural-Urban Migration, Surplus Labour, and the Relationship between Urban and Rural Wages." *Eastern Africa Economic Review* 1, no. 2 (December 1969): 1–27.

Stouffer, Samuel A. "Intervening Opportunities: A Theory Relating Mobility and Distance." *American Sociological Review* 5, no. 6 (December 1940): 845–67.

Sussman, Marvin B., and Burchinal, Lee. "Kin Family Network: Unheralded Structure in Current Conceptualizations of Family Functioning." In *Readings on the Family and Society,* edited by William J. Goode, pp. 170–76. Englewood Cliffs, N. J.: Prentice-Hall, 1964.

Todaro, Michael P. "A Model of Labor Migration and Urban Unemployment in Less Developed Countries." *American Economic Review* 59, no. 1 (March 1969): 138–48.

Vogel, Ezra F. "Kinship Structure, Migration to the City, and Modernization." In *Aspects of Social Change in Modern Japan,* edited by Ronald Philip Dore, pp. 91–111. Princeton: Princeton University Press, 1967.

Vogel, William M. *Is Labor Migration of Decreasing Significance in the Economies of East Africa?* Occasional Paper no. 34. Syracuse, N. Y.: Program of Eastern African Studies, Syracuse University, February 1968.

Wilkening, E. A.; Pinto, João Bosco; and Pastore, José. "Role of the Extended Family in Migration and Adaptation in Brazil." *Journal of Marriage and the Family* 30, no. 4 (November 1968): 689–95.

III. Materials on Zambia

A. General

Bolink, Peter. *Towards Church Union in Zambia: A Study of Missionary Co-operation and Church-Union Efforts in Central Africa.* Franeker, Netherlands: T. Wever, 1967.

Brelsford, William Vernon. *The Tribes of Zambia.* Lusaka: Government Printer, 1965.

Caplan, Gerald L. *The Elites of Barotseland, 1878–1969: A Political History of Zambia's Western Province.* Berkeley and Los Angeles: University of California Press, 1970.

Colson, Elizabeth, and Gluckman, Max, eds. *Seven Tribes of British Central Africa.* London: Oxford University Press, for the Rhodes-Livingstone Institute, 1951.

Davies, D. Hywel, ed. *Zambia in Maps.* London: University of London Press, 1971.

de Gaay Fortman, Bastiaan, ed. *After Mulungushi: The Economics of Zambian Humanism.* Nairobi: East African Publishing House, 1969.

Gann, Lewis H. *A History of Northern Rhodesia: Early Days to 1953.* London: Chatto and Windus, 1964.

Gelfand, Michael. *Northern Rhodesia in the Days of the Charter: A Medical and Social Study, 1878–1924.* Oxford: Basil Blackwell and Mott, 1961.

Hall, Richard [Seymour]. *The High Price of Principles: Kaunda and the White South.* New York: Africana Publishing Corp., 1970.

———. *Zambia.* New York: Frederick A. Praeger, 1966.

Kaunda, Kenneth David. "Address at the Official Opening of the Zambia Agricultural Show, August 7, 1971." Background 62/1971, Zambia Information Services, n.d.

———. "Address at the Opening of a Seminar on Rural Development Held in Lusaka on the 23rd March 1970." Background 24/1970, Zambia Information Services, n.d.

———. "Address at the Opening of the First Session of the Second National Assembly, 22 January 1969." In *Official Verbatim Report of the Debates of the First Session of the Second National Assembly, 21st January–23rd April 1969,* Hansard no. 17, pp. 30–50. Lusaka: Government Printer, 1969.

———. "Address to Parliament on the Opening of the 4th Session of the Zambia National Assembly, January 12, 1972." Background 2/1972, Zambia Information Services, n.d.

———. "Address to the U.N.I.P. National Council Held at Matero, Lusaka on the 11th August 1969." Zambia Information Services, Press Release, n.d.

————. *His Excellency the President's Address to Parliament on the Opening of the Second Session of the Second National Assembly, 7th January 1970*. Lusaka: Government Printer, 1970.

————. *His Excellency the President's Address to Parliament on the Opening of the Third Session of the Second National Assembly, 8th January 1971*. Lusaka: Government Printer, 1971.

————. *Humanism in Zambia and a Guide to Its Implementation*. Lusaka: Zambia Information Services, 1968.

————. *A Humanist in Africa: Letters to Colin M. Morris from Kenneth D. Kaunda, President of Zambia*. London: Longmans, Green, 1966.

————. "A Progress Report on the Re-organization of the Nation's Wealth since Independence; Speech to the UNIP National Council, March 4, 1972." Lusaka: Zambia Information Services, 1972.

————. "Speech at the Copperbelt Agricultural Show on June 4, 1971." Background 41/1971, Zambia Information Services, n.d.

————. *"Take Up the Challenge": Speeches Made by His Excellency the President Dr. K. D. Kaunda to the United National Independence Party National Council, Mulungushi Hall, Lusaka, 7–10 November, 1970*. Lusaka: Zambia Information Services, 1970.

————. *Zambia's Guideline for the Next Decade*. Lusaka: Ministry of Information, 1968.

Kay, George. *A Social Geography of Zambia: A Survey of Population Patterns in a Developing Country*. London: University of London Press, 1967.

Quiggin, A. H. *Trade Routes, Trade and Currency in East Africa*. Occasional Papers of the Rhodes-Livingstone Museum, no. 5. Livingstone: Rhodes-Livingstone Museum, 1949.

Simonis, Heide, and Simonis, Udo Ernest, eds. *Socioeconomic Development in Dual Economies: The Example of Zambia*. New York: Humanities Press, 1971.

Stokes, Eric, and Brown, Richard, eds. *The Zambesian Past: Studies in Central African History*. Manchester: Manchester University Press, for the Institute for Social Research, University of Zambia, 1966.

Taylor, John V., and Lehmann, Dorothea. *Christians of the Copperbelt*. London: SCM Press, 1961.

Thomson, J. Moffat. *Memorandum on the Native Tribes and Tribal Areas of Northern Rhodesia*. Livingstone: Government Printer, 1934.

B. On Luapula

"Alfred Sharpe's Travels in the Northern Province and Katanga." *Northern Rhodesia Journal* 3, no. 3 (1957): 210–19.

Burton, Sir Richard Francis. *The Lands of Cazembe: Lecerda's Journey to Cazembe in 1798*. London: John Murray, for the Royal Geographic Society, 1873.

Chiwale, Jacques Chileya. *Central Bantu Historical Texts, III: Royal Praises and Praise Names of the Lunda Kazembe of Northern Rhodesia*. Rhodes-Livingstone Communication no. 25. Lusaka: Rhodes-Livingstone Institute, 1962.

Cunnison, Ian George. *Central Bantu Historical Texts, II.* Rhodes-Livingstone Communication no. 23. Lusaka: Rhodes-Livingstone Institute, 1962.

————. *History on the Luapula: An Essay on the Historical Notions of a Central African Tribe.* Rhodes-Livingstone Papers, no. 21. London: Oxford University Press, for the Rhodes-Livingstone Institute, 1951.

————. "The Installation of Chief Kazembe XV." *Northern Rhodesia Journal* 1, no. 5 (June 1952): 3–10.

————. "Kazembe and the Arabs to 1870." In *The Zambesian Past: Studies in Central African History,* edited by Eric Stokes and Richard Brown, pp. 226–37. Manchester: Manchester University Press, for the Institute for Social Research, University of Zambia, 1966.

————. "Kazembe and the Portuguese, 1798–1832." *Journal of African History* 2, no. 1 (1961): 61–76.

————. *The Luapula Peoples of Northern Rhodesia: Custom and History in Tribal Politics.* Manchester: Manchester University Press, for the Rhodes-Livingstone Institute, 1959.

————. "The Reigns of the Kazembes." *Northern Rhodesia Journal* 3, no. 2 (1956): 131–38.

————, trans. and annotator. "Kazembe's Charter: An Extract from *Ifikolwe Fyandi na Bantu Bandi* by Mwata Kazembe XIV." *Northern Rhodesia Journal* 3, no. 3 (1957): 220–32.

Fryer, G. "Mwamfuli's Village: The New Fulcrum of the Bangweulu Fish Trade." *Northern Rhodesia Journal* 3, no. 6 (1958): 483–88.

Gammitto, A. C. P. *King Kazembe, Being the Diary of the Portuguese Expedition to that Potentate in the Years 1831 and 1832.* 2 vols. Translated by Ian Cunnison. Lisbon: Junta de Investigações do Ultramar, 1960.

Gore-Browne, Sir Stewart. "The Anglo-Belgian Boundary Commission, 1911–14." *Northern Rhodesia Journal* 5, no. 4 (1964): 315–29.

Jones, E. Averay. "Memories of Abandoned Bomas—No. 6: Kalungwishi." *Northern Rhodesia Journal* 2, no. 4 (1954): 46–48.

Kay, George. *Chief Kalaba's Village: A Preliminary Survey of Economic Life in an Ushi Village, Northern Rhodesia.* Rhodes-Livingstone Papers, no. 35. Manchester: Manchester University Press, for the Rhodes-Livingstone Institute, 1964.

————. *A Population Map (1:500,000) of the Luapula-Bangweulu Region of Northern Rhodesia with Notes on the Population.* Rhodes-Livingstone Communication no. 26. Lusaka: Rhodes-Livingstone Institute, 1962.

————, and Wright, D. M. "Aspects of the Ushi Iron Industry." *Northern Rhodesia Journal* 5, no. 1 (1962): 28–38.

Kazembe, Mwata, XIV. *Ifikolwe Fyandi na Bantu Bandi.* London: Macmillan, for the Northern Rhodesia and Nyasaland Publications Bureau, 1951.

Lammond, W. "The Luapula Valley." *Northern Rhodesia Journal* 2, no. 5 (1955): 50–55.

Lary, Peter H. "Aspects of Luapula Society and History in the Later Nineteenth Century." Paper presented to the Department of Political and Administrative Studies Seminar, University of Zambia, August 1973.

McGlashan, N. D., with Mulenga, James. "A Note on Traditional Attitudes towards Blindness in Chief Mununga's Area, Kawambwa." *Northern Rhodesia Journal* 5, no. 6 (1964): 583–87.

Macrae, F. B., and Paine, N. D. "Lake Bangweulu: Its Fish and Its Fishing." *Northern Rhodesia Journal* 1, no. 6 (December 1952): 3–19.

Marshall, H. C., and Lobb, Gordon. "Water Transport in the Bangweulu Swamps." *Northern Rhodesia Journal* 3, no. 3 (1957): 189–99.

Paine, Denis. "Lake Mweru, Its Fish and Fishing Industry." *Northern Rhodesia Journal* 1, no. 2 (1949): 7–13.

Slaski, J. *Peoples of the Lower Luapula.* In *Ethnographic Survey of Africa: East Central Africa*, pt. 2, edited by Cyril Daryll Forde. London: International African Institute, 1951.

Smith, Dean A. *Report of a Nutrition and Health Survey in the Kawambwa District.* Lusaka: Government Printer, 1950.

Thomson, Justice J. B. "Memories of Abandoned Bomas—No. 8: Chiengi." *Northern Rhodesia Journal* 2, no. 6 (1955): 67–77.

———. *Report on the Native Fishing Industry.* Livingstone: Government Printer, 1930.

Williams, S. "The Mweru-Luapula Fisheries." In *A Guide-Book to the Study of Sample Areas in Zambia*, by Republic of Zambia, Ministry of Education. Lusaka: Ministry of Education, 1966.

C. On the Growth of the Line of Rail

Baldwin, Robert E. *Economic Development and Export Growth: A Study of Northern Rhodesia, 1920–1960.* Berkeley and Los Angeles: University of California Press, 1966.

Bancroft, Joseph Austen. *Mining in Northern Rhodesia: A Chronicle of Mineral Exploration and Mining Development.* Bedford, Eng.: British South Africa Company, 1961.

Barber, William J. *The Economy of British Central Africa: A Case Study of Economic Development in a Dualistic Society.* Stanford: Stanford University Press, 1961.

Bates, Robert H. "Patterns of Uneven Development: Causes and Consequences in Zambia." *University of Denver Monograph Series in World Affairs* 11, no. 3 (1973–74): 1–59.

Berger, Elena L. *Labour, Race and Colonial Rule: The Copperbelt from 1924 to Independence.* Oxford: Clarendon Press, 1974.

Bettison, David G. "Factors in the Determination of Wage Rates in Central Africa." *Rhodes-Livingstone Journal*, no. 28 (December 1960): 22–46.

Beveridge, Andrew Alan. "African Urban Retailers." From the files of the Manufacturing and Trading Committee for the Second National Development Plan.

———. "Converts to Capitalism: The Emergence of African Entrepreneurs in Lusaka, Zambia." Ph. D. diss., Department of Sociology, Yale University, 1973.

———. "Economic Independence, Indigenization, and the African Businessman: Some Effects of Zambia's Economic Reforms." *African Studies Review* 17, no. 3 (December 1974): 477–90.

Bostock, R. M. "The Background to Participation." In *Economic Independence and Zambian Copper: A Case Study of Foreign Investment,* edited by Mark Bostock and Charles Harvey, pp. 107–30. New York: Praeger Publishers, 1972.

———. "The Transport Sector." In *Constraints on the Economic Development of Zambia,* edited by Charles Elliott, pp. 323–76. Nairobi: Oxford University Press, 1971.

———, and Harvey, Charles, eds. *Economic Independence and Zambian Copper: A Case Study of Foreign Investment.* New York: Praeger Publishers, 1972.

Bradley, Kenneth. *Copper Venture: The Discovery and Development of Roan Antelope and Mufulira.* London: Mufulira Copper Mines and Roan Antelope Copper Mines, 1952.

Brelsford, W. V. *Copperbelt Markets: A Social and Economic Study.* Lusaka: Government Printer, 1947.

Burawoy, Michael. *The Colour of Class on the Copper Mines: From African Advancement to Zambianization.* Zambian Papers, no. 7. Lusaka: Institute for African Studies, University of Zambia, 1972.

Coleman, Francis L. *The Northern Rhodesia Copperbelt, 1899–1962: Technological Development up to the End of the Central African Federation.* Manchester: Manchester University Press, for the Institute for African Studies, University of Zambia, 1971.

Collins, John. "The Evolution of Urban Housing Policies in Zambia with Particular Reference to Lusaka." M. Sc. thesis, Department of Urban Planning, Columbia University, April 1970.

Davis, John Merle, ed. *Modern Industry and the African.* 2d ed. New York: Negro Universities Press, 1969.

Dean, Edwin R. "Studies in Price Formation in African Markets." *Rhodes-Livingstone Journal,* no. 31 (June 1962): 1–20.

Deane, Phyllis. *Colonial Social Accounting.* Cambridge: At the University Press, 1953.

Dresang, Dennis Lee. "The Zambia Civil Service: A Study in Development Administration." Ph.D. diss., Department of Political Science, University of California at Los Angeles, 1971.

Drysdall, Alan. "Prospecting and Mining Activity, 1895–1970." In *Economic Independence and Zambian Copper: A Case Study of Foreign Investment,* edited by Mark Bostock and Charles Harvey, pp. 53–88. New York: Praeger Publishers, 1972.

Duff, C. E., ed. *First Report on a Regional Survey of the Copperbelt, 1959.* Lusaka: Government Printer, 1960.

Elliott, Charles, ed. *Constraints on the Economic Development of Zambia.* Nairobi: Oxford University Press, 1971.

Faber, Michael. "The Development of the Manufacturing Sector." In *Constraints on the Economic Development of Zambia*, edited by Charles Elliott, pp. 299–322. Nairobi: Oxford University Press, 1971.

Gielgud, Val. "Some Reminiscences of George Grey." *Northern Rhodesia Journal* 3, no. 2 (1956): 146–53.

Gifford, Prosser. "The Framework for a Nation: An Economic and Social History of Northern Rhodesia from 1914 to 1939." Ph. D. diss., Department of History, Yale University, 1964.

Goodman, Stephen. "The Foreign Exchange Constraint." In *Constraints on the Economic Development of Zambia*, edited by Charles Elliott, pp. 233–54. Nairobi: Oxford University Press, 1971.

Haefele, Edwin T., and Steinberg, Eleanor B. *Government Controls on Transport: An African Case*. Washington, D. C.: Brookings Institution, 1965.

Harvey, Charles R. M. "The Control of Inflation in a Very Open Economy: Zambia 1964–9." *Eastern Africa Economic Review* 3, no. 1 (June 1971): 41–61.

————. "Financial Constraints on Zambian Development." In *Constraints on the Economic Development of Zambia*, edited by Charles Elliott, pp. 121–51. Nairobi: Oxford University Press, 1971.

————. "The Fiscal System." In *Constraints on the Economic Development of Zambia*, edited by Charles Elliott, pp. 153–89. Nairobi: Oxford University Press, 1971.

————. "Tax Reform in the Mining Industry." In *Economic Independence and Zambian Copper: A Case Study of Foreign Investment*, edited by Mark Bostock and Charles Harvey, pp. 131–44. New York: Praeger Publishers, 1972.

Jolly, Richard. "The Seers Report in Retrospect." *African Social Research*, no. 11 (June 1971): 1–26.

————. "The Skilled Manpower Constraint." In *Constraints on the Economic Development of Zambia*, edited by Charles Elliott, pp. 21–56. Nairobi: Oxford University Press, 1971.

Kessel, Norman. "Mining and the Factors Constraining Economic Development." In *Constraints on the Economic Development of Zambia*, edited by Charles Elliott, pp. 257–68. Nairobi: Oxford University Press, 1971.

Lomas, P. K. "African Trade Unions on the Copperbelt." *South African Journal of Economics* 26, no. 2 (June 1958): 110–22.

Mihalyi, Louis James. "Charcoal from the Zambian Forests." *Geographical Magazine* 45, no. 3 (December 1972): 212–18.

Mitchell, J. Clyde. "Differential Fertility amongst Urban Africans in Zambia." *Rhodes-Livingstone Journal*, no. 37 (June 1965): 1–25.

————. "An Estimate of Fertility among Africans on the Copperbelt of Northern Rhodesia." *Rhodes-Livingstone Journal*, no. 13 (1953): 18–29.

Musakanya, Valentine. "Where to Spend our Scarce Resources." *African Development, Zambia Supplement* (October 1970): z18–z20.

Nyirenda, A. A. "African Market Vendors in Lusaka with a Note on the Recent Boycott." *Rhodes-Livingstone Journal*, no. 22 (September 1957): 31–63.

Prain, Sir Ronald L. "The Problem of African Advancement on the Copperbelt of Northern Rhodesia." In idem, *Selected Papers, 1953–1957*, 2: 19–34. London: Rhodesian Selection Trust Group, 1958.

————. "The Stabilization of Labour in the Rhodesian Copperbelt." In idem, *Selected Papers, 1953–1957*, 1: 99–109. London: Rhodesian Selection Trust Group, 1958.

Robinson, E. A. G. "The Economic Problem." In *Modern Industry and the African*, 2d ed., edited by John Merle Davis, pp. 131–224. New York: Negro Universities Press, 1969.

Rothchild, Donald. "Rural-Urban Inequities and Resource Allocation in Zambia." *Journal of Commonwealth Political Studies* 10, no. 3 (November 1972): 222–42.

Saffery, A. Lynn. *A Report on Some Aspects of African Living Conditions on the Copperbelt of Northern Rhodesia*. Lusaka: Government Printer, 1943.

Simmance, Allan J. F. *Urbanization in Zambia*. New York: Ford Foundation International Urbanization Survey, 1972.

Slinn, Peter. "The Legacy of the British South Africa Company: The Historical Background." In *Economic Independence and Zambian Copper: A Case Study of Foreign Investment*, edited by Mark Bostock and Charles Harvey, pp. 23–52. New York: Praeger Publishers, 1972.

United Nations, Economic Commission for Africa, Food and Agriculture Organization. *Report of the UN/ECA/FAO Economic Survey Mission on the Economic Development of Zambia*. Ndola: Falcon Press, 1964.

Young, Alistair. *Industrial Diversification in Zambia*. New York: Praeger Publishers, 1973.

————. "Patterns of Development in Zambian Manufacturing Industry since Independence." *Eastern Africa Economic Review* 1, no. 2 (December 1969): 29–38.

D. On Agriculture

Allan, William. "African Land Usage." *Rhodes-Livingstone Journal*, no. 3 (June 1945): 13–20.

————. *Studies in African Land Usage in Northern Rhodesia*. Rhodes-Livingstone Papers, no. 15. Capetown: Oxford University Press, for the Rhodes-Livingstone Institute, 1949.

————; Gluckman, Max; Peters, D. U.; and Trapnell, C. G. *Land Holding and Land Usage among the Plateau Tonga of Mazabuka District*. Rhodes-Livingstone Papers, no. 14. Capetown: Oxford University Press, for the Rhodes-Livingstone Institute, 1948.

Anthony, Kenneth R. M., and Uchendu, Victor C. *Agricultural Change in Mazabuka District, Zambia*. Stanford: Food Research Institute of Stanford University, 1970.

Beatty, D. M. F. *Results of a Fish Marketing Survey in Zambia, 1964–65*. Lusaka: Department of Wildlife, Fisheries, and National Parks, 1969.

Bessell, J. E. *Technical Systems of Maize Production in Africa*. Lusaka: University of Zambia, August 1973.

Colson, Elizabeth. *Life among the Cattle-Owning Plateau Tonga: The Material Culture of a Northern Rhodesia Native Tribe.* Occasional Papers of the Rhodes-Livingstone Museum, no. 6. Livingstone: Rhodes-Livingstone Museum, 1949.

———. "The Role of Cattle among the Plateau Tonga of Mazabuka District." *Rhodes-Livingstone Journal,* no. 11 (1951): 10–46.

———, and Chona, Mark. "Marketing of Cattle among Plateau Tonga." *Rhodes-Livingstone Journal,* no. 37 (June 1965): 42–50.

Dean, R. W. "Changes in Farming over the Past Fifty Years." *Farming in Zambia* 5, no. 4 (July 1970): 11–13.

de Gaay Fortman, Bastiaan. "Zambia's Markets: Problems and Opportunities." In *Constraints on the Economic Development of Zambia,* edited by Charles Elliott, pp. 191–232. Nairobi: Oxford University Press, 1971.

de Vries, E. "The Importance of Traditional Agriculture in Zambia." From the files of the Rural and Regional Planning Committee of the Second National Development Plan.

Elliott, C. M.; Bessell, J. E.; Roberts, R. A. J.; and Vanzetti, N. *Some Determinants of Agricultural Labour Productivity in Zambia.* Lusaka: University of Zambia, November 1970.

Gluckman, Max. "African Land Tenure." *Rhodes-Livingstone Journal.* no. 3 (June 1945): 1–12.

———. *Economy of the Central Barotse Plain.* Rhodes-Livingstone Papers, no. 7. Livingstone: Rhodes-Livingstone Institute, 1941.

Hadfield, James. *The Marketing of African Agricultural Produce in Northern Rhodesia.* Agricultural Bulletin no. 18. Lusaka: Government Printer, n.d.

———. *Report on the Peasant Farming Survey, 1960–1961.* Lusaka: Ministry of African Agriculture, Economics and Markets Advisory Branch, September 1962.

Hellen, John A. *Rural Economic Development in Zambia,1890 –1964.* New York: Humanities Press, 1968.

Johns, Sheridan. "Para-statal Bodies in Zambia: Problems and Prospects." In *Socioeconomic Development in Dual Economies: The Example of Zambia,* edited by Heide Simonis and Udo Ernst Simonis, pp. 217–52. New York: Humanities Press, 1971.

Johnson, C. E. *African Farming Improvements in the Plateau Tonga Maize Areas of Northern Rhodesia.* Agricultural Bulletin no. 11. Lusaka: Government Printer, 1956.

Kapteyn, R. C. E., and Emery, C. R. *Research Project on Administration for Rural Development: Draft Report for the First Year Study (July 1971-June 1972).* Lusaka: National Institute of Public Administration, 1972.

Kay, George. "Agricultural Progress in Zambia's Eastern Province." *Journal of Administration Overseas* 5, no. 2 (April 1966): 97–101.

———. *Social Aspects of Village Regrouping in Zambia.* Lusaka: Institute for Social Research, University of Zambia, 1967.

Lombard, C. Stephen. "Agriculture in Zambia since Independence." *East Africa Journal* 8, no. 3 (March 1971): 17–19.

———. *The Growth of Co-operatives in Zambia, 1914–71.* Zambian Papers, no. 6. Lusaka: Institute for African Studies, University of Zambia, 1971.

————, and Tweedie, A. H. C. *Agriculture in Zambia since Independence*. Lusaka: NECZAM, for the Institute of African Studies, University of Zambia, 1972.

Maimbo, Fabian J. M., and Fry, James. "An Investigation into the Change in the Terms of Trade between the Rural and Urban Sectors of Zambia." *African Social Research*, no. 12 (December 1971): 95–110.

Makings, S. M. *Agricultural Change in Northern Rhodesia/Zambia: 1945–1965*. Stanford: Food Research Institute of Stanford University, 1966.

————. "A Note on Crop Price Stabilization and Government Marketing Responsibilities with Reference to Conditions in Northern Rhodesia." Mimeographed. Lusaka: Department of Agriculture, January 1963.

Nadeau, E. G. "A Comparison of Two Farmers' Co-operative Unions in Northern Zambia: Problems of Productivity, Management, and the Role of the Members in Decision-Making." Occasional Paper. Mimeographed. University of Zambia, Rural Development Studies Bureau, December 1973.

Olund, G., and Russel, J. *Survey of Farming Co-operatives*. Lusaka: Ministry of Rural Development, 1970.

Pandawa, Abel. "Life in a Squatter Community." University of Zambia Sociological Association Paper no. 8. Mimeographed. April 1971.

Peters, D. U. *Land Usage in Serenje District*. Rhodes-Livingstone Papers, no. 19. London: Oxford University Press, for the Rhodes-Livingstone Institute, 1950.

Trapnell, Colin Graham. *The Soils, Vegetation and Agriculture of North-Eastern Rhodesia: Report of the Ecological Survey*. Lusaka: Government Printer, 1953.

————; Martin, J. D.; and Allen, W. *A Vegetation-Soil Map of Northern Rhodesia with Accompanying Memorandum*. Lusaka: Government Printer, 1950.

United Nations, Food and Agriculture Organization. *The Food Economy of Zambia*. Rome: United Nations Development Program, 1974.

————. *Report to the Government of Zambia on Agricultural Marketing and Pricing Policies*. Rome: United Nations Development Program, 1974.

Vaux, H. "Unusual Aspects of Native Land Tenure in the Mazabuka District." *Northern Rhodesia Journal* 2, no. 2 (1953): 18–27.

White, Charles M. N. "A Survey of African Land Tenure in Northern Rhodesia." *Journal of African Administration* 11, no. 4 (1959): 171–78; and 12, no. 1 (1960): 3–10.

Young, Charles E. "Rural-Urban Terms of Trade." *African Social Research*, no. 12 (December 1971): 91–94.

E. On Migration

Bates, Robert H., and Bennett, Bruce William. "Determinants of the Rural Exodus in Zambia: A Study of Inter-Censal Migration, 1963–1969." *Cahiers d'Études Africaines* 14, no. 3 (1974): 543–64.

Bettison, David G. *Numerical Data on African Dwellers in Lusaka, Northern Rhodesia*. Rhodes-Livingstone Communication, no. 16. Lusaka: Rhodes-Livingstone Institute, 1959.

Bond, George C. "Labour Migration and Rural Activism: The Yombe Case." *African Urban Notes*, ser. B, no. 1 (winter 1974–75): 21–33.

Breytenbach, W. J. *Migratory Labour Arrangements in Southern Africa.* Pretoria: Africa Institute, 1972.

Colson, Elizabeth. "Migration in Africa: Trends and Possibilities." In *Social Change: The Colonial Situation*, edited by Immanuel Maurice Wallerstein, pp. 107–13. New York: John Wiley and Sons, 1966.

Coulter, Charles W. "The Sociological Problem." In *Modern Industry and the African*, 2d ed., edited by John Merle Davis, pp. 31–127. New York: Negro Universities Press, 1969.

Fetter, Bruce. "Immigrants to Elisabethville: Their Origins and Aims." *African Urban Notes* 3, no. 2 (August 1968): 17–34.

Fielder, Robin J. "The Role of Cattle in the Ila Economy." *African Social Research* 15 (June 1973): 327–61.

———. "The Significance of the Accumulation of Wealth in Subsistence Economies." Paper presented to a seminar at the Department of Social Anthropology, Manchester University, 1969.

Gulliver, P. H. "Nyakyusa Labour Migration." *Rhodes-Livingstone Journal*, no. 21 (March 1957): 32–63.

Harries-Jones, Peter. "The Tribes in the Towns." In *The Tribes of Zambia*, by William Vernon Brelsford, pp. 124–46. Lusaka: Government Printer, 1965.

Heisler, Helmuth. "The Pattern of Migration in Zambia." *Cahiers d'Études Africaines* 13, no. 2 (1973): 193–212.

———. *Urbanisation and the Government of Migration: The Inter-relation of Urban and Rural Life in Zambia.* New York: St. Martin's Press, 1974.

Jackman, Mary Elizabeth. *Recent Population Movements in Zambia: Some Aspects of the 1969 Census.* Zambian Papers, no. 8. Lusaka: Institute for African Studies, University of Zambia, 1973.

Kay, George. "Sources and Uses of Cash in Some Ushi Villages, Fort Rosebery District, Northern Rhodesia." *Rhodes-Livingstone Journal*, no. 35 (June 1964): 14–28.

Kuczynski, Robert Rene. *Demographic Survey of the British Colonial Empire.* Vol. 2. London: Oxford University Press, for the Royal Institute of International Affairs, 1949.

———. "Population Movements: The Contribution of Demography to the Study of Social Problems." *Rhodes-Livingstone Journal*, no. 2 (December 1944): 16–34.

McCulloch, Merran. *A Social Survey of the African Population of Livingstone.* Rhodes-Livingstone Papers, no. 26. Manchester: Manchester University Press, for the Rhodes-Livingstone Institute, 1956.

Mitchell, J[ames] Clyde. *African Urbanization in Ndola and Luanshya.* Rhodes-Livingstone Communication, no. 6. Lusaka: Rhodes-Livingstone Institute, 1954.

———. "The Causes of Labour Migration." *Bulletin of the Inter-African Labour Institute* 6 (1959): 12–47.

———. "Demographic Appendix." In *Social Relations in Central African Industry*, Proceedings of the Twelfth Conference of the Rhodes-Livingstone

Institute for Social Research, edited by David Matthews and Raymond Apthorpe, pp. 9–14. Lusaka: Rhodes-Livingstone Institute, 1958.

———. "Distance, Transportation, and Urban Involvement in Zambia." In *Urban Anthropology: Cross-Cultural Studies in Urbanization*, edited by Aiden Southall, pp. 287–313. London: Oxford University Press, 1973.

———. "The Distribution of African Labour by Area of Origin on the Copper Mines of Northern Rhodesia." *Rhodes-Livingstone Journal*, no. 14 (1954): 30–36.

———. "Factors Motivating Migration from Rural Areas." In *Present Interrelations in Central African Rural and Urban Life*, edited by R. J. Apthorpe, pp. 12–23. Lusaka: Rhodes-Livingstone Institute, 1958.

———. *The Kalela Dance: Aspects of Social Relationships among Urban Africans in Northern Rhodesia*. Rhodes-Livingstone Papers, no. 27. Manchester: Manchester University Press, for the Rhodes-Livingstone Institute, 1956.

———. "A Note on the Urbanization of Africans on the Copperbelt." *Rhodes-Livingstone Journal*, no. 12 (1951): 20–27.

———. "Perceptions of Ethnicity and Ethnic Behavior: An Empirical Exploration." In *Urban Ethnicity*, edited by Abner Cohen, pp. 1–35. London: Tavistock Publications, 1974.

———. "Some Theoretical Approaches to the Sociological Interpretation of Labour Circulation." In *Contemporary Egyptian Nubia*, vol. 1, edited by Robert Allan Fernea, pp. 79–99. New Haven: Human Relations Area Files, 1966.

———. "Urbanization, Detribalization, and Stabilization in Southern Africa: A Problem of Definition and Measurement." In *Social Implications of Industrialization and Urbanization in Africa South of the Sahara*, by the International African Institute, pp. 693–711. Paris: UNESCO, 1956.

———. "Wage Labour and African Population Movements in Central Africa." In *Essays on African Population*, edited by Kenneth Michael Barbour and R. M. Prothero, pp. 193–248. New York: Frederick A. Praeger, 1962.

Ohadike, Patrick O. *Development of and Factors in the Employment of African Migrants in the Copper Mines of Zambia, 1940–66*. Zambian Papers, no. 4. Lusaka: Institute for Social Research, University of Zambia, 1969.

———. "Immigrants and Development in Zambia." *International Migration Review* 7, no. 3 (fall 1974): 395–411.

———. *Some Demographic Measurements for Africans in Zambia: An Appraisal of the 1963 Census Administration and Results*. Communication No. 5. Lusaka: Institute for Social Research, University of Zambia, 1969.

———. "Urbanization, Migration and Migrants in Zambia: A Survey of Patterns, Variations and Change in Lusaka." Paper presented to the International African Institute, Eleventh International African Seminar, in Association with the University of Zambia, Lusaka, September 1972.

Prain, Sir Ronald L. "The Stabilization of Labour in the Rhodesian Copperbelt." In idem, *Selected Papers, 1953–57*, 1: 99–109. London: Rhodesian Selection Trust Group, 1958.

Prothero, R. Mansell. "Foreign Migrant Labour for South Africa." *International Migration Review* 7, no. 3 (fall 1974): 383–94.

Richards, Audrey Isabel. *Land, Labour and Diet in Northern Rhodesia: An Economic Study of the Bemba Tribe.* London: Oxford University Press, for the International Institute of African Languages and Cultures, 1939.

Stephenson, J. E. "R. W. Yule: An Appreciation." *Northern Rhodesia Journal* 3, no. 2 (1956): 119–23.

van Velsen, J. "Labour Migration as a Positive Factor in the Continuity of Tonga Tribal Society." In *Social Change in Modern Africa*, edited by Aidan Southall, pp. 230–41. London: Oxford University Press, for the International African Institute, 1961.

Veitch M. D. "Employment and the Labor Force, Regional Analysis." From the files of the Rural and Regional Planning Committee of the Second National Development Plan.

Watson William. *Tribal Cohesion in a Money Economy: A Study of the Mambwe People of Northern Rhodesia.* Manchester: Manchester University Press, for the Rhodes-Livingstone Institute, 1958.

Wilson, Godfrey. *An Essay on the Economics of Detribalization in Northern Rhodesia*, pts. 1 and 2. Rhodes-Livingstone Papers, nos. 5 and 6. Livingstone: Rhodes-Livingstone Institute, 1941, 1942.

F. On Politics

Barber, William J. "Federation and the Distribution of Economic Benefits." In *A New Deal in Central Africa*, edited by Colin Leys and Cranford Pratt, pp. 81–97. London: Heinemann, 1960.

Bates, Margaret Rouse. "UNIP in Postindependence Zambia: The Development of an Organizational Role." Ph. D. diss., Department of Government, Harvard University, 1971.

Bates, Robert H. *Unions, Parties, and Political Development: A Study of Mineworkers in Zambia.* New Haven: Yale University Press, 1971.

Chabwera, Gerry G. "Rural Local Government in Lundazi." Paper no. 7. University of Zambia, Sociological Association, November 1970.

Davidson, James Wightman. *The Northern Rhodesian Legislative Council.* London: Faber and Faber, 1948.

Dresang, Dennis L. "Ethnic Politics, Representative Bureaucracy and Development Administration: The Zambian Case." *American Political Science Review* 68, no. 4 (December 1974): 1605–17.

Epstein, Arnold Leonard. *Politics in an Urban African Community.* Manchester: Manchester University Press, for the Rhodes-Livingstone Institute, 1958.

Gertzel, Cherry; Mutukwa, Kasuka; Scott, Ian; and Wallis, Malcolm. "Zambia's Final Experience of Inter-Party Elections: The By-elections of December 1971." *Kroniek van Afrika* 2 (June 1972): 57–77.

Gluckman, Max; Mitchell, J. C.; and Barnes, J. A. "The Village Headman in British Central Africa." *Africa* 19, no. 2 (April 1949): 89–106.

Hazlewood, Arthur, and Henderson, P. D. *Nyasaland: The Economics of Federation.* Oxford: Basil Blackwell, 1960.

Leys, Colin. " 'Partnership' as the Dismantling of the Colour Bar." In *A New*

Deal in Central Africa, edited by Colin Leys and Cranford Pratt, pp. 98–109. London: Heinemann, 1960.

————, and Pratt, Cranford, eds. *A New Deal in Central Africa*. London: Heinemann, 1960.

Meebelo, Henry S. *Reaction to Colonialism: A Prelude to the Politics of Independence in Northern Zambia, 1893–1939*. Manchester: Manchester University Press, for the Institute for African Studies, University of Zambia, 1971.

Molteno, Robert. "Cleavage and Conflict in Zambian Politics: A Study in Sectionalism." In *Politics in Zambia*, edited by William Tordoff, pp. 62–106. Berkeley and Los Angeles: University of California Press, 1974.

————, and Scott, Ian. "The 1968 General Election and the Political System." In *Politics in Zambia*, edited by William Tordoff, pp. 155–96. Berkeley and Los Angeles: University of California Press, 1974.

Mulford, David C. *The Northern Rhodesia General Election, 1962*. Nairobi: Oxford University Press, 1964.

————. *Zambia: The Politics of Independence, 1957–1964*. London: Oxford University Press, 1967.

National Institute of Public Administration. "Job Description for the Post of District Governor." Mimeographed. Lusaka: National Institute of Public Administration, January 1971.

————. "Job Description for the Post of District Secretary." Mimeographed. Lusaka: National Institute of Public Administration, January 1971.

————. "Job Description for the Post of Provincial Development Officer." Mimeographed. Lusaka: National Institute of Public Administration, February 1971.

Rasmussen, Thomas. "Political Competition and One-Party Dominance." *Journal of Modern African Studies* 7, no. 3 (October 1969): 407–24.

————. "The Popular Basis of Anti-Colonial Protest." In *Politics in Zambia*, edited by William Tordoff, pp. 40–61. Berkeley and Los Angeles: University of California Press, 1974.

Rotberg, Robert I. *The Rise of Nationalism in Central Africa: The Making of Malawi and Zambia, 1873–1964*. Cambridge: Harvard University Press, 1965.

————. "Tribalism and Politics in Zambia." *Africa Report* 12, no. 9 (December 1967): 29–35.

Scott, Ian, and Molteno, Robert. "The Zambian General Elections." *Africa Report* 14, no. 1 (January 1969): 42–52.

————. "The Functions of the Local Level Party since Independence." Unpublished manuscript.

Silverman, Philip Samuel. "Local Elites and the Image of a Nation: The Incorporation of Barotseland within Zambia." Ph.D. diss., Department of Anthropology, Cornell University, September 1968.

Taylor, P. L. "Decentralization for Co-ordinated Rural Development." Mimeographed. Lusaka: National Institute of Public Administration, March 1971.

Tordoff, William, and Molteno, Robert. "Introduction." In *Politics in Zambia*, edited by William Tordoff, pp. 1–39. Berkeley and Los Angeles: University of California Press, 1974.

————, and Scott, Ian. "Political Parties: Structures and Policies." In *Politics in*

Zambia, edited by William Tordoff, pp. 107–54. Berkeley and Los Angeles: University of California Press, 1974.

Watson, William. "The Social Background." In *A New Deal in Central Africa*, edited by Colin Leys and Cranford Pratt, pp. 138–57. London: Heinemann, 1960.

IV. Official Publications

A. Great Britain

Orde Browne, Major G. St. J. *Labour Conditions in Northern Rhodesia*. London: His Majesty's Stationery Office, 1938.

B. Federation of Rhodesia and Nyasaland

Report of the Commissioner of Taxes for the Year Ending 30 June 1963. Salisbury: Government Printer, 1963.

C. Northern Rhodesia

Commissioner for Native Development. *Better Living for Rural Africans: An Account of Rural Development in Northern Rhodesia*. Lusaka: Government Printer, 1954.

Department of African Affairs. *Annual Report[s] for the Year[s] 1947–1963*. Lusaka: Government Printer, 1948–1964.

Department of Native Affairs. *Annual Report[s] for the Year[s] 1929–1937*. Lusaka: Government Printer, 1930–1938.

Development Commissioner. *Recent Advances in the Northern and Luapula Provinces of Northern Rhodesia, Being a Report on Intensive Rural Development*. Lusaka: Government Printer, 1959.

Draft Development Plan for the Period 1st July 1961 to 30th June 1965. Lusaka: Government Printer, 1962.

Final Report of the Commission of Inquiry into the Cost of Living. Lusaka: Government Printer, 1950.

Preliminary Report of the May/June 1963 Census of Africans in Northern Rhodesia. Lusaka: Ministry of Finance, January 1964.

Report of the Chairman of the Native Labour Advisory Board. Lusaka: Government Printer, 1936.

Report of the Commission of Inquiry into the Future of the European Farming Industry in Northern Rhodesia and the Issue of Tenure of Agricultural Land. Lusaka: Government Printer, 1954.

Report of the Financial Relationship Committee. Lusaka: Government Printer, 1949.

Report of the Government Unemployment Committee, 1932. Livingstone: Government Printer, 1933.

Report of the Rural Economic Development Working Party. Lusaka: Government Printer, 1961.

Report of the Taxation Committee, April 1934. Livingstone: Government Printer, 1934.

Report of the Trades Licensing Committee. Lusaka: Government Printer, 1946.

Report on Intensive Rural Development in the Northern and Luapula Provinces of Northern Rhodesia, 1957–1961. Lusaka: Government Printer, 1961.

Report on Native Taxation. Lusaka: Government Printer, 1938.

Report on the Census of Population of Northern Rhodesia Held on 15th October, 1946. Lusaka: Government Printer, 1949.

Social Security in Northern Rhodesia, Part II: The Protection of Old Age. Lusaka: Government Printer, 1948.

Ten-Year Development Plan for Northern Rhodesia as Approved by Legislative Council on 11th February 1947. Lusaka: Government Printer, 1951.

D. *Republic of Zambia*

Agricultural Rural Marketing Board. "Fifth Annual Report of the Agricultural Rural Marketing Board for the Year Ended 31st December 1968." Mimeographed, n. p., n. d.

————. "Fourth Annual Report of the Agricultural Rural Marketing Board for the Year Ended 31st December 1967." Mimeographed, n. p., n. d.

Cabinet Office. "Government Organization: Working Instructions for Decentralized Administration." Circular no. 24 of 1970, 1 May 1970.

————. *Manpower Report: A Report and Statistical Handbook on Manpower, Education, Training and Zambianization, 1965–6.* Lusaka: Government Printer, 1966.

————. *Report of the Working Party Appointed to Review the System of Decentralized Administration.* Lusaka: Cabinet Office, May 1972.

————. *Report to the Government of Zambia on Incomes, Wages and Prices in Zambia: Policy and Machinery, by the International Labour Office, United Nations Development Programme, Technical Assistance Sector.* Lusaka: Government Printer, 1969.

Central Statistical Office. *Census of Population and Housing, 1969.* Lusaka: Central Statistical Office, 1970.

————. *Census of Production 1965 and 1966.* Lusaka: Central Statistical Office, 1968.

————. *Employment and Earnings 1966–68.* Lusaka: Central Statistical Office, 1970.

————. *Final Report of the May/June 1963 Census of Africans.* Lusaka: Central Statistical Office, January 1968.

————. *Fisheries Statistics (Natural Waters) 1965, 1968.* Lusaka: Central Statistical Office, 1966, 1969.

————. *Statistical Year-Book 1970.* Lusaka: Central Statistical Office, 1971.

————. *Survey of Occupations 1969.* Lusaka: Central Statistical Office, 1972.

Department of Agriculture. *Review of the Operations of the Agricultural Marketing Committee during the Year[s] Ending 30th June 1965 and 1967.* Lusaka: Government Printer, 1965, 1968.

Department of Community Development, Research Unit. *Ground Floor to Development: A Survey of Nguluwe Compound.* Lusaka: Department of Community Development, 15 March 1967.

―――. *Lodgers and Houses in New Kanyama: A Survey.* Lusaka: Department of Community Development, 10 September 1966.

―――. *The People of "Zambia City."* Lusaka: Department of Community Development, 10 September 1966.

―――. *The Rufunsa Area: A Socio-Economic Survey for Village Regrouping.* Lusaka: Department of Community Development, 1968.

―――. *A Socio-Economic Survey of Kalingalinga.* Lusaka: Department of Community Development, 30 June 1967.

Department of Co-operatives. *Annual Report of the Department of Co-operatives for the Year[s] 1965 and 1968.* Lusaka: Government Printer, 1966, 1969.

Department of Town and Country Planning, Development Planning and Research Unit. *Low Cost Residential Development in Lusaka: The Development and Characteristics of Official and Unauthorized Low Cost Housing in Lusaka.* Lusaka: Department of Town and Country Planning, August 1972.

―――. *Mwaziona: A Study of an Unofficial Housing Area.* Lusaka: Department of Town and Country Planning, July 1973.

Estimates of Revenue and Expenditure for the Year[s] 1965–1968. Lusaka: Government Printer, 1965–1968.

Financial Report for the Year[s] Ended 31st December 1969 and 1970. Lusaka: Government Printer, 1970, 1971.

First National Development Plan, 1966–1970. Lusaka: Office of National Development and Planning, 1966.

Ministry of Finance. *Economic Report[s], 1964–1970.* Lusaka: Government Printer, 1965–1971.

Ministry of Local Government and Housing. "Report on the Functions and Finances of Rural Local Authorities and the Financial Relationship between Central Government and Rural Authorities." By W. A. S. Lennox. Mimeographed. Lusaka: Ministry of Local Government and Housing, April 1965.

Ministry of Rural Development. *First Zambian National Food Congress, 29th and 30th April 1970.* Lusaka: Ministry of Rural Development, 1970.

―――. *Magoye Unit Farm Report, 1966–1971.* Lusaka: Ministry of Rural Development, October 1971.

―――. *A New Strategy for Rural Development in Zambia: Report of a Seminar on Rural Development Held in Lusaka from 23rd-25th March 1970.* Lusaka: Ministry of Rural Development, 1970.

―――. Land Use Services Division. *Farm Budgeting Handbook, Luapula Province.* Mansa: Ministry of Rural Development, February 1972.

Mulungushi Conference 1967: Proceedings of the Annual General Conference of the United National Independence Party Held at Mulungushi 14th-20th August, 1967. Lusaka: Zambia Information Services, 1967.

National Accounts and Input-Output Tables, 1969. Lusaka: Central Statistical Office, May 1972.

National Archives. *Calendars of the District Notebooks (Luapula Province)*

1798–1963. Vol. 1. Compiled by P. M. Mukula. Lusaka: Government Printer, 1973.

Office of the President. *Village Productivity and Ward Development Committees: A Pocket Manual.* Lusaka: Government Printer, 1971.

Office of Vice-President, Development Division. *Zambian Manpower.* Lusaka: Government Printer, 1969.

Report of the Commission of Inquiry into the Allegations Made by Mr. Justin Chimba and Mr. John Chisata. Lusaka: Government Printer, 1971.

Report of the Commission of Inquiry into the Mining Industry, 1966. Lusaka: Government Printer, 1966.

Report of the National Commission on the Establishment of a One-Party Participatory Democracy in Zambia. Lusaka: Government Printer, October 1972.

Report of the National Commission on the Establishment of a One-Party Participatory Democracy in Zambia: Summary of Recommendations Accepted by Government. Government Paper no. 1 of 1972. Lusaka: Government Printer, 1972.

Report of the Second National Convention on Rural Development, Incomes, Wages and Prices in Zambia: Policy and Machinery; Kitwe: 12-16th December 1969. Lusaka: Government Printer, 1970.

Second National Development Plan, January, 1972-December, 1976. Lusaka: Ministry of Development Planning and National Guidance, December 1971.

V. Files Consulted

A. National Level

Agriculture and Natural Resources Committee for the Second National Development Plan. "Minutes and Position Papers."

———. Department of Fisheries. "A Tentative Programme for Fisheries in the Second National Development Plan."

———. Ministry of Rural Development, Planning Unit. "Agriculture, Forestry, and Fisheries."

———. Ministry of Rural Development, Planning Unit. "Crop and Livestock Priorities."

———. Ministry of Rural Development, Planning Unit. "General Evaluation of the F[irst] N[ational] D[evelopment] P[lan]."

———. Ministry of Rural Development, Planning Unit. "The Rural Sector, Objectives and Strategies."

———. National Agricultural Marketing Board. "Preliminary Paper on Services to the Agricultural Industry."

———. National Agricultural Marketing Board. "A Short History of the Rural Marketing Department."

Mufulira Archives. Kawambwa District Files. AFN/7/4/1.

Office of National Development and Planning, Regional Planning Unit. Prov. L1, L2, L16, L22, L28, L31, L38.

B. Local Level

Kawambwa Rural Council Files. ADM/1; ADM/2, vols. 1-3; ADM/10; CON/1; FIN/4/2/1; HQ/FIN/4; LOC/Ele/123; POL/40; SOC/3/2, vols. 1 and 2.
————. Minutes of the Kawambwa Rural Council. AFN/27.
Lunda Native Authority Files, held by Kawambwa Rural Council. AFN/2; AGR/3; CUS/2; FIS/2; FIS/5; FIS/6; INF/2/1; LNA/LAN/2.
Nchelenge District Offices. ADM/4/6, vols. 1 and 2; ADM/5/1, vols. 1-3; COM/3/2; LP/ADM/14/1; LP/SOC/3/2, vols. 1-4; NC/CR/2.
————. Agricultural Finance Corporation. NE/70/S; NG/74/S.
————. Department of Co-operatives. Co-operative Unions, General.
————. Department of Co-operatives. Provincial Reports and Circulars.
————. Department of Co-operatives. Quarterly Reports of the District Co-operative Officer.
————. Fisheries Officer. FSH/5.
————. NAMBoard. Distribution and Buying Program, 1970, 1971, 1972.
Palace Files. AFN/PAL/16; LAN/2; LNA/AGR/4.
————. Minutes, Lunda Tribal Council.
Provincial Offices, Mansa. Provincial Fisheries Officer. DEV/7.

VI. Newspapers

Business and Economy of Central and East Africa. Ndola, 1967–72.
The Central African Mail. Lusaka, 1960–65.
Farming in Zambia. Ndola, 1968–72.
The Northern News. Ndola, 1956–65.
The Times of Zambia. Ndola, 1965–73.
The Zambia Mail. 1965–72.
Zambian Commercial Farming. Ndola, 1967–70.
The Zambia News. Ndola, 1963–72.

Index

Advisory Council, 33
African Farm Improvement Scheme, 38, 284
African Mineworkers' Union. *See* Mineworkers' Union
African National Congress (ANC): and constitutional commission, 335; and discrimination, 72, 74–76; and federation, 76; and hawkers, 72, 293; and party competition, 68–69, 126–27, 232, 234; and public investments, 127–29; rural support for, 72, 74, 77, 80–81, 87, 128, 236, 297; and United Progressive Party, 234, 238, 248, 250
African Representative Council, 34, 283
Agricultural Finance Company, 152, 223, 243, 333
Agricultural Rural Marketing Board, 117, 119–20. *See also* Marketing agency; National Agricultural Marketing Board
Agricultural Rural Marketing Service, 116–17. *See also* Marketing agency
Agriculture. *See* Farming
Anglo-American Corporation, 18

Balance of payments, 124, 246
Balance of trade, 124, 246, 247
Banda, Dingiswayo, 227, 329
Baptista, Pedro João, 10
Barotse Province: and African National Congress, 232, 234, 248; and British South Africa Company, 13, 20, 44, 295; and cattle, 22, 23; and maize, 125, 148; and marketing agency, 117; and migration, 44, 53, 55, 234; and politics, 227, 232; and rural development, 233–34, 236, 295; and United National Independence Party, 227–28, 232–34; and United Party, 233

Beatty, Alfred Chester, 18
Bemba: and Kasumpa village, 11–12, 14–15, 81; and the Lunda, 9, 12, 81; and Mwata Kazembe, 209–10
Bemba Native Authority, 82–83
Bloc vote, 223–24, 225
British South Africa Company (BSA): and commercial farming, 23; and Concession Companies, 17–18; investment patterns of, 16–18, 29–30, 42–44; and migration, 41–45, 266, 286; and mining industry, 12–14, 16–18, 31, 42, 108, 280, 286, 295, 336; and railways, 18–19; and taxes, 42–43, 44, 108
Broken Hill. *See* Kabwe
Broken Hill mine, 16, 17, 18
Bwana Mkubwa mine, 17, 18
Bwile, 9

Cattle: and cash crop farming, 21–22, 23, 128, 154; and migration, 174, 198–99, 313, 314, 317, 321; and retirement, 199; and rural incomes, 21–22, 23–24, 153–54, 168–69, 174, 198–99; and tsetse fly, 22, 24, 113, 280
Cement industry, 19
Central African Federation. *See* Federation of Rhodesia and Nyasaland
Central Province, 312; and employment, 161; and farming, 22, 38, 154, 164, 280, 281; and migration, 53; and politics, 128, 248, 329; wages in, 162
Chambeshi, Musonda, 238, 242, 331
Chambishi mine, 17
Chapoloko, Jameson, 238, 242, 331
Charcoal industry, 181, 182
Chewe, Huggins, 93
Chiengi, 14
Chimba, Justin, 227, 229, 237, 238, 331
Chisata, John, 237, 238, 242, 250, 331

Chishinga, 9
Chona, Mainza, 227, 329
Commercial farmers. *See* European settlers
Commonwealth Development Corporation, 19
Congo (L). *See* Katanga; Zaïre
Constitution: conference of (*1960*), 94–95, 335
Cooperatives: and bureaucracy, 138–39, 142–43, 224–25; and credit agency, 113–14, 132–33, 136–37; failure of, 132–33, 136–37, 141–44, 145, 150–51, 225, 243, 245, 307; formation of, 111–12; and government, 113, 131, 151; growth of, 113–14; incomes from, 132, 134–35, 204, 304–05; and loan repayments, 137, 143; and marketing agency, 137; and mechanization, 113; officers of, 131–36, 144, 145, 203, 301–02, 307; in peri-urban areas, 180; and rural development, 111, 112–13, 130–37, 151; and subsidies, 113–14; training for, 113–14, 145, *See also* Kasumpa village cooperatives
Copperbelt (Western) Province, 21*n*, 312; and employment, 161; and farming, 154, 180; and politics, 227, 228, 231, 233, 238, 248; and teachers training college, 219; wages in, 162
Copper Exports, Inc., 17
Copper industry: decline of, 246–47; and the depression, 31, 290; and discrimination, 71, 241–42; expansion of, 17–19; history of, 1, 11, 16–18; its labor force, 46, 47–49, 175–77, 241–42, 266, 290, 315, 318, 332; Mufulira disaster, 246; and other industries, 18–20, 22, 24–25, 89, 300; and prices, 17, 104, 108, 109, 117, 124, 246–47, 280; reserves of, 300; and retirement, 182–87, 317; and taxes, 104, 105, 108, 117–18, 246–47, 299–300, 301; and unions, 59, 176–77, 242, 290; and United Progressive Party, 241–42; wages in, 59, 176, 241–42, 284, 287, 290, 291, 315; and World War II, 31
Credit agency: beginnings of, 116–17; and cooperatives, 113–14, 132–33, 136–37; failure of, 152; and loan repayments, 137, 143, 147, 149, 152, 302, 308, 309; and red tape, 133, 142–43, 152; reform of, 119, 121, 243; and rural development, 137–41, 147, 152, 155. *See also* Agricultural Finance Company
Credit Organization of Zambia (COZ), 116, 152, 302

Davis, Sir Edmund, 17–18
Decentralization. *See* Public sector, decentralization
Development, Planning, and National Guidance, Ministry of, 268
Development plans, preindependence, 32, 35. *See also* First National Development Plan; Second National Development Plan
District development committees, 118–19, 215, 243, 268, 308–09; and decentralization, 221, 223

Eastern Province: and British South Africa Company, 13, 20; and cattle, 24; and farming, 22, 24, 281, 284; and land tenure, 281; and marketing agency, 117; and politics, 227–28, 229, 231, 232, 239; public investments in, 228; and roads, 220; and tsetse fly, 24
Economic reforms, 107, 121, 239–41, 247, 316–17
Education: costs of, 197–98, 321–22; and employment, 197–98; incentives for, 289; and migration, 51–52, 167–68, 289, 314, 321–22; and remittances, 197–98, 201, 321; and wages, 52, 168, 312
Elections: of *1959*, 68–69, 93; of *1964*, 109–10, 126–29; of *1968*, 118–19, 123, 126–29; to United National Independence Party Central Committee (*1967*), 227–28, 328–29
Electorate, 202–03, 275, 335; expansion of, 34, 67, 68, 109, 283; rural nature of, 109–10, 118
Employment: and education, 197–98; and mining, 46, 47–49, 175–77, 290, 315, 317, 332; off line of rail, 160–67 passim; on line of rail, 160–67 passim; peri-urban changes in, 180–82; and post-employment incomes, 179–81; rural-urban differences in, 20, 160–67 passim; and service industries, 164, 182; in shantytowns, 184
European settlers: and commercial farming, 23, 180, 280; and discrimination, 281, 291–92; distribution of, 20, 33, 294; and federation, 66, 67; and politics, 33–34, 65, 95, 303; and public investments, 32–33, 72–73. *See also* Farming, commercial
Executive Council, 33–34
Extension agents, 113, 122, 138, 147–49, 155, 307

Farming
—cash crop, 1, 2, 5, 6; and bureaucracy, 137–41; and cattle, 21–22, 23, 128, 154, 198; and credit agency, 38, 116, 146, 147, 243, 245, 308; and discrimination, 38–39, 281; and distance from market, 20–21, 24, 124, 169, 281; government support of, 110–29; incomes, 20–21, 146, 153, 274, 307, 309; and land tenure, 77; in Luapula valley, 21, 24, 39, 281, 284; and maize, 148–49, 303; and marketing agency, 116–17, 146; and mechanization, 115, 146; and migration, 22, 54, 168–69, 174, 312–13, 315; in peri-urban areas, 62, 180, 316; and pricing policies, 39, 122–24; and public investments, 307; training for, 115–16, 145, 146; and UN aid, 308. *See also* African Farm Improvement Scheme; Maize; Rural development
—commercial: and copper industry, 22–23; and credit agency, 38, 121; and Eastern Province, 281, 284; and government marketing policies, 37, 38–39, 120–21; history of, 22–23, 180; and land alienation, 23, 77, 78, 256; and maize, 123; and Northern Province, 281; and Northwestern Province, 281; and prices, 121–23; and pricing policies, 122–23; and rural development, 119, 120; by villagers, 23; and wages, 50. *See also* European settlers
—off line of rail, 21; earnings from, 164; and government agencies, 155; and investments, 156; and private markets, 155
—on line of rail, 5, 21, 22–23, 153–56; and cattle, 154; earnings from, 164; and government agencies, 155; and investments, 156; and marketing services, 156; and private markets, 155–56
—subsistence, 23, 39, 164, 281, 284
Federation of Rhodesia and Nyasaland, 66–70, 76, 94, 292; constitutional conference (*1960*), 94–95
Federation of Welfare Societies, 293. *See also* Welfare societies
First National Development Plan, 104–08, 126, 159, 219, 224, 268. *See also* Development plans, preindependence; Second National Development Plan
Fishing industry: and copper industry, 24–25, 89; decline of, 89–90, 157–58, 296; and Greek traders, 25; history of, 24–25; incomes from, 25–26, 310; and marketing agency, 158–59; and migra-

tion, 55; and political protest, 83–99 passim; and productivity, 25, 158; and prices, 157, 309–10; public investments in, 39–40, 158–59; regulation of, 83–99 passim, 157–58, 296; and tariffs, 88; and taxes, 83, 85, 258; and United Progressive Party, 245
Four Year Development Plan. *See* First National Development Plan

Gamitto, António Pedroso, 10
Gore-Browne, Sir Stewart, 67
Grain Marketing Board, 119, 120. *See also* Marketing agency
Great Britain, government of, 5; and constitutional conference (*1960*), 94–95; and federation, 66–67, 68, 69–70
Grey, George, 45

Hawkers, 72, 292–93
Housing, urban. *See* Retirement; Shantytowns
Humanism, 110

Ila, 198–99
Immigrants. *See* European settlers
Imports: of agricultural commodities, 122, 244, 284, 303
Incomes
—rural, 58–59; in Barotse Province, 234, 295; and cash crop farming, 20–22, 146–47, 179–81; and cattle, 21–22, 153–55, 198–99; and Central Province, 164; determinants of, 147–50; and fishing industry, 25–26, 26–27; levels of, 146–47, 160; and government agencies, 38, 99, 147–50, 155, 243, 258–59; measures of, 168–69, 314–15; and migration, 43–44, 168, 169, 188, 189–91, 192–93, 252, 311, 314–15; off line of rail, 153; on line of rail, 22, 23, 153, 155–56; and political protest, 87–91, 98–100, 103, 242–45; and politics, 202–25 passim; and pricing policies, 123–24; public investments in, 32, 169–71, 306; regional differences in, 153–56, 160, 164, 167, 258, 259; and remittances, 191–201, 320
—rural-urban differences in, 153–56, 160, 164, 167, 258, 259
—urban, 58–59, 146, 163, 284; and cost of living, 179–81; and remittances, 316. *See also* Wages
Indeco group, 107
Intensive development zones, 243, 306, 333

Investments, private
—postindependence: and government policies, 107–08; and rural development, 168–69
—preindependence: in Luapula valley, 39–40; patterns of, 16–28 passim
Investments, public
—postindependence: in Barotse Province, 233; and the bloc vote, 223–24; and cash crop farming, 110–29; and commercial farming, 122–23; and decentralization, 221–25; in Eastern Province, 228; and industrial diversification, 104–08; and intensive development, 243, 306, 333; in Luapula Province, 229–31; and migration, 169–71, 174, 314; in Northern Province, 228, 229; off line of rail, 110–59 passim, 204; on line of rail, 104–06, 108, 126, 333; patterns of, 103–29 passim; and political protest, 126–29, 216–17, 255; and politics, 202–25; reallocation of, 119–20; and regional conflicts, 217–21; and rural development, 130–59 passim, 169–74, 203, 243, 254, 258, 306, 333, 337; and rural-urban differences, 104–05, 260
—preindependence: determinants of, 282; and European settlers, 33; in fishing industry, 39–40; in Luapula valley, 39; and migration, 63–64; and native authority, 284–85; off line of rail, 30, 31–32, 36–40, 63, 99–100; on line of rail, 30, 34–36, 38–39; patterns of, 28–40 passim, 72–73; and World War II, 35. *See also* Credit agency; Marketing agency; Mechanization; Public sector; Rural development

Jehovah's Witnesses, 299
Johnston, Harry, 13
José, Amaro, 10

Kabwe (formerly Broken Hill): and migration, 47, 53, 56, 57, 178; and remittances, 58, 178–79. *See also* Broken Hill mine
Kakusa, Mama Katie, 297
Kalungwishi, 14
Kamanga, Reuben, 68, 227, 228, 231, 237, 329
Kanyembo, 11–12, 13–14, 15, 279, 325–26
Kapwepwe, Simon, 68, 329; detention of, 250; resignation of, 236–37, 239; and United Progressive Party, 238, 247, 249, 250, 331, 334; as Vice-President, 227, 229, 230, 231
Kariba dam, 19, 107
Kasenga, 25
Kashiba, 295
Kasumpa village: and cash crop farming, 114–15, 146–50, 214, 271, 308; and cash earnings, 190–91; and credit agency, 116, 149, 243; and decentralization, 224–25; and fishing industry, 27–28, 157; history of, 11–12, 14–15, 265–66; incomes in, 27–28, 146–47; and Lunda Native Authority, 81–82, 209–10; and market size, 149–50; measures of prosperity in, 192; and migration, 45–46, 188–201, 271, 272; and the National Agricultural Marketing Board, 213; and public investments, 205–06, 213–14; and remittances, 191–201, 321; as a research site, 6, 270–73, 282; and witchcraft, 197, 211–12, 324–25; and Zambia Highway, 214–17
—attitudes of: toward government, 205–07, 325–26; toward the Lunda, 209–11, 324; toward town, 188–89; toward village, 189–90
—and the family, 193–201 passim; child mortality rate, 212; children and migration, 190, 194–98; and the extended family, 195–97; its youth culture, 195
—and politics: and African National Congress, 81; disillusionment with government, 205–07, 325–26; and electoral tactics, 234–35; issues in, 209–17; and Nationalist Movement, 81–82, 85–87, 265, 267; and political protest, 97, 214–17, 271; and pressure group tactics, 212–17; and rewards, 203; and United National Independence Party, 81, 208–17, 326; and United Progressive Party, 244–45, 248–49; and Zambia African Nationalist Congress, 92–93
Kasumpa village cooperatives, 111–12, 113, 114, 130–37, 271
—Chikalamo, 111, 113, 136–37; failure of, 144–45; and government loans, 305, and marketing agency, 137; returns from, 136–37, 141–42, 305
—Katofyio, 28, 111, 130–36; failure of, 143–45; and fishing industry, 133–36, 144–45; government criticism of, 304; officers of, 131–36, 203, 304–05; and private markets, 134–36, 144–45; returns from, 132, 134, 135; and United

Progressive Party, 244–45, 249; and wages, 304
—Lukungwe, 111, 113, 136–37, 141–42, 189; failure of, 144–45; and marketing agency, 137; and red tape, 139, 142–43; returns from, 136–37, 305
Katanga, 9; and British South Africa Company, 13–14; and labor recruitment, 45; minerals in, 14, 16–17, 18–19, 42, 45; and railway development, 18–19; and secession, 88. *See also* Zaïre
Kaunda, Kenneth David (President of Zambia): and African National Congress, 68; and cooperatives, 111; and economic reforms, 239; and Humanism, 110; and Simon Kapwepwe, 236–37; and peri-urban farming, 180; and political appointments, 328; and political opposition, 230, 235, 236; resignation of, 329; and single-party state, 126; and United National Independence Party, 69, 94, 226, 227, 231, 237, 329
Kawambwa Rural Council, 203, 206–07
Kazembe, 27
Kitwe, 19; and United Progressive Party, 238, 240–41

Labor force: growth of, 163–64; stabilization of, 291; turnover of, 57–58, 175–77. *See also* Migration
Labor recruitment, 287
Labor unions: and copper industry, 59, 176–77, 241–42, 290, 332; and economic reforms, 240; and government policies, 241–42; and wages, 162–63, 241. *See also* Mineworkers' Union
Lacerda e Almeida, Francisco José de, 10
Lake Bangweulu, 9, 27
Lake Kariba, 78, 90
Lake Mweru, 9, 25, 40, 157, 159. *See also* Fishing industry; Mweru Wantipa
Lakes Fisheries of Zambia, Ltd., 159
Land reform, 255–56
Land tenure, 36–37, 62, 76–79, 145, 256–57, 283–84, 291, 294
Land use, urban, 179, 180, 181
Legislative Council, 33–34, 36
Lewanika, 13, 44
Lewanika, Godwin, 68
Livingstone, David, 10
Livingstone (town), 47, 52, 53, 55, 56
London Missionary Society, 77–78
Lozi, 13, 44
Luanshya, 19, 47, 58, 238

Luapula Province: and the bloc vote, 223–24; and British South Africa Company, 13; and cattle, 24, 269; and cattle-ranching scheme, 219; and cash crop farming, 21, 24, 39, 281, 284; and citrus fruit scheme, 219; and Congolese independence, 88–90; and cooperatives, 150–51; and credit agency, 152, 302; and decentralization, 221–22; and distance from market, 24, 269, 281; its ecologies, 270–71; exploration of, 10; and First Development Plan, 219; and fishing industry, 24–28, 39–40, 89–90, 157–59; and independence, 98–99; and intensive development zones, 333; and intraparty competition, 227–36; and labor recruitment, 45; and land tenure, 78–79; and maize, 125, 148–49, 284; and marketing agency, 117, 223; and mechanization, 151; and migration, 55–56; and Nationalist Movement, 65, 80–100 passim; and native authority, 295–96; and party propaganda, 75–76; and the pedicle, 24, 134, 220, 231; population of, 55–56; and pricing policies, 39–40; and public investments, 39–40, 99–100, 229–31; and recession, 87–100 passim; and regionalism, 217–21, 229–31; and roads, 219–21, 327; and rural development, 130–50; and subsistence farming, 39; and tariffs, 87–88, 296; and teachers training college, 219, 235; and tsetse fly, 22, 24, 113; and United National Independence Party Central Committee, 227, 228–31, 236, 330; and United Progressive Party, 238, 244–45, 248; wages in, 162; and Zambia African Nationalist Congress, 92. *See also* Kasumpa village
Luapula River, 9, 24, 25, 27
Lukwesa Mpanga, 11
Lunda Native Authority, 82–87, 266; and agriculture, 83, 84, 85, 114; and education, 83; and fishing industry, 83, 84, 90; and health, 83, 84, 85–86; and Kasumpa village, 81–82, 209–10; and mission lands, 77–78; resistance to, 92–94; revenues of, 82–83; and United National Independence Party, 99, 210. *See also* Native authority
Lunda tribe, 9–15, 81, 281
Lusaka, 47, 50, 52, 53, 58; Kapwepwe compound, 181–82; Nguluwe compound, 182; population of, 181

Macleod, Ian, 69, 95

Maize: and copper industry, 22, 24; and extension agents, 22, 148–49; "floor price" for, 124; importation of, 122, 244, 284, 303; and lack of regional specialization, 303; and mechanization, 152; and migration, 54; off line of rail, 123, 124, 302; on line of rail, 124, 125, 153–54, 156, 302; planting dates for, 305; prices of, 122, 123, 124, 125, 148–49, 244; and pricing policies, 37, 38–39, 155, 284; private sales of, 155; production, 122–23, 123–24, 148–49, 154, 302, 303, 309; and rural development, 122–24

Marketing agency: beginnings of, 37–38, 116–17; and cash crop farming, 155; and cooperatives, 137; and loan repayment, 137, 143, 155; and Luapula Province, 117, 223; and maize, 37, 122; and red tape, 139–41, 308–09; reform of, 119–21; and rural development, 137–41. *See also* Agricultural Rural Marketing Board; Grain Marketing Board; Investments, public; National Agricultural Marketing Board; Rural development

Maxwell, Sir James Crawford, 283

Mazabuka district, 23, 54–55, 153–56, 281

Mbereshi Mission, 77–78, 130–31, 145, 146, 266–67, 279

Mechanization, 137, 138, 139, 146; and cash crop farming, 115; costs of, 113, failure of, 151–52; inefficiencies of, 139–41

Migration: and age, 47–50, 167, 190, 288; and cash crop farming, 22, 54, 168–69, 174, 312–13, 315; and cattle, 166, 174, 198–99, 313, 314, 317, 321; changes in patterns of, 60, 62, 174–87, 286; costs of, 43–44, 52, 53, 285; demographic selectivity of, 47–51, 167–68, 169, 171–74; direction of, 165–66; and distance, 52–54, 169; economic basis of, 53, 166, 188–91, 253, 285–86, 320; and education, 51–52, 167–68, 289, 314, 321–22; and family separation, 56–57, 60, 175–77; and fishing industry, 55; hypotheses concerning, 3, 167–80, 198–201; and income, 43–44, 54–56, 58, 59–60, 62, 160–69 passim, 174, 188, 189–91, 192–93, 252, 253, 290, 311, 314–15; and Kasumpa village, 45–46, 188–201, 271, 272; to Katanga, 45–46; and labor recruitment, 43–45; and line of rail, 54–55, 56, 165–66, 283; motivations for, 2, 5, 41, 51–52, 166, 189–91, 253–54, 274–75, 285–86, 287, 320; and Nationalist Movement, 74–79; and political protest, 74–75, 79, 253–55; and population density, 166, 313–14; and public investment, 63–64, 169–71, 174, 314; regional selectivity of, 42–43, 44–45, 45–46, 165–66, 172–74; and remittances, 58, 60–64, 177–79, 191–201, 283, 320, 321–22; and retirement, 56–64, 286; and the role of the family, 193–201 passim; and sex, 47–51, 53, 166, 167, 174, 288, 313, 314; and social security, 62–64, 180–87, 194–99; and social ties with villages, 58–64 passim, 177–78, 188–201 passim; to South Africa, 45, 234; to Southern Rhodesia, 42–44, 75; and taxes, 42–43; and turnover, 57–58, 175–77. *See also* Shantytowns

Mineral rights, 13–14, 108, 336

Mineworkers' Union, 176–77, 241–42, 250, 332. *See also* Labor unions

Mining industry. *See* Copper industry

Missions, 50, 51, 77–78, 115, 288, 294, 301. *See also* Mbereshi Mission

Monckton Commission, 69, 94

Monteiro, José Correia, 10

Msidi (chief of the Yeke), 13

Msoni, Henry, 331

Mudenda, Elijah, 227, 329

Mufulira, 19, 238

Mufulira mine, 16, 52, 290

Mulungushi meetings, 69–70, 235

Mumba, Zilole, 331

Mundia, Nalumino, 233, 234

Mutima wa Jesu, 333

Mwabamukupa, 12, 14, 15, 81, 279

Mwamba (chief of the Bemba), 11, 12, 15

Mwanakatwe, John, 229–30

Mwansabombwe. *See* Kazembe

Mwata Kazembe, 76, 266; and Arab traders, 11, 12, 14; and the Bemba, 12, 15, 81, 209–10; and Dauti Yamba, 293; and foreign trade, 10–11; and headman of Kasumpa village, 15, 81, 209–10, 210–11; and Lunda tribe, 10, 281; and native authority, 82, 84; and United National Independence Party, 210

Mwata Yamvo, 9

Mweru Wantipa, 89, 134

Nakatindi, Princess Mukwae, 227, 233, 329

National Agricultural Marketing (NAM) Board, 120–21, 213, 223, 225, 302. *See also* Agricultural Rural Marketing

Board; Grain Marketing Board; Marketing agency

Nationalist Movement, 65–100 passim; chronology of, 65–70; and coercion, 299; and constitutional conference (*1960*), 94–95; and discrimination, 67, 70–71, 72, 74–76, 293; economic basis for participation in, 292–93, 298–99; and economic rewards, 203, 298; effect on rural areas, 98–100, 111–17 passim, 203–07; and federation, 72–73; and government regulation, 296; and hawkers, 292–93; and Kasumpa village, 81–82, 85–87, 265, 267; and land tenure reform, 77–79, 256; and migration, 74–79; and native authority, 85–87, 295; origins of, 34, 67–70, 277; and political protest, 1, 5, 87–92; and "positive action," 95–98; splits within, 68, 92; and tariffs, 88; and taxes, 85–87, 100, 103; and urban Africans, 70–74. *See also* African National Congress; United National Independence Party; Zambia African Nationalist Congress

Nationalization. *See* Economic reforms

Native authority: and Barotse Province, 295; and British South Africa Company, 295; and colonial government, 83–84; and fishing industry, 91, 98; and Luapula Province, 295–96; and migration, 266; opposition to, 85–87, 295–96; and political violence, 96–97; and public investments, preindependence, 284–85; and taxes, 85–86, 95–96, 98, 296, 298; and United National Independence Party, 96–97, 99, 210. *See also* Lunda Native Authority

Native Labor Association, 290

Native Labor Bureau, 43–44

Nchanga, 19

Nchanga mine, 16, 17, 52

Ndola, 47, 58, 316

Ng'andu, Victor, 331

Nkana mine. *See* Rokana mine

Nkumbula, Harry, 68, 74, 92

North-Eastern Rhodesia, 13, 43, 45

Northern Province: and British South Africa Company, 13; and cattle-ranching scheme, 219; and commercial farming, 281; and Committee of 24, 237; and labor force, 53; and marketing agency, 117; and politics, 227–51 passim; and public investments, 32, 228, 229; and railways, 219; and roads, 220; and taxes, 298; and United National Independence Party, 227–30, 237–38, 330; and United Progressive Party, 236–51, 331

Northern Rhodesia. *See* Investments, public, preindependence; Public sector

Northern Rhodesia African National Congress. *See* African National Congress

Northwestern Province: and commercial farming, 281; and land tenure, 281; and maize, 125, 148; and marketing agency, 117; and teachers training college, 219

North-Western Rhodesia, 13, 44

Nyirenda, Wesley, 227, 231, 237, 329

Oppenheimer, Ernst, 18

Opposition parties: banning of, 248–49; constitutional prohibition of, 250; government response to, 126–29, 231–32, 235–36; in Luapula Province, 235–36; in Northern Province, 236–51, 331; reasons for support of, 231–36, 238–39, 243–45; and rural development, 260. *See also* African National Congress; United Party; United Progressive Party

Oxen, 154, 156. *See also* Cattle

Pambashe Farmers' Union, 308

Party competition: and economic reforms, 240–41; end of, 335; incentives for, 231–34; instances of, 233–34, 235–36; inter-, 231–51 passim; intra-, 123, 225–38 passim, 244, 250; and public investments, 126–29, 269; and regionalism, 260; and rural development, 123, 202–03, 260; and violence, 234, 248–49. *See also* Opposition parties

Passfield Memorandum, 66, 291–92

Pedicle, the, 24, 134, 220, 231

Political parties. *See* African National Congress; Nationalist Movement; Opposition parties; Party competition; United National Independence Party; United Party; United Progressive Party; Zambia African Nationalist Congress

Political protest: basis of, 2, 3, 65, 66, 67–69, 81–82, 86–87, 90–92, 254–55, 275; and decentralization, 223–24, 225; and discrimination, 71, 72, 74–76; and economic reforms, 239–41; and electoral behavior, 68–69, 216–17, 231–32; and fishing industry, 81, 87, 91; "freedom fighters," 92–93; and land rights, 77, 79, 257–59; and migration, 74–75, 79, 253–55; and native authority, 85–87, 96–97, 295–96; and pressure group

(*Continued*)
    tactics, 212–17; and public services, 73–74, 212–17, 250; and roads, 214–17, 220; and rural development, 212–17, 234–35, 236; and rural incomes, 87, 91, 98–100, 103, 257–58; and tariffs, 87–88, 296; and taxes, 85–87, 95–96, 100, 103, 258, 296; and violence, 5, 70, 90, 92, 93–94, 95–98, 213, 214, 235, 248, 334. *See also* Nationalist Movement; Party competiton; Sectionalism; Taxes
Pombeiros. *See* Baptista, Pedro João; José, Amaro
Power industry, 19
Pricing policies: in agriculture, 38–39, 121–25
Provincial development committees, 118–19, 215, 268; and decentralization, 221–22, 224, 225
Public sector
—postindependence: and budget cut of *1972*, 247; and decentralization, 118–19, 217–25, 327, 337; and nationalization, 107; structure of, 103–29 passim; and Zambianization, 162
—preindependence: agricultural policies, 36–39; credit policies, 38; development plans, 32, 35; ideology, 30, 32; investment behavior, 28–29, 30–40; land policies, 36–38, 77; marketing policies, 37, 38–39; price policies, 38–39; structure of, 33–34
—*See also* African Representative Council; British South Africa Company; Economic reforms; Electorate; European settlers; Executive Council; First National Development Plan; Investments, public; Legislative Council; Native authority; Revenues of government; Second National Development Plan; Taxes
Puta, Robinson, 238, 242

Railways: and British South Africa Company, 18–19; and copper industry, 19; and discrimination, 71; and public investment, 107, 219
Regionalism. *See* Sectionalism
Remittances: and children, 195–98; determinants of, 62–63, 191–93; and education, 197–98, 201, 321; and the family, 193–201 passim; to Kasumpa village, 191–93; and land-use regulations, 62–63; levels of, 58, 191–92; and migration, 58, 60–64, 177–79, 191–201, 283, 320, 321; and retire-

ment, 62, 179, 183, 201, 317; from Rokana, 178–79; and rural development, 58, 63–64; and rural incomes, 191–201, 316, 320; and shantytowns, 62, 182, 186, 318; and social security, 194, 199; sources of, 197, 200–01; and urban stability, 58, 60–64, 174–87 passim; uses of, 191–93
Retail trade: decline of, 240; and discrimination, 292; and economic reforms, 239–41, 316–17; and taxes, 246–47
Retirement: attitudes toward, 183–84; and cattle, 199; and government regulations, 63; and migration, 56–64, 286; and mineworkers, 317; and remittances, 62, 179, 183, 201, 317; and shantytowns, 182, 184–85, 291
Revenues of government: changes in, 30–31, 35, 104, 108–09, 300; and copper industry, 35, 104, 105, 108, 117–18, 282, 301; decline of, 30–31, 246–47, 251; diversification of, 300; and pricing policies, 303; sources of, 31, 35, 82–83, 104–09; and tax holidays, 301. *See also* Taxes
Rhodes, Cecil John, 12–13
Rhodesia, 13, 42–44, 162, 244, 247
Rhodesian-Congo Border Power Corporation, 19
Rhodesian Native Labor Bureau, 290
Rhokana mine. *See* Rokana mine
Roads: in Barotse Province, 233, 236; development of, 107, 110; in Luapula Province, 231, 327; and political protest, 214–17, 220; politics of, 214–21; and rural development, 110, 139
Roan Antelope mine, 16, 17, 52, 242, 290, 315
Rokana mine, 16, 17
Rokana miners: and family separation, 175; and migration, 56, 57, 60; and protests, 242; and remittances, 178–79; and retirement, 182–87; and shantytowns, 184, 318; and turnovers, 175, 290; and United Progressive Party, 250, 334; and village connections, 177–78, 185–86
Rural development: and communal land rights, 257–59: and credit, 243, 333; and decentralization, 118–19, 217, 221–25; and education, 110; and the franchise, 109–10; and health and sanitation, 110; and income maximization, 275–76; and intensive development zones, 243, 333; and land reform,

256; and politics, 126–29, 202–60 passim; preindependence policies toward, 36–40, 63–64; and private investments, 168–69; and public investments, 130–59 passim, 204, 260, 278, 333; and red tape, 137–41, 245; reforms in, 117–24; and regional conflicts, 217–21; and revenues of government, 245–47; and roads, 110, 139; and single-party state, 251; and subsidies, 119, 125; and United Progressive Party, 242–45. *See also* Cooperatives; Credit agency; District development committees; Extension agents; Farming, cash crop; First National Development Plan; Incomes, rural; Investments, public, off line of rail; Maize; Marketing agency; Mechanization; Pricing policies; Provincial development committees; Public sector, decentralization; Second National Development Plan; Sectionalism
Rural Development, Ministry of, 119, 146–47, 151, 223, 268

Sandys, Duncan, 95
Second National Development Plan, 243, 334
Sectionalism: and decentralization, 217–25; and demands for public services, 217–18, 221–25, 260; and district development committees, 223; and interparty competition, 231–51 passim, 330; and intraparty competition, 218–21, 225–51 passim, 260; and locational disputes, 217–21; and Luapula Province, 229–31, 330; and provincial competition, 217–21; and provincial development committees, 221–22, 224, 225; and rural development, 217–21; and United National Independence Party, 226–31; vs. class conflict, 259–60. *See also* Barotse Province; Eastern Province; Northern Province; United Progressive Party
Seers Commission, 151
Selection Trust Ltd., 18
Settlers. *See* European settlers
Shantytowns: government policies toward, 62–63, 181, 291; growth of, 181–82; and incomes, 311; and peri-urban farming, 316; and remittances, 62, 186, 318; residents of, 182, 318; and retirement, 182, 184–85; and self-employment, 184; and village connections, 185–86

Sharpe, Alfred, 13–14
Shila, 9, 12
Sipalo, Munu, 68, 227, 233, 329
Social security, 62–64, 186–87, 194–99
Southern Province: and African Farm Improvement Scheme, 38; and cash crop farming, 23, 54–55, 153–56, 281; and cattle, 22; and citrus fruit scheme, 219; and commercial farming, 180; and employment, 161; and farm incomes, 164; and maize, 154; and migration, 54–55; and politics, 128, 217, 227, 233, 236, 248, 329; wages in, 162
Southern Rhodesia. *See* Rhodesia
Star of the Congo mine, 45
Subsidies, 113–14, 119, 124, 125, 142

Tabwa, 9, 11, 12
Tanganyika Concessions, Ltd., 45
Tariffs, 87–88, 296
Taxes: and British South Africa Company, 42–43, 44, 108; changes in, 126, 246–47; and copper industry, 104, 105, 108, 117–18, 246–47, 299–300, 301; and fishing industry, 258; and migration, 42–43; and native authority, 85–86, 95–96, 98, 296, 298; and political protest, 85–87, 95–96, 100, 103, 258, 296; and public services, 299; refusal to pay, 95–96, 98, 286, 298; sources of, 43, 104, 105–06, 299–300; and tax credit, 301. *See also* Revenues of government
Tobacco, 22
Tonga, Gwembe, 199
Tonga, Plateau, 23, 54, 55, 62–63
Tractors, 113, 115, 137, 138, 139, 151–52
Trade unions. *See* Labor unions
Tsetse fly, 22, 24, 113, 280

Union Minière du Haut Katanga, 45
Unions. *See* Labor unions
United Federal Party, 67, 95
United National Independence Party (UNIP): and Barotse Province, 232–34; Central Committee of, 226–31, 235, 236, 237, 330; and Committee of, 24, 237, 331; and constitution of, 237–38, 239; and cooperatives, 111–12, 203–04, 301–02; and economic reforms, 239–41; and elections (*1968*), 118–19; founding of, 69, 94; incomes of members, 204; and independence, 69–70; and intraparty competition, 123, 126–27, 208–09, 226–31, 234–36, 237–38, 244; and Jehovah's Witnesses, 299; and Simon Kapwepwe, 236–37; and

(*Continued*)

Kasumpa village, 81, 207–17, 323, 326; and Lunda Native Authority, 96–97, 99, 210; and Northern Province, 228–30; officers of, 203–04, 207–08, 226–27, 323; and party cards, 208–09, 248–49; and political cynicism, 204–07; and political opposition, 216–17, 237, 247–51, 335; and political rewards, 203–04; and "positive action," 95–98; and pressure group tactics, 212–17; and public investments, 99, 126–29, 216–17; and regionalism, 217–21, 226–31; and rural development, 110–29, 212–17; and single-party state, 126–28, 232, 248, 250–51; and Southern Province, 329; and taxes, 99; and United Progressive Party, 238–51, 333–34; and village headman, 209–12; and violence, 70, 95–98, 234, 248, 249, 334; and witchcraft, 211–12. *See also* Kasumpa village; Nationalist Movement; Opposition parties; Party competition; Sectionalism; Zambia African Nationalist Congress

United Nations Development Program, 334

United Party, 233, 234

United Progressive Party: and African National Congress, 238, 248; banning of, 248–49, 250; and economic reforms, 240–41, 247; executive committee of, 331; foreign assistance to, 335; and Luanshya, 238; and mineworkers, 241–42, 332; and Ndola, 238; and parliamentary elections, 250; rural organization of, 244–45; support for, 242–45, 333; and United National Independence Party, 238–51, 333–34. *See also* Opposition parties

Urban stabilization. *See* Migration

Villages: numbers of, 306; sizes of, 306

Wages: and British South Africa Company, 46; changes in, 162–63; and copper industry, 59, 176, 241–42, 284, 287, 290, 291, 315; determinants of, 58–59; and education, 52, 168, 312; and expatriates, 311; and the government, 241, 242; levels of, 50, 52, 60, 146, 304; and line of rail, 162–63; and political protest, 241–42; postindependence, 162–63; preindependence, 46; rural-urban differences in, 162–64, 167; and sex, 312. *See also* Incomes, rural; Labor unions

Welfare societies, 67–68, 283, 293, 316

Western Province: and maize, 155. *See also* Barotse Province; Copperbelt Province

Whites. *See* European settlers

Williams, Robert, 45

Wina, Arthur, 227, 233, 329

Wina, Sikota, 329

Witchcraft, 211–12

Yamba, Dauti, 83, 293

Yeke, 11, 12, 13–14

Yule, R.W., 45

Zaïre: independence of, 88–90, 91; Shaba Province of, 9. *See also* Katanga

Zambia African Nationalist Congress (ZANC): banning of, 93; and electoral boycotts, 68–69, 92, 93; founding of, 69, 92; and Jehovah's Witnesses, 299; and political protest, 92–94

Zambia City, 182

Zambia Highway, 214–17